V&R unipress

Schriften des Zentrums für Europäische
und Internationale Strafrechtsstudien

Band 3

Herausgegeben von Arndt Sinn

ZENTRUM FÜR EUROPÄISCHE UND
INTERNATIONALE STRAFRECHTSSTUDIEN

Stefano Ruggeri (ed.)

Liberty and Security in Europe

A comparative analysis of pre-trial precautionary
measures in criminal proceedings

With 3 figures

V&R unipress

Universitätsverlag Osnabrück

Bibliografische Information der Deutschen Nationalbibliothek

Die Deutsche Nationalbibliothek verzeichnet diese Publikation in der Deutschen
Nationalbibliografie; detaillierte bibliografische Daten sind im Internet über
http://dnb.d-nb.de abrufbar.

ISBN 978-3-89971-967-3

Veröffentlichungen des Universitätsverlags Osnabrück
erscheinen im Verlag V&R unipress GmbH.

Sponsored by the University of Messina and the University Consortium Megara Ibleo (CUMI).

Contents

Acknowledgements

This book is the result of comparative research on the right to liberty and security in Europe in relation to pre-trial measures of coercion. This research, which was promoted by my chair of criminal procedure at the Law School of the University of Messina and the University Consortium Megara Ibleo of Priolo Gargallo (Syracuse), has been carried out over more than one year by distinguished scholars of criminal law and procedure from four European countries, whom I sincerely wish to thank for their valuable contributions to this initiative. A special thank goes to Prof. Dr. Arndt Sinn for his generous hospitality in allowing us to publish in the ZEIS-Reihe, for which I feel highly honoured. I am very grateful to Prof. Dr. Richard Vogler for his irreplaceable support in conducting this research. Many people have collaborated, in different fashions, in this research and I would like to thank my entire chair team, especially Simona Arasi, Alessandro Arena, Giusy Laura Candito, Federica Crupi, Irene Giaimi, Letizia Lo Giudice. This book could not be completed without the extraordinary support of my wife Norma and my two daughters, Anna Lucia and Maria Isabel, whose patience and encouragement have compensated my inexperience and constantly accompanied me during the coordination of this research.

Stefano Ruggeri

Renzo Orlandi

Introduction. The protection of the right to liberty and security in the field of pre-trial precautionary measures in criminal matters

Table of Abbreviations

CPP   *Codice di procedura penale* (Code of Criminal Procedure)
EAW FD Framework Decision on the European Arrest Warrant
GC   German Constitution
IC   Italian Constitution
StPO   *Strafprozessordnung* (Code of Criminal Procedure)

Freedom and security: this topical binomial has become almost fashionable in legal publications of the last decade. Previously, the literature used to contrast individual freedom with the repressive function of the state; private versus public; the individual against authority. Today we prefer to set the value of individual freedom against the value of individual security. Each of us has the right to see his own freedom respected and can demand from the State that this right be made effective against external aggression. At the same time each one of us has the right to security, as citizens demand that the State guarantee protection against attack by third parties. It is a change that marks a turning point, at least in the context of continental European legal culture, worthy of careful consideration in an environment grounded for centuries on the city-state and the contraposition between authority and the individual. Today this antithesis is played out in the rights arena and has been narrowed to the individual sphere (freedom and security), while the State appears in the guise of a neutral guarantor of both these rights.

The need to ensure the security of one individual justifies limiting the freedom of another. Since the waning of the great Utopian matrix ideologies of the 19th and some of the 20th centuries, where the state was an institution immeasurably superior to individuals, criminal justice has been gradually stripped of its holy, authoritarian aura that garnered assent in the name of usefulness. This has not necessarily led the system to be any less harsh. It continues to seem cruel, and sometimes even "unfair." It has, however, led to the current idea that punishment is no longer tied to abstract state interests but rather linked to affirmed and contingent individual needs. It has transformed the entire field of security, in the many situations of life where it may be at risk. Security has become a constant requirement, tapped into by every ruling class to increase its political consensus and leverage. This aspect concurs to explain, in my view, the evolution towards prevention of modern criminal systems. An offence against a traditional legal right (property, health or physical integrity) is to be "compensated" by adequate remuneration. As an alternative, the security good must be ensured by pre-vention or at least by trying to avoid the many dangers threatening our lives. This transformation has also involved the criminal trial. Its institutions that have been moulded to comply with the increasing demand for security.

In this regard, the issue of pre-trial precautionary measures is highly re-vealing. Starting in the second half of the last century, we have been witnessing a gradual tendency for pre-trial precautionary measures to be increasingly given a preventive role.

In England, the first sentence justifying the refusal of bail with the argument of the danger of future crimes dates back to 1955.[1] This approach was then codified by the Bail Act of 1976.

In Germany, the trend started with 1964 legislation that for the first time included the *Wiederholungsgefahr* as a precautionary requirement in criminal proceedings for sexual offenses. A few years later in 1972, the rule would be extended to the widest range of crimes listed in the § 112 StPO, with the choice endorsed by the federal Constitutional Court, broadly equivalent to the pre-sumption of innocence.[2]

Similar considerations apply to Italy, where any consideration of a precau-tionary purpose was for a long time absent from mandatory detention for se-rious crimes.[3] The preventive purpose began to establish itself in certain pre-ventive measures of real coercion provided for by special laws (e. g. seizure of spoiled food, obscene press). The mid 70s saw explicit recognition of personal pre-trial precautionary measures with the denial of bail to people who endan-gered "the need for community protection."[4]

The marked preventive slant of precautionary measures is the most obvious manifestation of that "judicial substitution" denounced as pathological by the doctrine of the 1970s.[5] Indeed, this may be said to have become common practice.[6] Moreover, the phenomenon has understandably developed with par-

---

1 *Vogler, infra.*
2 *Sinn, infra.*
3 Art. 253 Italian CPP 1930.
4 Art. 1 Italian Law 152/1975.
5 Paradigmatic in this regard is the study of *Nobili*, pp. 51 ff.
6 *Di Chiara, infra.*

ticular virulence in countries like Italy, where time-to-trial is exceedingly lengthy. But even in situations where criminal proceedings have an unreasonable duration, the function of the precautionary institutions has gained increasing importance in concomitance with the increasing focus on prevention by anti-crime policies.[7]

How precautionary proceedings are played out anticipates the trial judgment of the main proceedings. Indeed, it is often the pre-trial precautionary approach that matters most, not least because it entails the swift, effective sacrifice of the very same right threatened by eventual punishment. Furthermore remedies, if any, against personal pre-trial precautionary measures do not have the effect of suspending enforcement.

Punishment and pre-trial precautionary measures are of course placed on separate planes on account of the presumption of innocence principle that is widely acknowledged and celebrated in all systems to which the contributions in this volume relate. But formal recognition of the principle does not prevent limitations on freedom or a precautionary measure from acquiring the con-notations of punishment. This particularly applies to precautionary measures enacted on the grounds of the likelihood of committing future crimes, a motive now codified in almost all contemporary legal proceedings and one in which it is difficult to distinguish preventive from effective punishment.

It must be admitted that personal freedom is now threatened by the process rather than by the execution of the sentence. This deserves careful consideration. Indeed it is difficult to deny that during the pre-trial proceeding the merits of the case are discussed in advance, a fact that is confirmed by the daily bickering we constantly witness over the rules governing the precautionary procedure. The Italian example is very meaningful. No section of the code has developed so copiously and with such detailed case law as personal precautionary measures. Interventions by entire criminal units have been very frequent. The central data-processing unit of the Italian Court of Cassation has about three hundred results for the enquiry entry "personal precautionary measure!" Is this a sign of the feverish vitality of precautionary institutions? This vitality that is also reflected in the frequent positions taken by the Italian Constitutional Court and the ceaseless work of legislative reform on the provisions contained in Book IV of CPP.

The studies presented in this volume confirm that other European systems face the same situation. In Spain, Germany, England and Wales, precautionary measures have increased in importance from the very moment in which the value of personal liberty had to square with security concerns in their multiple

---

7 Enlightening, in this regard, is the essay by *Hassemer*, pp. 321 ff.

forms: security in the suburbs, in crowded spaces (airports, stations, stadiums etc.), but also on the streets or in the work place.

Comparing the practice of different legal systems provides us with a deeper knowledge of each national legislative framework. Being able to look beyond our own sphere and connect it to the wider world enriches our vision and capacity to comprehend because we are forced to take a step beyond our own juridical origins. In so doing, the similarities between institutes become even more important and gain increasing significance. In addition, the doctrines elaborated on the comparison among the institutes can be unexpectedly useful to improve an understanding of our own normative background.

This should be kept in mind when reading and interpreting the present work. However, one should not remain merely on the surface of these similarities.

For example, the issue of *fumus commissi delicti*, (i.e. the circumstantial threshold imposed in order to resort to measures of personal coercion), is referred to in various procedural systems with a standard lexicon whose meaning appears identical: *probable cause, gravi indizi di colpevolezza, dringender Verdacht, indicios suficientes de un hecho criminal imputado*, all of which seem to allude to the same phenomenon. In reality, as soon as we delve into the meaning of these wordings in the case-law, we note unexpected differences; differences, however, that present to the scholar precious opportunities for growth and refinement.

The same holds true for *pericula libertatis*, which have with time been arranged in a way that reveals curious parallels in the evolution of the different normative statutes. For example, questions of the genuine evidence, the risk of flight, and the risk of repeated offence nearly everywhere justify the restriction of personal liberty within the framework of the presumption of innocence. But are we sure that these terms are understood in the same manner? For example, the Italian *pericolo di fuga*[8] usually refers to the risk that once sentenced, the defendant might avoid enforcement of the sentence. *Fluchtgefahr*, on the other hand, as provided by § 112.2 StPO, refers to the risk that the defendant might escape from juridical authorities during trial. Hence the attendant precautionary measure motivated by *Fluchtgefahr* serves to ensure the presence of the defendant at the hearing.

Another superficial similarity is evident in the series of grave crimes for which the limitation of personal liberty is conceded, provided there is a precautionary measure to be observed.[9]

Similar rules are found in England and Wales.[10] The difference lies in the

---

8 Art. 274(b) Italian CPP.
9 See respectively Art. 275.3 Italian CPP and § 112.3 German StPO.
10 *Vogler, infra.*

series of crimes the measures aim to prevent, whose gravity moreover differs in the different countries. Since 11th September 2001, however, it can be said that international terrorism has become an obsession shared by all western countries and contrasted with precautionary measures.

Also of note is the theory of the principle of proportionality set down by the German federal Constitutional Court at the beginning of the 1950s and gradually developed by European criminal procedural doctrines on the limitation of fundamental rights. It is a principle of practical rationality whose dissemination in European doctrines and jurisprudence has been possible thanks to the common principles underpinning the constitutions of post-World War II continental Europe, built around the fundamental value of human dignity[11] and the inviolable rights of the human person.[12] The principle of proportionality may be broken down into three categories of suitability (*Geeignetheit*), strict proportionality (*Proportionalität im engeren Sinne*) and adequacy or necessity (*Erforderlichkeit*). As a principle it has become an essential criterion used mostly by constitutional judges (also in Italy) and by the Court of Strasburg to balance the need for repression with concerns for individual human rights.[13] It has proved a much more congruent instrument of rational justification than the (exclusively political) criterion of reasonableness used for years by the jurisprudence.

Yet a mere comparison of precautionary measures would be a very limited exercise and should entail much more than speculative interest. Looking at foreign solutions serves to better understand one's own situation. In the case of precautionary measures, it can have very real consequences in terms of practice and application.

Today, the FD EAW requires that criminal law magistrates of the Member States know the rules governing precautionary measures applied by the states involved in the request. Of importance to these ends are all the details contained in the precautionary measures procedure: from the premises required (serious circumstantial evidence of guilt), and the precautionary requirements (the so-called *pericula libertatis*), to the series of defence guarantees set down by procedural laws.[14]

In a recent case coming before the Italian Court of Cassation, the question arose of the possibility of transferring a suspect to a country (Germany) whose system does not set maximum time limits of detention.[15] An accurate examination of the norms contained in the StPO, particularly §§ 117 – 122, was nec-

---

11 Art. 1 GC.
12 Art. 2 IC.
13 See respectively *Marzaduri and Maggio, infra*.
14 *Rafarci, infra*.
15 Cass. (SU), Decision of 30. 1. 2006, Ramoci, in: Cass. pen. 2007, p. 911.

essary to establish that the German legal system does provide a limit to the duration of preventive detention even if in a different way to the measures envisaged by Articles 303 ff. of the Italian CPP.

Another thorny application problem regards the value to be attributed to preventive detention when other countries are involved. Under Article 33 of Italian Law 69/2005, time is counted according to Articles 303.4 and 304 CPP. However, according to the Italian Constitutional Court,[16] in addition to the overall time limit set by the mentioned Article 303.4 CPP, the computation must also include the phases mentioned under the previous paragraphs of the same article and may imply an attentive consideration of any investigation phase entailing a criminal process outside Italy.

In conclusion, the EAW constitutes a powerful factor of interaction and harmonization of European procedural systems. It is largely thanks to the EAW that we have been encouraged to broaden our perspective and consider how each of our particular systems deals with the issues of liberty and security against the backdrop of the normative framework of other European countries, their doctrines and jurisprudence. The studies contained in this volume are a precious contribution in this direction.

Bibliography

Hassemer, Winfried, Sicherheit durch Strafrecht, in: Strafverteidiger (2006), pp. 321 ff.
Nobili, Massimo, La procedura penale tra "dommatica" e sociologia: significato politico d'una vecchia polemica, in: La questione criminale (1977), pp. 51 ff.

The chapter contributions of this book are quoted with the only reference to the Author's surname, *infra*.

---

16 Constitutional Court, Decision 143/2008.

I. The supranational frameworks

A) The ECHR system of protection of personal freedom

Enrico Marzaduri

The application of pre-trial precautionary measures

Table of Contents

Table of Abbreviations

ACHR   American Convention on Human Rights
ECHR   European Convention on Human Rights
ECtHR European Court of Human Rights
GM   *Giurisprudenza di merito*
ICCPR International Covenant on Civil and Political Rights
LP   *La Legislazione penale*
RIDPP *Rivista italiana di diritto e procedura penale*

1.   The aim of Article 5 ECHR: to ensure that no one is arbitrarily deprived of his liberty

Unlike the provisions of Article 9 ICCPR and Article 7 ACHR, in Article 5 ECHR the assertion of everyone's right to personal liberty and security is accompanied by a list of instances in which this right may be legitimately limited.[1]

The structure of the provision described thus displays a relationship between rule and exception, in the sense that the situations where the deprivation of personal liberty may take place are no more than exceptions to a general principle of individual protection. This is a fundamental right at the top of the scale of values consecrated in the ECHR, which occupies a crucial place in democratic societies,[2] so much so that the protection it offers is not optional, as European case-law soon had an opportunity to establish, when it ruled that just because a person had intended to turn himself in voluntarily, this could not prejudice the need to review the legality of a precautionary measure.[3]

The judges in Strasbourg also stressed that the list found in Article 5.1 ECHR, that authoritative commentators have however deemed "rather extensive,"[4] is an exhaustive list for Member States and that "only a narrow interpretation of those exceptions is consistent with the aim of that provision, namely to ensure that no one is arbitrarily deprived of his liberty."[5]

In effect, Article 5 ECHR, in contrast with the corresponding provisions of the ICCPR and ACHR, does not explicitly prohibit a person's arbitrary arrest or detention, but merely requires that lawful arrest or detention fall within the

---

1 See *Trechsel*, pp. 405 ff.
2 Of many examples, see ECtHR, Grand Chamber, Decision of 8.4.2004, Assanidzé v. Georgia, Application No. 71503/01, § 169, EctHR, Decision of 19.3.1972, De Wilde, Ooms and Versyp v. Belgium, Applications No. 2832/66; 2835/66, 2899/66, § 37. See *Mazza*, pp. 46 f.
3 See ECtHR, De Wilde, Ooms and Versyp v. Belgium (fn. 2), § 65, where it is established that such an occurrence does not exempt the competent bodies from checking the legality of the deprivation of liberty imposed on the individual. On this issue, see *Pisani*, p. 117; *Ubertis*, p. 98. *Trechsel*, p. 414, this sentence "is misleading and contradictory in that the very notion of detention implies the absence of consent," but "the passage reveals its meaning, however, when read in its context: detention cannot be justified by relying on the fact that the person concerned *initially* agreed to enter and stay in a particular institution if he or she later wishes to leave."
4 *Trechsel*, p. 407.
5 See ECtHR, Decision of 21.6.2011, Shimovolos v. Russia, Application No. 30194/09, § 51. This approach, although formulated differently, appeared for the first time in ECtHR, Decision of 24.10.1979, Winterwerp. v. Netherlands, Application No. 6301/73, § 39, where it was observed that in Article 5 ECHR "lawfulness" presupposes conformity with the domestic law in the first place and also, as confirmed by Article 18, conformity with the purpose of the restrictions permitted by Article 5.1(e)."

scope of Article 5 ECHR and are adopted in accordance with a procedure pre-scribed by the law.

This wording may seem to restrict the scope of the reference to compliance with the law to compliance with national law, but actually stresses the sig-nificance of the Convention's concern with a measure's legitimacy, in its refer-ence to the list of the situations in which personal liberty may be restricted.[6]

On this point, the Court of Strasbourg has observed that it is true that:

"Where the lawfulness of detention is in issue, including the question as to whether 'a procedure prescribed by law' has been followed, the Convention refers essentially to national law and lays down the obligation to conform to the substantive and procedural rules thereof. Compliance with national law is not, however, sufficient: Article 5.1 requires in addition that any deprivation of liberty should be in keeping with the purpose of protecting the individual from arbitrariness. [...] the Court must further ascertain in this connection whether domestic law itself is in conformity with the Convention, including the general principles expressed or implied therein, notably the principle of legal certainty."[7]

The reference to the lawfulness of the deprivation of personal liberty, therefore, requires a check on the actual compliance with the provisions of national law, since:

"... although it is in the first place for the national authorities, notably the courts, to interpret and apply domestic law, under Article 5.1 failure to comply with domestic law entails a breach of the Convention and the Court can and should therefore review whether this law has been complied with."[8]

But this check cannot be considered exhaustive, because it is also necessary to check that the provisions of the State comply with the primary purpose of Article 5 ECHR,[9] which is that, as already noted, of protecting personal freedom from arbitrary intervention by public authorities.[10] In this latter perspective:

"... it is particularly important that the general principle of legal certainty be satisfied. In laying down that any deprivation of liberty must be 'lawful' and be effected 'in accordance with a procedure prescribed by law,' Article 5.1 does not merely refer back

---

6 See, in particular, *Trechsel*, p. 421.
7 ECtHR, Decision of 12.01.2008, Mooren v. Germany, Application No. 113647/03, § 72. See previously ECtHR, Winterwerp v. Netherlands (fn. 5), § 45, and later, ECtHR, Decision of 2.9.1998, Erkalo v. Netherlands, Application No. 23807/94, § 52.
8 ECtHR, Mooren v. Germany (fn. 7), § 73, which *inter alia* refers to EctHR, Decision of 10.6.1996, Benham v. United Kingdom, Application No.19380/92, § 41.
9 *Mazza*, pp. 48–49.
10 See *Chiavario* [2], p. 315, who appropriately points out, in line with the guidelines from the outset expressed in European case-law, that the protection of security referred to in Article 5 ECHR, constitutes a guarantee against the "arbitrary interference of public authorities in the freedom of an individual."

to domestic law; like the expressions 'in accordance with the law' and 'prescribed by law' in the second paragraphs of Articles 8 to 11, it also relates to the 'quality of the law,' requiring it to be compatible with the rule of law. [...] 'Quality of the law' in this sense implies that where a national law authorises deprivation of liberty it must be sufficiently accessible, precise and foreseeable in its application, in order to avoid all risk of arbitrariness."[11]

Basically, according to the Court:

"It is [...] essential that the conditions for deprivation of liberty under domestic law be clearly defined and that the law itself be foreseeable in its application, so that it meets the standard of lawfulness set by the Convention, a standard which requires that all law be sufficiently precise to allow the person – if need be, with the appropriate advice – to foresee, to a degree that is reasonable in the circumstances, the consequences which a given action may entail."[12]

The importance placed on the concept of arbitrariness, however, inevitably brings with it room for interpretive discretion[13] and the Court has noted how in this assessment "great weight [should be given] to the circumstances" of each specific instance of detention.[14]

The need to prevent arbitrary deprivations of liberty from being imposed on individuals has been appreciated, moreover, in rulings tending towards the opposite direction, i. e. aiming to limit rather than extend the boundaries within which we can speak of illegal arrest or detention. In fact, the recent case-law of the Strasbourg Court has on various occasions ruled out a violation of Article 5 ECHR in the presence of detected infringements of national law, where these have been considered such as not to cause "a breach of the Convention under Article 5.1," without forgetting that "the core task of the Court is to detect manifest cases of arbitrariness."[15]

---

11 ECtHR, Mooren v. Germany (fn. 7), § 76. See also ECtHR, Decision of 25.6.1996, Amuur v. France, Application No. 19776/92, § 50.

12 See, recently, ECtHR, Decision of 28.3.2000, Baranowski v. Poland, Application No. 28358/95, § 52.

13 Of a different opinion *Trechsel*, p. 421, who feels there should be a link between the arbitrary nature of measures regarding freedom and their non-necessary nature.

14 See, ECtHR, Decision of 2.10.1987, Bozano v. France, Application No. 9990/82, § 59.

15 Most recently, ECtHR, Decision of 31.5.2011, Khodorkovskiy v. Russia, Application No. 5829/04, § 156. On this topic, above § 5.

2.   The cases of arrest or detention during criminal proceedings

The cases of deprivation of personal liberty connected to a pending criminal proceeding[16] are covered in Article 5.1(c) ECHR, which considers "the lawful arrest or detention of a person effected for the purpose of bringing him before the competent legal authority."[17]

The provision, therefore, refers both to cases where the precautionary measure was ordered by the court, and in cases where this decision was issued by the police.

In this latter regard, also those situations where the police stop an individual for a few tens of minutes in order to search him should also fall within in the scope of the Convention's provision.[18] So, a measure whereby a person was taken to the police station under the threat of force, and was unable to leave without permission was considered as constituting a deprivation of personal liberty. This element of coercion, "notwithstanding the short duration of the arrest" – 45 minutes – "was indicative of a deprivation of liberty within the meaning of Article 5.1."[19]

By contrast, the simple restrictions of freedom of movement are not significant in this area, being regulated separately under Article 2.1 of Protocol No. 4.[20] However, according to the Court of Strasbourg:

> "… the starting-point must be the concrete situation of the individual concerned and account must be taken of a whole range of factors arising in a particular case such as the type, duration, effects and manner of implementation of the measure in question. The distinction between deprivation of, and a restriction upon, liberty is merely one of degree or intensity and not one of nature or substance."[21]

---

16 In the sense that for all the hypotheses covered by Article 5.1(c) ECHR the guarantees provided for under Article 5.3 ECHR must be applied, thus excluding an interpretation that allows the issue of a measure involving deprivation of liberty generally aimed at preventing a person from committing an offence. See the first case decided by the ECtHR, Decision of 1.7.1961, Lawless v. Ireland (merits), Application No. 332/57, § 14. See *Chiavario* [1], p. 196 – 197.

17 It should here be remembered that in the French version of the Convention there is no reference to the need for the arrest or detention to be legal, but this has not affected the interpretation of the provision: *Trechsel*, p. 408, which explains the omission as a simple oversight. See also *Fawcett*, p. 6. On this issue see ECtHR, Decision of 27.11.1991, Kemmache v. France, Application No. 12325/86, 14992/89, § 42, which clarifies that the reference to lawfulness (or *régularité*) refers to a general notion applicable to the whole of Article 5.1 ECHR, so that the omission in the French version is insignificant in terms of exegesis.

18 Cf., among the various rulings, ECtHR, Decision of 3.5.2011, Iliya Stefanov v. Bulgaria, Application No. 32438/96, § 71.

19 ECtHR, Shimovolos v. Russia (fn. 5), § 50.

20 See, for example, ECtHR, Decision of 28.5.1985, Ashingdane v. United Kingdom, Application No. 8225/78, § 41.

21 EctHR, Shimovolos v. Russia (fn. 5), § 49. See also ECtHR, Amuur v. France (fn. 11), § 42; ECtHR, Ashingdane v. United Kingdom (fn. 20), § 41; ECtHR, Decision of 6.11.1980, Guz-

As far as regards meanwhile the deprivations of liberty resulting from a measure issued by the judicial authority, we should note that a conviction at first instance prevents us from considering the detention subsequently suffered as being relevant under Article 5.1(c) ECHR. In fact, according to a well-established interpretation, even if the defendant has filed an appeal and is awaiting the final decision, we must refer to sub-paragraph a) of the aforementioned provision, concerning "the lawful detention of a person after conviction by a competent court."[22] Moreover, point 94.2 of Recommendation Rec (2006) 2 on the European Prison Rules states that: "a state may elect to regard those who have been convicted and sentenced as untried prisoners if their appeals have not been disposed of finally." In clearer terms, in point 1.2 of the Recommendation Rec(2006)13 on the use of remand in custody, it is established that "remand in custody also includes any period of detention after conviction whenever persons awaiting either sentence or the confirmation of conviction continue to be treated as unconvicted persons." We cannot therefore rule out that in the near future, also in the wake of the aforementioned documents of the Committee of Ministers of the Council of Europe, there may be changes in Strasbourg case-law regarding inclusion in the categories under Article 5.1 ECHR of defendants convicted but awaiting a final sentence.[23]

3.   The reasonable suspicion of having committed an offence

Of the situations described in Article 5.1(c) ECHR, the first refers to the arrest or detention of those for whom there is reasonable suspicion that they have committed an offence.

As reported by legal scholars, for several decades there has been little discussion of this assumption, since "the assumption was rather that the test would

---

zardi v. Italy, Application No. 7367/76, § 92–93. In this case, rightly called "the most critical borderline case decided" (in this sense *Trechsel*, p. 414), it was held that the application of the preventive measure of the forced stay in a circumscribed area of the island of Asinara, accompanied by a system of strict surveillance and control of communications, was to be seen as constituting a deprivation of liberty, even if Guzzardi could move in an area of approximately 2.5 square kilometres.

22 ECtHR, Decision of 27.6.1968, Wemhoff v. Germany, Application No. 2122/64, § 9. Subsequently, Decision of 6.4.00, Labita v. Italy, Application No. 26672/85, § 147; ECtHR, Decision of 30.11.2004, Klyakhin v. Russia, Application No., § 57. *Trechsel* is highly critical of this case-law, pp. 519 f.

23 We may also note that "almost all Member States of the European Union have chosen to regard this category of prisoners as pre-trial detainees." In this sense see *van Kalmthout et al.* (eds.), p. 57.

be met in all but those cases where the suspicion was shown to be of an entirely arbitrary nature."[24]

A significant change in approach was recorded in 1990, when, with respect to a series of arrests under section 11(1) of the Northern Ireland (Emergency Provisions) Act 1978, which allowed any constable to arrest without warrant any person suspected of being a terrorist, the Strasbourg Court had to clarify the meaning to be attributed to the expression in which the suspicion required by the ECHR to justify the deprivation of personal liberty was considered reasonable. Having stressed the importance of the "'reasonableness' of the suspicion," that "forms an essential part of the safeguard against arbitrary arrest and detention," the Court observed that a reasonable suspicion rather than a genuine and *bona fide* suspicion "presupposes the existence of facts and information which would satisfy an objective observer that the person concerned may have committed the offence."[25] And in this perspective, while recognising the difficulties inherent in the investigation of terrorist offences, so much so as to assert that "the reasonableness justifying such arrests cannot always be judged according to the same standards as are applied in dealing with the conventional crime," the decision ruled out that the needs of fighting terrorist crime could "justify stretching the notion of 'reasonableness' to the point where the essence of the safeguard secured by Article 5.1(c) is impaired."[26] And in the case in hand this had no doubt happened, since the only grounds for the arrest were previous convictions of the defendants for acts of terrorism connected with the IRA, which however dated back to about seven years previously.[27]

This approach was subsequently confirmed and clarified several times in the decisions of the Court,[28] decisions which, moreover, are bound to reflect the uncertainty characterising the concept of suspicion in assessing evidence.[29] Consequently it was established that:

"... the standard imposed by Article 5.1(c) does not presuppose that the police have sufficient evidence to bring charges at the time of the arrest," in consideration of the fact that "the object of questioning during detention [...] is to further the criminal

---

24 See *Trechsel*, pp. 423 f.
25 ECtHR, Decision of 30. 8. 1990, Fox, Campbell and Hartley v. United Kingdom, Application No. 12244/86, 12245/86, 12383/86, § 32.
26 ECtHR, Fox, Campbell and Hartley v. United Kingdom (fn. 25), § 32.
27 For other legal proceedings related to terrorism in Northern Ireland, see ECtHR, Decision of 28. 10. 1984, Murray v. United Kingdom, Application No. 14310/88, §§ 55 – 63; ECtHR, Decision of 16. 10. 2001, O'Hara v. United Kingdom, Application No. 37555/97, §§ 40 – 41, in which the questionable restrictive measures adopted by the police are clearly viewed favourably. In this regard, see the synthesis of *Trechsel*, pp. 424 f.
28 See recently ECtHR, Decision of 21. 4. 2011, Nechiporuk and Yonkalo v. Ukraine, Application No. 420/04, § 175.
29 *Trechsel*, p. 424.

investigation by way of confirming or dispelling the concrete suspicion grounding the arrest."[30]

Thus, "the fact that an applicant has not been charged or brought before a court does not necessarily mean that the purpose of his detention was not in accordance with Article 5.1(c)."[31] With regard to statements made by the *pentiti*, it was considered that although they should be seen as requiring corroboration, they could nevertheless justify the initial detention of the suspect. However, although they could be used to justify an application for a coercive measure, they could not subsequently constitute valid grounds for the measure's extension.[32]

4. The meaning of the other situations provided for by Article 5.1(c) ECHR

It is no simple matter to pinpoint the meaning of the other two situations covered by Article 5.1(c) ECHR which justify the deprivation of personal liberty in order to bring a person before the judicial authorities.

Indeed, the arrest or detention of a person when it is reasonably considered necessary to prevent his committing an offence, could lead us, at least initially, to believe that this thus envisages the adoption of a preventive measure intended in the strict sense.[33]

The link identified since the first decision by the European Court among the cases applying Article 5.1(c) and Article 5.3 ECHR, however, makes it impossible to follow this path and requires a reading whereby the provision may be implemented only within criminal proceedings.[34] In the few examples from case-law in which this specific issue has been dealt with, therefore, it has been justly ruled out that the provision may:

> "permit a policy of general prevention directed against an individual or a category of individuals who are perceived by the authorities, rightly or wrongly, as being dangerous or having propensity to unlawful acts. It does no more than afford the Contracting States a means of preventing a concrete and specific offence."[35]

---

30 In these terms, see recently, ECtHR, Decision of 23.9.2008, Lexa v. Slovakia, Application No. 54334/00, § 50.
31 ECtHR, Labita v. Italy (fn. 22), § 155; ECtHR, Decision of 22.10.1997, Erdagoz v. Turkey, Application No. 21890/93, § 51.
32 ECtHR, Labita v. Italy (fn. 22), § 159.
33 See, for instance, among Italian scholars, *Amodio*, p. 874.
34 On this issue, see clearly ECtHR, Decision of 31.7.2000, Jécius v. Lithuania, Application No. 34578/97, § 50.
35 See recently ECtHR, Shimovolos v. Russia (fn. 5), § 54. See previously ECtHR, Guzzardi v. Italy (fn. 21), § 102; Decision of 22.2.1989, Ciulla v. Italy, Application No. 11152/84, § 40.

This could be seen "both from the use of the singular (an offence) and from the object of Article 5, namely to ensure that no one should be dispossessed of his liberty in an arbitrary fashion."[36]

Having to connect the possibility of the commission of a crime to the fact of a pending criminal proceeding, we must determine situations in which a person's conduct has constituted acts punishable at least as an inchoate offence, for which there must be concrete, specific information regarding "the place and time of their commission and their victims."[37]

Strictly speaking, then, it seems that the applicative scope for the hypothesis in question is similar to that already examined for cases where a reasonable suspicion exists that a person has committed a crime, or has attempted to do so.[38]

Moreover, albeit in a case defined by the Court itself as exceptional, the provision was held to be applicable even though it was impossible to talk of reasonable suspicion of the commission of an offence in the form of a punishable attempt.[39] In fact, in consideration of the nature and extent of the applicant's previous convictions for threatening behaviour and physical assault and his mental state at the relevant time, the European judges maintained that "there were substantial grounds for believing that he would commit further similar offences" and that "the offences apprehended were thus sufficiently concrete and specific to meet the standard enunciated by the Court."[40]

The third case considered for the purposes of the deprivation of personal liberty in Article 5.1(c) ECHR refers to arrest justified by the risk of someone who has committed a criminal act escaping. "Beyond the all too easy irony to

---

36 ECtHR, Decision of 13.1.2011, Haidn v. Germany, Application No. 6587/04, § 76; ECtHR, Guzzardi v. Italy (fn. 21), § 102.

37 ECtHR, Decision of 17.12.2009, M. v. Germany, Application No. 19359/04, § 102.

38 *Trechsel*, p. 426.

39 See, moreover, in the sense that the scope of the provision could encompass not only the possibility of arrest during an attempted crime, but also arrest before this phase of those guilty of "agreeing to or inciting commission of a crime," and finally those in which the deployment of public forces actually makes the crime "impossible," *Chiavario* [1], p. 198, although this is a situation in which judgment is aimed at the possible adoption of a security measure and not the infliction of a punishment.

40 ECtHR, Decision of 27.5.1997, Eriksen v. Norway, Application No. 102/1995/608/696, § 86, where it is noted that, "as a rule, Article 5.1(c) would not provide a justification for the re-detention or continued detention of a person who has served a sentence after conviction of a specific criminal offence where there is a suspicion that he might commit a further similar offence. However, in the Court's opinion the position is different when a person is detained with a view to determining whether he should be subjected, after expiry of the maximum period prescribed by a court, to a further period of security detention imposed following conviction for a criminal offence. In a situation such as that in the present case, the authorities were entitled, having regard to the applicant's impaired mental state and history as well as to his established and foreseeable propensity for violence, to detain the applicant pending the determination by a Court of the Prosecutor's request."

which the wording of the rule lays itself open," in relation to the presumption of innocence under Article 6.2 ECHR,[41] we must rule out that this situation is effectively different to that in which there is the reasonable suspicion that a crime has been committed. "It can only be assumed that the drafters intended to cover a scenario where the suspect was caught in the act."[42] In fact, they were unable to assume that just because someone tries to get away from the scene of a crime, this may be an independent reason for suspicion justifying arrest,[43] since the text of the Convention seems to relate the commission of the crime to the person subjected to the precautionary measure, regardless of any attempt to escape.

5.   The arbitrary deprivation of the accused's liberty

In order to determine whether the arrest or detention of the defendant are lawful, however, the existence of a reasonable suspicion that a crime has been committed is not the only aspect to be assessed. As already mentioned, compliance with national law in substantive and procedural terms originates from the reference made to it in Article 5.1 ECHR. This reference also requires assessment of whether the legislation "is in conformity with the Convention, including the general principles expressed or implied therein." In other words, the Strasbourg Court is asked to assess the quality of the national law, which must be "sufficiently accessible, precise and foreseeable in its application, in order to avoid all risk of arbitrariness."[44]

In this respect, according to the European Court it is impossible to find "a global definition as to what types of conduct on the part of the authorities might constitute 'arbitrariness' for the purpose of Article 5.1," since "key principles have been developed on a case-by-case basis."[45] Thus:

> "... one general principle established in the case-law is that detention will be arbitrary where, despite complying with the letter of national law, there has been an element of bad faith or deception on the part of the authorities or where the domestic authorities neglected to attempt to apply the relevant legislation correctly."[46]

---

41 *Chiavario* [1], p. 200.
42 *Trechsel*, p. 428.
43 See *Chiavario* [1], p. 200.
44 ECtHR, Mooren v. Germany (fn. 7), § 76.
45 *Ibid.*, § 77.
46 For this summary, see ECtHR, Mooren v. Germany (fn. 7), § 78, which refers, among others, to ECtHR, Bozano v. Italy (fn. 14), § 59; ECtHR, Decision of 4.3.2008, Marturana v. Italy, Application No. 63154/00, § 80.

Moreover:

> "… the reasoning of the decision ordering detention is a relevant factor in determining whether a person's detention must be considered as arbitrary. The Court has considered the absence of any grounds given by the judicial authorities in their decisions authorising detention for a prolonged period of time to be incompatible with the principle of the protection from arbitrariness enshrined in Article 5.1. Conversely, it has found that an applicant's detention could not be said to have been arbitrary if the domestic court gave certain grounds justifying the continued detention on remand, unless the reasons given are extremely laconic and without reference to any legal provision which would have permitted the applicant's detention."[47]

However, we may not consider as lawful those cases of detention enforced "solely on the basis of the fact that a bill of indictment has been submitted to the trial court,"[48] precisely because in such cases there is no specific reason to support the restrictive measure.

Moreover, the concept of arbitrariness can also help circumscribe cases of lawful detention, to the extent that, as highlighted by the recent case-law of the European Court, "not every fault discovered in a detention order renders the underlying detention as such unlawful with the purposes of Article 5.1."[49]

This approach has led to distinguish between *ex facie* invalid detention orders – for example, given by a court in excess of jurisdiction[50] or where the interested party did not have proper notice of the hearing[51] – and detention orders which are prima facie valid and effective unless and until they have been overturned by a higher court. Only violations of national law which have given rise to a "gross and obvious irregularity," then, could support a claim that the detention is unlawful with regard to the primary goal pursued by the Convention: to prevent the arbitrary deprivation of personal liberty.[52]

As a result of this differentiation, a measure in which the facts and evidence establishing the grounds for the strong suspicion that the applicant was guilty are not described in sufficient detail does not in itself give rise to unlawful detention.[53] In fact, the order in question did not suffer from any serious and

---

47 See ECtHR, Mooren v. Germany (fn. 7), § 79, which should be referred to for extensive references to Strasbourg case-law.
48 ECtHR, Decision of 10.2.2011, Kharchenko v. Ukraine, Application No. 40107/02, § 71.
49 ECtHR, Mooren v. Germany (fn. 7), § 74. But see also ECtHR, Benham v. United Kingdom (fn. 8), § 42; ECtHR, Decision of 4.8.1999, Douiyeb v. Netherlands, Application No. 31464/96, § 45; ECtHR, Decision of 24.10.2003, Minjat v. Switzerland, Application No. 38223/97, § 41; ECtHR, Decision of 8.12.2005, Khudoyorov v. Russia, Application No. 6847/02, § 128.
50 ECtHR, Marturana v. Italy (fn. 46), § 78.
51 ECtHR, Khudoyorov v. Russia (fn. 49), § 129; ECtHR, Decision of 26.7.2011, Liu v. Russia, Application No. 29157/09, § 79.
52 ECtHR, Mooren v. Germany (fn. 15) § 75.
53 *Ibid.*, §§ 83–85.

obvious defect that rendered it null and void, but remained valid until overturned by a higher court, since the basic conditions for the detention existed and
the formal defects could not be considered such as to render the measure null
and void. On another occasion, the Court did not find that there was an infringement of Article 5.1(c) ECHR in the failure to make precautionary proceedings public, which were held behind closed doors in violation of the correct
interpretation of the relevant legislation.[54] The European judges stressed:

> "… the fact that the Convention case-law itself does not include the requirement of a
> public hearing in the list of 'core' procedural guarantees inherent to the notion of
> 'fairness' in the specific context of detention proceedings."[55]

This means that the irregularity in question could not be deemed "gross and
obvious."[56]

In short, by developing the concept of the arbitrariness of arrest or detention,
European case-law seems to reduce the significant role in terms of guarantees
under the convention played by the necessary compliance with national provisions, subordinating it to a judgment on the importance of the breach, which
could turn out to be excessively discretionary. Not only is the guarantee that
should be ensured by the intervention of the Strasbourg Court compromised, in
terms of verifying compliance with internal regulations, but sometimes the legal
certainty itself may be compromised by the kind of interpretation just mentioned.[57]

6.   Reasonable grounds for justifying the continued deprivation of personal liberty

As is apparent from the analysis of the convention in terms of the adoption of
measures involving the deprivation of liberty in criminal proceedings, in contrast to what usually occurs in European countries, the legality of arrest or
detention is not subordinated to the protection of specific precautionary needs,[58]

---

54 ECtHR, Khodorkovskiy v. Russia (fn. 15), § 158 – 165.
55 *Ibid.*, § 159.
56 *Ibid.*, § 159.
57 On this point, it should be remembered that "the principle of legal certainty may be com-
    promised if domestic courts introduce exceptions in their case-law which run counter to the
    wording of the applicable statutory provisions:" ECtHR, Mooren v. Germany (fn. 7), § 93.
58 See the careful examination carried out on the states of the European Union by *van Kalm-
    thout et al.* (eds.), pp. 71 – 74. Nor may we overlook, moreover, at the level of the Council of
    Europe, the meaning of Recommendation Rec(2006)13 of the Committee of Ministers to
    member states on the use of remand in custody, which at Article 7 establishes that "a person
    may only be remanded in custody where all of the following four conditions are satisfied: a)

but refers only to the need for there to be a reasonable suspicion of having committed an offence.

In fact, according to the Court of Strasbourg, detention may well be based solely on the suspicion of guilt, but after some time has elapsed,[59] this condition, while still necessary, is no longer sufficient to justify continuation of the coercive measure.[60]

We should start with the consideration whereby "under Article 5 of the Convention the presumption is in favour of release."[61] Thus, "continued detention may be justified in a given case only if there are clear indications of a genuine public interest which, notwithstanding the presumption of innocence, outweighs the right to liberty."[62]

In this regard, European case-law has developed four basic acceptable reasons for refusing bail (or any other measure of restraint not related to deprivation of liberty): the risk that the accused will fail to appear for trail,[63] the risk that the accused, if released, would take action to prejudice the administration of justice[64] or commit further offences[65] or cause public disorder.[66]

In assessing the existence of these reasons:

"... the national judicial authorities must examine all the facts arguing for or against the existence of a genuine requirement of public interest, and must set them out in their

---

there is reasonable suspicion that he or she committed an offence; and b) there are substantial reasons for believing that, if released, he or she would either (i) abscond, or (ii) commit a serious offence, or (iii) interfere with the course of justice, or (iv) pose a serious threat to public order; and c. there is no possibility of using alternative measures to address the concerns referred to in b.; and d. this is a step taken part of the criminal justice process." In this regard, however, some might object that the importance of precautionary needs is nevertheless related to a danger that could become concrete only if the accused has been released, and thus not when the detention order is issued.

59 As observed by *Trechsel*, p. 522, "there is no precise indication of how long the certain lapse of time during which suspicion suffices to justify detention on remand may last." Here too, we cannot fail to express concern about the wide-ranging discretionary powers of interpretation of the Strasbourg Court in establishing when the judicial authorities must justify detention in terms of precautionary needs.

60 See, *inter alia*, ECtHR, Decision of 17.3.1997, Muller v. France, Application No. 21802/93, § 35; ECtHR, Labita v. Italy, (fn. 22), § 153. See more recently ECtHR, Decision of 28.10.2010, Knebl v. Czech, Application No. 20157/05, § 77; ECtHR, Nechiporuk and Yonkalo v. Ukraine (fn. 28), § 219.

61 ECtHR, Khodorkovskiy v. Russia (fn. 15), § 182.

62 See recently ECtHR, Nechiporuk and Yonkalo v. Ukraine (fn. 28), § 219.

63 On this point, see ECtHR, Decision of 10.11.1969, Stögmüller v. Austria, Application No. 1602/62, § 15.

64 See ECtHR, Wemhoff v. Germany (fn. 22), § 14.

65 See in particular ECtHR, Decision of 10.11.1969, Matznetter v. Austria, Application No. 2178/64, § 9.

66 Among the first decisions see ECtHR, Decision of 26.6.1991, Letellier v. France, Application No. 12369/86, § 51.

decisions. Arguments for and against release must not be 'general and abstract', but contain references to the specific facts and the applicant's personal circumstances justifying his detention."[67]

In this perspective, the danger of absconding cannot only be based on the severity of the possible sentence, but must be related to objective factors that may confirm the need for a precautionary measure. Consequently, "regard must be had in particular to the character of the person involved, his morals, his assets, his links with the State in which he is being prosecuted and his international contacts."[68] As far as regards, meanwhile, the risk of interfering with the ascertainment of truth, "with the passage of time this ground inevitably becomes less and less relevant and even disappears completely with the passing of time."[69] When assessing the risk of committing further offences, the reference to the accused's criminal record may not in itself justify continued detention,[70] although it may be useful to assess the long-term continuation of unlawful conduct by the accused and the extent of damage thus caused.[71] The Court has also recognized that the severity of a crime and the relative reaction of the public may "give rise to public disquiet capable of justifying pre-trial detention for a certain time,"[72] provided that the accused's release would actually prejudice public order.[73]

In a decision on personal freedom, however, even when there are the above reasons, the court is not obliged to continue holding the accused in custody. Indeed, "the Court is prepared to tolerate an implicit rejection of the alternative measures at the initial stages of the investigation,"[74] in line, moreover, with the idea that the measure can only be based on reasonable suspicion.[75] In fact, from this point of view we cannot appreciate a difference of treatment of the accused based on his different levels of dangerousness. But when enough time has elapsed for the judicial authorities to be in a position to determine whether less invasive measures may be taken, it is the court's duty to verify whether the

---

67 For a summary, see ECtHR, Khodorkovskiy v. Russia (fn. 15), § 185.
68 *Ibid.*, § 185.
69 *Ibid.*, § 187, which provides useful references to the earlier ECtHR case-law.
70 ECtHR, Decision of 12.10.1991, Clooth v. Belgium, Application No.12718787, § 40; ECtHR, Muller v. France (fn. 59), § 44.
71 See especially ECtHR, Matznetter v. Austria (fn. 64), § 9.
72 ECtHR, Decision of 13.3.1990, Tomasi v. France, Application No.12850/87, § 91.
73 *Trechsel*, p. 527.
74 ECtHR, Khodorkovskiy v. Russia (fn. 15), § 195.
75 In the sense that at the beginning of the proceedings, "the existence of suspicion provides a sufficient ground for detention and any unavailability of bail has not been seriously challengeable," ECtHR, Decision of 3.10.2006, McKay v. United Kingdom, Application No. 543/03, § 46.

application of alternative measures would have been sufficient to reduce or eliminate entirely the precautionary risks posed by the defendant.
However:

> "... the Court acknowledges that in some circumstances, for example where the suspect allegedly belongs to a gang implicated in violent crimes, or, probably, in terrorist cases, the unavailability of bail can be self-evident, although even in such circumstances detention should not be automatic."[76]

Moreover, European case-law has not been oblivious to the need for the special regulation of detention during proceedings, when the defendant is particularly dangerous, such as in the case of the suspected membership of organised crime rings. In fact, it has been stated that the fight against this type of crime authorises a legal presumption of risk that can be justified, in particular, even when this is not absolute but may be countered with evidence to the contrary.[77] However, even in these cases it seems we should give adequate space to the principle of proportionality.[78] Recently, in fact, it has been recognised that this presumption must also contend with the time of the proceedings, in the sense that in the absence of a "specific substantiation" or "any other factor" capable of demonstrating the existence of a precautionary risk, the arguments supporting such measures cannot "be accepted in the context of the whole period."[79]

Bibliography

Amodio, Ennio, La tutela della libertà personale dell'imputato nella Convenzione europea dei diritti dell'uomo, in: Rivista italiana di diritto e procedura penale (1967), pp. 810 ff.

Chiavario, Mario, [1] La Convenzione europea dei diritti dell'uomo nel sistema delle fonti normative in materia penale, Giuffrè (1969), [2] Processo e garanzie della persona, II, Le garanzie fondamentali, 3rd ed., Giuffrè (1984).

Fawcett, James, The Application of the European Convention on Human Rights, 1st ed., Oxford University Press (1969).

Filippi, Leonardo, Libertà personale e garanzie europee, in: Corso, Piermaria / Zanetti, Elena (eds.), Studi in onore di M. Pisani, II vol., Diritto processuale penale e profili internazionali, La Tribuna (2010), pp. 225 ff.

Mantovani, Giulia, Corte europea dei diritti dell'uomo e criminalità organizzata: un delicato equilibrio tra garanzie ed efficienza, in: La legislazione penale (2008), pp. 49 ff.

---

76 ECtHR, Khodorkovskiy v. Russia (fn. 15), § 196.
77 ECtHR, Decision of 6.11.2003, Pantano v. Italy, Application No. 60851/00, § 69. On this decision, see especially *Mantovani*, pp. 52 ff.
78 For an interesting attempt to assess the principle of proportionality within the discipline of the Italian precautionary measures, see *Valentini*, pp. 446 ff.
79 ECtHR, Decion of 3.3.2009, Hilgartner v. Poland, Application No. 37976/06, § 32. In this regard, see the findings of *Ruggeri*, pp. 450 f.

Pisani, Mario, Art. 5, in: Bartole, Sergio et al. (eds.), Commentario alla Convenzione europea per la tutela dei diritti dell'uomo e delle libertà fondamentali, Cedam (2001), pp. 115 ff.

Ruggeri, Stefano, Art. 2 Decreto legislativo 11/2009, in: La legislazione penale (2009), pp. 429 ff.

Trechsel, Stefan, Human Rights in Criminal Proceedings, Oxford University Press (2005).

Ubertis, Giulio, Principi di procedura penale europea, 2nd ed., Milano (2009).

Valentini, Elena, Principio di proporzionalità e durata della cautela, in: Giurisprudenza di merito (2010), pp. 446 ff.

van Kamlthout, Anton, Introductory Summary, in: van Kamlthout, Anton et al. (eds.), Pre-trial Detention in the European Union. An Analysis of Minimum Standards in Pre-trial Detention and the grounds for Regular Review in the Member States of the EU, Wolf Legal Publishers (2009).

Paola Maggio

Judicial reviews against deprivation of liberty

Table of Contents

Table of Abbreviations

CPP   *Codice di procedura penale* (Code of Criminal Procedure)
ECHR   European Convention on human rights
ECtHR European Court of human rights

1.   Grounds and reasons of arrest

Article 5.2 ECHR provides that anyone who is arrested shall have the right to be informed of the reasons for his arrest and the charge against him. If the national authorities fail to comply, the arrest or detention is unlawful. Violation of this paragraph often also implies a violation of the fourth paragraph of this article. Article 5.2 ECHR in fact grants anyone deprived the right to freedom the right to take proceedings to ensure that the lawfulness of such deprivation of liberty be reviewed speedily by a Court and release ordered if detention is deemed un-lawful.

With regard in particular to judicial review, the ECtHR observes the need for a specific, comprehensive motivation for depriving a person of his liberty that must be correlated to the content of the review of the merits of the temporary measure. Equally important is a person's crucial right to be informed promptly in a language he understands of the reasons for his arrest and of any charge against him.[1]

The triple notion of protection – of a substantial, formal and temporal nature – that derives from this principle affects not only the formal subject matter of the motivation but also the timing of the communication.

European case-law has proved extremely precise on this point, intending arrest in the wide sense of the term and also resolving any ambiguity deriving from the rule that mentions both the "reasons for the arrest" and the "charge," in that it clarifies the essential need for the interested party to be provided with detailed information regarding the definition of the charge and anything else which he or she may need to discuss when the lawfulness of his arrest is debated speedily by a court.[2] As the right to know the contents of the custodial measure and the reasons given for it, the ECtHR has instead chosen a more "realistic" interpretative approach. The language used, albeit not necessarily the detainee's mother tongue, must, for instance, be understandable to him. This means that although the written form is considered unessential,[3] on a number of occasions the Court has stressed the detainee's right to an interpreter.[4] If we then look at the temporal aspect and the need for prompt information, the Court has stressed that this must be correlated to arrest, confirming that the provision of such information may not be delayed.[5]

---

1 Art. 5.2 ECHR.

2 In these terms *Ubertis*, p. 108; *Russo / Quaini*, p. 136, in addition to the case-law mentioned, ECtHR, Decision of 30.08.1990, Fox, Campbell, and Hartley v. United Kingdom, Application No. 12383/86, § 40.

3 Cf. ECtHR, Decision of 30.03.1989, Lamy v. Belgium, Application No. 10444/83, § 31, which, however, maintained that there was no obligation to inform the interested party of the contents of the procedural case file.

4 ECtHR, Decision of 19.12.1989, Kamasinski v. Austria, Application No. 9783/82, § 74; ECtHR, Decision of 19.12.1989, Brozicek v. Italy, Application No. 10964/84, § 41. More recently, ECtHR, Decision of 19.10.2004, Makhfi v. France, Application No. 59335/00, § 32.

5 ECtHR, Decision of 21.2.1990, Van der Leer v. Netherlands, Application No. 11509/85, §§ 30 – 31, criticised the change in a patient's custodial status, which was not communicated until ten days after the judge's decision. See also ECtHR, Decision of 11.7.2006, Saadi v. United Kingdom, Application No. 13229/03, § 55; ECtHR, Grand Chamber, 29.1.2008, Saadi v. United Kingdom, Application No. 13229/03, § 84. The Court found that a delay of 76 hours in providing reasons for detention is not compatible with the requirement of the provision that such reasons should be given "promptly," with violation of Article 5.2 ECHR.

2. The right to be brought promptly before a judicial authority and the need for subsequent reviews of the remand detention

Article 5.3 ECHR basically establishes the right of every person arrested or detained to be brought before a judge or officer authorised by law to exercise judicial power.[6]

This right is combined with the recognised alternative of the need for a person to be judged in a reasonable time or to be released during the investigation phase. It is also combined with the guarantee that the detainee must appear at the release hearing.[7] Equally important is the European Court's case-law upholding the automatic and prompt nature of custodial review. Unlike the measure provided for under Article 5.4 ECHR, which establishes the interested party's right to take proceedings, paragraph 3 asserts the need that the assessment of lawfulness be conducted with all due haste (*promptly*).[8]

---

6 *Klip*, p. 262. The case-law of the European Court has specified the characteristics of the body before which a detained person should appear, holding that it need not possess all the requirements of jurisdictionality, provided it is independent of the executive and the interested parties. In this sense ECtHR, Decision of 28.10.1998, Assenov et al. v. Bulgaria, Application No. 24760/94, § 146. Moreover, there must be a clear separation between the prosecution and the body responsible for issuing decisions on preventive custody. In this sense see ECtHR, Decision of 26.5.1988 Pauwels v. Belgium, Application No. 10208/82, § 38, according to which the fact that a judge responsible for deciding on detention could subsequently assume the role of prosecutor violates the precepts laid down under the Convention. This principle was recently confirmed by ECtHR, Decision of 6.11.2008, Yeloyev v. Ukraine, Application No. 17283/02, § 47; ECtHR, Decision of 23.11.2010, Moulin v. France, Application No. 37104/06, § 61. On the independence, efficiency and responsibilities of judges, see also the Recommendation Rec(2010)12 of the Committee of Ministers of the Council of Europe.
7 On the need for prompt contact between the accused and the judge see ECtHR, Decision of 27.7.2004, Ikincisoy v. Turkey, Application No. 26144/95, § 100, according to which "article 5.3 aims to avoid the arbitrariness and to secure the rule of law by requiring judicial control of the interference by the executive." Albeit in a different field, it has been maintained in Italy that the absence of a decision by the supervisory court on appeals brought against the measures of the Ministry of Justice adopted pursuant to Article 41bis Law 354/1975, violates, according to Article 6 ECHR, the right of those whose personal liberty is restricted to have access to a Court. See ECtHR, Decision of 30.10.2003, Ganci v. Italy, Application No. 41576/98, § 31.
8 See *Ubertis*, p. 111. The reference is to a decision regarding terrorist crimes, which criticised the unlawfulness of custody extended without judicial review, respectively, according to the interested parties, for four days and six hours, and for six days and 16.5 hours. Even in the case of departures from standard procedure in special cases, the Court still retains the power to review excessive delays in bringing the accused before the judicial authority. In this sense ECtHR, Decision of 29.11.1988, Brogan et al. v. United Kingdom, Application No. 11209/84, § 62. In the field of terrorist crimes see also ECtHR, Assenov et al. v. Bulgaria (fn. 13), § 146. This decision represents a precedent to which the Court has constantly appealed. See, for instance, ECtHR, Decision of 02.11.2004, Abdülsamet Yaman v. Turkey, Application No. 32446/96, § 74, on the maximum time limit of four days and six hours. Similarly, ECtHR, Decision of 22.7.2004, Sarikaya v. Turkey, Application No. 36115/97, § 59. More in general, on

The procedural repercussions of this right strongly condition the character-istics of reviews of custodial measures. The prevalent European case-law has in fact clarified that immediately following arrest an individual has the right to be heard personally by the judicial authority, even though his or her lawyer is not present.[9] Moreover, the circumstances weighing for and against the defendant must be assessed on the merits and adequate grounds for them must be pro-vided.[10] Finally, if there are insufficient reasons to support the charge, the magistrate must be able to order the detainee's immediate release.[11]

With particular regard to the time of custody, the first period of paragraph 3 significantly asserts the right to be tried in a reasonable time as an alternative to the right to be released during the investigation phase. This difference must be intended in the sense that the release of the defendant is necessary whenever custody exceeds the threshold of "reasonableness" in proportion to the concrete information of the case and with regard to the presumption of innocence.[12]

Assessment in this direction extends as far as checking the reasonable con-tinuation of custody and imposes a review attentive to the applications for release submitted during proceedings, examining the reasons submitted by the defendant together with those of the national authority[13] and taking into ac-count, in concrete terms, the justifications for rejection of an application for

---

the speedy assessment of the lawfulness of the detention, ECtHR, Decision of 25.10.1989, Bezicheri v. Italy, Application No. 11400/85, § 26.

9 ECtHR, Grand Chamber, Decision of 29.4.1999, Aquilina v. Malta, Application No. 25642/94, § 54.

10 ECtHR, Grand Chamber, Decision of 18.2.1999, Hood v. United Kingdom, Application No. 27267/95, § 60. On the need to avoid stereotyped supporting arguments, ECtHR, De-cision of 22.7.2008, Getiren, v. Turkey, Application No. 10301/03, §§ 105 ff.

11 ECtHR, Decision of 22.5.1984, Duinhof and Duijf v. Netherlands, Application No. 9626/81, §§ 32 ff. In this light, for instance, the Italian system has appeared open to criticism for two types of reasons. It delays the moment of contact between the judge and the detained person until the beginning of the trial; incorporating this examination into the trial does not satisfy the need for automatic review. Moreover, in the investigation phase, the rapidity of contact between the arrested person and the judge is compromised by Article 294.1 of the Italian CPP, which sets the time limit for examining whether the detainee shall remain on remand (*interrogatorio di garanzia*), at five days from the beginning of preventive custody, i.e. more than the maximum time-frame of four days and six hours established by the ECtHR case-law. On this topic see *Mazza*, p. 62. Cf. Constitutional Court, Decision 230/2005. On similar lines, see subsequently Constitutional Court, Decision 267/2008.

12 For example, ECtHR, Decision of 27.6.1968, Wemhoff v. Germany, Application No. 2122/64, § 5. Article 5.3 would also be violated in the case of detention based on the legitimate need for a precautionary measure, but whose duration is disproportionate to the effective complexity of the trial and the conduct of the appellant. See ECtHR, Decision of 27.8.1992, Tomasi v. France, Application No. 12850/87, § 102. In the same sense ECtHR, Decision of 8.10.2009, Naudo v. Francia, Application No. 35469/06, § 47.

13 ECtHR, Wemhoff v. Germany (fn. 13), § 12.

release, also in terms of the effective prevalence of public interest over individual liberty.[14]

However, the provision laid down in paragraph 3 is independent of the more general one envisaged under paragraph 1 regarding lawfulness of arrest.[15] The question of legitimacy has already been clarified, in the sense that detention fully complies with national law, as well as with the principles and exceptions envisaged under the Convention.[16] Moreover, the aforementioned conformity should not be assessed in abstract terms but with regard to the particularities of individual cases.[17] Conformity is not achieved in the event of the "special diligence" required of judges in dealing with proceedings involving charged detainees being absent.

Finally, the Court of Strasbourg requires a review of lawfulness at reasonable intervals.[18] This principle has been applied to the problem of the duration of custody before conviction. As the Italian Court of Cassation has observed,[19] these rules also imply that during the whole period prior to conviction states need to adopt systems of continuous review, "at regular intervals," of the need for continued detention in order to avoid an excessive length thereof, a goal that

---

14 ECtHR, Decision of 24.8.1998, Contrada v. Italy, Application No. 92/1997, § 54. Public interest needs include a judicial system that ensures the right to defend oneself and an impartial judge. See ECtHR, Decision of 6.11.2003, Pantano v. Italy, Application No. 60851/00, § 74.

15 According to ECtHR, Decision of 24.9.1992, Kolompar v. Belgium, Application No. 11613/85, § 45, since these are distinct orders, compliance with the former does not imply consequential observance of the latter.

16 ECtHR, Decision of 29.8.1990, E. v. Norway, Application No. 11701/85, § 49; ECtHR, Decision of 10.6.2010, Borer v. Switzerland, Application No. 22493/06, § 47, with regard to Article 5.1 ECHR. See also ECtHR, Decision of 13.1.2011, Haidn v. Germany, Application No. 6587/04, § 94, according to which "in order to be 'lawful,' detention must conform to the substantive and procedural rules of national law, which must, moreover, be of a certain quality and, in particular, must be foreseeable in its application, in order to avoid all risk of arbitrariness."

17 ECtHR, Decision of 17.2.2005, Sardinas Albo v. Italy, Application No. 56271/00, § 97. The Court considers that the duty of "special diligence" enshrined in Article 5.3 was not observed.

18 ECtHR, Decision of 22.5.1984, De Jong, Baljet and Van Den Brink v. Netherlands, Application No. 8805/79, § 58. See also ECtHR, Decision of 24.10.1979, Winterwerp v. Netherlands, Application No. 6301/73, § 61, in a case of detention of a person of unsound mind.

19 Cass. (SU), Decision of 30.1.2007, Ramoci, in: CP 2007, p. 911, which, with regard to Art. 18(e) Law 69/2005, regarding the issue of European arrest warrants, deemed that the Italian judicial authority should, for the purposes of delivery, check whether "the legislation of the issuing Member State expressly establishes a term of duration of the preventive custody until conviction at first instance, or failing this, if an implicit time limit can in any case be deduced from other procedural mechanisms that establish, as obligatory and at pre-established intervals, judicial review to confirm the legitimate continuance of preventive custody or, alternatively, order release."

can be usefully (albeit not necessarily) pursued limiting custody to pre-established "maximum periods."[20]

3.   The *Habeas Corpus* guarantee

3.1.   The right to take proceedings under Article 5.4 ECHR

Examining more closely the dictates regarding the assessment of the lawfulness of arrest or detention, the provision contained in Article 5.4 ECHR stresses the difference with regard to the right to be brought before the judicial authority laid down under Article 5.3 ECHR. Undoubtedly, this implies that the two needs may be jointly protected.[21]

Salient observations on custodial reviews point up the possibility of jurisdictional appeal,[22] which must possess sufficient certainty in the national legal system to avert the risk of non-compliance with the conditions laid down under Article 5.4 ECHR[23] and permit an assessment of the lawfulness of the measure including the possibility of directly ordering the release of the detained person.[24]

Naturally, the judge given responsibility for this assessment must be independent of the Executive and equidistant with respect to the interested parties.[25] Regarding the incompatibility of the judge, the European Court has not deemed it necessary that the bodies ordering preventive custody and those subsequently called to review its legitimacy be different.[26] However, this rule is only valid for the very first phase of assessing the lawfulness of detention.

These European principles were considered as respected by an order of a

---

20 On this point, see the Recommendation Rec(2006)13 of the Committee of Ministers of the Council of Europe. Cf. recently the Green Paper of the Commission of 14.6.2011 on the application of EU criminal justice legislation in the field of detention. Strengthening mutual trust in the European judicial area (COM(2011) 327 final).

21 ECtHR, Decision of 26.6.1991, Letellier v. France, Application No. 12369/86, § 46.

22 According to *Spagnolo*, p. 55, the value of the precept underlying Article 5 ECHR lies in "the series of guarantees that renders a procedure jurisdictional."

23 ECtHR, Decision of 24.8.1998, Soumare v. France, Application No. 48/1997, § 42. The Court reiterates that the existence of a remedy must be sufficiently certain, failing which it lacks the accessibility and effectiveness required for the purposes of Article 5 § 4. The accessibility and effectiveness of the remedy were remarked on by ECtHR, Decision of 13.3.2003, Öcalan v. Turkey, Application No. 46221/99, §§ 100 ff.

24 Along these lines, see ECtHR, Decision of 02.03.1987, Weeks vs. United Kingdom, Application No. 9787/82, § 61 ff.

25 ECtHR, Decision of 26.5.1968, Neumeister v. Austria, Application No. 1936/63, § 24.

26 On this point cf. *Ubertis*, p. 119. This assumption is confirmed in the English version of the text, which talks of the right "to take proceedings" and makes no mention of the concepts of "appeal," "recourse" or "remedy." Along the same lines, see ECtHR, Decision of 18.06.1971, De Wilde, Ooms and Versyp v. Belgium, Application No. 2832/66, § 79.

jurisdictional authority following a judicial procedure in which the minimum fair trial guarantees are respected, particularly with regard to participation of the interested party,[27] even if the review of detention is incorporated in the decision.[28] Vice versa, for every matter subsequent to the custody order – with particular regard to circumstances subject to change over time – the detained person has the right to have recourse to a jurisdictional authority at regular, shortly spaced intervals in order to contest the lawfulness of his detention.[29]

Moreover, forms of incompatibility have been found when a magistrate, in order to issue a preventive custody writ, is obliged, pursuant to his national legislation, to refer to the ascertained existence of "particularly significant suspicions" regarding the commission of the alleged facts by the defendant. In such situations, the difference between the analysis performed for the purposes of pre-trial detention and that required to arrive at a judicial decision is significantly reduced.[30]

3.2.   Fair trial guarantees in the Habeas Corpus procedure

In terms of liberty, the minimum guarantees of a fair trial regard above all the observance of the adversarial process[31] and ensuring an even playing field.[32]

This leads to the need for the effective participation of the interested party in

---

27 Regarding the necessary presence of the interested party or his counsel see ECtHR, Decision of 25.10.1990, Keus v. Netherlands, Application No. 12228/86, § 27.

28 ECtHR, Decision of 24.10.1995, Iribarne Pérez v. France, Application No. 16462/90, § 30.

29 Cf. ECtHR, Assenov et al. v. Bulgaria (fn. 13), § 162. For example, it was deemed reasonable for the defendant held in pre-trial custody to contest the lawfulness of the detention – by means of a new request for release – one month after a previously rejected application. In this sense ECtHR, Decision of 25.10.1989, Bezicheri v. Italy, Application No. 11400/85, §121.

30 Particularly important is ECtHR, Decision of 24.5.1989, Hautschildt v. Denmark, Application No. 10486/83, § 53, regarding the violation of Article 6.1.

31 ECtHR, Decision of 21.2.1996, Hussain v. United Kingdom, Application No. 21928, § 57 ff.; ECtHR, Decision of 1.6.2006, Fodale v. Italy, Application No. 70148/01, § 41 ff., which established that "a court examining an appeal against detention must provide guarantees of a judicial procedure. The proceedings must be adversarial and must always ensure 'equality of arms' between the parties, that is, the prosecutor and the detained person. Equality of arms is not ensured if counsel is denied access to those documents in the investigation file which are essential in order to challenge effectively the lawfulness of his client's detention."

32 On various occasions the European Court has recognised that the defendant's right to be tried "on an even playing field" also applies to appeals against preventive custody. In this sense ECtHR, Decision of 13.7.1995, Kampanis v. Greece, Application No. 17977/91, § 58; ECtHR, Decision of 12.12.1991, Toth v. Austria, Application No. 11894/95, § 84; ECtHR, Decision of 30.3.1989, Lamy v. Belgium, Application No. 10444/83, § 29.

the proceedings[33] and, in the event of remand detention, a decided preference for an actual hearing in court (equality of arms).[34]

Great attention has also been given to the presence of the detained person and whether he or she is effectively cognisant of the details of the charge.[35] Any inversion of the burden of proof to the disadvantage of the defendant has also been criticised.[36] In relation to these aspects it has been maintained that failure to issue the defence counsel with notice fixing the date of the hearing before the Court of Cassation, as provided for under the Italian system, renders an even playing field between the prosecution and defence impossible.[37] This omission seriously compromises the adversarial nature of the process guaranteed under Article 6 ECHR, implying, both for the prosecution and detained person, the opportunity to be informed of the observations or evidence produced by the adverse party and to discuss them. According to the ECtHR case-law, the text of Article 6 – and especially the independent sense attributed to the notion of "criminal charge" – means that this provision may be applied to the phases prior to the proceedings.[38] Taking into consideration the dramatic consequences of the deprivation of liberty for the fundamental rights of the person concerned, any procedure that falls within the field of application of Article 5.4 of the Convention must in principle also comply, as far as is possible in the context of an investigation, with the fundamental requirements of due process. National legislation can satisfy this requirement in various ways, but the method it adopts must in any case ensure that the adverse party is kept informed of observations filed and has a real possibility to comment on them.[39]

Less clear are the "secondary issues" of the right to legal assistance, acknowledged above all in situations of protecting weak persons, such as minors, or whenever the examination of the interested party's personality is important.[40]

---

33 ECtHR, Decision of 2.3.1987, Weeks v. United Kingdom, Application No. 9787/82, § 40.
34 ECtHR, Grand Chamber, Decision of 25.3.1999, Nikolova v. Bulgaria, Application No. 31195/96, § 65.
35 ECtHR, Decision of 9.1.2003, Shishkov v. Bulgaria, Application No. 38822/97, § 54.
36 ECtHR, Decision of 20.2.2003, Hutchison Reid v. United Kingdom, Application No. 50272/99, § 81. The Court convicted the United Kingdom for violation of Article 5.4 ECHR, due to the fact that the burden of proof weighed upon the appellant in the course of preventive custody proceedings and due to the excessive duration of the proceedings themselves.
37 ECtHR, Decision of 1.6.2006, Fodale v. Italy, Application No. 70148/01, § 41.
38 ECtHR, Decision of 1.6.2006, Fodale v. Italy, Application No. 70148/01, § 41; ECtHR, Decision of 24.11.1993, Imbrioscia v. Switzerland, Application No. 13972/88, § 36.
39 ECtHR, Decision of 13.2.2001, Garcia Alva v. Germany, Application No. 23541/94, § 39, according to which the court examining appeal against detention must provide guarantees of judicial procedure. On "equality of arms" and fairness between the parties, the prosecutor and the detained person see ECtHR, Decision of 30.3.2010, Allen v. United Kingdom, Application No. 18837/06, § 47.
40 On the necessary presence of defence counsel in the case of minors, see ECtHR, Decision of

The implicit assent to free legal aid also during the review of the legitimacy of custodial measure was confirmed by a court decision which, although denying the existence of a violation of Article 5.4 ECHR, upheld the right to free legal aid[41] as being one of the guarantees of liberty.

With regard to the specific characteristics of the measure, the Court maintained that external publicity in the pre-trial interlocutory phase did not benefit the interests of the accused.[42]

Regarding the cognizance of the body responsible for remand detention, the European Court, while underlining the distinction between this and a judgment on the merits,[43] has specified the need to ascertain properly that the conditions exist to justify custody, noting that this assessment should not be confined to mere consideration of whether the body issuing the measure is competent to do so.[44]

The decision must also be made "speedily," and the time established for the decision correlated with the essential limit for presenting an appeal.[45] In the cases examined, the supranational judges took into consideration the specific complexities of the dispute or the behaviour of the interested party during the proceedings.

The time required for assessment naturally varies according to whether the individual national systems provide for appeals against the order,[46] or for forms of periodical review;[47] as a rule, the timeframes necessary to produce expert witnesses' reports are considered unjustified.[48]

29.2.1988, Bouamar v. Belgium, Application No. 9106/80, § 60 ff. Regarding the case in which the personality of the defendant must be assessed following long periods of detention, see ECtHR, Decision of 21.2.1996, Singh v. United Kingdom, Application No. 23389/94, § 68 ff.

41 ECtHR, Grand Chamber, Decision of 18.2.1999, Hood v. United Kingdom, Application No. 27267/95, § 65, underlines that in the case in point, the detained person had enjoyed access to legal assistance and had not asked for free legal aid.

42 ECtHR, Neumeister v. Austria (fn. 30), § 24.

43 ECtHR, Decision of 5.11.1981, X v. United Kingdom, Application No. 7215/75, § 58.

44 ECtHR, Decision 29.11.1988, Brogan et al. vs. United Kingdom, Application No. 11209/84, § 65.

45 ECtHR, Decision of 22.5.1984, De Jong, Baljet and Van Den Brink v. Netherlands, Application No. 8805/79, § 58, found a violation of Art. 5 § 4 ECHR in a case in which six days had passed since the beginning of detention before the person was given the opportunity to present an appeal against the decision.

46 In these cases the overall nature of the proceeding itself must be assessed. In this sense ECtHR, Decision of 23.11.1993, Navarra v. France, Application No. 13190/87, § 28 ff. On the need to decide on any appeals once they have been made, ECtHR, Decision of 26.10.2006, Khudobin v. Russia, Application No. 59696/00, § 124.

47 ECtHR, Decision of 24.9.1992, Herczegfalvy v. Austria, Application No. 10533/83, § 77, maintained that reasonable regularity had not been complied with in the case of an initial review 15 months after the decision ordering internment in a psychiatric hospital and subsequent review after two years. On the essentially periodical nature of review, also in the

Moreover, general warnings are contained in all the requests addressed to Member States aimed at establishing the correct and effective organisation of jurisdiction over personal liberty, indicating factors to be taken into account such as workload,[49] judicial holidays,[50] and requirements related to the federal structure[51] of some nations.

When applying the notion of reasonable time to the system of assessing precautionary measures, the European Court condemned Turkey for its delay in issuing decisions on requests for the review of precautionary measures.[52] The restricted time limit considered "reasonable" by the Court for such decisions can be deduced from rulings that found a violation of Article 5.4 ECHR in a decision on the lawfulness of provisional detention issued 17 days after the defendant's request.[53] Furthermore, the European parameters not only show the Italian system as testing positive but also would call into question any prospective future legislation should it interfere with this value by shifting forward the aforementioned time limit.

Indeed, the ECtHR has already handed down harsh criticism of Italy's current

---

event of restriction of a person's freedom to circulate, see ECtHR, Decision of 21. 10. 2008, Bessenyei v. Hungary, Application No. 37509 / 06, § 23 ff.

48 ECtHR, Grand Chamber, Decision of 25. 3. 1999, Musial v. Poland, Application No. 24557 / 94, § 46.

49 ECtHR, Decision of 25. 10. 1989, Bezicheri v. Italy, Application No. 11400 / 85, §25.

50 ECtHR, Decision of 29. 8. 1990 E. v. Norway, Application No. 11701 / 85, § 66.

51 ECtHR, Decision 26. 9. 1997, R. M. D. v. Switzerland, Application No. 81 / 1996, § 54.

52 The meaning of "reasonable time" is discussed in *Amodio*, p. 797, and, with different emphasis, in *Grevi*, p. 3204. See also *van Dijk et al.*, p. 373. See ECtHR, Decision of 6. 2. 2003, Zeynep Avci v. Turkey, Application No. 37021 / 97, § 54, condemned Turkey for its tardy decisions in reply to requests for review made by the appellant. Previously, on the violation of Article 5.3, see ECtHR, Decision of 5. 12. 2002, Dalkilic v. Turkey, Application No. 25756 / 94, § 23, which had criticised the delay whereby the detainee was not brought before the judge until after 15 days of provisional detention. A similar perspective can be found in ECtHR, Decision of 10. 10. 2002, Gündogan v. Turkey, Application No. 31877 / 96, § 23; ECtHR, Decision of 20. 6. 2002, Igdeli v. Turkey, Application No. 29296, § 30 ff.; ECtHR, Decision of 9. 1. 2003, Kadem v. Malta, Application No. 55263 / 00, § 54; ECtHR, Decision of 30. 01. 2003, Nikolov v. Bulgaria, Application No. 38884 / 97, § 77. The Court found that there had been a violation of the applicant's right, under Article 5.3 ECHR, to trial within a reasonable time or to release pending trial. In this sense ECtHR, Decision of 13. 12. 2007, Mooren vs. Germany, Application No 11364 / 03, § 74. This was confirmed by ECtHR, Decision of 9. 7. 2009, Mooren v. Germany, Application No 11364 / 03, § 107. The Court considered that the German courts, and in particular the Court of Appeal, failed to make a "speedy" decision on the lawfulness of the applicant's detention on remand. This constituted a breach of Article 5.4 ECHR.

53 See ECtHR, Decision of 9. 1. 2003, Kadem v. Malta, Application No. 55263 / 00, § 44. Similarly, ECtHR, Decision of 30. 1. 2003, Nikolov v. Bulgaria, Application No. 38884 / 97, §§ 77 – 92, upheld the ruling that Art. 5 § 4 ECHR had been violated both on account of the delay with which the request for review had been examined, and because the defence was denied access to the file for review.

precautionary system[54] with specific regard to the requirement that the many remedies designed to assess the lawfulness of detention in Italy comply with the absolute and non-negotiable value of promptness.

The Court warns that decisions must be taken "speedily" regardless of the specific procedural systems regulating multiple or repeatable remedies.

The contents of the guarantee enshrined in Article 5.4 thus seem to require prompt assessment in general terms, a requirement that applies to all courts in which it is to be adopted. The aforementioned strict, substantialist approach seems to reject the possibility of so-called incorporated assessment since it weakens the right to promptness although the detention measure has already been subject to an initial review in a reasonable time in compliance with fair trial principles.[55]

In effect, the intrinsic evolution of the precautionary system requiring constant review of the premises for detention confirms the need recognised by the European Court that no room be left "for variable compositions or balancings between the need for prompt assessment and its systematic collocation in the individual system that provides for it."[56]

The case-law assessment of the European Court allows it to rule from time to time on the absolute nature of the right claimed by means of concrete assessment of the procedural progress and the duration of individual cases. These individual cases do not, however, compromise the general need asserted by the European Court that preventive detention reviews be prompt and effective and as a consequence, nor do they lessen the precise burdens of liability for Member States failing to comply with this generally affirmed principle.

---

54 Cf., ECtHR, Decision of 19.5.2005, Rapacciuolo v. Italy, Application No. 76024/01, § 37, criticising the failure to observe the obligation of speed with regard to appeal and appeal to the Court of Cassation. ECtHR, Decision of 3.7.2007, Naranjo Hurtado v. Italia, Application No.16508/04, § 32, maintained that the decision in appeal proceedings against custody, issued after 33 days, was excessively late. Cf. ECtHR, Decision of 4.3.2008, Marturana v. Italia, Application No. 63154/00, § 114, on the violation of Article 5.4, due to the "significant delays" of the Court of Cassation in examining the appeals against the lawfulness of his detention (in particular, the two appeals to Cassation had been decided "only" five months later and eight months later).

55 On this controversial topic, see *Pisani*, pp. 141 ff.; *Defilippi*, pp. 193 ff.; *Mazza*, p. 69. The hypotheses in consideration are traditionally those of detention following conviction (Art. 5.1(a) ECHR) or of custody followed by appearance before the judge (Art. 5.3 ECHR).

56 This is the well-reasoned opinion of *Rafaraci*, p. 288.

Bibliography

Amodio, Ennio, Ragionevole durata del processo, *abuse of process* e nuove esigenze di tutela dell'imputato, in: Diritto penale e processo (2003), pp. 797 ff.

Defilippi, Claudio, Art. 5, in: De Filippi, Claudio / Bosi, Debora / Harvey, Rachel (eds.), La Convenzione europea dei diritti dell'uomo e delle libertà fondamentali, ESI (2005), pp. 193 ff.

Filippi, Leonardo, Libertà personale e garanzie europee, in: Corso, Piermaria / Zanetti, Elena (eds.), Studi in onore di Mario Pisani, II, Diritto processuale penale e profili internazionali, La Tribuna (2010), pp. 225 ff.

Grevi, Vittorio, Il principio della "ragionevole durata" come garanzia oggettiva del "giusto processo" penale, in: Cassazione penale (2003), pp. 3204 ff.

Klip, Andr, European criminal law, Intersentia (2009).

Manes, Vittorio / Zagrebelsky, Vladimiro, La Convenzione Europea dei diritti dell'uomo nell'ordinamento penale italiano, Giuffrè (2011).

Mazza, Oliviero, La libertà personale nella Costituzione europea, in: Aimonetto, Maria Gabriella (ed.), Profili del processo penale nella Costituzione europea, Giappichelli (2005), pp. 45 ff.

Pisani, Mario, Art. 5, in: Bartole, Sergio / Conforti, Benedetto / Raimondi, Guido (eds.), Commentario alla Convenzione europea per la tutela dei diritti dell'uomo e delle libertà fondamentali, Cedam (2001), pp. 114 ff.

Rafaraci, Tommaso, Le garanzie del procedimento *de libertate*, in: Kostoris / Roberto E. / Balsamo, Antonio (eds.), Giurisprudenza europea e processo penale italiano, Giappichelli (2008), pp. 272 ff.

Russo, Carlo / Quaini, Paolo, La Convenzione europea dei diritti dell'uomo e la giurisprudenza di Strasburgo, Giuffrè (2006).

Spagnolo, Paola, Il tribunale della libertà tra normativa nazionale e normativa internazionale, Giuffrè (2008).

Spangher, Giorgio, Evoluzione e involuzione del sistema cautelare, in: Corso, Piermaria / Zanetti, Elena (eds.), Studi in onore di Mario Pisani, II, Diritto processuale penale e profili internazionali, La Tribuna (2010), pp. 792 ff.

Ubertis, Giulio, Principi di procedura penale europea. Le regole del giusto processo, 2th ed., Raffaello Cortina (2009).

van Dijk, Peter et al. (eds.), Theory and practice of the European Convention of Human Rights, 4th ed., Intersentia (2006).

B) The harmonization at European Union level

Sabela Oubiña Barbolla*

The European Arrest Warrant in Law and Practice

Table of Contents

Table of Abbreviations

CGPJ	*Consejo general del poder judicial* (General Council of the Judiciary)
EEW	European Evidence Warrant
EAW	European Arrest Warrant
ECHR	European Court of Human Rights
ECJ	European Court of Justice
EJN	European Judicial Network
FD	Framework Decision
EAW FD	Framework Decision on the European Arrest Warrant
TEU	Treaty of the European Union
LOPJ	*Ley orgánica poder judicial* (Organic Law of the Judicial System)

* This paper is written in the context of two research projects. The first, funded by the European Commission, is titled "The European Arrest Warrant in law and in practice: a comparative study for the consolidation of the European law-enforcement area" (reference JLS/2007/JPEN/245 and ABAC 30-CE-0178645/00–20). The second, funded by Spanish Ministry of Education and Science, is entitled "Restrictions on personal freedom of terrorists in criminal proceedings" (DER 2008\06178).

REJUE   *Red judicial española de cooperación judicial internacional* (Spanish
         Judicial Network of Mutual Assistance in Judicial Matters)
SCC   Spanish Criminal Code
SIS   Schengen Information System

1.   Introduction: the EAW Framework Decision and its history

On 13th June 2002, the Council of the European Union adopted the Framework
Decision[1] on the EAW[2] and the Surrender Procedures between Member States
(2002/584/JAI, FD EAW). The FD EAW established 31st December 2003 as the
deadline for transposition into Member States' national law (art. 34).

On 14th February 2002 Spain, France, Belgium, Portugal, Germany and Lux-
emburg stated their intention to revise their national law during the first quarter
of 2003 in order to implement the EAW as soon as possible.[3] In this chronological
context Spain was the first EU Member State to transpose the FD and, moreover,
the only Member State to meet the deadline agreed upon unofficially by the
aforementioned group of six Member States. By the time of the FD deadline
(art. 25) on 1st January 2004, only eight countries had adopted the necessary legal
measures. The remaining Member States[4] had also consented, meaning that the
process of effective transposition of the FD was held up[5] beyond the official
deadline initially envisaged by the Commission.

The EAW is a judicial instrument issued by a Member State requiring another
Member State to detain and surrender a requested person. The EAW may be
issued for two different purposes: either to conduct a criminal prosecution or to
execute a custodial sentence or detention order (art. 1 FD EAW).

In general, a FD implies a certain regulatory standardisation of the subject
under regulation, even if on some points it allows States freedom in the transposition[6] to their respective internal legal systems; hence the different national

---

1 On the nature of the EAW FD, see *Kaunert*, p. 390; *Vogel*, pp. 937–943; *Fennelly*, pp. 519–520.
2 We highly recommend as a practical reference for all researchers interested in the EAW the
   detailed report on the EAW across EU, VVAA, The European Arrest Warrant in Law and in
   Practice: a comparative study for the consolidation of the European law-enforcement area,
   Coimbra, 2010, available in English at http://opj.ces.uc.pt/pdf/EAW_Final_Report_
   Nov_2010.pdf (European research project JLS/2007/JPEN/245 and ABAC 30-CE-
   0178645/00–20).
3 *Irurzun Montoro* [1], pp. 58–61.
4 Especially conspicuous was the late transposition by Italy (1 year, 3 months and 27 days); Czech
   Republic (1 year and 19 days later) and the Republic of Germany (6 months and 22 days).
5 Report from the Commission, Brussels, 23.2.2005, COM (2005) 63 final, based on art. 34 FD
   EAW.
6 One of the last and most complete for its detailed analysis by *Gomes/Fernandes/Borges Reis*
   [1], pp. 40–62.

legal solutions envisaged for the different practical issues.[7] The differences we find in each of the national experiences of the EAW are, as we will explain, inherent to the choice of the FD as a legal instrument.[8]

The Court of Justice expressly endorsed the use of the FD as the particular legal instrument in the EAW in the Advocaten voor de Wereld case[9] since article 31.1(a) and (b) TEU did not indicate a specific type of legal instrument. This means that the Council had the power of "choice between several instruments to regulate the same subject-matter," and in this case it decided to use the vehicle of a FD.

2.   Competent judicial authorities

The EAW FD gives Members States freedom to choose the authorities competent to issue and execute an EAW, on one condition, however. According to Article 6 EAW FD, they must be *judicial authorities*.[10] This simple fact is the first and distinctive feature of an EAW compared to extradition since the EAW abandons political-governmental procedures, including the intervention of different Ministries. Surprisingly, however, the concept of judicial authority is not always the same around the EU. It includes obviously Courts, but may also include Public Prosecutors, Police Forces, etc. The EAW FD left the Member States free to establish their *competent judicial authorities*, but as Fichera observes[11], some of them have interpreted it rather broadly (for instance, Denmark, Germany, Cyprus). The upshot, however, is that governments will no longer have the role they traditionally played in extradition matters.

One of the main issues of interest concerning authorities is the degree of centralisation chosen by states, especially on the execution procedure. From the issuing judicial authority perspective, the general rule is that any court might be a legitimate issuing authority. However, there are some partial exceptions, like

---

7   For example, the transposition into Spanish Law required two laws to be approved. The first and more important one for its content is Law 3/2003 very simply entitled "on the EAW" (to which we refer as EAW Spanish Law). Second is Law 2/2003, whose more organic nature complements the previous one. While, unlike other Member States, Spain did not have to revise its Constitution in order to transpose the FD (*Combeaud*, pp. 187–194), it did, however, have to change on the same date (14th March) Articles 65.4 and 88 LOPJ, so that the law establishing the jurisdiction of all Spanish judicial bodies could also encompass the new powers of the Criminal Division of the National Court and the Central Preliminary Investigation in the execution of the EAW procedure.

8   *Peers*, pp. 1–14; *Wagner*, pp. 695–712; *Mackarel*, p. 46.

9   ECJ, Decision of 3.5.2007, Advocaten voor de Wereld VZW v. Leden van de Ministerraad, Case C-303/05.

10 *López Ortega*, pp. 28–33.

11 *Fichera*, p. 88.

Italy, where courts are compelled to channel their contacts abroad through the Ministry of Justice.

As for the execution or decision of the EAW, some Member States leaned towards a centralised system; others preferred a decentralised or mixed one. Much of the doctrine and some experts[12] see centralisation as an advantage for judicial security and the unification of the EAW criteria because it avoids having differing decisions in similar cases. For this reason, the executing countries that do not have a centralized judicial authority might be working within the parameters of an extradition case because they will only decide on a few isolated EAWs. Centralisation therefore avoids problems caused by the lack of experience of some judicial bodies, the lack of harmonised criteria, etc. However, the same drawback might be had by those countries that give the power of decision of an EAW to the same judicial authority competent in the extradition procedure. Another plus of centralized structure is that communication between judicial authorities is easier.

Disagreeing with the above mentioned criteria, other sectors[13]consider that a concentrated system is inconsistent on the grounds that there is no reason to surrender material and territorial competence to execute a detention and surrender act to a specific judicial authority simply because an EU judicial authority is involved, while a national detention and surrender act is executed by the nearest judicial authority to the requested person. Another problem with centralisation of competence is that sometimes the transporting of suspects to the centralised judicial authority in some countries might be difficult due to the climatic variety and size of the country.

However, in our opinion, the numerical factor is a relevant component that must be taken into account when considering decentralising reforms. The risks of conferring this power on a large number of judicial bodies must not be underestimated. For example, according to the latest data[14] from the Spanish CGPJ, Spain has 453 Courts of Preliminary Investigation in Spain, to which another 1065 mixed courts must be added (called *Juzgados de 1ª Instancia e Instrucción*) with jurisdiction in both civil and criminal matters. Consequently, we do not share the thesis of absolute decentralisation of EAW execution because that would mean that some Member States might have more than 1500 execution judicial authorities. A more reasonable alternative, as suggested by Moreno

---

12 Regarding the opinion expressed by Fernando Grande Marlaska (Magistrate of the Central Preliminary Investigation Court), González Mota (Prosecutor of the National Court), Guajardo (Prosecutor of the International Cooperation Section) in several interviews conducted during the European Research project mentioned at the beginning.

13 Within this group, among others, *De Miguel Zaragoza*, p. 144.

14 La Justicia dato a dato 2009, Madrid, CGPJ, p. 10.

Catena and Conde-Pumpido Tourón,[15] would be restricted decentralisation in favour of a specific number of judicial bodies. It would be a compromise solution between a single judicial body and thousands of execution judicial authorities. Some countries, like Spain[16] or the Netherlands,[17] have opted for a single all-encompassing national authority[18] to execute an EAW. In contrast, Italy[19] and Portugal[20] have a mixed system, i. e., half way between concentrated and scattered competence. In both countries the EAW execution decision is not the responsibility of a single judicial body but is shared by a very limited number of judicial bodies. In Italy,[21] execution judicial authorities are the appeal courts (known as *Corte di appello*) in the region where the requested person has his address (fixed or temporary). Of a subsidiary character, in cases when this "forum" or territorial circumstance is unknown, the decision is taken by the appeal court of Rome. In Portugal,[22] the EAW's execution is again the responsibility of the appeal courts, known there as *Tribunal de Relação*. In both cases there is a limited number of jurisdictional bodies: Italy has 29 *Corti di Appello* and Portugal has only 5 *Tribunais de Relação*.

Finally, each Member State can also designate a central authority charged with administrative transmission and reception of the EAW and all related communications (art. 7 FD). In general, countries have chosen administrative and governmental authorities. In Spain[23] and Italy,[24] it is the Ministry of Justice, while in Portugal[25] it is the Public Prosecutors Office. Some authors[26] put forward arguments against this choice on the grounds that the involvement in an EAW procedure of a government authority – even as a central authority – is contrary to the spirit of the FD since the exclusion of governments is, as has already been noted, the most important difference between the EAW and extradition. The

---

15 *Moreno Catena / Conde-Pumpido Tourón*, www.uclm/espaciojudicialeuropeo.es. *Moreno Catena*, pp. 11 – 38; *Conde-Pumpido Tourón*, pp. 39 – 48.
16 *Oubiña Barbolla / González Vega*, pp. 473 – 596.
17 *Langbroek / Kurtovic*, pp. 245 – 347.
18 See art. 2. Spanish Law 3 / 2003, as well as Arts. 1 and 20 of the Dutch Surrender Act of 29 April 2004.
19 *Velicona / Fabri*, pp. 119 – 243.
20 *Gomes / Fernandes / Borges Reis* [2], pp. 349 – 471.
21 Art. 5 Italian Law 69 / 2005.
22 Art. 15 Portuguese Law 65 / 2003.
23 Art. 2 Spanish Law 3 / 2003.
24 Art. 4 Italian Law 69 / 2005.
25 Art. 9 Portuguese Law 65 / 2003.
26 *Castillejo Manzanares*, p. 3; *Jimeno Bulnes*, p. 4. Also working group on EAW comprising expert magistrates of the National Criminal Court, General Prosecutor, Legal assistance from the Judicial Ministry and Home Affairs Ministry. For more information: http://www.mjusticia.es/cs/Satellite?pagename=Portal_del_Derecho/InternacionalPrincipal/ TplInternacional&idCInter=1075994483764&tipoCInter=PT&cid=1075994483764&c= InternacionalPrincipal&p=1151913189285&menu_activo=1151913189285.

EAW is a procedural not a political decision. It is an exclusively legal procedure where there is direct communication between judicial authorities, with no governmental involvement, which is the reason behind the idea that the role of the central authority should be performed by other bodies. Opinions differ as to which these should be. In Spain Jimeno Bulnes[27] suggests that the REJUE should be this authority, while the Spanish CGPJ alleges it should have the role of Central Authority. In this scenario, we agreed with Plachta,[28] who points out that in the EAW system the role of the "central authority" has been significantly diminished and does not have special competences or significant responsibilities. So there is little reason for concern: national EAW judicial authorities may forego this role.

3.   Scope of application

Article 2 FD establishes the scope of the EAW. In general the EAW is pertinent to criminals punishable by the law of the issuing Member State with a maximum deprivation of freedom of at least 12 months if they are still under prosecution, or with a prison sentence of at least 4 months if they have already been sentenced. In other words, if an EAW is issued for prosecution purposes, the requested person must be a suspect under investigation for crimes punishable with a *custodial sentence* (prison sentence) of 12 months or more. On the other hand, if an EAW is issued to execute a sentence, the requested person must have been convicted to a custodial sentence of 4 months or more. Obviously, qualification of the facts and valid penalty procedures are those established by the State issuing the request.

Although apparently clear, the wording of Article 2.1 FD in an EAW for prosecution purposes could cause some confusion in its reference to acts punishable "by a custodial sentence *or detention order* of at least 12 months." *Detention* is not defined in the FD and when it is used, refers to keeping a person in prison during an investigation until he / she is convicted.

Over and above this question, the EAW is essentially sustained by two elements. The first is the "type of criminal offence" or "offence" underpinning the EAW. Second, and closely linked to it, is the "penalty" entailed by the offence or that has been effectively handed down. The "class of offence" distinguishes the EAW according to whether it is included or not in the list of Article 2.2 FD (henceforth the EAW catalogue). The second factor, "the period of the detention order or custodial sentence" makes a distinction between the above-mentioned cases according to certain minimum limits. On this basis, the EAW system may be split into two groups: a) EAW requests referring to offences included in the

---

27 *Jimeno Bulnes*, [2], p. 4.
28 *Plachta*, p. 188.

EAW catalogue, which must also be punishable with a custodial sentence of three or more years; b) EAW requests for a offence not listed in the EAW catalogue, in which case the "limit of penalty" varies depending on the aim of the EAW. If the EAW has been issued to launch or continue proceedings against the requested person, the offence should be punishable with a custodial sentence of 12 months or more. If the EAW has been issued for execution of sentence, the conviction must be of at least four months.

In terms of execution, this division determines whether the principle of double incrimination is at stake.[29] The EAW FD abolishes double criminality checks that routinely take place for extradition, for the first group (a). It follows that the executing state cannot refuse surrender, even of its own nationals, on the grounds that it does not recognise the offence as a crime under its jurisdiction. In fact, this is an example of the principle of mutual recognition at work. For offences outside the EAW catalogue, the FD the double-criminality check is to the discretion of the Member States.

The schema may seem straightforward, but it is not so easy in practice. We shall now make a brief critical summary of some of the controversial points. First of all, the EAW FD leaves a legal gap for those offences falling within the scope of the list but under the three-year threshold. Obviously, in this case double criminality remains by omission.

On the other hand, the EAW catalogue[30] has been criticised by the doctrine on several counts. First, for the lack of logical order with which the offences are listed, arguing that they should have been grouped together following logical criteria,[31] for example, the legal interest being protected and / or the seriousness of the crime.

Considering specific offences included in the list, other problems may arise. Surprisingly or not, not all the categories listed are considered crimes throughout the EU. Some national criminal law systems do (or did) not envisage one or two crimes within the catalogue. Therefore, these countries would never be able to issue an EAW for these behaviours, but in the opposite case they would be obliged to surrender a requested person for these crimes. For example, illicit trade in human organs and tissues was not a crime in Spain until recently. This gap was corrected in the last reform of the SCC,[32] but it will only become effective

---

29 On the content and significance of the double incrimination principle see *Cezón González*, pp. 88 – 90 as well as *Manzanares Samaniego*, pp. 48 – 55 in connection with Art. 2 of said convention signed on 13 December 1957. *Cuerda Riezu*, pp. 541 – 566. *Gómez-Jara Díez*, pp. 1 – 6. *González-Cuéllar Serrano*, pp. 1 – 6.

30 In any case, the EU Council can change the EAW catalogue after consultation with the EU Parliament (art. 2 FD EAW).

31 Concerning this, *Arangüena Fanego*, p. 28.

32 See new Art. 176bis SCC.

when the reform enters into force on 23rd December 2010.[33] The crime of swindling is also unknown in English and Scottish Criminal Law. In other Member States, these issues have resulted in some Member States excluding some offences from the list on the grounds that they are not punishable under their own criminal codes. This is the case for abortion and euthanasia in Belgium, or the generic exclusion by Austria, until 31st December 2008, if the act for which the EAW has been issued is not punishable under Austrian Law. However, the Court of Justice[34] notes that the only valid definition is that given by the issuing judicial authority according to its domestic law.

From another point of view, the FD list terminology is sometimes too abstract,[35] for example, corruption,[36] computer-related crime,[37] swindling, terrorism, racketeering,[38] etc. As suggested by a group of doctrine experts,[39] it would be (and would have been) useful for each member state to publish a record / catalogue of all those acts that their national laws would include under the offences listed.

In other cases the difficulty arises because the maximum penalty under national law for some listed offences is always lower than three years. For example, in Spain the illegal trafficking of an endangered plant species has a maximum penalty of two years imprisonment.[40] Therefore, although the offence is listed, in Spain it would be automatically excluded because of the penalty duration, and, in the end, an EAW of this type of offence would depend on the requirements of offences not included on the list.

All in all, the majority (if not all) the thirty-two offences on the EAW list are punishable in all Member States.[41] In our opinion, this highlights further that the new EAW system is innovative in its exclusion of government authority involvement rather than for doing away with the principle of double incrimination checks.[42] If the principle of controlling double incrimination is successfully

---

33 Organic Law 5/2010, modifying Organic Law 10/1995, SCC, does not, however, enter into force until 23 December 2010.
34 See Decision of 3.5.2007, Advocaten voor de Wereld VZW v. Leden van de Ministerraad, Case C-303/05.
35 See *Ormazabal Sánchez*, p. 2. *De Hoyos Sancho* [1], p. 11. Art. 2.2 FD EAW has been also criticised for its vagueness, see *Pérignon / Daucé*, p. 207. *Mackarel*, p. 44. Same critique, *Fichera*, pp. 79–80.
36 *Jiménez Villarejo*, pp. 1–5.
37 Some authors remark on the need for clarification based on the diverging international praxis and domestic laws on what constitutes this crime, the activities included in "cyber crime," etc., see in particular, *Pocar*, p. 32, more pp. 34–37.
38 *Plachta*, p. 190.
39 See *Fonseca Morillo*, p. 89.
40 Art. 332 SCC.
41 *De Miguel Zaragoza*, pp. 139–236.
42 See *Jimeno Bulnes* [2], p. 4. Of the same author [1], pp. 235–253. See also *Mackarel*, p. 40.

implemented for the majority of listed offences because they are punished by
both countries (the issuing and executing), what advance or improvement would
provide the removal of the double incrimination principle? This is what the
Advocate General explained in his allegation to the case voor de Wereld. In Ruiz
Jarabo's view:

> "... the acts listed are classed as offences in all the Member States, so it is not the double
> criminality requirement, which is set aside but rather only the requirement of its
> verification."[43]

## 4.	Grounds for refusal and other guarantees

Notwithstanding these limits, the executing judicial authority still enjoys some
leeway to refuse an EAW request on mandatory grounds of non-execution or
non-mandatory grounds of non-execution. Even forwarding execution to the
issuing state implies some guarantees.

Article 3 EAW FD establishes the grounds for non-execution of an EAW and
distinguishes mandatory from non-mandatory elements. An EAW must be refused by the executing judicial authority if the sentence has been already served
elsewhere, if the offences are covered by amnesty under the jurisdiction of the
executing state, or if the requested person's age exempts him/her from criminal
liability. In other words, an executing judicial authority may refuse to comply
with an EAW in the event of *non bis in idem*,[44] age (requested person is a minor)
and pardon.

In addition, the EAW FD envisages seven cases in which the executing judicial
authority may refuse to execute the EAW.[45] The non-mandatory grounds for
refusal are: 1) offences subject to double criminality check that are not a crime in
the executing state (although mismatch of tax regimes between countries is not a
valid ground for refusal in the case of tax crimes); 2) acts already under prosecution in the executing state; 3) acts the executing state has decided not to

---

43	They are offences where the verification of double criminality is regarded as superfluous
because the acts concerned are punished throughout the Member States. Paragraph 90. See
also footnote No. 86. Advocate General's opinion. Decision of 3.5.2007, Advocaten voor de
Wereld VZW v. Leden van de Ministerraad, Case C-303/05.

44	See, *López Barja de Quiroga*, pp. 14 – 17; *De Hoyos Sancho* [2], pp. 1 – 22; *Cedeño Hernan*,
pp. 75 – 106; *Irurzun Montoro* [2], pp. 1 – 12. *Vervaele*, pp. 100 – 118. *Bailin*, pp. 103 – 120.
Wasmaier/Thwaites, pp. 65 – 78. *Van der Wilt*, pp. 99 – 117; ECJ jurisprudence about the
non bis in idem: Criminal Proceedings v. Miraglia, Decision of the 10.3.2003, Case C-
469/03. Criminal Proceedings v. Decision of 9.3.2006,Van Esbroeck, Case C-436/04. Criminal Proceedings v. Decision of 28.9.2006, Gasparini and others, Case C-467/04. Decision
of 28.9.2006,Van Straaten, v. Netherland and Italy, Case C-105/05.

45	Art. 4 EAW FD.

prosecute or that have already been sentenced elsewhere; 4) acts within the jurisdiction of the executing state whose punishment is statute-barred; 5) acts already prosecuted, sentenced or served in another state, other than the issuing state (*ne bis in idem*); 6) in the case of a warrant for sentence execution, decision of the executing state to execute the sentence itself instead of surrendering the requested person for him to serve it abroad; 7) acts committed, in whole or part, in the executing state, or outside the issuing state.

Regardless of the specific optional cause, what does an optional cause of denial actually signify for the executing judicial body? Is the judicial body obliged *sua sponte* to control each of these, i. e., to know if in each case they may be applied or not? In other words, must be the executing judicial body be aware of the existence of an optional ground whether or not it intends to apply it? Are the executing judicial bodies obliged to verify their possible existence even if the judge does not intend to refuse the EAW?

Members States are free to decide whether to consider these circumstances optional grounds or, on the contrary, as mandatory. For instance, although most Members States generally enforce double criminality checks for crimes outside the EAW catalogue, there are some exceptions like Spain[46] where it remains optional. Under Spanish EAW Law, even the decision of whether to surrender a requested person for crimes outside[47] the EAW catalogue that are not offences under Spanish law is left to the discretion of the executing judicial body.

Furthermore, nothing has prevented some national transpositions from extending the grounds for non-execution of an EAW. Obviously from a mutual recognition principle point of view[48] this is highly debatable, especially when there exist mandatory grounds for non-execution. Perhaps, the most paradigmatic case is the Italian system[49] where all optional grounds have been turned into mandatory elements, with even some additional new mandatory grounds added. As a whole, the Italian law has twenty mandatory grounds for refusal, three mandatory and seven optional grounds more than provided for by the FD. These include: consent of the person whose right has been infringed; whether under Italian law, the offence could be considered as committed in order to exercise a right, fulfil a duty, or was determined by chance or *force majeure*; if there are no limits to preventive detention in the issuing state; if the object of the EAW is a political offence; if there is reason to believe the underlying sentence does not respect the minimum rights of the requested person; if the requested person is pregnant or the mother of children under the age of three; if the

---

46 Art. 4.6 Spanish Law 3 / 2003.
47 Art. 9.2 Spanish Law 3 / 2003.
48 *Alegre / Leaf*, pp. 208 – 209.
49 Art. 20 Italian Law 69 / 2005.

coercive measure underlying the warrant lacks justification; if the sentence underlying the warrant is contrary to the fundamental principles of the Italian legal system.

The Dutch Law[50] turns most optional grounds for refusing an EAW into mandatory elements, with three exceptions: 1) for acts under prosecution in the Netherlands, the Minister of Justice can decide, on advice of the public prosecutor's office, to suspend the Dutch prosecution and enable surrender abroad; 2) on acts the Netherlands has decided not to prosecute, either because its criminal law is inapplicable or a trial abroad is preferred; 3) on acts committed in the Netherlands or outside the issuing state, refusal of surrender can be waived on a reasoned request by the public prosecutor.

It is evident from the above that the unequal application of the EAW throughout Member States is a major issue.[51] The legal and practical power of executing judicial authority in each Member State is not always very clear. The belief that the EAW will function harmoniously is therefore not enough to ensure its implementation. In our opinion these problems, sometimes more serious than others, uncover another major point of concern: the guarantees for surrender. In short, judicial insecurity generated by the double incrimination configuration, like a surrender denial contingent on offences not included in the list, could seriously endanger the principles of equality, legality and the fundamental rights of interdiction of defencelessness and due process.

Article 5 FD allows the executing state to demand three different kinds of guarantees: a) retrial if the requested person was sentenced *in absentia*; b) review in the case of a lifetime sentence; c) the possibility to serve the sentence at home for nationals or residents of the executing state; in the event of an EAW issued for prosecution this means that surrender may be subject to the condition of returning to the executing country to serve the eventual custodial sentence or detention order if the requested persons so desires.

The last guarantee seems reminiscent of the traditional right not to be extradited from one's home country and be able to serve the sentence at home. However, there is a slight difference depending on the purpose of the EAW. In the event of an EAW for prosecution, the executing state can demand this guarantee. However, if the EAW is to execute a sentence, the executing judicial authority has the option to refuse the surrender if it decides to execute the sentence itself.

In practice, these guarantees may function as further grounds for non-execution if the issuing country does not ensure them. However, it is up to the national transpositions to make specific mention of such guarantees and, obviously, whether they are mandatory or optional.

---

50 Arts. 8–9 and 13 of Dutch Surrender Act 2004.
51 As *Guild.*

For example, Portuguese EAW Law has converted two optional guarantees into mandatory ones:[52] retrial for decisions rendered *in absentia* and review of lifetime sentences. Similarly, the Netherlands[53] where mandatory guarantees are retrial for sentences *in absentia* and the opportunity to serve sentence at home.

All in all, Dutch law is one of the most protective of its nationals, only allowing surrender for prosecution with the guarantee that the requested person may return to serve any eventual sentence in the Netherlands. Dutch nationals may never be surrendered to serve a sentence abroad since in such cases the Netherlands will always execute the sentence itself. Indeed the EU Council has rightly considered this attitude a discriminatory practice against non-Dutch citizens and contrary to the spirit of the EAW FD.[54]

Spain only envisages as mandatory the guarantee[55] of review of lifetime sentences and as optional the guarantee of return after surrender in a prosecution request. Indeed the guarantee of a retrial in the event of sentence rendered *in absentia* has received much attention for its surprising absence in the Spanish EAW Act. Initially this was interpreted as an obligation on Spanish judicial authorities to surrender the requested person even if the custodial sentence had been rendered in the issuing country *in absentia*. The confusion was resolved subsequently by the Spanish Constitutional Court pointing out that under Spanish constitutional doctrine, review of a judgement rendered *in absentia* is mandatory for every surrender decision whatever the procedure, be it for extradition or an EAW request. On this point, the Constitutional Court stated that although a Spanish National Court does not require any preconditions to be provided by the issuing authority before approving an extradition or EAW, the order granting surrender must include the guarantee that the issuing state accepts the requested person's right of appeal. In this way the issuing state takes full responsibility for compliance with the guarantee. The Legal Basis 7 of Judgement 177 / 2006 of 27th June states that although the EAW FD and the EAW Spanish Law 3 / 2003 do not establish this requirement as a *sine qua non* condition for surrender, this does not mean the executing judicial authorities may ignore it since it is an essential part of the fundamental right to trial with full guarantees recognised by Article 24.2 of the Spanish Constitution, and therefore must be respected implicitly or explicitly by any Spanish law. The FD EAW does not make it mandatory for Member States to establish such conditions for surrender, but forwards the matter to the national legal systems. In fact, al-

---

52 Art. 17 Portuguese Law 65 / 2003 of 22 August 2003.
53 Art. 6 Dutch Surrender Act of 29 April 2004.
54 Council of the EU, 2009, p. 46.
55 Art. 11 Spanish Law No. 3 / 2003 of 14 March 2003.

though the EAW Spanish Law does not envisage any specific rules in this respect, the right to trial with full guarantees is enshrined in the Spanish legal system.

Finally and despite its restrictive legislation, the Italian EAW Law considers all these guarantees as optional.

5.   EAW procedure

Most of the FD deals with EAW procedure. For obvious reasons neither this nor the specific system of each Member State can be examined in depth here. Focus shall rather be given to the following sequential phases: 1) EAW transmission; 2) Arrest of the requested person; 3) Hearing; 4) Surrender Decision; and finally, 5) The effective transfer of the requested person.

In general, according to the EAW FD, the EAW executing procedure is dealt with as a matter of urgency and within preclusive time-limits,[56] the requested person is entitled to a hearing,[57] to be assisted by a lawyer and an interpreter,[58] to the rights available to arrested persons and, where appropriate, to provisional release in accordance with the executing state's law.

The procedure starts when a Member State issues an EAW. The transmission of the EAW may be,[59] either directly to an executing judicial authority (with possible mediation of the national's central authority or the EJN) where the requested person is known or believed to be located; and/or generically by introducing an alert on the SIS, in which case any enforcement agency of the Member States may carry out the arrest directly if the requested person resides or is found in its territory. In practice, most EAWs are issued and received through this last channel. This seems logical since most EAWs are issued by judicial authorities, which do not really know the whereabouts of the requested person.

The rare cases of direct transmission are generally for one reason, i.e. so as not to renounce the speciality rule. These are EAW requests for persons who have previously been claimed in an EAW for other facts. The decision on the previous EAW may be pending or even may have been executed, but the issuing judicial authority already knows where the requested person is to be found.

When the executing judicial authority receives the EAW through one of these channels, it verifies its legitimacy according to the above-mentioned require-

---

56 Arts. 17 and 23 EAW FD.
57 Arts. 14 and 19 EAW FD.
58 Art. 11.2 EAW FD.
59 Art. 9 EAW FD.

ments, such as the nature of the offences, the length of penalty, principle of double criminality, grounds for refusal, guarantees, etc.

At this stage, the executing judicial authority may consider the EAW invalid and refuse its execution. The EAW may also prove to be incomplete. In this case the executing judicial authority must ask the issuing authority for further clarifications. Only when these problems have been resolved can the EAW request move on to next stages: arrest and hearing.

On an initial reading of the FD, the arrest or detention and consecutive hearing of the requested person may appear somehow intermingled due to their proximity in time. In any event, when the requested person is arrested, he or she has the right to be informed of the warrant, its contents, the possibility of consenting to surrender, and assistance by a legal counsel and an interpreter in compliance with local law.[60]

These stages encompass two major decisions of the EAW procedure: a) the consent decision,[61] where the requested person chooses whether to consent to his surrender; b) the provisional imprisonment decision, where the executing authority chooses whether to keep the requested person incarcerated, or release him/her provisionally until the final EAW surrender decision. The executing judicial authority must take this decision according to its national laws and consequently take the necessary measures to prevent absconding.[62]

If the requested person acquiesces voluntarily, fully aware of what his/her choice to surrender entails, the executing procedure is shorter and simpler. The surrender decision should be taken within a period of 10 days after consent has been given.[63]

When the requested person does not consent to his/her surrender, any surrender decision may be taken only after a hearing and within a period of 60 days after the arrest of the requested person.

However, according to Article 17 EAW FD, in both cases (consent and contested cases) the time limits for the surrender decision may be extended by a further 30 days if the grounds are considered reasonable.

The timeframes and content of the hearing stage are surprisingly underspecified by the FD. For example, according to Article 14 EAW FD, it is clear that if the requested person does not consent to surrender, he/she is entitled to a hearing. However, nothing is said in the EAW FD about the consequences if the requested person consents to surrender. As a result, many transnational laws envisage a hearing in both cases. The EAW FD also establishes that a repre-

---

60 Art. 11 EAW FD.
61 *De Prada Solaesa*, pp. 355–362.
62 Art. 12 EAW FD.
63 Arts. 13 and 17 EAW FD.

sentative of the issuing country may be present at the hearing,[64] but some national transpositions do not recognise this ruling.

The content of this hearing differs in each case. For example, in the case of an EAW issued for prosecution purposes, the requested person must either be heard or temporarily transferred to the executing state under conditions agreed by both states, with the right to return to the issuing state being guaranteed before the surrender decision.[65]

In conclusion, the executing judicial authority follows its national EAW law. While details of each EAW system cannot be given here, it may be affirmed that as a rule, the hearing will also consider previously mentioned elements such as information of the warrant, provisional imprisonment or detention decision, consent decision, etc.

Likewise, the EAW FD recognizes other circumstances that may also condition the surrender decision process. For example, in the event of multiple surrender requests for one person,[66] the executing judicial authority must choose one on the basis of their gravity, the date of the requests, and also their purpose. On the other hand, the countdown on the time limits referred to in article 17 does not start until any privileges or immunity enjoyed by the requested person are waived.[67] If the requested person has been extradited from a third state, the executing judicial authority must first ask this third state for authorisation to surrender him. By the same token, the deadlines set are not taken into account until such authorisation is received and the previous speciality rules relinquished.[68]

Once a decision to surrender has been taken, the procedure enters the final stage of *transfer*. The requested person is surrendered as soon as possible on a date agreed between the authorities concerned. In any event, the effective surrender should be no later than 10 days after the decision on the EAW execution.[69] Any delay must be reported with justification to Eurojust.[70] On this point, some authors[71] see an incongruence in the legislation since although the EAW FD fixes short time limits to decide and proceed with the surrender; it is surprisingly silent about the consequences of non-fulfilment the surrender once the execution has been approved.

---

64 Art. 9 EAW FD.
65 Art. 18 EAW FD.
66 Art. 16 EAW FD.
67 Art. 20 EAW FD.
68 Art. 21 EAW FD.
69 Art. 23.2 EAW FD.
70 Art. 17 EAW FD.
71 See *Hoyos Sancho* [3], pp. 303–315; *Jimeno Bulnes* [3], p. 303. The authors criticise the fact that no kind of juridical sanction or penalty is contemplated.

6. Personal reflection: usefulness of the EAW for future criminal justice cooperation instruments

With the EAW FD, traditional mechanisms of judicial cooperation have to resort to a new method based on mutual trust[72] and relations among the judicial systems of Member States. Indeed the principle of mutual recognition[73] has become the cornerstone of judicial cooperation. No one doubts that the EAW is a highly significant first legal instrument to further European judicial cooperation. However, it is fair to say that from a practical point of view flaws and irregularities have emerged in the theoretical model of the Framework Decision and the ensuing national EAW laws. The EAW has existed for nearly seven years (2004 – 2011), so this is a good time to take stock of its practical[74] application on the basis of yardsticks like legality, effectiveness, and (3) respect of fundamental rights.

Close judicial cooperation between Member States is definitely necessary for an effective European area of freedom, security and justice. The background of the EAW can help us plan or design a better European Area of Justice with instruments that have come into force, such as the Directive on the "European Protection Order", which was approved last 13th December 2011 (DO L 338/02, 21.12.2011), as well as the Framework Decisions on the mutual recognition of supervision measures,[75] EEW,[76] supervision of sentenced persons or persons on conditional release,[77] mutual recognition of custodial sentences and measures

---

72 As the heart of the European Union, as the European Constitutional Law Review explains, see "Editorial", *European Constitutional Law* Review, 2006, Vol. 2, pp. 1 – 3. See clause 33, Tampere Conclusions European Council, Special Meeting, 15 and 16 October 1999, available at http://www.europarl.europa.eu/summits/tam_en.htm#c. The importance of recognizing judicial decision was previously highlighted many times. See De Kerchove / Weyembergh, and the Préface of Lenarts to the De Kerchove / Weyembergh's book.

73 See *Gutiérrez Zarza*, pp. 17 – 52; *De la Quadra-Salcedo Janini*, pp. 279 – 321.

74 In this sense, the research report of the EAW is indispensable as a source VVAA, The European Arrest Warrant in Law and in Practice: a comparative study for the consolidation of the European law-enforcement area, Coimbra, 2010, available in English in http://opj.ces. uc.pt/pdf/EAW_Final_Report_Nov_2010.pdf European research project JLS / 2007 / JPEN / 245 and ABAC 30-CE-0178645 / 00 – 20.

75 Council FD 2009 / 829 / JHA on the application, between Member States of the European Union, of the principle of mutual recognition of decisions on supervision measures as an alternative to provisional detention.

76 The EEW FD 2008 / 978 / JHA replaces the system of mutual assistance in criminal matters between Member States for obtaining objects, documents and data for use in criminal proceedings.

77 Council FD 2008 / 947 / JHA on the application of the principle of mutual recognition to judgments and probation decisions with a view to the supervision of probation measures and alternative sanctions [see amending act(s)].

involving deprivation of liberty,[78] recognition and execution of confiscation orders,[79] mutual recognition of pre-trial supervision measures,[80] mutual recognition of financial penalties.[81]

Bibliography

Alegre, Susie / Leaf, Marisa, Mutual recognition in European judicial co-operation: a step too far too soon? Case Study – the European Arrest Warrant, commentary to art. 7 ECHR "Double Criminality and Retrospective Application", in: 10 European Law Journal (2004), pp. 208 – 209.

Arangüena Fanego, Coral, La orden europea de detención y entrega. Análisis de las Leyes 2 y 3 de 14 de Marzo de 2003, de transposición al ordenamiento jurídico español de la Decisión Marco sobre la "euroorden", in: 10 Revista de Derecho Penal (2003), pp. 11 – 98.

Bailin, Alex, Double jeopardy, in: Leaf, Marisa (ed.), Cross border crime, Justice Publication (2006), pp. 103 – 120.

Castillejo Manzanares, Raquel, El procedimiento español para la emisión y ejecución de una orden europea de detención y entrega, in: 587 Actualidad Jurídica Aranzadi (2003), pp. 1 – 5.

Cedeño Hernan, Marina, La orden de detención y entrega europea. Especial consideración del non bis in idem como motivo de denegación, in: Gascón Inchausti, Fernando et al. (eds.), El Derecho Procesal en la Unión Europea, Tirant lo blanch (2006), pp. 75 – 106.

Cezón González, Carlos, Derecho Extradicional, Dykinson (2003).

Combeaud, Sebastian, Implementation of the European Arrest Warrant and the Constitutional Impact in the Member States, in: Guild, Elspeth (ed.), Constitutional challenges to the European Arrest Warrant, Wolf Legal Publisher (2006), pp. 187 – 194.

Conde-Pumpido Ferreiro, Candido, La orden de detención y entrega europea. La perspectiva española, in: Arroyo Zapatero, Luis et. al (eds.), La orden europea de detención y entrega europea, Universidad Castilla La Mancha (2006), pp. 39 – 48.

Cuerda Riezu, Antonio, Los principios de legalidad, doble incriminación e igualdad en la orden europea de detención y entrega, in: Cuerda Riezu, Antonio / Jiménez de Parga,

---

78 Council FD 2008/909/JHA on the application of the principle of mutual recognition to judgments in criminal matters imposing custodial sentences or measures involving deprivation of liberty for the purpose of their enforcement in the European Union [see amending act(s)].

79 Council FD 2006/783/JHA on the application of the principle of mutual recognition to confiscation orders [see amending act(s)].

80 Proposal for a Council FD of 29 August 2006 on the European supervision order in pre-trial procedures between Member States of the European Union [COM(2006) 468 final – Not published in the Official Journal]. The Commission has put forward a series of initiatives to enhance the protection of fundamental rights in the European law-enforcement area.

81 Council FD 2005/214/JHA on the application of the principle of mutual recognition to financial penalties [see amending act(s)]. This Framework Decision extends the principle of mutual recognition, the cornerstone of judicial cooperation, to financial penalties.

Manuel (eds.), Nuevos desafíos del derecho penal internacional: terrorismo, crímenes internacionales y derechos fundamentales, Tecnos (2009), pp. 541 – 566.

De Hoyos Sancho, Monserrat, [1] Cooperación judicial en la Unión Europea. Reflexiones en torno al nuevo sistema de extradición simplificada, in: Calonge Velázquez, Antonio (ed.), Actas del II Congreso Internacional "El futuro de Europa a debate", Instituto de Estudios Europeos (2004), pp. 66 – 78; [2] Eficacia transnacional del *non bis in idem* y denegación de la Euroorden, in: 6330 Diario La Ley (2005), pp. 1 – 22; [3] Il nuovo sistema di estradizione semplificata nell'Unione Europea. Lineamenti della legge spagnola sul mandato d'arresto europeo, in: XLV Cassazione Penale (2005), pp. 303 – 315.

De la Quadra-Salcedo Janini, Tomás, La Orden europea de detención y el principio constitucional de reciprocidad, in: 18 Civitas Revista Española de Derecho Europeo (2006), pp. 279 – 321.

De Miguel Zaragoza, Juan, Algunas consideraciones sobre la Decisión Marco relativa a la orden de detención europea y a los procedimientos de entrega en la perspectiva de extradición, in: 4 Actualidad Penal (2003), pp. 139 – 236.

De Prada Solaesa, Jose Ricardo, Consentimiento a la entrega. Renuncia al principio de especialidad, in: Arroyo Zapatero, Luis et. al (eds.), La orden europea de detención y entrega europea, Universidad Castilla La Mancha (2006), pp. 355 – 362.

De Kerchove, Gilles / Weyembergh, Anne, La Reconnaissance Mutuelle des Décisions Judiciaires Pénales dans l'Union Européenne, Éditions de l'Université de Bruxelles (2001).

Fennelly, Nial, The European Arrest Warrant: Recent Developments, in: 8 ERA Forum (4 / 2007), pp. 519 – 520.

Fichera, Massimo, The European Arrest Warrant and the Sovereign State: A Marriage of Convenience?, in: 15 European Law Journal (1 / 2009), pp. 70 – 97.

Fonseca Morillo, Francisco, La orden de detención y entrega europea, in: 14 Revista Española de Derecho Comunitario Europeo (2003), pp. 69 – 96.

Gomes, Conceiçao / Fernandes, Diana / Borges Reis, Jose, [1] The European Arrest Warrant: comparative analysis, in: The European Arrest Warrant in law and in practice: a comparative study for the consolidation of the European law enforcement area, Permanent Observatory of Portuguese Justice (11 / 2010), pp. 40 – 62. In: http://opj.ces.uc. pt/pdf/EAW_Final_Report_Nov_2010.pdf); [2] The European arrest warrant in Portugal, in: The European Arrest Warrant in law and in practice: a comparative study for the consolidation of the European law- enforcement area, Permanent Observatory of Portuguese Justice (11 / 2010), in: http://opj.ces.uc.pt/pdf/EAW_Final_Report_ Nov_2010.pdf, pp. 349 – 471.

Gómez-Jara Díez, Carlos, Orden de Detención Europea y Constitución Europea: reflexiones sobre su fundamento en el principio de reconocimiento mutuo, in: 6069 Diario La Ley (2004), pp. 1 – 6.

González-Cuéllar Serrano, Nicolás, La "euroorden:" hacia una Europa de los carceleros, in: 6619 Diario La Ley (2006), pp. 1 – 6.

Guild, Elspeth, Introduction, in: Guild, Elspeth (ed.), Constitutional challenges to the European Arrest Warrant, Wolf Legal Publisher (2006).

Gutiérrez Zarza, María Ángeles, La Orden de Detención Europea y el futuro de la cooperación judicial penal en la Unión Europea: reconocimiento mutuo, confianza recíproca y otros conceptos clave, in: 42 Manuales de formación continuada, CGPJ (2007), pp. 17–52.

Irurzun Montoro, Fernando, [1] El proceso de adaptación de la Decisión Marco a los quince Estados miembros, in: Arroyo Zapatero, Luis et. al (eds.), La orden europea de detención y entrega europea, Universidad Castilla La Mancha (2006), pp. 58–61; [2] El espacio judicial europeo en una encrucijada?, in: 6532 Diario La Ley (2006), pp. 1–12.

Jiménez Villarejo, Carlos, Reflexiones sobre el concepto de corrupción a propósito de la orden de detención europea, in: 560 Actualidad Jurídica Aranzadi (2002), pp. 1–5.

Jimeno Bulnes, Mar, [1] After September 11th: the Fight Against Terrorism in National and European Law. Substantive and Procedural Rules: Some Examples, in: 10/2 European Law Journal (2004), pp. 235–253; [2] La orden europea de detención y entrega: aspectos procesales, in: 5979 Diario La Ley (2004), pp. 1–7; [3] The Enforcement of the European Arrest Warrant: A Comparison Between Spain and the UK, in: 15/3 European Journal of Crime, Criminal Law and Criminal Justice (2007), pp. 263–308.

Kaunert, Christian, Without the Power of Purse or Sword: The European Arrest Warrant and the Role of the Commission, in: 29/4 European Integration (2007), pp. 387–404.

La Justicia dato a dato 2009, Madrid, CGPJ, p. 10. Also available online: http://www.poderjudicial.es/eversuite/GetDoc?DBName=dPortal&UniqueKeyValue=153903&-Download=false&ShowPath=false.

Langbroek, Philip/Kurtovic Elina, The EAW in the Netherlands, in: The European Arrest Warrant in law and in practice: a comparative study for the consolidation of the European law-enforcement area, Permanent Observatory of Portuguese Justice (November/2010), in: http://opj.ces.uc.pt/pdf/EAW_Final_Report_Nov_2010.pdf, pp. 245–347.

López Barja de Quiroga, Jacobo, El principio *non bis in idem*, Dykinson (2004).

López Ortega, Juan José, La orden de detención europea: Legalidad y jurisdiccionalidad de entrega, in: 45 Jueces para la Democracia (2002), pp. 28–33.

Mackarel, Mark, The European Arrest Warrant – the Early Years: Implementing and Using the Warrant, in: 15/1 European Journal of Crime, Criminal Law and Criminal Justice (2007), pp. 37–65.

Manzanares Samaniego, José Luis, El Convenio Europeo de Extradición, Bosch (1986).

Moreno Catena, Víctor, La orden europea de detención en España, in: 78 Revista del poder judicial (2005), pp. 11–38.

Moreno Catena, Víctor/Conde-Pumpido Tourón, Candido, in: Round Table Conference, La Orden de Detención Europea, Toledo (2003), in: www.uclm/espaciojudicialeuropeo.es.

Oubiña Barbolla, Sabela/González Vega, Ignacio, The European arrest warrant in Spain, in: The European Arrest Warrant in law and in practice: a comparative study for the consolidation of the European law- enforcement area, Permanent Observatory of Portuguese Justice (November/2010), in: http://opj.ces.uc.pt/pdf/EAW_Final_Report_Nov_2010.pdf, pp. 473–596.

Ormazabal Sánchez, Guillermo, La Orden europea de detención y entrega y la extradición de nacionales propios a la luz de la jurisprudencia constitucional alemana. [Especial consideración de la Sentencia del Tribunal Constitucional alemán de 18 de julio de 2005 (2 BvR 2236/2004)], in: 6394 Diario La Ley (2006), pp. 1–7.

Peers, Steve, Proposed Framework decision on European Arrest Warrant, in: 3 Statewatch post (11.09.01), available at www.statewatch.org.

Pérignon, Isabelle / Daucé, Constance, The European Arrest Warrant a growing success story, in: 8 ERA Forum (2007), pp. 203 – 214.

Plachta, Michael, European Arrest Warrant: Revolution in Extradition?, in: 11 / 2 European Journal of Crime, Criminal Law and Criminal Justice (2003), pp. 178 – 194.

Pocar, Fausto, New challenges for international rules against cyber-crime, in: 10 European Journal on Criminal Policy and Research (2004), pp. 27 – 37.

Van der Wilt, Harmer, The European Arrest Warrant and the principle *ne bis in idem*, in: Bleckxtoon, Rob / Van Ballegooij, Wouter (eds.), Handbook on the European Arrest Warrant The Hague (2005), pp. 99 – 117.

Velicona, Marco / Fabri, Marco, The European arrest warrant in Italy, in: The European Arrest Warrant in law and in practice: a comparative study for the consolidation of the European law-enforcement area, Permanent Observatory of Portuguese Justice (November / 2010), in: http://opj.ces.uc.pt/pdf/EAW_Final_Report_Nov_2010.pdf, pp. 119 – 243.

Vervaele, John, The transnational *ne bis in idem* principle in the EU: mutual recognition and equivalent protection of human rights, in: 1 Utrecht Law Review (2005), pp. 100 – 118.

Vogel, Joachim, Abschaffung der Auslieferung? Kritische Anmerkungen zur Reform des Auslieferungsrechts in der Europäischen Union, in: 56 / 19 Juristenzeitung (2001), pp. 937 – 943.

VVAA, The European Arrest Warrant in law and in practice: a comparative study for the consolidation of the European law-enforcement area, Permanent Observatory of Portuguese Justice (November / 2010), European research project JLS / 2007 / JPEN / 245 and ABAC30-CE-0178645 / 00 – 20. http://opj.ces.uc.pt/pdf/EAW_Final_Report_Nov_ 2010.pdf.

Wagner, Wolfgang, Building an Internal Security Community: The Democratic Peace and the Politics of the Extradition in Western Europe, in: 40 / 6 Journal of Peace Research (2003), pp. 695 – 712.

Wasmeier, Martin / Thwaites, Nadine, The development of *non bis in idem* into a transnational fundamental right in EU law: comments on recent developments, in: 31 European Law Review (2006), pp. 65 – 78.

Tommaso Rafaraci

The application of the principle of mutual recognition to decisions on supervision measures as an alternative to provisional detention

Table of Contents

Table of Abbreviations

EAW FD	Framework Decision on the European Arrest Warrant
EEW FD	Framework Decision on the European Evidence Warrant
EU FRCh	Charter of the fundamental rights of the European Union
ECHR	European Convention on human rights
ECtHR	European Court of Human Rights
EU	European Union
FD	Framework Decision
TFEU	Treaty on the functioning of the European Union

1. Objectives of the FD 2009/829/JHA

According to the Programme of Measures to implement the principle of mutual recognition of decisions in criminal matters,[1] and following the FD 2002/584/JHA on the European arrest warrant, the Council has recently adopted the FD 2009/829/JHA on the application, between Member States of the European

---

1 OJ C 12/10 of 15.1.2001 (Measure No. 10).

Union, of the principle of mutual recognition to decisions on supervision measures as an alternative to provisional detention.[2]

This FD applies when a person is resident in one Member State but subject to criminal proceedings in a second Member State; it lays down rules according to which one Member State (the executing State) shall recognise a decision on supervision measures issued in another Member State (the issuing State) as an alternative to provisional detention, monitor the supervision measures imposed on a natural person and surrender the person concerned to the issuing State in case of breach of these measures.[3]

One of the main objectives of this Framework Decision is to prevent discrimination between those who are resident in the trial State and those who are not. In fact there is a risk that a non-resident might be remanded in custody pending trial in circumstances in which a resident would not. Not surprisingly, before the adoption of this Framework Decision, in the absence of a legal instrument with which to recognise and execute a supervision measure as an alternative to provisional detention within the EU, the competent authorities of the trial State have often remanded in pre-trial custody non-residents accused of offences in other Member States just because of the greater perceived risk of flight. Thus measures alternative to detention have been an option available to residents in the trial State only. This has posed serious questions of discrimination that could no longer be tolerated in an area of freedom, security and justice where free movement of persons is fully granted.[4]

Besides preventing discrimination, the FD at issue aims at enhancing the right to liberty and the presumption of innocence in the EU by promoting, where appropriate, the use of non-custodial measures as an alternative to provisional detention.[5] The FD also aims at enhancing the protection of the general public, thereby giving further effect to the right of law-abiding citizens to live in safety and security by enabling a person to be supervised by the authorities of the Member State of residence while awaiting trial in another Member State.[6] Together with the purpose of promoting the principle of *favor libertatis* to its

---

2 On the draft of this Framework Decision COM(2006) 468, see *Ljungquist* p. 169, and *Aran-güena Fanego*, p. 224. On the Green Paper, COM(2004) 562 final, on mutual recognition of non-custodial pre-trial supervision measures that preceded the FD at issue, see *Fragalà*, p. 721, and Justice response to the European Commission green paper on mutual recognition of non-custodial pre-trial supervision measures COM (2004) 562 final, available at http://www.justice.org.uk/images/pdfs/ecbail.pdf.

3 Art. 1 FD 2009/829/JHA.

4 Recital No. 5 FD 2009/829/JHA.

5 Recital No. 4 FD 2009/829/JHA. This issue is of utmost importance if one considers the great use, if not abuse, made of pre-trial detention across the EU. On this topic see *Stevens*, p. 165; *Cid Moliné*, p. 268.

6 Recital No. 3 and Art. 2 FD 2009/829/JHA.

maximum extent, the FD fulfils a humanitarian objective, since the execution of a measure in the Member State where the person concerned is resident allows family and social ties to be preserved.

In this respect, the FD at issue is coherent with other instruments adopted at EU level, where the main objectives are rehabilitation and reintegration into society of the sentenced person. The reference is to FD 2008/947/JHA on the application of the principle of mutual recognition to judgments and probation decisions with a view to the supervision of probation measures and alternative sanctions,[7] and to FD 2008/909/JHA on the application of the principle of mutual recognition to judgments in criminal matters imposing custodial sentences or measures involving deprivation of liberty for the purpose of their enforcement in the EU.[8] Undoubtedly, there are strong connections as well as significant analogies between these two FDs and the one under consideration.[9]

The objective of facilitating rehabilitation and reintegration into society of the sentenced person through preservation of family and social ties is pursued also by the EAW FD, which provides that where a person who is the subject of a European arrest warrant for the purposes of prosecution is a national or resident of the executing Member State, surrender may be subject to the condition that the person, after being heard, is returned to the executing Member State to there serve the custodial sentence or detention order passed against him in the issuing Member State.[10] Similarly, the executing judicial authority may refuse to execute the European arrest warrant issued for the purposes of execution of a custodial sentence or detention order where the requested person is staying in, or is a national or a resident of the executing Member State and that State undertakes to execute the sentence or detention order in accordance with its domestic law.[11]

---

7 This FD shall, in relations between Member States, replace the corresponding provisions of the Council of Europe Convention of 30.11.1964 on the supervision of conditionally sentenced or conditionally released offenders. On this FD see *Sanz Morán*, p. 290.

8 This FD shall replace the corresponding provisions of the international conventions listed under Article 26, most of which have never been ratified (see, for example, the European Convention on the transfer of sentenced persons of 21.3.1983). On the FD see: *Plastina* [1], p. 2633. The FD has been recently implemented in Italy, with the Legislative Decree 161/2010. On the Italian implementing law, see *Plastina* [2], pp. 4409 ff. Prompt implementation reveals the expectations that the enforcement of custodial sentences in other Member States may contribute to address the issue of overcrowded prisons in Italy.

9 The draft Directive on the European protection order, presented in 2010 by the Council falls outside the rehabilitation and reintegration objectives, however. Its main purpose is to prevent victims from suffering further offences committed by the same person. The order should be recognised by all Member States and should be enforced in their territories. It could be issued on request of the victim and on the basis of a decision that applies a protection measure in the issuing Member State. On this subject-matter see *Eucrim* 2009, n. 4, p. 138.

10 Art. 5 No. 3 EAW FD.

11 Art. 4 No. 6 EAW FD.

With regard to this, the European Court of Justice has explained that, when the European arrest warrant is issued for the purpose of execution of a custodial sentence or detention order, the notion of residence should not be strictly construed: what counts is that the connection with the executing Member State is stable and continuous.[12] In line with this principle, the Italian Constitutional court declared the illegitimacy of Article 18(r) of the Law 69/2005 implementing the Framework Decision on the European arrest warrant in Italy on the grounds that it was contrary to Articles 11 and 117.1 of the Italian Constitution.[13]

2.   Scope of application

The FD on supervision measures as an alternative to provisional detention covers all criminal offences and is not restricted to particular types or levels of crime. However, it is likely to cover mostly cases of less serious offences, where supervision measures are generally applied.[14]

Minimum penalty thresholds are not provided. In particular, minimum penalty thresholds as provided under Article 2.1 of the EAW FD are not foreseen. This implies that recognition and supervision will apply to any offence for which, in the issuing Member State, the competent authorities are allowed to issue a supervision measure. This wide scope of application would appear sound: it would be unreasonable and discriminatory to grant the benefits stemming from the execution of a non-custodial measure in the Member State of residence only when the offence in question is serious. As a consequence, the executing Member State may be asked to recognise and supervise non-custodial measures as an alternative to provisional detention, even where, according to the law of the executing Member State, provisional detention may not be imposed. However, the fact that non-custodial measures are not the same across the EU should not be an obstacle to the implementation of the FD under consideration.

---

12 ECJ, Dominic Wolzenburg, Case C-123/08. The operative part of the judgment is published in OJ C 282/8, of 21.11.2009. The European Court of Justice claimed, *inter alia*, that Article 4.6 EAW FD "must be interpreted as meaning that, in the case of a citizen of the Union, the Member State of execution cannot, in addition to a condition as to the duration of residence in that State, make application of the ground for optional non-execution of a European arrest warrant laid down in that provision subject to supplementary administrative requirements, such as possession of a residence permit of indefinite duration." For a comment on this judgment see: *Calvanese/De Amicis*, p. 1191.

13 Constitutional Court, Decision 227/2010. On this ruling, see: *Colaiacovo* [1], p. 4156. More in general on this topic, see: *Colaiacovo* [2], p. 671; *Spagnolo*, p. 456. Indeed, the Italian implementing law provided grounds for non-execution of a European arrest warrant only where the requested person was a national; no ground for refusal was provided where the requested person, although a national of another Member State, was resident in Italy.

14 Recital No. 13 FD 2009/829/JHA.

Differences may be smoothed out on the basis of the tolerance rule,[15] typical of mutual recognition instruments, as well as on the basis of the positive results for the person subject to criminal proceedings.

The supervision measures covered by the FD are listed under Article 8.1: a) an obligation for the person to inform the competent authority in the executing State of any change of residence, in particular for the purpose of receiving a summons to attend a hearing or a trial in the course of criminal proceedings; b) an obligation not to enter certain localities, places or defined areas in the issuing or executing State; c) an obligation to remain at a specified place, where applicable during specified times; d) an obligation containing limitations on leaving the territory of the executing State; e) an obligation to report at specified times to a specific authority; f) an obligation to avoid contact with specific persons in relation with the offence(s) allegedly committed. However, Article 8.2 provides that each Member State shall notify the General Secretariat of the Council, when transposing the FD, or at a later stage, which supervision measures, apart from those listed under paragraph 1, it is prepared to monitor. These measures may include: a) an obligation not to engage in specified activities in relation with the offence(s) allegedly committed, which may include involvement in a specified profession or field of employment; b) an obligation not to drive a vehicle; c) an obligation to deposit a certain sum of money or to give another type of guarantee, which may either be provided through a specified number of instalments or in a lump sum; d) an obligation to undergo therapeutic treatment or treatment for addiction; e) an obligation to avoid contact with specific objects in relation with the offence(s) allegedly committed.

3.   Procedure of recognition

The procedure is based on direct contacts between the competent authorities of the issuing and executing Member State[16]. These authorities should be judicial authorities. However, non-judicial authorities may exceptionally be designated as competent, provided they have competence for taking decisions of a similar nature under their national law and procedures.[17]

The initiative of the competent authority of the issuing Member State does not

---

15 *Fragalà*, pp. 731 f.
16 Each Member State may designate a central authority or, where its legal system so provides, more than one central authority to assist its competent authorities. Central authorities shall be responsible for the administrative transmission and reception of decisions on supervision measures, together with the certificates, as well as for all other official correspondence relating thereto (Art. 7 FD 2009/829/JHA).
17 Art. 6 FD 2009/829/JHA.

lie in a request for, but simply in the transmission of the decision on supervision measures (or a certified copy of it) to another Member State, accompanied by a certificate, the standard form of which is annexed to the FD. The certificate must be signed, and its content certified as accurate, by the competent authority in the issuing Member State.[18]

The competent authority in the executing Member State shall, as soon as possible and in any case within 20 working days of receipt of the decision[19], recognise the decision on supervision measures forwarded in accordance with the rule and procedure laid down in the FD, and without delay take all necessary measures to monitor the supervision measures. The recognition procedure provides that the decision taken by the competent authority of the issuing Member State to order the supervision measure as an alternative to provisional detention must be accompanied by a certificate, the standard form of which is annexed to the FD. It is noteworthy that this procedure partially differs from the procedure provided under the EAW FD, where only the standard form needs to be sent by the issuing authority, without the need to attach the domestic decision.

The competent authority in the executing Member State may refuse to recognise the decision on supervision measures and invoke one of the grounds for non-recognition envisaged under Article 15 FD 2009/829/JHA. In particular, the executing authority must check the existence of the substantial conditions for recognition. First of all, it must be checked whether the person concerned lawfully and ordinarily resides in the executing Member State, and whether, on being informed of the measures, consents to return to that State.[20] In this context the consent of the person concerned is therefore indispensable for recognition and execution of the measure in the State of residence, and not merely optional, as is the case with the surrender procedure under the Framework Decision on the European arrest warrant. Secondly, the certificate must be ascertained to refer to measures expressly covered by Article 8.1 FD 2009/829/JHA, or to the measures

---

18 Art. 10 FD 2009/829/JHA.
19 The time limit for recognition of the decision on supervision measures shall be extended by another 20 working days, if a legal remedy has been introduced against the decision (Art. 12.2 FD 2009/829/JHA). If, under exceptional circumstances, the competent authority in the executing State is unable to comply with the given time limits, it shall immediately inform the competent authority in the issuing State by any means of its choosing giving reasons for the delay and indicating how long a final decision is expected to take (Art. 12.3 FD 2009/829/JHA).
20 Art. 9.1 FD 2009/829/JHA. It is, however, possible that, at the request of the person concerned, the competent authority in the issuing State forwards the decision on supervision measures to the competent authority of a Member State other than the Member State in which the person is lawfully and ordinarily residing, on condition that the latter authority has consented to such forwarding (Arts. 9.2 and 9.3 FD 2009/829/JHA).

the executing Member State has declared it is prepared to recognize and supervise according to Article 8.2 2009/829/JHA.

As to the grounds for non-recognition, other than those strictly relating to the absence of formal conditions or the material prerequisite for recognition,[21] these may be reduced or limited[22] in consideration of the objective of the FD, which is to favour the position of the person concerned, who would otherwise be remanded in pre-trial custody. In particular, non-recognition on account of the offence not being considered such in both countries (double incrimination) raises some concern. However, in line with the EAW FD, double incrimination is no longer required for thirty-two criminal offences listed under Article 14 FD 2009/829/JHA, if they are punishable in the issuing State by a custodial sentence or a measure involving deprivation of liberty for a maximum period of at least three years. Nonetheless, Member States may, for constitutional reasons, declare that they will not apply the abolition of double incrimination in respect of some or all of the offences expressly listed.[23] For any other offence, the executing State may proceed to recognise the decision on supervision measures subject to the condition that the decision relates to acts which also constitute an offence under the law of the executing State, whatever the constituent elements or description of the offence.[24] This provision is expected not to facilitate recognition of supervision measures issued in relation to less serious crimes to which the Framework Decision is likely to apply more frequently.

A characteristic ground for non-recognition is provided for by Article 15.1(h) FD 2009/829/JHA: the competent authority in the executing State may refuse to

---

21 Art. 15.1(a) and (b) FD 2009/829/JHA. The competent authority in the executing Member State may refuse to recognise the decision on supervision measures if: a) the certificate referred to in Art. 10 is incomplete or obviously does not correspond to the decision on supervision measures and is not completed or corrected within a reasonable period set by the competent authority in the executing Member State; b) the criteria laid down in Arts. 9.1, 9.2 or 10.4 FD 2009/829/JHA are not met.

22 The other grounds for non-recognition provided under Article 15 FD 2009/829/JHA may apply when: recognition of the decision on supervision measures would contravene the *ne bis in idem* principle (c); the decision on supervision measures relates, in the cases where double criminality is required, to an act which would not constitute an offence under the law of the executing Member State, save in tax, customs and currency matters (d); criminal prosecution is statute-barred under the law of the executing Member State and relates to an act which falls within the competence of the executing Member State under its national law (e); there is immunity under the law of the executing Member State, which makes it impossible to monitor supervision measures (f); under the law of the executing Member State, the person may not, on account of his age, be held criminally responsible for the act on which the decision on supervision measures is based (g); the executing authority would, in the case of breach of the supervision measures, have to refuse to surrender the person concerned in accordance with a European arrest warrant (h).

23 Art. 14.1 FD 2009/829/JHA.

24 Art. 14.3 FD 2009/829/JHA.

recognise the decision on supervision measures if, in the event of breach of the supervision measures, it would be obliged to refuse to surrender the person concerned in accordance with the EAW FD.[25] However, even if the executing authority believes that, in the case of breach of the supervision measures, it would refuse to surrender the person concerned according to a European arrest warrant, it may nevertheless recognize and monitor the supervision measures, after informing the competent authority in the issuing State of the reasons for the possible future refusal of surrender, should the issuing authority not withdraw the certificate.[26]

4. Execution of supervision measures and surrender of the person

To be welcomed is provision under Article 13 FD 2009/829/JHA according to which, if the nature of the supervision measures is incompatible with the law of the executing Member State, the competent authority in that Member State may adapt them to align with the types of supervision measures applying to equivalent offences under the law of the executing Member State. Since the provision allows adaptation of the measure issued, not its conversion into a different measure, the adapted supervision measure must correspond as far as possible to that imposed in the issuing State.[27] In any event, the adapted supervision measure may not be more severe than the supervision measure originally imposed.[28] The adaptation procedure may not be successful, however. Indeed the competent authority in the executing Member State must inform the competent authority in the issuing Member State of any decision to adapt the supervision measures[29] and the competent authority in the issuing Member State may decide to withdraw the certificate provided monitoring of the supervision procedure has not yet been initiated by the executing Member State.[30] In other words, adaptation of the supervision measure cannot be imposed on the issuing authority but must be agreed on.

---

25 Arts. 19.3 and 18.1(c) FD 2009/829/JHA.
26 Art. 15.3 FD 2009/829/JHA.
27 Art. 13.1 FD 2009/829/JHA.
28 Art. 13.2 FD 2009/829/JHA.
29 Art. 20.2(f) FD 2009/829/JHA.
30 Art. 13.3 FD 2009/829/JHA. The competent authority in the issuing State may decide to withdraw the certificate also following receipt of information referred to in Article 20.2(b) FD 2009/829/JHA. The authority in the executing State shall inform the competent authority in the issuing State of the maximum length of time during which the supervision measures can be monitored in the executing State, if the law of the executing State provides such a maximum (Art. 13.3 FD 2009/829/JHA).

Execution of a supervision measure in the Member State of residence may not jeopardize the objective of the FD, which is to ensure the due course of justice and, in particular, that the person concerned will be available to stand trial.[31] This is the reason why the competent authority in the executing Member State shall – using the standard form expressly provided – immediately notify the competent authority in the issuing Member State of any breach of a supervision measure, and any other finding which may result in a subsequent decision being taken,[32] such as renewal, review, withdrawal, modification of the supervision measures,[33] issuing of an arrest warrant or any other enforceable judicial decision having the same effect.[34]

The competence for taking all subsequent decisions relating to a decision on supervision measure rests with the authority of the issuing Member State,[35] whose law shall apply.[36] The monitoring of supervision measures, however, shall be governed by the law of the executing Member State.[37] In this respect, it is noteworthy that, while the competence of the authority in the issuing Member State for any subsequent decision following a supervision measure decision is in line with the rationale of mutual recognition, the competence of the authority in the executing Member State for the execution of supervision measures is typical of so-called primary judicial cooperation[38].

---

31 Art. 2.1 FD 2009 / 829 / JHA. With a view to hearing the person concerned, the procedure and conditions contained in instruments of international and European Union law provide for the possibility of using telephone and videoconferences for hearing persons (Art. 19.4 FD 2009 / 829 / JHA).

32 Art. 19.3 FD 2009 / 829 / JHA.

33 In this case the measure may be adapted according to Article 13 FD 2009 / 829 / JHA. However, the authority in the executing Member State may refuse to monitor the modified supervision measures if these measures do not fall within the types of supervision measures referred to in Article 8.1 FD 2009 / 829 / JHA and / or within those notified by the executing State concerned in accordance with Article 8.2 FD 2009 / 829 / JHA. It follows that the measure, even after modification, must be a non-custodial measure.

34 Art. 18.1 FD 2009 / 829 / JHA.

35 Recital No. 9 FD 2009 / 829 / JHA: "The competent authority in the issuing State should have jurisdiction to take all subsequent decisions relating to a decision on supervision measures, including ordering a provisional detention. Such provisional detention might, in particular, be ordered following a breach of the supervision measures or a failure to comply with a summons to attend any hearing or trial in the course of criminal proceedings."

36 Arts. 18.1 and 18.2 FD 2009 / 829 / JHA.

37 Art. 16 FD 2009 / 829 / JHA.

38 The traditional distinction between primary and secondary cooperation depends on the competences assigned to the requested State. Under secondary cooperation, the requested State shall carry out activities that do not imply transfer of powers (extradition and legal assistance are typical examples of this type of cooperation). Under primary cooperation, the requesting State shall delegate the requested State for certain powers. In the case under consideration, the delegation concerns supervision powers during the execution of a measure as an alternative to detention. See *Fragalà*, p. 730.

Should the competent authority of the issuing Member State issue a European arrest warrant or any other judicial decision having the same effect following a breach of a supervision measure, the person concerned must be surrendered in accordance with the EAW FD. As a result, the grounds for refusal[39] and the guarantees to be granted in certain circumstances are applicable as provided for by Articles 5.2 and 5.3 2009/829/JHA.[40] Only Article 2.1 EAW FD may not be invoked by the competent authority of the executing State to refuse to surrender the person.[41] The reason for this provision is clear. The aim is to avoid any potential refusal of surrender in the event of breach of a supervision measure discouraging the use of non-custodial measures. In other words, the exception is not intended to jeopardize the objectives of the FD on supervision measures as an alternative to provisional detention.

However, each Member State may notify that it will also apply Article 2.1 EAW FD in deciding on the surrender of the person concerned. The general application of the EAW FD is, however, likely to impair the effectiveness of the FD under consideration.

It would have been preferable to provide for a surrender procedure not linked to the European arrest warrant procedure, thereby alleviating concern regarding refusal of surrender in the event of the breach of supervision measures ordered as an alternative to provisional detention. All in all, the obligation to respect fundamental rights and fundamental legal principles, and the non-discrimination clause provided under the FD on supervision measures,[42] would be sufficient safeguard against having to surrender a person who is in some way in a prejudiced situation.

5.   Effectiveness of the new instrument

In light of this overview, the question now is whether the FD on supervision measures as an alternative to provisional detention may be considered effective. Effectiveness is undeniably desirable. As already pointed out, the aims include promoting free movement of persons in the EU, reducing recourse to detention measures, and safeguarding the right to liberty and the presumption of in-

---

39 As already underlined, where the competent authority in the executing State is of the opinion that it may refuse to surrender the person concerned following a European arrest warrant, but is nevertheless willing to recognise the decision on supervision measures (Art. 15.1(h) FD 2009/829/JHA), it shall inform the competent authority in the issuing State (Art. 15.3 FD 2009/829/JHA).

40 Recital No. 13 FD 2009/829/JHA.

41 Art. 21.2 FD 2009/829/JHA.

42 Recital No. 16 and Art. 5 FD 2009/829/JHA.

nocence (in line with Arts. 5.1 and 6.2 ECHR), without, however, jeopardising security or the due course of justice. Thanks to this Framework Decision, the principle of proportionality of supervision measures virtuously enters the area of freedom, security and justice. Importantly, once implemented at national level, this FD will probably have the effect to reduce the frequent and unjustified use made of European arrest warrants, especially in the context of petty crimes.[43]

These considerations may represent a good response to opponents of mutual recognition on account of the diversity of the 27 Member States' legal systems. The issue is nonetheless quite delicate and the fact that provisional measures are a bone of contention does not make things any easier. It cannot be affirmed that mutual trust is any stronger because mutual recognition applies to provisional measures. Indeed, provisional measure decisions are taken by procedures that are less guaranteed than those governing trial, and moreover are very different from one Member State to another.

It is true that the ECHR and the ECtHR case-law have set common standards binding upon Member States; but such standards are only minimum and not always respected, as the jurisprudence of the Court of Strasbourg clearly shows. Furthermore, the ECtHR does not assess respect of the ECHR in relation to single national provisions but with reference to the overall proceedings of a specific case.

The marked differences between national legal systems and procedural guarantees constitute an impediment to mutual recognition as they cast into question the *a priori* existence of mutual trust between Member States, an indispensable element on which mutual recognition must be founded. On the other hand, trust is a dynamic and mutual process that requires effort and predisposition, especially in the criminal law sector. Indeed, trust may well be placed by a Member State in another Member State; it first must be deserved, however.[44] It is therefore undeniable that reducing such differences through harmonization of procedural safeguard standards across the EU would contribute substantially to the coherence and efficacy of mutual recognition measures. It has been pointed out that the degree of procedural law harmonization and mutual trust is directly proportional.[45]

---

43 On 11th April 2011, justice commissioner Viviane Reding said that "the European arrest warrant is an important tool to catch criminals, but member states should ensure that it is used correctly [...] not issued mechanically for crimes that are not very serious such as bicycle theft." Figures published by the EU commission on the same day show that Poland is the most eager to issue the warrants, with 4,844 put out in 2009 compared to the UK's 220. In total, Member States issued 54.689 European arrest warrants between 2005 and 2009, leading to 11,630 suspects being surrendered.
44 See *Vernimmen-VanTiggelen et al.*, p. 550.
45 *Ibid.*, p. 560.

However, the only initiative taken to set common minimum standards for certain procedural rights in criminal proceedings throughout the EU[46] failed. This has rekindled criticism especially on the lack of attention by the EU to procedural safeguards compared with the huge focus given to security issues, of which the European arrest warrant is the preeminent result. Added to that, the lack of common rules in several areas, not least that pertaining to evidence, has been one of the main reasons leading to the limited scope of application of the instrument adopted (i. e. EEW FD 2008 / 978 / JHA).

6. Mutual recognition and harmonization after the Treaty of Lisbon

Following the Treaty of Lisbon, the new legal framework of the EU takes into serious consideration the need for approximation of procedural and substantive legislations,[47] with the precise purpose of facilitating mutual recognition. Article 82.1 TFEU provides that:

> "Judicial cooperation in criminal matters in the Union shall be based on the principle of mutual recognition of judgments and judicial decisions and shall include the approximation of the laws and regulations of the Member States in the areas referred to in paragraph 2 and in Article 83."

Thanks to Article 82, the principle of mutual recognition has been formally affirmed for the first time and given a legal basis in the Treaty. Mutual recognition is now a principle regulating the important (concurrent) competence of the EU in the area of judicial cooperation in criminal matters. In this framework, the initiative of the EU is not dependent on previous harmonization of national legislations, although it demands the accomplishment of a minimum level of harmonization, considered to be the necessary prerequisite for the functioning of mutual recognition.[48]

In light of these considerations, it may be said that under the Treaty of Lisbon the principle of mutual recognition is strongly affirmed and becomes essential for EU action in the area of judicial cooperation in criminal matters. At the same time, this principle has a dynamic dimension that entails the consolidation of mutual trust. Such consolidation can be pursued in many ways; a key approach is approximation.

In line with this objective, Article 82.2 TFEU provides that:

---

46 Proposal of FD on common minimum standards for certain procedural rights in criminal proceedings throughout the EU, Brussels, 28.4.2004 COM(2004) 328 final, 2004 / 0113 (CNS). On this, see below.
47 Art. 82 TFEU. With regard to harmonization of substantive criminal laws see Art. 83 TFEU.
48 See *Cerizza*, p. 65.

"To the extent necessary to facilitate mutual recognition of judgments and judicial decisions and police and judicial cooperation in criminal matters having a cross-border dimension, the European Parliament and the Council may, by means of directives adopted in accordance with the ordinary legislative procedure, establish minimum rules."

Minimum rules may concern:

"(a) Mutual admissibility of evidence between Member States; (b) the rights of individuals in criminal procedure; (c) the rights of victims of crime; (d) any other specific aspects of criminal procedure which the Council has identified in advance by a decision; for the adoption of such a decision, the Council shall act unanimously after obtaining the consent of the European Parliament."

Of course, the establishment of minimum rules shall be limited to the fulfilment of mutual recognition and shall concern the areas of particularly serious crime with a cross-border dimension.[49] In addition, only the introduction of "minimum rules" is envisaged, which explains why Article 82 TFEU provides that "adoption of the minimum rules [...] shall not prevent Member States from maintaining or introducing a higher level of protection for individuals." Precautions are also granted with Article 82 providing that "such rules shall take into account the differences between the legal traditions and systems of the Member States."

Expectations concerning EU action to foster approximation of national legislations cannot disregard the important institutional progress achieved by the Treaty of Lisbon.[50] According to Article 82.1 TFEU, approximation shall be carried out by means of directives adopted in accordance with the ordinary legislative procedure, which implies majority-voting rules (unanimity within the Council no longer applies). However, Article 82.3 TFEU provides for an "emergency break" procedure:[51] just one dissenting Member State may lead to the suspension of the ordinary legislative procedure and the withdrawal of the draft directive concerned, save when at least nine Member States wish to establish enhanced cooperation. Certainly, enhanced cooperation is not desirable

---

49 These areas of crime are those listed under Article 83.1 TFEU.
50 On the main changes brought about by the Treaty of Lisbon see *Serzysko*, p. 69; *Herlin-Karnell*, p. 59.
51 Where a member of the Council considers that a draft directive would affect fundamental aspects of its criminal justice system, it may request that the draft directive be referred to the European Council. In that case, the ordinary legislative procedure shall be suspended. After discussion, and in the event of a consensus, the European Council shall, within four months of this suspension, refer the draft back to the Council, which shall terminate the suspension of the ordinary legislative procedure (Art. 82.3 TFEU). As to draft directives aimed at the approximation of substantive criminal law, the same procedure is foreseen under Art. 83.3 TFEU.

as it reveals little cohesion within the EU. Yet the provision regarding this extraordinary procedure shows a realistic approach, which might be the only possible approach in certain circumstances.

It follows that not only is approximation limited in its scope of application, but no few doubts arise as to its success. In this regard, Article 82 TFEU is a step forward in the process of EU integration, even though unanimity remains a key feature. Notwithstanding these limits, there is space for relevant initiatives. The subject-matters for which approximation is already authorized by Article 82.2 TFEU (mutual admissibility of evidence between Member States, the rights of individuals in criminal procedure, the rights of victims of crime) are wide and crucial. The issue concerning the rights of individuals in criminal proceedings is perhaps the area that should be first tackled by the EU, thereby responding to the criticisms levelled at mutual recognition measures, especially with regard to the Framework Decision on the European arrest warrant. The conclusions of the European Council held in Tampere in 1999 already demanded the adoption of common minimum standards for certain aspects of procedural law considered necessary to facilitate the application of the principle of mutual recognition while respecting the fundamental legal principles of Member States (§ 37). In line with this objective, in 2003 the Commission presented a Green Paper on procedural safeguards for suspects and defendants in criminal proceedings throughout the EU,[52] and, in 2004, the Council submitted a Framework Decision proposal on certain procedural rights in criminal proceedings throughout the EU.[53] This initiative failed, however, because the Council failed to achieve unanimity.

After this experience and some time before the Treaty of Lisbon, it became clear that a more gradual approach was necessary. The first step in this direction was the 2009 draft Framework Decision on the right to interpretation and to translation in criminal proceedings.[54] Given the essential and uncontroversial nature of these rights, a political agreement was easily reached on this draft in 2009. However, since the adoption of the Treaty of Lisbon was by that time very close, it was decided to propose the initiative once again within the new institutional and legal framework that was better designed to incorporate these provisions safeguarding individual rights. Indeed, important changes in the law-making process,[55] the legal binding character of the EU FRCh, as well as the possible accession of the EU to the ECHR have all been provided for under the reform Treaty.

---

52 Brussels, 19.2.2003, COM(2003) 75 final.
53 Brussels, 28.4.2004 COM(2004) 328 final, 2004/0113 (CNS).
54 Brussels, 8.7.2009, COM(2009) 338 final, 2009/0101 (CNS).
55 A greater involvement of the European Parliament and the majority-voting rule are provided under the ordinary legislative procedure.

According to the gradual approach, on 30th November 2009, the Council adopted a roadmap for strengthening procedural rights of suspected or accused persons in criminal proceedings[56] – subsequently inserted in the Stockholm Programme (§ 2.4)[57] – where the Commission is invited to submit proposals regarding the following subject-matters: a) translation and interpretation; b) information on rights and charges; c) legal advice and legal aid; d) communication with relatives, employers and consular authorities; e) special safeguards for vulnerable suspects or charged persons; f) a Green Paper on pre-trial detention.

Following this roadmap and in accordance with a proposal of Directive of 9th March 2010, approved in June by the European Parliament, on 7th October 2010 the Council adopted the Directive 2010 / 64 / EU on the right to interpretation and translation in criminal proceedings.[58] On 20th July 2010, the Commission presented its draft Directive on the right to information in criminal proceedings[59] (according to letter b of the subject-matters listed in the roadmap). The Council adopted a general approach to this draft Directive on 3rd December 2010 and negotiations with the European Parliament have been initiated with a view to reaching an agreement.[60] As to the other subject matters envisaged by the roadmap, initiatives by the Commission are expected in 2011.

Directive 2010 / 64 / UE has a symbolic value. It constitutes the very first measure establishing common minimum standards for the safeguard of defence rights in criminal proceedings, thereby remedying the repeatedly underlined lacunas in the relationship between prosecution and defence within the scope of judicial cooperation in criminal matters at EU level. The content of this Directive repeats some indications stemming from the case-law of the ECHR; this content will soon be applied at national level following the obligation to implement the Directive. The scope of application of the Directive is quite wide: the right to interpretation and the right to translation apply both to criminal proceedings and proceedings for the execution of a European arrest warrant (with regard to this, Article 11 FD 2002 / 584 / JHA does not provide for any guarantees but refers to the national legislation of the executing Member State). The right to interpretation is granted in the relationship between the defendant and the judicial authority, as well as in the relationship between the defendant and the defence

---

56 OJ C 295 of 4.12.2009.
57 OJ C 115 of 4.5.2010. In the Stockholm Programme the European Council invites the Commission to examine further elements of minimum procedural rights for suspected and accused persons, and to assess whether other issues, for instance the presumption of innocence, need to be addressed to promote better cooperation in this area.
58 OJ L 280 of 26.10.2010.
59 Brussels, COM(2010) 392 / 3.
60 Brussels, 6.12.2010, 17503 / 10, 2010 / 0215 (COD).

lawyer. Of course, some margin of appreciation rests with Member States.[61] This Directive is to be welcomed. In the context of swifter, more effective cooperation in criminal matters between Member States, it responds to the need for the protection of fundamental rights and guarantees as established under the ECHR (especially Articles 5 and 6) and under the Charter of Fundamental Rights of the European Union (especially Articles 47 and 48).

In conclusion, it may be said that there is still a long way to go before judicial cooperation in criminal matters becomes smoother and more efficient, especially as far as pre-trial detention is concerned. Negotiations on future instruments are not expected to be simple given the striking differences in national legislations. These difficulties explain the reason why the roadmap invites the Commission to submit an initial Green Paper to enable open debate.

Bibliography

Arangüena Fanego, Coral, De "la orden europea de vigilancia" al reconosimiento muto de resoluciones iudicia essobremedidas sustitutivas de la prisión provisional: primera aproximación a la decisión marco 2009/829/JAI del Consejo, in: Arangüena Fanego (ed.), Espacio europeo de libertad, seguridad y justicia: últimos avances en cooperación sudicia penal, Lex Nova (2010), pp. 224 ff.

Calvanese, Ersilia / De Amicis, Gaetano, Mandato d'arresto europeo e consegna "esecutiva" del cittadino nell'interpretazione della Corte di giustizia: verso la declaratoria di incostituzionalità dell'art. 18 lett. r), della l. n. 69/2005?, in: Cassazione penale (2010), pp. 1191 ff.

Cerizza, Solutions Offered by the Lisbon Treaty, in Eucrim (2/2010).

Cid Moliné, José, La política criminal europea en materia de sanciones alternativas a la prisión y la realidad española: una brechaquedebesuperarse, in: Arangüena Fanego (ed.), Espacio europeo de libertad, seguridad y justicia: últimos avances en cooperación sudicia penal, Lex Nova (2010), pp. 224 ff.

Colaiacovo, Guido, [1] Euromandato e cittadini extracomunitari residenti: ancora dubbi dopo la pronuncia della Corte costituzionale, in: Cassazione penale (2010), pp. 4156 ff.; [2], La mancata previsione del rifiuto di consegna del residente non cittadino, in: Cassazione penale (2010).

Fragalà, Alfio Gabriele, Considerazioni sul Libro verde in tema di mutuo riconoscimento delle misure cautelari non detentive, in: L'area di libertà, sicurezza e giustizia: alla ricerca di un equilibrio fra priorità repressive ed esigenze di garanzia, Rafaraci (ed.), Giuffré (2007), pp. 721 ff.

Gialuz, Mitja, Novità sovranazionali, in: Processo penale e Giustizia (2011), pp. 9 ff.

Herlin-Karnell, Ester, The Lisbon Treaty. A Critical Analysis of Its Impact on EU Criminal Law, in: Eucrim (2/2010), pp. 59 ff.

---

61 See *Gialuz*, p. 9.

Ljungquist, Thomas, Mutual recognition of non custodial pre trial supervision measures in the European Union, in: 77 Revue Internationale de droit pénal (2006), pp. 169 ff.

Plastina, Nadia, [1] La Decisione Quadro del Consiglio dell'Unione europea relativa al trasferimento dei condannati approvata a Bruxelles, in: Cassazione penale (2009), pp. 2633 ff.; [2], L'ordine europeo di trasferimento delle persone condannate, in: Cassazione penale (2009), pp. 4409 ff.

Sanz Morán, Ángel José, Reflexiones en torno a la idea de "libertad vigilada," in: Arangüena Fanego (ed.), Espacio europeo de libertad, seguridad y justicia: últimos avances en cooperación sudicia penal, Lex Nova (2010), pp. 290 ff.

Serzysko, Agnieszka, European Criminal Justice Under the Lisbon Treaty, in: Eucrim (2/2010), pp. 69 ff.

Spagnolo, Paola, La consegna esecutiva dello straniero "straniero": mera discrasia rispetto al mandato processuale o lesione del principio di uguaglianza?, in: Giurisprudenza di merito (2009), pp. 456 ff.

Stevens, Lonneke, Pre-Trial Detention: The Presumption of Innocence and Article 5 of the European Convention on Human Rights Cannot and Does Not Limit its Increasing Use, in: 17 European Journal of Crime, Criminal Law and Criminal Justice (2009), pp. 165 ff.

Vernimmen-VanTiggelen, Giselle et al. (eds.), The future of mutual recognition in criminal matters in the European Union / L'avenir de la reconnaissance mutuelle en matière pénale dans l'Union européenne, Editions de l'Université de Bruxelles (2009).

II. The perspective of domestic legal systems

Richard Vogler

England and Wales

Table of Contents

Table of Abbreviations

BASS	Bail Accommodation and Support Scheme
CAR	Commonwealth Arbitration Reports
CPD	Law Reports, Common Please Division
EBS	Effective Bail Scheme
ECHR	European Convention on Human Rights
ECtHR	European Court of Human Rights
LJQB	Law Journal Reports, Queen's Bench
LT	Law Times Reports (1859 – 1947)
PACE	Police and Criminal Evidence Act 1984

1.   The right to liberty

According to a former Lord Chancellor of England, the refusal of pre-trial release is the solitary exception to *Magna Charta*; "… the only example in peace time where a man can be kept in confinement without a proper sentence following conviction after a proper trial."[1]

Seven hundred and eighty four years after *Magna Charta,* the UK government finally decided to enact another charter of rights by introducing the Human Rights Act 1998, which effectively domesticated the provisions of the ECHR, which hit her to had not been part of our law. Measured against this new standard, the English law on pre-trial custody, we are told by our Law Commission, was entirely compliant. There were, apparently "no provisions (in the domestic legislation) which, upon analysis, cannot be applied compatibly nor which, given appropriate training, decision-makers would be likely to apply in a way which would violate Convention rights."[2]

The purpose of this short chapter is to question this assumption and to suggest that the last few decades in England and Wales have seen a radical departure from the use of pre-trial precautionary measures exclusively to support the main criminal process (the sole justification for the derogation from *Magna Carta* and Article 5 ECHR) to policing and control objectives which are completely unconnected with the trial process itself. One of the paradoxes of this assertion is that, despite these deficiencies, the absolute numbers of defendants remanded in custody in England and Wales has remained stable over recent years and, as a percentage of the overall prison population, has declined sharply. This is notwithstanding successive moral panics about "Bail Bandits," which have prompted more and more repressive legislation in this area. The percentage of the overall prison population in England and Wales which consists of unconvicted or unsentenced individuals is 17 %, comparing very favourably with the rates in both our European sister jurisdictions, some of which have percentages as high as 52 % and with those of other Common law countries.[3]

The question of "pre-trial precautionary measures" in the common law world is usually referred to, for historical reasons, in terms of "bail" (conditional release) and "custody." This is a profoundly anomalous area of our law which has caused, and continues to cause, serious disquiet. Not only is the bail/custody decision anomalous in terms of human rights protections but in almost no other circumstances is the court called upon to make predictions about future conduct rather than to determine and to punish events which have taken place in the past.

---

1 *Cavadino/Gibson*, p. 69.
2 *Law Commission* [1], p. 3.
3 *Hucklesby* [4], pp. 3–23; *Player et al.*, pp. 1–21.

Typically they are asked to perform this Solomon-like task in the briefest of time-frames and on the basis of the most speculative assertions and little hard evidence. It is not surprising that bail has predominantly been seen as a political rather than a judicial issue in English history. Nothing could be more calculated to undermine the right to liberty and the presumption of innocence than to incarcerate an unconvicted person. Nothing could do more damage to the adversarial principle than to imprison one adversary so that the logistical difficulties of case preparation are magnified and he or she will appear in court robbed of any opportunity of appearing as an innocent person. For this reason it seems fundamental that the decision to remand in custody should be taken only in circumstances where release would threaten the whole object of the criminal proceedings.

1.1. A history of the right to liberty

The right to bail in England is, according to Sir James Stephen "as old as the law of England itself and is explicitly recognised by our earliest writers."[4] Because of the presence of the jury in English procedure, the trial was central and there was no pre-trial of any kind until 1554[5] and therefore no necessity to detain defendants for interrogation as was common in the continental Roman-Canon practice.[6] Bail was therefore exclusively for the purpose of securing attendance at trial and was based on a contractual relationship between the court and the accused for the payment of a money bond or security which would be forfeited in the event of non-appearance. The hearing to consider the amount of money bail to be demanded in exchange for release was always held in public.[7] Nevertheless, politically motivated bail refusal became a matter of the greatest importance in the constitutional struggles of the seventeenth century and the resulting legislation ensured that a refusal of bail or a delay in granting bail by a judge was a criminal offence under the Habeas Corpus Act 1679[8] and the Bill of Rights 1688.[9] Moreover, the same Bill of Rights enacted the rule that "excessive bail ought not to be required,"[10] a provision of such fundamental significance for the freedom of the individual that it was reproduced verbatim in the Eighth Amendment to the United States Constitution.

---

4 *Stephen*, p. 233.
5 Bail Statute of 1554, 1 & 2 Philip and Mary, c. 13.
6 *Langbein*.
7 *Corre / Wolchover*, p. 31.
8 31 Car. 2, ch. 2 (1679).
9 1 W. & M. (2d. Sess.) (1688).
10 Ch. 2, s. 10.

Another ancient and powerful legal instrument for the protection of the liberty of the individual was the "Great Writ" of *Habeas Corpus*. Established by *Magna Carta* in 1215, the first use of the writ is recorded by Blackstone as occurring in 1305. *Habeas Corpus* is a summons with the force of a court order, which can be requested by a private individual. It is addressed to any custodian (e. g. a prison official), demanding that a prisoner be taken before the High Court for the lawfulness of the detention to be examined. Unless the custodian can establish lawful authority to the satisfaction of the court, the prisoner will be released immediately. According to Justice Brennan:

> "It is perhaps the most important writ known to the constitutional law of England, affording as it does a swift and imperative remedy in all cases of illegal restraint or confinement."[11]

Habeas Corpus proved of critical importance in such constitutional landmarks as *Bushell's Case* in 1670.[12] Its continuing role is well illustrated by the 2006 US case of *Hamdan v. Rumsfeld*[13] in which a Guantanamo Bay prisoner petitioned for a writ, claiming that the military commissions "violated both the Uniform Code of Military Justice and the four Geneva Conventions." The weakness of the writ is that it is a common law remedy which can be overruled by statute and withdrawn in time of war or political unrest. Its limitations have recently been criticised by the European Court of Human Rights.[14]

Until 1898 the defendant in a criminal trial was not competent to give evidence and so there was little point in detaining him beforehand except to ensure his attendance.[15] According to Lord Russell:

> "It cannot be too strongly impressed on the magistracy that bail is not to be withheld as a punishment but that the requirements of bail are merely to secure the attendance of the prisoner at his trial."[16]

The test for pre-trial release laid down by Coleridge J in 1855[17] required the magistrates to direct their minds exclusively to this issue, recognising the inadequacies and dangers of any cursory enquiry into the accused's character or future behaviour. Instead, only three criteria could be considered: the gravity of the offence charged, the probability of conviction and the severity of any likely punishment. The same principle operated in the US and the Supreme Court, in *Stack v. Boyle* in 1951, reaffirmed the doctrine that risk of flight was the sole

---

11 *Shoenberger*, pp. 47–66.
12 1670, 124, Eng. Rep. 1006 (CPD).
13 548 U.S. 557 (2006).
14 *Shoenburger*, op. loc. cit.
15 Criminal Evidence Act 1898. See *Vogler* [3], pp. 149–150.
16 In *R. v. Rose* (1898) 78 LT 119.
17 In *Re Robinson* (1854) 23 LJQB 286.

legitimate justification for pre-trial remand. They pointed out that "unless the right to bail is preserved, the presumption of innocence, secured after centuries of struggle, would lose its meaning."[18] The pre-trial precautionary measures of this period were accordingly entirely determined (in law at least) by the requirements of the main proceedings.

This law remained settled in England for a century until one of our least liberal judges, Lord Goddard, introduced an entirely new and unprecedented ground for the refusal of bail. In his view, bail could in future be refused solely to prevent a defendant "having the opportunity of committing further offences."[19] This was a completely novel development, for the first time using bail systematically as preventative detention to stop future crime in a way unconnected with the main proceedings. It was argued forcefully at the time that the proper means of deterring crime was the threat of trial and punishment, not prior imprisonment. Nevertheless this justification for the refusal of bail was enshrined in law by the Bail Act 1976.

This legislation, which continues to regulate pre-trial remand in England and Wales, in itself represented another revolutionary change in practice. It ended the historic procedure of money bail and personal sureties offered by the defendant and for the first time created a criminal offence of "failing to answer bail." A free-market contractual relationship between state and bailee was replaced by a penal relationship, thereby further decoupling bail from the main proceedings and creating the potential for fresh, Bail Act offences to be committed.

There were sound reasons for this change since the drawbacks of the old system, which still continues in the US, were considerable.[20] First it permitted draconian and extra-judicial powers to anyone standing as contractual security for a bailed defendant (particularly, commercial bail-bondsmen), to use force if necessary to bring him or her to court. Second, although the amount of bail was set in accordance with a defendant's financial means, the system was inevitably unfair to the impecunious defendant and, in its most extreme American manifestation was "... at best a system of chequebook justice (and) at worst a highly commercialized racket."[21]

It is worth noting that, despite the impact of the Federal Bail Reform Act 1984,[22] the US has continued to emphasise the contingency of the bail decision to the main proceedings. According to Metzmeier, the United States remains

---

18 342 U.S. 1 (1951) at 4.
19 *R. v. Wharton* [1955] CLR 565.
20 *Bottomley.*
21 *Goldfarb*, p. ix.
22 *Metzmeier*, pp. 409–410; *Wiseman*, pp. 121–157.

"… unique among common law nations in the primacy it still places on appearance at trial as the basis of bail."[23]

1.2. The current situation

The Bail Act 1976 was introduced following a Working Party Report[24] as a means
of "enabling courts to release more persons on bail without diminishing the
protection of the public."[25] Because it created in s. 4.1 a presumption in favour of
bail, it was subjected to vigorous police criticism at the time, as a "notorious Act"
aimed merely at the release of "hardened criminals."[26]

   This is clearly not the case. Under Schedule 1, Part 1, paragraph 2 of the Act, a
defendant charged with an imprisonable (e. g. serious) offence *must* be granted
unconditional bail unless the court is satisfied that there are substantial
grounds[27] for believing that one of the three rebutting conditions apply. These
are that the defendant, if released on bail (whether subject to conditions or not)
would (a) fail to surrender to custody, or (b) commit an offence while on bail, or
(c) interfere with witnesses or otherwise obstruct the course of justice, whether
in relation to himself or any other person.

   Since condition (b) rapidly came to represent the single most likely ground
for the refusal of bail,[28] the major importance of the bail / custody decision has
clearly shifted from judicial to policing objectives. Significantly, whereas the Law
Commission concluded that exceptions (a) and (c) above were "plainly compatible"[29] with the ECHR, provision (b) concerning the likelihood of future
offending was only considered "capable of being applied in a Convention-
compliant manner."[30]

   Other criteria for the refusal of bail which are unrelated to the main proceedings include where a defendant ought to be kept in custody for his own
protection or, if he is a child or young person, for his own welfare or where he or
she is already serving a sentence of custody or where insufficient information is
available to reach a proper decision.[31]

   Guidance for the courts in applying these provisions was provided by the

---

23 *Metzmeier*, p. 412.
24 *Graham-Harrison.*
25 House of Commons Debates, Vol. 912. See also *Graham-Harrison.*
26 See citations in *Vogler* [1], pp. 11 ff.
27 Recent studies have suggested that this test is not used in a consistent way. See *Dhami*,
     pp. 349 – 360.
28 *Vogler* [1], p. 11.
29 *Law Commission* [1], para. 1.46.
30 *Ibid.*, para. 1.47.
31 Bail Act 1976, Schedule I, Part 1, para. 2 A.

criteria set out in paragraph 9 of the First Schedule to the Act, which indicates that "the court shall have regard to such of the following considerations as appear to it to be relevant," including (a) the nature and seriousness of the offence or default (and the probable method of dealing with the defendant for it) (b) the character, antecedents, associations and community ties of the defendant (c) the defendant's record as respects the fulfilment of his obligations under previous grants of bail in criminal proceedings (d) (except in the case of a defendant whose case is adjourned for inquiries or a report), the strength of the evidence of his having committed the offence or having defaulted, as well as to any others which appear to be relevant.[32]

In view of the correlation of trial outcomes with the initial bail or custody decision, the impact of police decision-making on this process gives cause for concern. Research evidence suggests that courts have a strong tendency to accept the recommendation on bail, conditional bail or custody proposed by the Crown prosecutor. There is also a strong correlation (85 %) between the advice of the police and the recommendations of the Crown prosecutor.[33] Hucklesby has found that bail was contested in only one in ten cases and was granted in only a third of such cases.[34] This indicates a very strong influence for the police perspective in a hearing in which it is very difficult to challenge their version of the alleged facts. A refusal of bail may well set up a chain of perceptions, which will lead ultimately to a conviction.

Since the enactment of the Bail Act in 1976, a number of attempts have been made to reverse the presumption in favour of bail in respect of certain classes of offender. These provisions, which are summarised below, demonstrate again a significant shift away from the role of bail in supporting the main proceedings towards the role of bail in policing certain groups of alleged offenders. Four important exceptions to the usual bail regime have been developed over recent years. These include:

(1) Alleged Terrorism defendants, for whom the maximum pre-trial detention (without appearance before a judicial authority) is 28 days.[35]

(2) Defendants who have allegedly committed one or more serious offences (murder, manslaughter, and rape, for example) and who have a record of similar offences. In these circumstances the courts are required to provide written reasons for granting bail.[36]

(3) Defendants who have been charged with a serious offence, which was allegedly committed while on bail for another serious offence. These in-

---

32 *Ibid.*, Schedule 1, Part I, paras. 9 (a–d).
33 *Phillips*, p. 135.
34 *Hucklesby* [2], p. 219.
35 Ss. 23–24 of the Terrorism Act 2006.
36 S. 153 of the Criminal Justice Act 1988.

dividuals cannot be granted bail at all unless the court believes that there is no significant risk of offences being committed on bail.[37]

(4) Defendants for whom there is drug test evidence of Class A drug use need not be granted bail if the offence is drug-related and he or she does not agree to undergo assessment and / or follow-up treatment for drug dependency.[38]

Attempts by the UK government to adopt even more serious derogations from the presumption in favour of bail established by the 1976 Act have not been entirely successful. In the 1990s, following a series of moral panics about alleged "Bail Bandits" (criminals facing custody and with nothing to lose, committing further offences while on bail) the government attempted to reverse the presumption in favour of bail in such circumstances. However, it was obliged to withdraw this provision when it became clear that it would inevitably be condemned by an unfavourable judgement of the ECtHR. There have been no subsequent attempts to reverse completely the presumption in favour of bail but the above provisions nevertheless come very close![39]

2.   Limitations to the right to liberty

2.1.   Pre-trial supervision measures as an alternative to custody

As will be seen from the above, money bail has for many centuries been the sole supervision measure in respect of pre-trial release. However, radical new approaches were developed in the 1960s. A seemingly innocuous amendment to the 1967 Criminal Justice Bill introduced a unprecedented new power for courts to impose conditions other than financial sureties on the grant of bail. The clearly expressed intention was to enable more people to be released from prison than was hitherto the case.[40] Under s. 6 of the Bail Act 1976, the court can now impose any condition which it considers "necessary" in order to address exceptions to bail which it believes would otherwise exist. Since 1994 the police as well as the courts have been empowered to impose conditions on police bail[41] and the rise in the use of conditions has been exponential. Conditions which are commonly used include *inter alia*, residence, curfew, reporting to the police station, sur-

---

37 S. 25 of the Criminal Justice and Public Order Act 1994 as amended by the Criminal Justice Act 2003.

38 S. 4.9 of the Bail Act 1976, as inserted by s. 58 of the Criminal Justice and Court Services Act 2000.

39 *Huckesby* [4], p. 4.

40 House of Commons Debates, Vol. 745, 26th April 1967, 1621.

41 *Hucklesby* [3], pp. 441–463.

render of passport, money security (surety) paid by another person (but not by the defendant), keeping away from particular places or persons (including prosecution witnesses), monitoring by electronic tagging (introduced in 2005), and drug testing.[42]

The general impact of the use of bail conditions has been net-widening and there is no doubt that conditions are frequently imposed on defendants who otherwise would have received unconditional bail. During the 1990s conditional bail was imposed in approximately 30 % of cases but nowadays over half of all defendants are released on conditional bail.[43] Conditions are commonly offered by the defence as a means of encouraging the grant of bail and are not always relevant to the objectives of the Bail Act or the type of offending involved.[44] Electronic tagging has been adopted for approximately 3,500 defendants by March 2009, rising from 2,000 for the whole of 2007 / 8.[45] Some research tends to suggest that compliance with bail conditions is improved by tagging[46] but overall the data are inconclusive and the lessons learned do not seem to have been well applied.[47] Certainly there is insufficient evidence about the impact of tagging on the individuals concerned.[48] Bail with a condition of drug treatment has also been introduced since 2007 with variable success.[49] Clearly, the outcome of this growth in the use of conditions has been to extend the bail regime yet further into the realm of policing and control.

2.2. Custody

The ultimate test of any system of pre-trial precautionary measures is not only the justifications advanced for their use but also the extent of their use. Despite the enactment of legislation designed to reduce the availability of bail, there has been surprisingly little change in the absolute number of persons in custody awaiting trial in the period 1994 to 2008. Because this was at a time during which the overall number of prisoners increased by around two-thirds, the percentage of unconvicted or unsentenced prisoners within that population declined sharply from 26 % in 1994 to 16 % in 2008.[50] It is also worth noting that during

---

42 *Hucklesby* [1], pp. 258–270; *Raine / Willson*, pp. 256–270.
43 *Hucklesby* [4], p. 11.
44 *Ibid.*, loc. ult. cit.
45 *Ibid.*, p. 12.
46 *Cassidy et al.*
47 *Mair*, pp. 257–277.
48 *Nellis*, pp. 41–65 .
49 *Hucklesby* [5].
50 Player et al., p. 6; *Hucklesby et al.* [4], p. 5.

the same period, the number of women who were remanded in custody increased by 80 %[51] whereas the numbers of remanded young people aged between 11 – 17 declined by 25 % between 2002 and 2008.[52]

Some further evidence of the differing priorities of the pre-trial custody system other than the mere support of the trial process can be found in the fact that in 2007 (a typical year), only 52 % of the 75,000 defendants who had been remanded in custody were subsequently sentenced to custody. A further 15 % of remanded defendants were acquitted, while 29 % were convicted but not sentenced to custody.[53] Moreover, there is further evidence that changes in the percentages of individuals remanded in custody have not been occasioned by the priorities of the trial process but by completely extraneous factors. According to Hucklesby there has been a quiet (and sometimes not so quiet) revolution taking place in remand policy:

> "As a consequence of government concerns over prison overcrowding generally, pressure has been applied to remand decision-makers to make less use of custody. A policy of quiet persuasion has been used to cajole decision-makers into conforming. The specific mechanisms that have been used vary and include the introduction of Restriction on Bail and bail accommodation and support schemes. More direct pressure has been brought to bear through the use of memoranda and letters sent to courts asking decision-makers to think carefully before remanding defendants in custody."[54]

Moreover, there are no effective time limits in England and Wales on either the main proceedings[55] or the length of time a person can be held in custody. An attempt to introduce time limits was made under the Prosecution of Offences Act 1985, as amended, but these are easily circumvented.[56] Unlike England, Scotland has historically operated a 110 day rule within which serious cases must be brought to trial.[57]

However, in practice, the pre-trial procedure in England and Wales is relatively rapid and is becoming faster and more streamlined following the successful implementation of the recommendations of the Narey Committee.[58] Indeed, some of the explanation for the recent stabilisation in remand numbers may relate to the reduction in waiting times for trials. Such reductions have certainly made a very significant contribution to the fall in the average time spent

---

51 *Hucklesby et al.* [4], pp. 8 – 11.
52 *Ibid.*, p. 11.
53 *Ibid.*, p. 12.
54 *Ibid.*, p. 18.
55 *Jackson / Johnstone*, pp. 3 – 23 .
56 *Samuels*, pp. 260 – 268 .
57 Now under s. 65 of the Criminal Procedure (Scotland) Act 1995.
58 *Narey.*

on remand from 58 days in 2006 to 55 days in 2007.[59] The absence of effective time limits in English jurisprudence represents a significant defect in our trial process, one which has been concealed by the relative rapidity (in most cases) of the strongly adversarial pre-trial.

Once remanded a defendant may no longer be interviewed by the police or any other authority in connection with the case except in exceptional circumstances. However, the position of the defendant at trial is materially undermined by custody and the wearing of handcuffs and the presence of escort officers is very likely to prejudice a court in their disfavour. Remand in custody also has a strongly negative impact on the capacity of the defence to mount a successful defence in an adversarial setting. The difficulties of access to legal advisers, according to H.M. Inspector of Prisons, constitute "an obstacle to the fair and just treatment of unsentenced prisoners."[60] Since less than half of defendants who appear in court for their trial in custody actually receive a sentence of custody, it is highly likely that courts tend to view the period of time spent in prison on remand as "punishment enough" in many cases and tailor their decisions accordingly.

3. Procedures

3.1. Domestic Procedures

Individuals have the right (subject to the restrictions mentioned below) to ask for bail at any point in the proceedings. This is described as a "bail application" although clearly this is an inappropriate description in view of the presumption in favour of bail.[61]

The first opportunity to be released occurs in the police station. The police themselves, acting under s. 47.3 of the Police and Criminal Evidence Act 1984 (PACE) have the power to (a) release a suspect on bail during the course of an investigation, requiring him or her to attend at such police station at such time,[62] as the custody officer may appoint or (b) where the investigation has been completed, can order bail for a defendant to appear before a Magistrates' Court at such time and such place as he or she shall appoint. Since 1994 the police also

---

59 *Hucklesby et al.* [4], p. 16.
60 *H.M. Inspector of Prisons*, p. 52.
61 The right to bail exists independently of any application.
62 There is no maximum time limit despite a Recommendation from a Standing Committee of the House of Commons. See http://www.parliament.the-stationery-office.co.uk/pa/cm 200203/cmselect/cmhaff/83/8306.htm.

have been authorised to attach conditions to these two types of bail[63] under s. 27 of the Criminal Justice and Public Order Act 1994 and s. 37 of PACE respectively.[64] The priority in these bail decisions are necessarily investigation and control and mark another step away from the original purpose of bail. Cape and Edwards have argued that the police powers to impose bail conditions on uncharged individuals are not appropriately regulated and represent a clear breach of Article 5 of the ECHR.[65]

The Police can also remand a defendant in custody for a very brief period (usually overnight) to appear at the next available Magistrates' Court. Normally, defendants make their first appearance at the Magistrates' Court, which sits with three lay magistrates or one (professional) District Judge. This court can remand a defendant in custody or impose conditional or unconditional bail subject to the conditions set out below. A single lay magistrate, sitting alone can order bail or conditional bail but not custody. The question of bail, conditional bail or custody will initially be dealt with on first appearance at what is described (again inaccurately) as a "remand hearing." This is an adversarial procedure in open court at which the defendant is entitled to be represented. At the first hearing (the "duty lawyer hearing"), he or she will, in all probability be represented by a lawyer whose services are provided free. There will be a rota of local lawyers willing to undertake this work on the basis of government remuneration.

The Bail Act 1976 guaranteed the right of a remanded defendant to ask for bail each time he or she appeared in court (which was once every week until trial). This was considered to be wasteful of resources if exactly the same issues were being re-argued on each occasion. S. 154 of the Criminal Justice Act 1988 therefore codified the practice of restricting effective bail applications to two, unless new circumstances arose. As a result, defendants are entitled to an automatic remand hearing when they first appear in court at the initial "duty-lawyer hearing" and a subsequent, usually more detailed consideration, after a week, if they are not granted bail, with or without conditions, on the first occasion. Thereafter the defendant will not have to be produced in court for 28 days, albeit with a right of appeal against the decision to remand in custody. A fresh bail application may not be made after the first two have been unsuccessful, unless there is a material change of circumstances. Where appropriate, bail hearings can be conducted by a live video link to a prison or police station under Part 3 A of the Crime and Disorder Act 1998.[66]

The only information available to the decision-making court is that presented

---

63 With the exception of residing at a bail hostel.
64 As amended by s. 28 and schedule 2 of the Criminal Justice Act 2003.
65 Cape / Edwards, pp. 529 – 560.
66 As amended by s. 145 of the Police and Justice Act 2006.

by the prosecution and defence in the form of oral submissions rather than (usually) hard evidence given under oath. Objective Bail Information Schemes were introduced in the 1990s on the model of the Vera Institute in the US. The aim was to provide factual, verified information, in addition to that otherwise available to the Crown Prosecution Service (and the defence) to assist it to decide whether there are grounds for asking the court to release a defendant on bail rather than remand him or her in custody. Although these early court-based schemes were discontinued for lack of funding,[67] they have continued to operate successfully in prisons,[68] primarily in order to support the Bail Accommodation and Support Scheme (BASS) and the Effective Bail Schemes (EBS) set up in 2007. BASS was established in order to provide a network of privately funded bail hostels for low-level offenders to supplement the existing hostels which are now monopolised by higher level offenders.[69]

Bail information schemes address the specific concerns expressed in opposition to bail and also aim to draw attention to the defendant's character, antecedents, community ties which are relevant to the remand decision. Bail information is not, simply a case of providing details of suitable accommodation, but also looks for factors such as the defendant's reliability, employment record, family responsibilities and support services in the community.

Appeal against a decision by the Magistrates' Court on bail, conditional bail or custody is made, on motion to a Judge of the Crown Court, sitting alone. This judge can also rule on bail, conditional bail or custody in respect of defendants appearing in the Crown Court. Appeal against a decision by a Crown Court Judge lies to the Court of Appeal. There are further opportunities for appeal. Decisions of either of these courts may be reviewed for their legality by an appeal "by way of case stated" to the Divisional Court of the High Court or by Writ of *Habeas Corpus* in some circumstances.

The integrity of the trial process clearly remains central to the formal requirements under Schedule 1, Part 1, Paragraph 2 of the Bail Act 1976, since two of the three grounds for overturning the presumption in favour of bail concern this issue (failure to surrender and interfering with witnesses or obstructing the course of justice). The wording of paragraph 9 of the same Part of the Schedule also reinforces the centrality of the main proceedings to the decision on pre-trial precautionary measures as two of the four material considerations to be addressed by the court relate to this issue. The court is told specifically to consider "the nature and seriousness of the offence or default (and the probable method of

---

67 *Hucklesby* [4], pp. 13–14.
68 See *Prison Service Order* 6101, Bail Information Scheme. Issued 02.09.1999.
69 *National Probation Service* (2008), Accommodation and Support Scheme for Bail and HDC. Briefing No. 42 Home Office London at: www.probation.homeoffice.gov.uk/files/pdf/NPS%20Briefing%2042 %20.pdf.

dealing with the defendant for it)" as well as "the strength of the evidence of his having committed the offence or having defaulted." This approach is entirely consistent with the historical position, which is set out above, and the traditional justifications for the custody exception. The situation in practice is unfortunately likely to be very different. Since no hard evidence is likely to be forthcoming at the decision-making stage for pre-trial measures, this consideration can be a speculation at best.

As a result, preventive detention, completely unconnected with the main proceedings, has become increasingly a factor in bail and custody decisions in recent years, particularly during periods of unrest. Examples are numerous. During the inner city uprisings in 1981, the police flooded the courts in Liverpool, Manchester and London with large numbers of defendants arrested for minor public order offences, in the expectation that custodial remand and heavy bail conditions, including curfews would be imposed to discourage further rioting. It was apparent that for a short period at least, the presumption in favour of bail was completely reversed in these courts and the major, most severe penalty inflicted became the custodial remand or bail with heavy conditions, rather than the post-conviction sentence. Indeed, many cases were abandoned once the riots subsided.[70] Similar events took place during the Miners' Strike in 1984,[71] with climate protesters in 2009[72] and in other similar incidents of civil disorder. They demonstrate clearly that once pre-trial precautionary measures become de-coupled from the main proceedings, they will inevitably be determined by policing priorities and therefore the potential for abuse is considerable.

3.2.   International Procedures

Originally the Bail Act 1976 did not apply to international "fugitive offenders" but the situation was changed dramatically by the adoption of the Framework Decision on the European Arrest Warrant by the Crime (International Cooperation) Act 2003. S. 198 of the Extradition Act 2003 specifically applies the provisions of s. 4 of the Bail Act 1976 (as set out above) to extradition proceedings. This provision applied to unconvicted defendants only and convicted persons (or, after 1996, those "unlawfully at large after conviction")[73] were specifically excluded. Bail has been granted to a number of high profile in-

---

70   *Vogler* [2], pp. 143–144.
71   *Percy Smith / Hillyard*, pp. 345–354.
72   See *The Guardian*, 27.10.2009. Police use Bail Restrictions to Stifle Climate Protests'.
73   Police and Justice Act 2006, s. 42, and Schedule 13, para. 34.

dividuals for whom extradition is sought. These include the "Nat West Three" in 2004[74] and Julian Assange, the founder of "*Wikileaks*" in January 2011.[75]

4.   Recent reform and proposals of reform

The pressure to use the bail/custody system for policing rather than judicial purposes continues unabated. It was renewed in 2008 after Garry Weddell, a police officer on bail for the alleged murder of his wife, apparently killed his mother in law. In response, the Ministry of Justice released "snapshot" figures to show that out of 455 murder suspects, 60 had been released on bail whereas 35 out of 41 manslaughter suspects were on bail.[76] The Ministry of Justice commissioned a Report *Bail and Murder,* which in June 2008 set out a range of options to prevent defendants charged with murder being granted bail.[77] As a result, s. 115 of the Coroners and Justice Act 2009 prohibits Magistrates' Courts (but not other courts) from granting bail in murder cases. The Criminal Justice and Immigration Act 2008 also contains provisions[78] designed to ensure that custodial remands in minor cases are targeted where there is a risk of further offences involving injury or fear of it.

There has also been considerable academic interest in reform. Mandeep Dhami has called for the quantification of the otherwise nebulous concept of "substantial grounds" for believing that one of the three grounds for refusing bail exist.[79] Cape and Edwards have suggested a major revision of the rules on police bail to ensure their compliance with the ECHR[80] while more fundamentally, Hucklesby has criticised the "disjuncture between the bail law and its practical operation".[81] Player et al. have argued that the major failing of the system is the lack of transparency in relation to cases where the defendant is remanded in custody but does not receive a prison sentence and they suggest that this "requires careful scrutiny and the development of principled guidelines."[82]

It has been argued here that pre-trial security measures are an important derogation from the international obligations of the state to respect the right to

---

74 *BBC News*, 28.12.2004, http://news.bbc.co.uk/1/hi/business/3695958.stm.
75 *BBC News*, 16.12.2010, http://www.bbc.co.uk/news/uk-12005930.
76 *The Guardian*, 25.2.2008.
77 http://www.justice.gov.uk/consultations/cp1108.htm.
78 S. 52 and Schedule 12.
79 *Dhami*, loc. cit.
80 *Cape/Edwards*, loc. cit.
81 *Hucklesby* [4], p. 19.
82 *Player et al.*, p. 16.

liberty of unconvicted or unsentenced individuals, expressed in almost every charter of human rights from *Magna Charta* to the ECHR and ICCPR. The justification for this derogation has historically been the preservation of the integrity of the main court proceedings but increasingly refusal of bail or the imposition of bail conditions has been authorised for the purposes of preventative detention, wholly unconnected or only tangentially connected with the main proceedings. Some authors have linked these developments, particularly the widespread use of electronic surveillance of a target population, with Foucault's disciplinary panopticism,[83] although Crawford's concept of "contractual governance" of deviancy, supplanting the penal sanction, is perhaps more apposite.[84] These evolutions of policy should be viewed with concern not only because they represent a dangerous undermining, which has hitherto passed largely unchallenged, of the role of human rights precepts in criminal justice but also because they present a standing opportunity for serious abuse of procedure for political purposes.

Bibliography

Bottomley, Allan Keith, Imprisonment Before Trial. Occasional Paper in Social Administration, No. 39, Bell & Son (1970).

Cape, Ed / Edwards, Richard A., Police Bail without Charge: The Human Rights Implications, in: The Cambridge Law Journal (2010), pp. 529 ff.

Cassidy, Davnet et al., Understanding Electronic Monitoring of Juveniles on Bail or Remand to Local Authority Accommodation, Home Office (2005).

Cavadino, Paul / Gibson, Bryan, Bail. The Law, Best Practice and the Debate, Waterside Press (1993).

Corre, Neil / Wolchover, David, Bail in Criminal Proceedings, Oxford University Press (2004).

Crawford, Adam, "Contractual Governance" of Deviant Behaviour, in: Journal of Law and Society (2003), pp. 479 ff.

Dhami, Mandeep K., Lay Magistrates' Interpretations of "Substantial Grounds" for Denying Bail, in: The Howard Journal of Criminal Justice (2010), pp. 349 ff.

Goldfarb, Ronald L., Ransom: A Critique of the American Bail System, Harper & Row (1965).

Graham-Harrison, Francis Laurence Theodore, Bail Procedures in Magistrates' Courts. Report of a Working Party, HMSO (1974).

H.M. Inspector of prisons, Unjust Deserts A Thematic Review by HM Chief Inspector of Prisons of the Treatment and Conditions for Unsentenced Prisoners in England and Wales, Home Office (2000).

---

83 See discussion in *Nellis*, pp. 57 – 60.
84 *Crawford*, pp. 479 – 505.

Hucklesby, Anthea, [1] The Use and Abuse of Conditional Bail, in: Howard Journal of Criminal Justice (1994), pp. 258 ff.; [2] Bail or Jail? The Practical Operation of the Bail Act 1976, in: Journal of Law and Society (1996), pp. 213 ff.; [3] Police Bail and the Use of Conditions, in: Criminology and Criminal Justice (2001), pp. 441 ff.; [4] Keeping the Lid on the Prison Remand Population: The Experience in England and Wales, in: Current Issues in Criminal Justice (2009), pp. 3 ff.

Hucklesby, Anthea et al., The Evaluation of the Restriction on Bail Pilots: Final Report. Home Office Online Report 06. Vol. 7, Home Office (2007).

Jackson, John / Johnstone, Jenny, The Reasonable Time Requirement: an Independent and Meaningful Right, in: Criminal Law Review (2005), pp. 3 ff.

Langbein, John H., Torture and the law of Proof: Europe and England in the Ancien Régime, University of Chicago Press (1977).

Law Commission, [1] Bail and the Human Rights Act 1998: Item 10 of the Seventh Programme of Law Reform, Law Commission 2001; [2] Bail and the Human Rights Act 1998: Item 10 of the Seventh Programme of Law Reform: Criminal Law, Law Commission.

Mair, George, Electronic Monitoring in England and Wales, in: Criminal Justice (2005), pp. 257 ff.

Metzmeier, Karl X., Preventive Detention: A Comparison of Bail Refusal Practices in the United States, England, Canada and Other Common Law Nations, in: Pace International Law Review (1996), pp. 399 ff.

Narey, Martin, Review of Delay in the Criminal Justice System, Home Office (1997).

Nellis, Mike, Surveillance and Confinement: Explaining and Understanding The Experience of Electronically Monitored Curfews, in: European Journal of Probation (2009), pp. 41 ff.

Percy-Smith, Janie / Hillyard, Paddy, Miners in the Arms of the Law: A Statistical Analysis, in: Journal of Law and Society (1985), pp. 345 ff.

Phillips, Coretta et al., Entry into the Criminal Justice System: A Survey of Police Arrests and their Outcomes, Home Office (1998).

Player, Elaine et al., Remanded in Custody: An Analysis of Recent Trends in England and Wales, in: The Howard Journal of Criminal Justice (2010), pp. 1 ff.

Raine, John W. / Willson, Michael J., The Imposition of Conditions in Bail Decisions: From Summary Punishment to Better Behaviour on Remand, in: Howard Journal of Criminal Justice (1996), pp. 256 ff.

Samuels, Alec, Custody Time Limits, in: Criminal Law Review (1997), pp. 260–268.

Shoenberger, Allen E., The Not So Great Writ: The European Court of Human Rights Finds Habeas Corpus an Inadequate Remedy: Should American Courts Re-examine the Writ, in: Catholic University Law Review (2006), pp. 47 ff.

Stephen, Sir James Fitzjames, A History of the Criminal Law of England (3 Vols.), Macmillan (1883).

Vogler, Richard K., [1] The Changing Nature of Bail, in: Legal Action Group Bulletin (1982), pp. 11 ff.; [2] Reading the Riot Act. The Police, Army and Magistracy in Civil Disorder, Open University Press (1991); [3] A World View of Criminal Justice, Ashgate (2005).

Wiseman, Samuel, Discrimination, Coercion, and the Bail Reform Act of 1984: The Loss of the Core Constitutional Protections of the Excessive Bail Clause, in: Fordham Urban Law Journal (2009), pp. 121 ff.

Arndt Sinn

Germany

Table of Contents

Table of Abbreviations

AuslG	*Ausländergesetz* (Aliens Act)
BGBl.	*Bundesgesetzblatt* (Federal Law Gazette)
BGHR	*BGH-Rechtsprechung* (Federal High Court Case-law)
BVerfG	*Bundesverfassungsgericht* (Federal Constitutional Court)
BVerfGE	*Entscheidungen des Bundesverfassungsgerichts*
ECHR	European Convention on Human Rights
EGStPO	*Einführungsgesetz zur Strafprozessordnung* (Introductory Act to the Code of Criminal Procedure)
GG	*Grundgesetz* (Constitution)
GVG	*Gerichtsverfassungsgesetz* (Courts Constitution Act)
IRG	*Internationale-Rechtshilfe-Gesetz* (International Mutual Assistance Act)
JGG	*Jugendgerichtsgesetz* (Youth Courts Law)
LG	*Landesgericht* (Regional Court)
NJW	*Neue Juristische Wochenschrift*
NStZ	*Neue Zeitschrift für Strafrecht*
OLG	*Oberlandesgericht* (Higher Regional Court)
StA	*Staatsanwaltschaft* (Public Prosecutor's Office)
StPO	*Strafprozessordnung* (Code of Criminal Procedure)
StV	*Strafverteidiger*
UDHR	Universal Declaration of Human Rights

1.   The right to liberty

1.1.   Introduction

A criminal prosecution is the most intrusive measure that the state can take against individuals. Even if it ends in acquittal, albeit for lack of sufficient evidence to convict, the prosecution itself has factually irreversible consequences. In order to minimize the impact on defendants of prosecutions even before their conclusion, the state must provide guarantees in its legal system to protect the freedoms of the defendant in reasonable proportion to the charges against him and the prosecuting power over which the state holds a monopoly. These guarantees serve as evidence of the rule of law. In particular, since pre-trial detention serves not as a punishment but as a means of securing the integrity of the trial, the tension between the right to liberty and the state's prosecutorial interest is particularly palpable.

1.1.1. The goal of a criminal investigation

Criminal investigations serve to determine and carry out the state's duty to punish wrongdoing, to guarantee due process under the rule of law, and to reinforce the peace of a law-abiding society. The German penal system approaches these aims through the so-called inquisitorial model: investigations are focused around the search for the truth, not on a solution acceptable to the involved parties, as is the case for the adversarial model.

1.1.2. Stages of German criminal procedure

The German law of criminal procedure distinguishes between five stages: investigation, pre-trial litigation, the trial itself, appeals, and sentencing.

Criminal procedure begins with the investigative stage. This stage serves to assess whether there is adequate suspicion that a particular suspect has committed a punishable act.[1] Investigations are led by the StA, the state prosecution service, working in conjunction with the police. Investigations end either through termination[2] or with an indictment.[3]

Issuance of an indictment opens the pre-trial litigation stage.[4] At this stage, the court with jurisdiction over the indictment must decide whether the case should proceed to trial. Courts will forward cases to trial where they have determined that sufficient suspicion exists that the accused has committed the acts described in the indictment.

The pre-trial stage is accordingly quite short, though its filter function is not always fully realized. The goal is that the accusations of the indicting authority be independently examined and the defendant afforded a further opportunity to defend himself.

Should the court decide to send the case for trial, the trial phase begins. The trial phase decides the facts necessary to determine guilt and pass sentence.

1.1.3. Constitutional guarantees of freedom of the person

The right to freedom is guaranteed by the Constitution. The protections of Article 104 GG correspond broadly to the protections captured by the term *habeas corpus*. Custody, representing as it does a serious restriction of a person's liberty, is in all the more acute need of justification at the pre-trial stage. Article 104.1 limits restrictions on liberty of the person, permitting them "only pur-

---

1 §§ 151 ff. StPO.
2 See §§ 170.2 and 153 ff. StPO.
3 § 170.1 StPO.
4 §§ 199 ff. StPO.

suant to a formal law and only in compliance with the procedures prescribed therein." Article 104.2 states that "Only a judge may rule upon the permissibility or continuation of any deprivation of liberty. If such a deprivation is not based on a judicial order, a judicial decision shall be obtained without delay. The police may hold no one in custody on their own authority beyond the end of the day following the arrest. Details shall be regulated by a law." Article 104.3 specifies time limits and confers a right to be heard. Personal liberty is also addressed in Articles 2.1 and 11 GG.

The German code of criminal procedure, the StPO, satisfies the constitutional requirement of "formal law." § 125 StPO requires a judicial order for the issue of an arrest warrant, and § 115a StPO calls for review by the judge of the nearest local court. The procedure is laid out in §§ 114 – 130 StPO.[5]

1.2.   History of the right to liberty

German constitutional history was strongly influenced by the American Declaration of Independence, the American constitution of 1787 and the French declaration of 1789. Constitutions in the south of Germany began to include a right to *habeas corpus* review starting from the beginning of the nineteenth century. The draft Imperial Constitution of 1849 called for imprisonment only in the cases of justified judicial order (§ 138.2 – 3), but the provision was absent from the final constitution of 1871.

The Weimar Constitution recognized freedom of the person as a fundamental right (Art. 114), though it stopped short of explicitly requiring a judicial basis for detention. An "emergency declaration" in 1933 suspended the enforcement of Article 114, laying the groundwork for arbitrary detentions under the National Socialist regime. The lawful basis for detention and the guarantee of personal freedom was the subject of much lively discussion during the Parliamentary Assembly following the fall of the National Socialists. Today's constitutional protection comes from Article 104 GG, and consists of a substantive fundamental right coupled with a procedural guarantee of the review of any restrictions on it.[6]

---

5 For more details, see below.
6 Cf. on the historical development *Rüping*, points 1 – 11.

1.3.   Current situation

Each year, the Federal Statistical Office publishes data[7] on the number of inmates and detainees in Germany. As of 30 November 2008, there were 11,577 people in pre-trial detention, whereas on the same day in 2003 the number was 16,785. From 2001 to 2008, the number of pre-trial detainees has continually fallen.

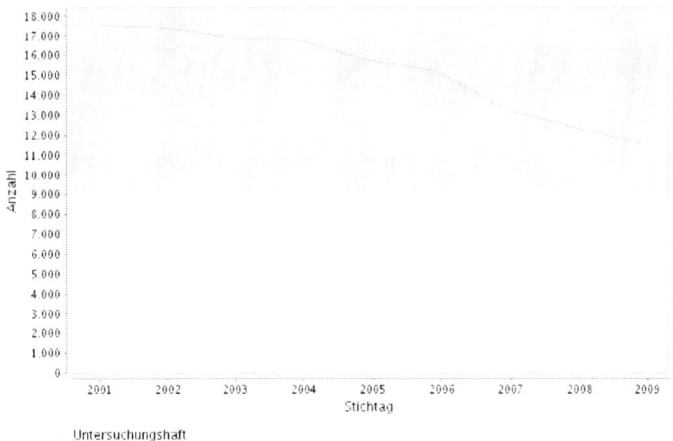

Source: Statistisches Bundesamt, Wiesbaden 2010

The number of individuals in detention at any one time, however, is not representative of the total number of people held in pre-trial detention. In 2009, pre-trial detention was ordered in respect of 28,309 suspects. Almost half were accused of financial crimes. 6,609 were drugs cases, and a further 5,260 were cases of crimes against the person. Flight risk dominates the reasons given for ordering detention (25,779 cases), followed closely by the risk that the defendant could destroy evidence (1,908 cases). Detention was ordered in 452 cases because of the severity of the accusations. The danger of repeat offence led to detention in 380 cases of alleged sex crimes and in 1,553 cases of other alleged serious offences.[8]

In a majority of cases (8,151), detention lasted up to a month. 4,918 cases of detention lasted between six months and one year, and in 1,428 cases, pre-trial

---

7 Cf. https://www-genesis.destatis.de/genesis/online;jsessionid=9F0DF2E1BAAA02475C3729 E03F477DC4.tomcat_GO_1_1?operation=abruftabelleBearbeiten&levelindex=2&levelid= 1292664979440&auswahloperation=abruftabelleAuspraegungAuswaehlen&auswahlverzeich nis=ordnungsstruktur&auswahlziel=werteabruf&selectionname=24321-0002&auswahltext =&werteabruf=starten (18.12.2010).
8 Cf. Statistisches Bundesamt, Fachserie 10, Reihe 3, 2009, p. 364.

detention lasted more than one year. There were 2,010 cases in which pre-trial detention lasted longer than the eventual custodial sentence.[9]

2.   Limitations to the right to liberty

German law permits the restriction of liberty through pre-trial detention,[10] psychiatric detention orders,[11] temporary arrest[12] and trial detention.[13] An order for detention in a psychiatric or rehabilitation facility is a temporary measure for the protection both of the subject of the order and of the general public.[14] Temporary arrest does not require the order of a court, and is therefore subject to the strictest statutory standards. Trial detention, which may only last a week and has not yet proven popular in practice, supplements the rules on accelerated court procedures;[15] it does not require the giving of reasons.

Pre-trial detention is one of several types of detention and arrest. The so-called "disobedience detention" (*Ungehorsamshaft*) serves to ensure the attendance of the defendant at trial.[16] In furtherance of order during the sittings of the court, detention orders can be issued against the defendant, witnesses, experts, or observers.[17] If a suspended sentence is to be put into effect, the court can order the subject of the sentence to be secured in detention.[18] Interference with the administration of justice[19] or the commission of an offense in a sitting of a court[20] can lead to immediate temporary detention. The StPO further prescribes, in part 9a, additional measures for the facilitation of prosecution and the carrying out of sentences,[21] such as surveillance, bail, and service of court papers by proxy if the requirements for an arrest warrant are not met.

---

9 *Ibid.*, p. 365.
10 §§ 112 ff. StPO.
11 § 126a StPO.
12 § 127 StPO.
13 § 127b StPO.
14 *Lemke* [1], point 1.
15 §§ 417 ff. StPO.
16 See §§ 230.2; 236, 329.4(1); 412.1 StPO.
17 See §§ 177.1; 178.1(1) GVG.
18 § 453c StPO.
19 § 164 StPO.
20 § 183.2 GVG.
21 See §§ 131 and 132 StPO.

2.1. Conditional release and supervision measures alternative to custody

The opportunity to set aside an arrest warrant is a particular instance of the principle of proportionality. Where the defendant presents a flight risk, an arrest warrant can be set aside when other, less severe measures will adequately address the risk of flight. These include:

a) an obligation to register with the police;[22]
b) restrictions on residence;[23]
c) prohibitions on leaving one's residence without supervision;[24]
d) the posting of bail.[25]

If the court considers the defendant likely to destroy evidence or have evidence destroyed, it can additionally order that the defendant have no contact with specific persons[26] and can order additional conditions if it considers repeat offense likely.[27]

The contents of these judicially-set conditions can significantly limit the exercise of fundamental rights, especially general freedom of movement,[28] mobility,[29] free exercise of profession,[30] freedom of expression and assembly,[31] and the right to property.[32]

2.2. Custody

2.2.1. Pre-trial detention and the presumption of innocence

Pre-trial detention is not in anticipation of custodial sentence. It is strictly a measure ordered to assure the attendance of the defendant at trial or to facilitate investigative measures. The presumption of innocence applies even to people in pre-trial detention. The constitutional justification for the presumption of innocence is the rule of law,[33] as well as Articles 11.1 UDHR and 6.2 ECHR. It is also mentioned explicitly in several individual statutes of the federal states.

---

22 § 116.1(2)(1) StPO.
23 § 116.1(2) StPO.
24 § 116.1(3) StPO.
25 §§ 116.1(4) and 116a StPO.
26 § 116.2 StPO.
27 § 116.1 (2)(1) StPO.
28 Art. 11.2 GG.
29 Art. 11.1 GG.
30 Art. 12 GG.
31 Arts. 5.1 and 8.1 GG.
32 Art. 14.1 GG.
33 Art. 20 GG.

If there is no justification for pre-trial detention, the defendant enjoys the right to await the outcome of the criminal process as a free man.[34] Respecting the presumption of innocence is an element of a fair trial,[35] and measures equivalent[36] to those of a custodial sentence are prohibited even during the course of pre-trial detention. The law nonetheless permits restrictions necessary for the maintenance of order within a particular detention facility.

The presumption of innocence does not prevent a prosecuting authority from making a pre-conviction assessment of the degree of suspicion a defendant is under;[37] such evidence-based assessments are an integral[38] part of any criminal procedure which respects the rule of law. It is therefore not a violation of the accused's fundamental rights, either under Article 104 GG or the ECHR, to make a determination of suspicion for the purpose of pre-trial decisions in the criminal process.[39]

2.2.2. Pre-trial detention's place in the criminal process

Ordering pre-trial detention is possible at every stage of the criminal process. As the locus of responsibility changes from stage to stage, so does the primary responsibility for applying for a detention order. At the investigation stage, detention grounds are raised and amended by the StA,[40] with applications reviewed and warrants issued by a district judge. After the indictment has been issued, pre-trial detention can only be ordered by the court responsible for the indictment. These courts can order detention of their own initiative, but must consult the prosecutor's office beforehand. During the appellate stage, the court of original jurisdiction retains responsibility for ordering or ending detention. When a case is remanded to a lower court, that court takes responsibility for the detention as well. If the appeal is subject to *de novo* review, the appellate court takes over jurisdiction when the case reaches it. The prosecutor's office may,

---

34 Cf. BVerfG, Decision of 15.8.2007 – 2BvR 1485/07, in: StV (2008), p. 25; OLG Oldenburg, Decision of 28.11.2007 – 1 Ws 639/07, in: StV (2008), p. 84.
35 *Lemke* [1], point 12.
36 BVerfG, Decision of 16.5.1973 – 2BvR 590/71, in: BVerfGE 35, p. 320.
37 Cf. BVerfG, Decision of 26.3.1987 – 2 BvR 589/79, 740/81, 284/85, in: BVerfGE 74, pp. 358 ff. (372) (= NJW 1987, p. 2427); BVerfG, Decision of 23.4.1994 – 1 BvR 1170/90, 1174/90, 1175/90, in: BVerfGE 84, pp. 106 ff.
38 Cf. for example BVerfG, Decision of 15.12.1965 – 1 BvR 513/65, in: BVerfGE 19, pp. 342 ff. (347 f.) (= NJW 1966, p. 243 – on detention); BVerfG, Decision of 23.4.1994 – 1 BvR 1170/90, 1174/90, 1175/90, in: BVerfGE 84, pp. 106 ff.
39 BVerfG, Decision of 23.4.1994 – 1 BvR 1170/90, 1174/90, 1175/90, in: BVerfGE 84, pp. 106 ff.
40 § 125.1 StPO.

however, issue such warrants as are necessary to execute a sentence legally in force.[41]

With this division of responsibility, the consistent principle is that the decision on detention rests with the body with which the decision regarding guilt or innocence also rests. This is on the one hand procedurally economical—the court in the best position to decide on detention is certainly the one already familiar with the substantive case, and can make decisions with the benefit of its prior knowledge quickly without having to brief other judges or courts on the case. On the other hand, it must not be overlooked that courts will decide on detention without approaching the facts freshly, and that the confirmation of suspicion inherent in a detention order might represent the beginnings of an opinion being formed about the ultimate factual questions and thus be indicative of bias.

2.2.3. Substantive requirements for a detention order

Detention orders rest on two substantive requirements: urgent suspicion and grounds for detention. Furthermore, pre-trial detention must not be disproportionate to the case itself and to the maximum allowable sentence for the crime alleged.

2.2.3.1. Urgent suspicion

§ 112 StPO pins the issuance of a detention order to a specific degree of suspicion: urgent suspicion (*dringender Tatverdacht*). Suspicion is considered urgent when the present state of the investigation indicates a high probability that the defendant was the perpetrator or a conspirator in a punishable offense. Considerations of defences, justifications, and reduced culpability already have a role to play here, but not for curable procedural defects.[42] The analysis is thus one of prognosis, and the conclusion the judge must arrive at is "merely" that the totality of the investigation has concluded that there is a "high probability" that the defendant is guilty. It is not a statement of the likelihood of conviction;[43] suspicion can ebb and flow as the process drags on. Suspicion must be founded on facts; presumptions are not sufficient. The silence of the accused may not be used against him.[44]

---

41 § 457 StPO.
42 OLG Dresden, Decision of 26.7.2001 – 3 AK 0056/01, in: StV 2001, pp. 519 ff.
43 Decision of 6.4.1979 – 1 BJs 205/78/StB 16/79.
44 *Lemke* [2], point 7.

2.2.3.2. Grounds for detention

There are four grounds for detention:
a) flight or risk of absconding;[45]
b) the risk that the defendant may destroy evidence or have it destroyed;[46]
c) that the offense is classified by statute as particularly severe;[47]
d) risk of repeat offense.[48]

These too must have their bases in fact, and the examination may include the history of the accused, his economic and personal situation, as well as his milieu and interpersonal relationships.

"Flight" is defined as departure from a previous (geographic) focal point for the purpose of being unreachable by the prosecuting authorities. According to a decision of the Court of Appeal in Stuttgart,[49] this is not available as a ground for detention where the presence of the defendant is not required, as at the appellate stage.[50]

Risk of absconding may be presumed when particular facts in the circumstances of the given case give rise to the danger that the accused may attempt to escape the criminal process. But this threshold is not met, for example, simply because the defendant has his legal residence abroad.[51]

There may also be grounds for detention if the accused seeks to remove himself other than physically[52] from the criminal process, for example through drug use or refusing to take critical medications. Whether the risk of suicide constitutes grounds for detention is a matter of conflicting[53] authorities.[54]

The risk of destruction of evidence (Verdunkelungsgefahr) consists of facts which point to an urgent suspicion that the defendant or someone acting on his instructions may destroy, hide, change, or forge evidence, or may attempt to exert untoward influence over witnesses or experts, and thus make the investigation more onerous.

---

45 § 112.2(1) StPO.
46 § 112.2(3) StPO.
47 § 112.3 StPO.
48 § 112a StPO.
49 OLG Stuttgart, Decision of 24.7.1981 – 3 Ws 208/81, in: NStZ 1982, pp. 217 ff.
50 § 329 StPO.
51 OLG Dresden, Decision of 24.2.2005 – 1 Ws 29/05, in: StV 2005, pp. 224 ff.
52 OLG Oldenburg, Decision of 11.5.1989 – 1 Ws 78/89, in: StV 1990, pp. 165 ff.
53 OLG Oldenburg, Decision of 5.8.1961 – 1 Ws 274/61, in: NJW 1961, pp. 1984 ff.
54 OLG Hamburg, Decision of 27.8.1993 – 2 Ws 429/93, in: StV 1994, pp. 142 ff.

2.2.3.3. Detention for certain serious crimes

The wording of § 112.3 StPO permits a detention order for certain named offenses (crimes against humanity, homicide, terrorism) even in the absence of other grounds for detention. This rule is widely seen as systematically contradictory, permitting as it does detention even when there are no risks to the integrity of the criminal process. The Constitutional Court has thus required that, for these types of detention orders, the possibility of flight or destruction of evidence must at least not be excludable.[55] This is nevertheless a considerably lower threshold than in § 112.2 StPO. Here, it suffices that the concrete circumstances of the case do not exclude the risk of flight or evidence tampering, or if there is credible suspicion that the accused is likely to offend again.[56] It is necessary and sufficient that a relatively mild or remote danger of this sort can be attested.[57] If the circumstances of the case point conclusively away from a risk of flight, evidence tampering, or repeat offense, detention per § 112.3 is not permissible.[58] It was for these reasons that the Third Criminal Senate of the Federal Supreme Court lifted the detention order against suspected RAF member Verena Becker in December 2009: she did not pose a flight risk.[59]

For minor offenses – those not subject to imprisonment for more than six months or to a fine of more than 180 days' wages – evidence tampering does not constitute a ground for detention. In these cases, flight risk is furthermore only available under very limited conditions as a ground.[60]

2.2.3.4. Detention and the risk of repeat offending

For specific offenses such as sexual offenses, the risk of repeat offense may within certain strict parameters itself serve as a ground for detention. Detention in these cases is not for securing the integrity of the criminal process but instead for the protection of the general public: a preventative measure, and thus often referred to as "preventative detention" (*Sicherungshaft*). Because of the overwhelming interest in the protection of the general public, the Constitutional Court has declared this practice permissible.[61] The risk of repeat offense is also allowed as a justification for detention in the ECHR (Art. 5.1(c)), but several

---

55 BVerfG, Decision of 15.12.1965 – 1 BvR 513/65, in: BVerfGE 19, pp. 342 ff.
56 LG Kiel, Decision of 2.7.2001 – VIII Ks 7/01, in: StV 2001, pp. 687 ff.
57 BGHR StPO, § 112(3) Fluchtgefahr 1; *Meyer-Goßner*, point 38.
58 OLG Frankfurt, Decision of 18.01.2000 – Ws 3/00, in: StV 2000, pp. 374 f.; OLG Düsseldorf, Decision of 09.08.1982 – Ws 617/82, in: StV 1982, pp. 585 ff.; OLG Köln; Decision of 05.09.1994 – 2 Ws 399/94, in: StV 1994, pp: 584 ff. See also *Graf*, point 42.
59 Decision of 23 December 2009 – StB 51/09.
60 § 113 StPO.
61 BVerfG, Decision of 15.12.1965 – 1 BvR 513/65, in: BVerfGE 19, pp. 342 ff. (349); Decision of 30.05.1973 – 2 BvL 4/73, in: BVerfGE 35, pp. 185 ff. (188).

commentators have argued that this may violate the presumption of innocence in Article 6.2 ECHR.[62]

2.2.3.5. Proportionality

The constitutional guarantee of proportionality dominates the entire criminal process. § 112.2 StPO mentions it explicitly, and a detention order cannot be made in cases where it is out of proportion to the significance of the case and the expected punishment. Judges are not, however, bound to make a positive finding of proportionality; instead, disproportionality functions as a factor excluding detention. The significance of this is that detention is only barred when disproportionality can be determined by the court. Doubt about the proportionality of detention is not sufficient to prevent it. The role that proportionality has to play for minor offenses is explicitly set out in § 113 StPO.[63]

2.2.4. Detention of minors

Detention orders may be made against minors, but the rules on arrest warrants in respect of young people are subject to a subsidiarity requirement in § 72 JGG: detention is thus only available where its goal cannot be achieved through instructions from a family court or other less-intrusive measures. For minors under 16, the "flight risk" ground for detention is subject to further qualifications.

3.   Procedures

3.1.   Domestic

3.1.1. Measures to secure the integrity of the criminal process

Apart from a few narrow exceptions, the defendant is expected to be personally present for the duration of the trial. The court is entitled to a direct impression of the defendant personally, in his appearance, and of his explanations.[64] The attendance requirement is considered part of the inquisitorial search for the truth, and this search requires that the court be able to count on the presence of the accused. Detention is ordered in furtherance of this goal.

---

62 *Paeffgen*, point 5; *Deckers*, point 6; *Wolter*, pp. 485 f.
63 In evidence-tampering cases this is not permissible; in others only under very strict conditions as laid out above.
64 *Beulke*, point 382.

3.1.2. Execution of the arrest warrant

An arrest warrant is executed by detaining the person named in it, and the arrested person is to be brought before the responsible judge immediately.[65] In this sense, "brought before" does not require that the prisoner be brought into the personal presence of the judge, but rather that he is secured in a location over which the judge has direct custodial control. This is usually a detention facility, information on the defendant's delivery into which is then relayed to the judge and the prosecutor's office. "Immediately" means within a day, and within a day of being "brought before" the judge, the judge must question the accused. If this is impossible, the defendant must be brought before the nearest district court.[66]

3.1.3. Challenging an arrest warrant

A detainee may issue Detention Complaint proceedings[67] or apply for judicial review of his detention,[68] in both cases with a view to the lifting of the arrest warrant. The complaint procedure permits the court either to address the complaint or pass it to a review court (*Beschwerdegericht*); further appeal may in turn be lodged against the decision of this review court. As long as the accused is in detention, he may apply for judicial review of his detention and for the setting aside either of the warrant itself or of its execution pursuant to § 116 StPO.[69] Both procedures cannot be initiated simultaneously, but appeal can be lodged against the result of the judicial review.[70]

The reform of the law on pre-trial detention in 2010 introduced the requirement that an accused have access to counsel even at the pre-trial stage.[71] This replaces a requirement in § 117.5 that the court review detention of its own initiative every three months in case the defendant was not represented by counsel.

§ 117.3 StPO permits the judge to order individual investigations that may produce relevant information for the initiation or continuation of detention, and to review the detention anew in light of the result of these investigations.

As long as no verdict has been reached that permits the imposition of a custodial sentence, detention may not exceed six months. Exceptions to this arise only when the particular severity of the offense in the indictment or the

---

65 § 115 StPO.
66 § 115a StPO.
67 See §§ 304 ff. StPO.
68 § 117.1 StPO.
69 Cf. §§ 126 and 117.1 StPO.
70 § 117.2 StPO.
71 § 140.1(4) StPO.

particular scope of the investigation or some further important factor justify the continuation of the detention.[72] Detention for longer than six months requires the approval of the circuit Court of Appeal (*Oberlandesgericht*), which must then review the case every three months.

Detention based on the danger of repeat offence[73] cannot be sustained for longer than a year.[74] After the maximum allowable time, the court must lift the detention order.

3.1.4. Lifting the detention order

The court and the prosecutor's office are obliged to continually review the conditions for the detention order and to lift it should these no longer be fulfilled. Additionally, review of detention is explicitly required at the start of the trial phase and when a verdict is reached.[75] Statute also prescribes a number of factors which result in the lifting of the order: acquittal, rejection of the indictment for trial, and other than temporary suspension of proceedings.[76]

3.2. International

Detention can be ordered in extradition proceedings if necessary to secure the extradition,[77] transit[78] or repatriation[79] to a foreign country. Pre-deportation detention also bears mentioning,[80] though it is not permissible as an additional justification for detention in a criminal process.[81] The European Arrest Warrant is valid in Germany, even for the extradition of German citizens.

---

72 § 121.1 StPO.
73 § 112a StPO.
74 § 122a StPO.
75 See §§ 207.4 and 268b StPO.
76 See §§ 120.1, 120.3, 122a StPO.
77 § 15 IRG.
78 § 45 IRG.
79 § 68 IRG.
80 § 57.2(1) AuslG.
81 Cf. OLG Frankfurt, Decision of 18.01.2000 – Ws 3/00, in: StV 2000, p. 377.

4.   The current direction of reform

The latest reform[82] of the law on detention came in the form of a revision of the rules on the carrying out of the detention itself. Before 2010, few regulations governed pre-trial detention despite the legislative competence of the federal government. The StPO mentioned certain specific areas, but the majority was handled by secondary legislation consisting mainly of practice directions aimed at prison officials but which had nonetheless come to dominate in practice. As part of the constitutional reform of federalism, § 119 StPO was repealed in favour of a new version[83] of Article 74.1(1) GG, assigning regulatory competence for detention to the federal states.

In the absence of any state legislation at the time of the reform, however, the federal legislature introduced transitional regulations. Article 13 EGStPO directs that the provisions of § 119 StPO relating to pre-trial detention remain in force pending the passage of state legislation. Limitations for the purpose of maintaining order in detention facilities are therefore permitted under the current legal structure. The new law permits only such restrictions as are necessary to prevent flight, evidence tampering, or repeat offending, but the transitional measures are in force until at least 31st December 2011.

5.   Concluding remarks

Germany's system of measures to secure the integrity of trials, of which detention is one, is highly developed. But it is not without theoretical weaknesses, particularly with regard to the presumption of innocence and the impartiality of the trial court. It must also not be overlooked that securing the integrity of the criminal process is often teleologically confused with crime prevention in general; and that in practice, the statutory restrictions on pre-trial detention are not always respected. It is commonplace that the time limits set out in § 115 StPO are stretched to their maximum for tactical reasons. Nor can the possibility be ignored of preventive detention being used as leverage to compel a confession.[84] Resisting these impulses is the job of the courts, which must through evidence arrive at a suitable balance.

---

82 BGBl. I 2274 of 1.1.2010.
83 Constitutional Amendment Act of 28.8.2006 (BGBl I p. 2034).
84 *Schünemann*, p. 107, even speaks of a "notoriously misused pressure-instrument." See also *Gieg*, p. 477.

Bibliography

Beulke, Werner, Strafprozessrecht, 10th ed., C.F. Müller (2008).

Deckers, Rüdiger, § 112a StPO, in: Wassermann, Rudolf (ed.), Reihe Alternativkommentare, Kommentar zur Strafprozessordnung, vol. 2 / 1, Leuchterhand Verlag (1996).

Gieg, Georg, Letzter Anlauf für eine gesetzliche Regelung von Verständigungen im Strafverfahren?, in: Goltdammer's Archiv für Strafrecht (2007), pp. 469 ff.

Graf, Jürgen-Peter, § 112 StPO, in: Hannich, Rolf (ed.), Karlsruher Kommentar zur Strafprozessordnung, 6th ed., Beck (2008).

Lemke, Michael et al. (eds.), [1] At §§ 112 ff. StPO; [2] § 112 StPO, Heidelberger Kommentar zur Strafprozessordnung, 3rd ed., C.F. Müller (2001).

Meyer-Goßner, Lutz et al. (eds.), Strafprozessordnung, § 112 StPO, 53rd ed., Beck (2010).

Paeffgen, Hans-Ullrich, § 112a StPO, in: Rudolphi, Hans-Joachim et al. (eds.), Systematischer Kommentar zur Strafprozessordnung und zum Gerichtsverfassungsgesetz, vol. II, Carl Heymanns Verlag (2007).

Rüping, Hinrich, Art. 104 GG, in: Dolzer, Rudolf et al. (eds.), Bonner Kommentar zum Grundgesetz (Zweitbearbeitung), 135th upd., Vahlen (2008).

Schünemann, Bernd, Ein deutsches Requiem auf den Strafprozess des liberalen Rechtsstaats, in: Zeitschrift für Rechtspolitik (2009), pp. 104 ff.

Wolter, Jürgen, Untersuchungshaft, Vorbeugehaft und vorläufige Sanktionen, in: Zeitschrift für die gesamte Strafrechtswissenschaft, vol. 93 (1981), pp. 452 ff.

Giuseppe Di Chiara

Italy

Table of Contents

Table of Abbreviations

Cost.	Costituzione della Repubblica italiana (Italian Constitution)
CPP	Codice di procedura penale (Code of Criminal Procedure)
CPP 1930	Codice di procedura penale (1930) (Code of Criminal Procedure 1930)
Cass.	Corte di cassazione (Court of Cassation)
Cass. (SU)	Sezioni Unite penali della Corte di Cassazione (Joint Criminal Divisions of the Court of Cassation)
ECHR	European Convention on Human Rights
ECtHR	European Court of Human Rights

1. The constitutional protection of personal freedom

"Since it is a punishment, the deprivation of liberty may not precede the sentence except when there is a need for it," wrote Cesare Beccaria in the second half of the 18th century in one of the most famous passages of the Italian legal Enlightenment.[1] The general philosophical view during the Enlightenment and of the later so-called classical school was influenced by an awareness of the suffering inflicted by the deprivation of liberty. When this deprivation takes place in the preliminary stage of proceedings, prior to the final determination of guilt, even more difficult problems arise in terms of protecting personal liberty and dignity.[2] The crucial problem lies precisely in identifying the "need" for measures restricting liberty referred to by Beccaria and therefore – in more direct terms – in standardising precautionary needs in such a way as to justify a restriction of personal liberty in the course of proceedings. Given the crucial nature of the interests involved, which fall within the category of fundamental human rights, the matter has historically been governed by constitutional norms.

1.1. The historical background: united Italy and the Albertine Statute

Historical research on the constitutional protection of individual liberty shows it to originate with the Statute of the Kingdom of Sardinia of 1848, which was subsequently extended to all Italy after unification in 1860. Although this was of

---

1 *Beccaria*, § XIX.
2 One of the most important examples of classical thought is *Carrara*, pp. 297 ff.

course not the first instance of constitutional protection of individual freedom in the geographical area of Italy, the previous division of the Italian peninsula into many states of varying size, legal traditions and civilizations would make an analytical study here very fragmented.

The Albertine Statute, granted for the Kingdom of Sardinia by King Charles Albert of Savoy following the 1848 uprisings, was a flexible constitution for the entire period in which it was in force, and its rank within the system of sources was equal to that of ordinary law. Article 26 of the Statute contained a fundamental rule that, although perhaps somewhat insufficient to our modern eyes, established that "individual freedom is guaranteed." The principle of the legality of measures limiting liberty was established in a provision whereby "no one can be arrested or brought to trial, except in cases envisaged by law, and in the forms prescribed thereby." It is worth stressing that the 1848 Statute consecrated the home (Art. 27) and "property" (Art. 29) as "inviolable," but not individual freedom, which was only "guaranteed." The terms of this guarantee were furthermore delegated to the ordinary law.

1.2.   The current situation: the Constitution of 1948

Much more substantial guarantees were laid down in the Republican Constitution of 1948: the experience of serious violations of individual freedoms under fascism had led the Constituent Assembly, during the intense preparatory work of the new Charter between June 1946 and December 1947, to dedicate ample space and particular care to the protection of personal liberty.

1.2.1. Inviolability of personal freedom

The regulation of personal freedom hinges on the complex system of Article 13 of the Constitution, which draws three concentric circles. The basis of protection is contained in the formula "personal liberty is inviolable."[3] This is followed by statements regarding restrictions on liberty, permitted "as a result of justified acts on the part of the judicial authorities, and only in the cases and manner provided for under law,"[4] and regarding instances where, in "exceptional cases of necessity and urgency, strictly established by law," it is possible for "public security authorities" to adopt "interim measures," which must be confirmed by the judicial authorities within a very short time limit, established by the constitution itself. The system therefore extends radially from the central tenet of

---

3 Art. 13.1 Cost.
4 Art. 13.2 Cost.

the inviolability of individual freedom, the key criterion. The two outer concentric circles are exceptions to the rule and are based on: restrictions of law (it is the law that establishes those cases where limitation of liberty is permissible); restrictions of jurisdiction (it is the task of the judicial authority, within the framework of legality established generally and theoretically by law, to apply specifically and in practice any measure restricting personal liberty); and the obligation of grounds (any measure restricting personal liberty, issued by judicial authorities within the scope of cases and procedures established by law, must be justified).

The reasoning behind the second exception – police powers in exceptional cases of necessity and urgency provided for under law – is due to the technical impossibility in such cases of obtaining court intervention. In practical terms, the rule covers cases of arrest *in flagrante delicto* and detention of those about to commit a crime, where the need to intervene urgently prevents normal procedures being followed. Unable to intervene *a priori*, the court nonetheless reacquires its role of guarantor through the confirmation process, which aims to assess, within the very short time limits set by the Constitution itself, whether the police has exercised its powers in accordance with the provisions of law: the request for confirmation is made within 48 hours of arrest or detention, and the relative decision must be taken within the following 48 hours; failure to do so will render detention ineffective.

Moreover, Article 13 of the Constitution completes the regulations with two crucial provisions. First it establishes that "any act of physical and moral violence inflicted on individuals subjected to a restriction of liberty shall be punished."[5] This is a direct implication of the connections between the principle of the inviolability of freedom and the restriction of law regarding permitted limitations of liberty. This guarantee falls within the field of the protection of fundamental human rights[6] and, ultimately, of the protection of human dignity. Since the restriction of personal liberty affects an inviolable right, it is only permitted within the confines of strict legality; any additional restrictions not provided for and not permitted constitute abuses of the inviolable tenet of human dignity, and therefore are not only prohibited but also punished.

Finally, the law establishes the "maximum period of preventive custody."[7] The system lays down essential time limits, based on reasonableness, for the restriction of personal liberty pending trial, thereby underlining its precautionary nature and ultimately defending the inviolability of personal liberty that is the crux of the entire system.

---

5 Art. 13.4 Cost.
6 Art. 2 Cost.
7 Art. 13.5 Cost.

1.2.2. Presumption of innocence and rule of treatment

Although thorough, Article 13 of the Constitution says nothing, however, about the fundamental aims of precautionary measures, a failing which triggered the academic "lack of purpose" debate of the last century.[8] This lacuna was filled by the constitutional presumption of innocence established under Article 27.2 of the Constitution, which serves as a rule of treatment.

It has already been shown that the Italian constitutional formula, albeit using different language, can be traced back to the core concept of the presumption of innocence,[9] outlined by the liberal culture and classical school and established in European terms by Article 6.2 ECHR. Where the text of the European Convention and the Italian Constitution differ is in the threshold beyond which the presumption is reversed. The ECHR sets this threshold, in general terms, at the moment when the guilt of the person charged with a criminal offence has been "legally established." The Italian Constitution sets the guarantee bar higher at the moment when a conviction becomes *res judicata.*

The presumption of innocence operates on various levels: as a rule of proof (the burden of proving the defendant's guilty lies with the prosecution); as a rule for resolving uncertainties (the court must acquit the defendant if his guilt has not been proven beyond reasonable doubt); and as a rule of treatment, where the law makes it possible to compensate for that "lack of purpose" found in a close reading of Article 13 of the Constitution. The presumption of innocence as a rule of treatment means that until a conviction has become *res judicata*, the person charged with a criminal offence is necessarily considered innocent, and should thus be treated as not guilty. Any mechanism that results in even a surreptitious infliction of punishment in advance is therefore prohibited. Since the penalty can be enforced only when the guilt of the person has been established by a definitive conviction, any device that seeks to bring forward implementation of the punishment to a time prior to sentencing would inevitably be tantamount to judging the defendant guilty, and would thus conflict with the constitutional guarantee.

Lastly we should remember the guarantee of appeal to the Court of Cassation for violation of the law by all measures affecting personal liberty:[10] every ruling affecting personal liberty may always be subjected to a review of legality to further protect the defendant during proceedings.

---

8 In this regard see *Elia*, p. 951.
9 See, among others, although with differences of emphasis, *Grevi* [1], pp. 24 ff.; *Illuminati* [1]; *Nobili*, pp. 829 ff.; *Paulesu*; *Fiandaca/ Di Chiara*, pp. 310 ff.
10 Art. 111.7 Cost.

2.   Active enforcement: the system of personal precautionary measures

The current Italian CPP, in force since 1989, devotes much more attention to the personal liberty of the defendant than the previous code of 1930. Previously regulations on warrants and orders fell within the broader context of the preliminary inquiry, whereas today, Book IV of the Code is entirely devoted to precautionary measures, covering the rules governing the restriction of personal freedom and, in the last part, precautionary measures.

With its lengthy and systemic treatment of protection of liberty during trial, the new Code has introduced many innovations. Examples include the shift from "sufficient" to "serious" evidence of guilt, clearer regulation of precautionary proceedings and appeals against precautionary measures, and the introduction of a mechanism of redress for unfair or unlawful detention. However, what especially stands out is, among the various innovations, the transition from a single-module system that hinged for practically the entire lifespan of the 1930 Code on the sole measure of custody in prison (then referred to as preventive detention), to a system, embodied by the 1988 Code, based on a scale of precautionary measures of increasing severity. The consequences of this Copernican revolution are obvious. Previously, once the threshold of the evidence of guilt had been clearly established and one or more precautionary requirements evidenced, the court clearly applied the only measure provided for, namely pre-trial detention, which in some cases, such as particularly serious crimes, was obligatory. Today, apart from the exceptions we will discuss, once the court has found serious evidence of guilt and at least one precautionary need, it also has to decide, according to specific criteria outlined by the law, which of the standard measures should be applied to the case in hand.

2.1.   Non-custodial precautionary measures

The system therefore no longer consists of a single measure (the old system of pre-trial detention) but on a range of precautionary measures, all analytically standardised in observance of the restriction of law established under Article 13.2 of the Constitution.

A distinction must first be made, within the field of the personal precautionary measures, between coercive (*misure coercitive*) and control measures (*misure interdittive*). Coercive precautionary measures are those that directly relate to personal liberty, such as the freedom of self-determination also in terms of movement,[11] while control measures affect certain powers of the person but are not strictly related to the "freedom from arrest."[12] Control measures include the suspension of parental authority,[13] suspension from a public office or service[14] and the temporary prohibition from exercising certain occupations or business activities.[15]

Coercive measures are those that most directly affect the person's freedom of physical self-determination. Developed over time, the system is the result of a layering of rules introduced since the 1988 Code came into force. A traditional classification distinguishes between mandatory and custodial coercive measures. Custodial measures, which include house arrest and detention, are those that most clearly restrict a person's physical freedom and are at the top end of the scale of severity. Mandatory measures are at the lower end of the scale and aim to satisfy precautionary needs while at the same time safeguarding the physical liberty of the defendant as much as possible.

A look at the different types of coercive measures envisaged highlights their graded scale nature. At one end we have the ban against leaving the country, and on the other, custody in prison or a place of care. The intermediate levels of the scale are occupied by a range of further measures, each more restrictive of a person's physical self-determination than the one before, culminating with the most restrictive, last resort measure of pre-trial custody.

A) The least severe type of precautionary measure consists in a ban on travel abroad.[16] The person subjected to this ban will be forbidden to leave the Italian state, although he/she is free to travel at will within the country. Clearly this measure has a limited impact on individual self-determination: within national boundaries, the person maintains full freedom of movement.

B) The ban on foreign travel is followed by the obligation to report to the police.[17] The judge will establish the days and times at which the defendant must report to a specific police station to sign a special register. The contents of the measure are flexible and may be adapted to the needs of the individual case. The judge shall specify how frequently the person is obliged to report: reporting twice a week has clearly different implications to reporting every day.

---

11 On the essential configuration of the personal liberty of the defendant in terms of freedom from arrest, see *Amato* [2], p. 6.
12 On the topic of control measures, see *Peroni*.
13 Art. 288 CPP.
14 Art. 289 CPP.
15 Art. 290 CPP.
16 Art. 281 CPP.
17 Art. 282 CPP.

C) The measure of removal from the family home was introduced in 2001.[18] It is designed to protect the victims in criminal investigations for domestic violence, and requires the defendant to leave the family home or not return without permission of the court. The flexibility of the measure allows the emotional aspects involved to be taken into account and ensures the best interest of the victims by specifying eventual visiting rights.

D) The prohibition of approaching the places frequented by the victim[19] is another recent innovation. It is designed to operate in cases of persistent harassment,[20] and requires the defendant not to come close to certain places usually frequented by the victim, their close relatives or persons bound to them by emotional relationships, or to maintain a certain distance from these places or such persons.

E) The last of the non-custodial coercive measures is the prohibition and obligation of residence.[21] The great flexibility of the measure, whose terms may be changed and adapted to the individual circumstances of the case, is evident from its multifaceted content. The court may, if it sees fit, opt for a ban on staying in certain places or for a more restrictive obligation not to leave the territory of the municipality of habitual residence or other municipality or fraction thereof.

2.2. Custodial precautionary measures

The top end of the range of coercive measures is occupied, as we have seen, by custodial tools that most severely restrict physical self-determination.

A) Under the CPP 1930, house arrest was merely conceived as an alternative form of preventive detention. Departing from the basic one-track approach of the previous system,[22] the 1988 code views house arrest[23] as an autonomous measure, intended as the penultimate step in terms of severity in the scale of coercive measures. House arrest requires the defendant not to leave his or her home, other private house, public place of care or assistance or, if appropriate, protected accommodation. The measure is compatible with the administration of so-called windows of freedom: permission granted the defendant to be absent during the day from the place of house arrest to engage in employment or to

---

18 Article 282bis CPP was introduced by Article 1.2 Law 154/2001.
19 Art. 282ter CPP.
20 Article 282ter CPP was introduced by Article 9.1(a) of Legislative Decree 11/2009, converted into Law 38/2009. This legislation also introduced the crime of stalking into the Italian criminal system.
21 Art. 283 CPP.
22 See above, § 2.
23 Art. 284 CPP.

follow other essential living needs. The use of electronic monitoring instruments is also envisaged,[24] making house arrest more secure and therefore avoiding custody in prison.

B) Pre-trial custody[25] is at the top of the scale of coercive measures and is the maximum restriction of liberty during proceedings. It may also be implemented for mentally ill defendants, in which case an appropriate place of care will be indicated.[26]

2.3.   The operational core of the system

Despite the thoroughness of the rules contained in Book IV of the CPP, the system of active precautionary measures is built around an operational framework of core elements. The rule of law,[27] as the cornerstone of such a system, makes it possible – by implementing the provision of Article 13.2 of the Constitution – to limit the personal freedom of the defendant only under the circumstances and in the manner provided for under the Code. Within these limits, the court is first of all required to show serious evidence of guilt and the existence of precautionary needs in the case at hand. Having clarified that in practice this may give rise to a restriction of the defendant's liberty, the court will subsequently have the task of deciding which measure to apply in accordance with standardised parameters that guide the choice of judicial discretion in the field.

2.3.1.   The requirement of proof: serious evidence of guilt

A basic requirement for measures restricting liberty consists of evidentiary grounds: no one may be subjected to precautionary measures without "serious evidence of guilt."[28] Although the CPP 1930 merely required the existence of "sufficient" evidence of guilt, towards the end of its lifespan the threshold of evidentiary requirements was raised and arrest or detention warrants had to be supported by "serious" the evidence of guilt.[29]

The issue of serious evidence has been the subject of complex case law interpretation. The upshot has been a consensus whereby "evidence" is not interpreted as restricting precautionary measures just to those cases in which there is logical

---

24 Art. 285bis CPP.
25 Art. 285 CPP.
26 Art. 286 CPP.
27 Art. 272 CPP.
28 Art. 273 CPP.
29 See in this regard Art. 252 CPP 1930, as amended by Art. 12 Law 330 / 1988. On this issue, for a perceptive discussion, see *Chiavario* [3], p. 496.

or indirect evidence.[30] Representational evidence, such as statements by people with information on the facts, or statements by accomplices, may well serve as the basis for a restrictive precautionary measure.[31] As to the assessment of this assumption whereby evidence is considered as already acquired, serious evidence of guilt refers to all those logical or representational elements that contain the essence (or even only some of the structural elements) of the evidence to which they refer. Although these elements do not suffice *per se* to prove the suspect's involvement beyond all doubt, they are sufficiently solid to suggest that with the future acquisition of additional elements, they will demonstrate such involvement, and at the same time establish qualified probability of guilt.[32] The assessment of serious evidence of guilt thus involves assessing whether the crime may reasonably be attributed to the defendant and whether the items of evidence already filed are likely to lead to sufficient further developments.

2.3.2. Precautionary needs

We have seen[33] that the presumption of innocence, in its capacity as a rule of treatment, can compensate for the alleged "lack of purpose" of Article 13 of the Constitution. It is presumption of innocence principle that renders any attempt, however surreptitious, to anticipate punishment before conviction unconstitutional.

Having clarified what the Constitution forbids, we now must indicate what precautionary objectives are constitutionally allowed. The liberal tradition[34] considers limitations of liberty in the course of the proceedings as having a "functional three-dimensionality."[35] The three *pericula libertatis* that severally justify the issuance of a precautionary measure are danger of tampering with evidence, risk of escape and protection of the public.[36]

A) The code starts with the protection of evidentiary authenticity. This is the most typical aim of precautionary measures, classified as an "instrumental

---

30 See Cass., Decision of 23. 4. 1993, Surrenti, in: Ced Cass., No. 194270; Cass., Decision of 19. 1. 1994, Iamonte, in: Ced Cass., No. 196654. For a clear systematic assessment, see *Dominioni*, p. 5.
31 See recently on this issue Cass., Decision of 1. 4. 2010, Iannicelli, in: Ced Cass., No. 247206, and Cass., Decision of 9. 4. 2010, Sacco, in: Ced Cass., No. 246948. On the rules of assessment applicable to complicity in the perspective of serious evidence of guilt, see especially Cass. (SU), Decision of 30. 5. 2006, P.m. in c. Spinnato, in: Ced Cass., No. 234598.
32 In these terms see Cass. (SU), Decision of 21. 4. 1995, Costantino, in: Ced Cass., No. 202002.
33 See above, § 1.2.2.
34 See, in this sense, *Beccaria*, § XIX.
35 The expression was coined by *Chiavario* [4], p. 43.
36 Art. 274 CPP.

procedural precaution"[37] since its effects are expressed, by definition, entirely within the confines of the performance of the trial. In this case the restriction of liberty is justified because there is a concern, based on specific concrete grounds, that if released, the defendant might engage in activities that would prejudice the authenticity of the sources of evidence (intimidation or suppression of persons informed of the facts, destruction of documents, etc.).

B) The risk of flight is the second precautionary aim. The reason for the restriction of freedom in this case is to prevent the person from absconding, which would render any future custodial sentence unenforceable. For this reason it is usually classified as a "final procedural precaution."[38]

C) Protection of the public completes the list of protective aims in the code and is the most problematic. Restriction on the defendant's freedom is justified in this case by the risk that if released, he or she might commit serious crimes of the kind expressly listed, or crimes similar to those of which he or she is accused. It is clear that this third precautionary need – and statistically most frequent – is not always perfectly compatible with the presumption of innocence until definitive conviction. The fear that a person may commit *further* crimes carries the risk of considering the defendant guilty, which is inconsistent with the constitutional guarantee.[39] Nevertheless, the need to protect society has always outweighed any doubts raised regarding on the measure's constitutionality.[40]

2.3.3. The selection criteria

Once it has found serious evidence of guilt and at least one of the precautionary needs allowed by the system and consequently the need to limit the defendant's personal freedom, the court shall determine the measure to be implemented in the case in point from the range of measures standardised by law. This is a typical discretionary ruling that the judge implements in accordance with established guidelines.[41]

The measures must first of all be applied in the light of the criteria of proportionality and appropriateness. The judge will ensure that the chosen measure is proportionate to the offence and the punishment that has been or, he believes, may be imposed. The measure, however, should be selected according to the principle of the least necessary sacrifice, meaning that the judge will apply the measure that allows the precautionary objectives of the case in question to be pursued with minimal sacrifice of personal freedom. For example, if house arrest

---

37 *Grevi* [1], p. 51.
38 *Grevi* [1], p. 59.
39 See, on this issue, among others, *Pisani* [2], p. 224; *Vassalli*, pp. 1 ff.
40 Constitutional Court, Decision 1 / 1980.
41 Art. 275 CPP.

is sufficient to protect the specific precautionary needs, an application for prison custody will not be allowed, since the excessive sacrifice imposed on the liberty of the defendant would, in this case, not be instrumental to the precautionary aim pursued, and to the extent that the sacrifice imposed is pointless, it would be tantamount to anticipating punishment, in violation of the constitutional presumption of innocence.

The ordinary assessment of sufficiency is, however, in certain cases, subject to exceptions under law,[42] which result in normal selection criteria being suspended. This occurs when dealing with a series of specific and particularly serious crimes. In such cases the ordinary system gives way to a special procedure based on the presumption that precautionary needs exist (which may be overturned if it can be proved, on the basis of specific, concrete elements, that none of these needs apply to the case in hand), and that any measure other than custody in prison would be insufficient. So-called mafia crimes (mafia-type association, crimes committed using the typical conditions of mafia association and crimes of so-called mafia abetting) are not subject to ordinary assessment of sufficiency and treated as exceptions in a system that has been ruled as not in conflict with the Constitution[43] and in practice compliant with Article 6 ECHR.[44] However, given the somewhat disordered approach to the range of crimes falling outside the ordinary precautionary system,[45] the Constitutional Court has reduced the scope of the exceptional mechanism.[46]

Additional guidance criteria grounded in the view that custody in prison is a last resort are aimed to protect minors under the age of six, persons aged over seventy, and those suffering from AIDS or severe immune deficiency.

3.   Precautionary proceedings

3.1.   Internal regulations

The multiple aspects regarding application of precautionary measures set down in the Italian code occupy most of the rules contained in Book IV. On the level of precautionary dynamics, the principle of the request is one of the pivots of the entire system; particular space is also dedicated to events following the issuance of the precautionary measure and to appeals against precautionary measures.

---

42 Art. 275.3 CPP.
43 Constitutional Court, Decisions 450/1995; 40/2002; 130/2003.
44 ECtHR, Decision of 6.11.2003, Pantano v. Italy, Application No. 60851/00.
45 Art. 275.3 CPP, as amended by Art. 2.1(a-bis) of Legislative Decree 11/2009, converted into Law 38/2009.
46 Constitutional Court, Decisions 265/2010; 164/2011.

3.1.1. The procedural core: the principle of application, decision on custody and review examination

It is up to the public prosecutor to ask the judge (i. e., in the course of pre-trial stages, the judge in charge of preliminary inquiries), to issue a precautionary measure. The representative of the prosecution will attach the documents deemed appropriate to support the request, any evidence in favour of the suspect and any deductions and briefs already filed.[47] The procedural judge will issue the order, analytically justified according to the challenging (and sometimes cumbersome) model provided by law,[48] in which he will allow the prosecutor's request, entirely or in part, or reject it.

The issue of the precautionary order is not subject to an adversarial procedure, and no alternatives have seemed adequate,[49] since the current system of a decision followed by a debate once the order has already been issued remains unchanged. This debate takes the form of a questioning of the defendant, which must be conducted by the judicial authority.[50] It is the duty of the judge, until the debate begins, to question the accused subjected to the precautionary measure within five days (in the case of custody in prison) or within ten days (in the case of any other measure), starting from the time of implementation of the measure. This examination aims to ensure that the defendant has the right to submit arguments regarding the grounds and legality of the measure in progress, in order to obtain a reduction or cancellation of the precautionary measures implemented. Failure to implement the order within the time limit laid down by law entails the lapse of the precautionary measure, and thus obliges the prosecuting authorities to release the defendant unless he or she is held for other reasons.

3.1.2. The mechanism for amending or revoking the measure

The functional *iter* of the measure needs to be constantly coordinated with the developments of the main investigative proceedings and with the possible emergence of new facts or circumstances that change the factual framework of reference. Precisely for this reason the system provides a device[51] that ensures, at the instigation of a party, or in some cases even *ex officio*, continuous review of the factual and legal grounds on which the precautionary measure is based. The measure should be withdrawn immediately where the applicable conditions or

---

47 Art. 291 CPP.
48 Art. 292 CPP.
49 See, for interesting reflections *de jure condendo*, *Illuminati* [2], pp. 23 ff.; *Spangher*, pp. 43 ff.; *Riccio*, pp. 685 ff.
50 Art. 294 CPP.
51 Art. 299 CPP.

precautionary needs fail or cease to exist, including as a result of events occurring subsequently. The initial measure may, however, be replaced by another
less, severe measure if the precautionary needs are attenuated or the measure no
longer seems proportionate to the magnitude of the fact or the penalty that may
be imposed. At the request of the public prosecutor, the measure may also be
made more severe.

3.1.3. Contesting precautionary orders

It has already been stressed[52] that the guarantee of appeal to the supreme court
for violation of the law governing precautionary measures is a constitutional
right (Art. 111. 7 Cost.), introduced to further safeguard the inviolability of
personal liberty. This guarantee is further dealt with in the procedural code that
regulates it.[53] For some time, however, it has been observed that in almost all
cases, appeals against the contents of the precautionary measure have not been
upheld when the merits of the case could not be assessed. This shows the in-
adequacy of a system that attributes a crucial role within the system of guarantees to entitlement to appeal to the Court of Cassation.[54]

Aware of this, and in line with the provisions of Article 5.4 ECHR regarding
the judicial review of restrictive measures "within a tight deadline," a new
remedy – a judicial complaint (*riesame*) – had already been introduced during
the final period of application of the 1930 Code. Here review was characterised
by incisive, strictly circumscribed time limits and wide-ranging powers on the
part of the review judge.[55]

The 1988 Code reiterated the central role of the judicial complaint within the
framework allowing precautionary measures to be challenged, which included
appeal procedures[56] (Art. 310 CPP) also to the Court of Cassation.[57]

3.1.3.1. Judicial complaint

Since the outset, the fundamental need pursued by judicial complaint can be
summed up as the intention to ensure a wide-ranging re-examination, at the
request of the interested party, of a precautionary measure within a specified,
strictly circumscribed timeframe. This was achieved by structuring the complaint in the form of an appeal, thus making it devolutive, and at the same time
imposing an extremely limited time on the court in charge of complaint to reach

---

52 See above, § 1.2.2.
53 Art. 311 CPP.
54 See, for example, *Pisapia*, p. 89; *Pisani* [2], pp. 250 ff.; *Marzaduri* [1], p. 771.
55 See Arts. 263bis and 263ter CPP 1930, in the form introduced by Arts. 7 – 8 Law 532 / 1982.
56 Art. 310 CPP.
57 Art. 311 CPP.

a decision, on pain of the annulment of the contested precautionary measure if such time limits are not observed. The salient features of the system can be summarised as follows:

A) Only the interested party and his lawyer may make a request for complaint, and review may be requested of only those precautionary measures applying a coercive precautionary measure for the first time. Complaint must be requested, under penalty of inadmissibility, within ten days of the performance or service of the contested measure. In contrast any other decision regarding the defendant's liberty must be challenged by means of an appeal.

B) The jurisdiction to hear the request for review lies with a judicial review court (*tribunale della libertà*), represented by the court, sitting en banc, of the provincial capital of the court of appeal in whose district the judge who issued the contested measure is based. This jurisdiction, as has been stated in case law, is exclusive,[58] since even if the coercive order is pronounced by the court of appeal, the court is entitled to be informed of the relative request for review.

C) The presiding judge of the court ensures that immediate notice of the request is given to the prosecuting authority, which, by the next day and in any event within five days, is required to forward the files originally accompanying the request for a precautionary measure to the court, together with all the evidence presented in favour of the defendant. Failure to observe the time limit of five days causes the contested precautionary order to lapse, with the consequence that the person must be released unless held for other reasons.

D) Within ten days of receiving the files, the court, unless it declares the request inadmissible, may cancel, amend or confirm the precautionary order appealed against also on the basis of events occurring in the meantime and submitted by the parties at the hearing in chambers for discussion of the request. The contested decision may be annulled or amended in a manner favourable to the defendant for reasons other than those set forth by the party, or can be confirmed also for reasons other than those set out in the grounds for the precautionary order under review. Failure to reach a decision within the terms renders the contested precautionary order ineffective, and consequently obliges the release of the person unless detained for other reasons.

3.1.3.2. Appeals against precautionary measures and appeal to the Court of Cassation

A) If judicial complaint is not envisaged by law, the defendant and his or her lawyer may lodge an appeal within ten days of the performance or service of the precautionary order. The public prosecutor, who may not legitimately request complaint, has similar rights. Traditionally, the appeal against a precautionary

---

58 Cass. (SU), Decision of 22. 10. 1996, Di Francesco, in: Ced Cass., No. 205618.

measure is seen as strictly devolutive: the structure of the appeal is, therefore, significantly different from that of a request for complaint.

Jurisdiction over appeals against precautionary orders lies with the same court having jurisdiction over the complaint of coercive measures. The presiding judge of the court ensures that the prosecuting authority is immediately informed. By the end of the following day the latter must deliver the order appealed against along with the files on which it is based. The court then has 20 days from receipt of such files to decide on the appeal. While failure to observe the deadline for appeal is a cause of inadmissibility, the other terms are merely ordinative: delay in the transmission of files by the competent authority, or delay in the decision on appeal, does not affect the contested measure, which thus continues to be effective.

B) In terms of its chronological aspects, appeals to the Court of Cassation follow a similar system. This strictly devolutive instrument may be used by the interested party, defence counsel or public prosecutor against measures issued by the court in charge of complaint as a result of the complaint or appeal against a precautionary measure. The person concerned and his or her lawyer may also appeal immediately to the Court of Cassation only against those measures that may be subject to review. The judge who issued the contested order, at whose office the appeal to the Court of Cassation is filed, notifies the prosecuting judicial authorities, and by the end of the following day, the latter must deliver the contested measure and the documents on which it is based. A ruling on the appeal is made by the Court of Cassation, sitting in chambers, within 30 days of receiving the files. The deadline for submitting the dossier and the decision is, also in this case, merely ordinative, and any failure to observe them does not compromise the precautionary order subject to appeal.

3.1.4. Remedies for false imprisonment

Introduced for the first time by the procedural code of 1988,[59] the mechanism of redress for unfair or unlawful detention is governed by Article 5.5 ECHR and fills a legal vacuum rightly criticised on various occasions in the past.[60]

The device covers two distinct situations: first, the remedy can be requested by those who, after suffering a custodial measure, have been acquitted by an irrevocable decision because there was no case to answer; because they did not commit the crime; because the act committed was not a crime, or is not con-

---

59 There is, in fact, a historical precedent dating back to the laws of the Kingdom of the Two Sicilies in the 18th century. See, on the issue, *Di Chiara,* pp. 1412 ff. See on this institution, among others, *Coppetta, Turco, Zanetti.*
60 Arts. 314–315 CPP. On this topic see, among others, *Grevi* [1], pp. 370 ff.

sidered a crime under law; or because there has since been an order to close the case. This mechanism can also be used in cases where an irrevocable decision has established that the precautionary measure was issued or maintained in the absence of serious evidence of guilt or of the legal framework required for the implementation of coercive measures, regardless of the fact that the subject was subsequently, on the merits, convicted of the offence with regard to which the precautionary measure was unlawfully issued.

The application for a remedy must be submitted, under penalty of inadmissibility, within two years of final conviction or acquittal, or of the date when the ruling of no case to answer becomes unappealable, or of notification of the order to dismiss the case. Jurisdiction lies with the court of appeal of the district in which the judge who issued the judgment or order to dismiss the case is based. There is a limit to compensation, which may not exceed EUR 516,459.90.

3.2.   International relations: passive extradition and precautionary mechanisms

Brief mention should be made of the system of precautionary measures applicable in the context of extradition to other countries. The field is governed by Book XI of the procedural code,[61] which, as is known, applies only to those relations not regulated by international conventions.[62] This is a largely unsatisfactory discipline, which still suffers from a statist vision subsequently superseded by conventions and above all by regional cooperation within the European Union.[63]

Under this system, the person whose extradition is sought may, "at all times," be subjected to coercive measures at the request of the minister of justice. These will be issued by the court of appeal or, for proceedings at cassation, the Court of Cassation, which in this case rules on the merits of the precautionary measure. Reference, in the compatibility clause, to the provisions of Book IV of the Code, which govern "common" precautionary measures, specifically excludes the applicability of the rule of serious evidence of guilt and of the legal framework of coercive measures.[64] Coercive measures may not be applied if there are reasons to believe that the conditions for a ruling granting extradition do not exist. Any

---

61 Arts. 714–719 CPP.
62 Art. 696 CPP.
63 For solid fundamental considerations, see, among others, *Marzaduri* [2].
64 Articles 273 and 280 CPP do not apply.

measures issued are revoked if the specifically established deadlines have passed without an extradition order being issued.

Ordinary means of appeal provided by relevant legislation may not be used to appeal against orders to implement measures, and the only meagre remedy allowed is an appeal to the Court of Cassation for violation of the law.

Bibliography

Amato, Giuliano, [1] Individuo e autorità nella disciplina della libertà personale, Giuffrè, 1976; [2] Commento all'art. 13 Cost., in: Branca, Giuseppe (ed.), Commentario della Costituzione, Rapporti civili, Zanichelli-Il Foro Italiano (1977), pp. 1 ff.

Aprile, Ercole, [1] Le impugnazioni delle ordinanze sulla libertà personale, Giuffrè, Milano, 1996; [2] Le misure cautelari nel processo penale, Giuffrè (2006).

Beccaria, Cesare, Dei delitti e delle pene, Società dei Filosofi (1774) (rist. anastatica, Fondazione Giangiacomo Feltrinelli, 2001).

Carrara, Francesco, Immoralità del carcere preventivo, in: Carrara, Francesco, Opuscoli di diritto criminale, IV vol., 2nd ed., Tipografia Giusti (1874), pp. 297 ff.

Chiavario, Mario, [1] Processo e garanzie della persona, II, Le garanzie fondamentali, 3rd ed., Giuffrè (1984); [2] Problemi attuali della libertà personale. Tra "emergenza" e "quotidiano" della giustizia penale, Giuffrè (1985); [3] Una legge "anticipatrice" sui generis in tema di libertà personale, in: La legislazione penale (1988), pp. 491 ff.; [4] Arts. 272 ff., in: Chiavario, Mario (ed.), Commento al nuovo codice di procedura penale, III vol., Utet (1990), pp. 23 ff.; [5] Le misure cautelari nel nuovo codice: una "carta delle libertà" equilibratamente coraggiosa con qualche sgualcitura (e qualche... patinatura di troppo), in: Chiavario, Mario (ed.), Commento al nuovo codice di procedura penale, III vol., Utet (1990), pp. 3 ff.

Coppetta, Maria Grazia, La riparazione per ingiusta detenzione, Cedam (1993).

De Luca, Giuseppe, Lineamenti della tutela cautelare penale. La carcerazione preventiva, Cedam (1953).

Di Chiara, Giuseppe, Attualità del pensiero di Francesco Carrara in tema di riparazione dell'ingiusto "carcere preventivo", in: Rivista italiana di diritto e procedura penale (1988), pp. 1412 ff.

Dominioni, Oreste, Misure cautelari personali, in: Amodio, Ennio/Dominioni, Oreste (eds.), Commentario del nuovo codice di procedura penale, III vol. (pt. II), Giuffrè (1990), pp. 1 ff.

Elia, Leopoldo, Le misure di prevenzione tra l'art. 13 e l'art. 25 della Costituzione, in: Giurisprudenza costituzionale (1964), pp. 951 ff.

Fiandaca, Giovanni/Di Chiara, Giuseppe, Una introduzione al sistema penale. Per una lettura costituzionalmente orientata, Jovene (2003).

Grevi, Vittorio, [1] Libertà personale dell'imputato e Costituzione, Giuffrè (1976); [2] Il sistema delle misure cautelari personali nel nuovo codice di procedura penale, in: Grevi, Vittorio (ed.), La libertà personale dell'imputato verso il nuovo processo penale, Cedam (1989), pp. 263 ff.

Fontana, Filippo / Guadalupi, Stefano, Le impugnazioni delle misure cautelari personali, Giappichelli (2005).

Illuminati, Giulio, [1] La presunzione d'innocenza dell'imputato, Zanichelli, 1979; [2] Relazione, in: Riccio, Giuseppe (ed.), G.i.p. e libertà personale. Verso un contraddittorio anticipato?, Jovene (1997), pp. 23 ff.; [3] Presupposti e criteri di scelta delle misure cautelari, in: Conso, Giovanni (ed.), Il diritto processuale penale nella giurisprudenza costituzionale, ESI (2006), pp. 389 ff.

Marzaduri, Enrico, [1] Riesame dei provvedimenti restrittivi della libertà personale, in: VI N.moDI Appendice, Utet (1986), pp. 771 ff.; [2] Libertà personale e garanzie giurisdizionali nel procedimento di estradizione passiva, Giuffrè (1993); [3] Considerazioni sul significato dell'art. 27, comma 2, Cost.: regola di trattamento e regola di giudizio, in AA.VV., Processo penale e Costituzione, Giuffrè (2010), pp. 303 ff.

Negri, Daniele, Fumus commissi delicti. La prova per le fattispecie cautelari, Giappichelli, 2004.

Nobili, Massimo, Spunti per un dibattito sull'articolo 27 comma 2° della Costituzione, in: Il Tommaso Natale, Scritti in memoria di Girolamo Bellavista (1978), II vol., pp. 829 ff.

Paulesu, Pier Paolo, La presunzione di non colpevolezza dell'imputato, Giappichelli (2009).

Peroni, Francesco, Le misure interdittive nel sistema delle cautele penali, Giuffrè (1992).

Pisani, Mario, [1] Libertà personale e processo, Giuffrè (1974); [2] Libertà personale e processo penale, in: Indice penale (1987), pp. 209 ff.

Pisapia, Gian Domenico, Orientamenti per una riforma della custodia preventiva nel processo penale, in: Rivista italiana di diritto e procedura penale (1965), pp. 89 ff.

Polvani, Michele, Le impugnazioni de libertate, Cedam (1999).

Riccio, Giuseppe, Nuovi spazi legislativi e ruolo della dogmatica, in: Politica del diritto (1997), pp. 685 ff.

Spagnolo, Paola, Il tribunale della libertà tra normativa nazionale e normativa internazionale, Giuffrè (2008).

Spangher, Giorgio, Relazione, in: Riccio, Giuseppe (ed.), G.i.p. e libertà personale. Verso un contraddittorio anticipato?, Jovene (1997), pp. 43 ff.

Turco, Elga, L'equa riparazione tra errore giudiziario e ingiusta detenzione, Giuffrè (2007).

Vassalli, Giuliano, Libertà personale dell'imputato e tutela della collettività, in: Giustizia penale (1978), I, pp. 1 ff.

Zanetti, Elena, La riparazione dell'ingiusta custodia cautelare. Aspetti sistematici e questioni applicative, Cedam (2002).

Víctor Moreno Catena*

Spain

Table of Contents

* This paper is written in the context of a research project funded by the Spanish Ministry of Education and Science with the title "Restrictions on personal freedom of terrorists in criminal proceedings" (DER 2008\06178) and directed by Victor Moreno Catena.

5. Recent reform and proposals of reform
    5.1. Preventive detention
    5.2. Interim measures, protective measures and other measures

Table of Abbreviations

ACHR   American Convention on Human Rights
CE   *Constitución española* (Spanish Constitution)
EAW   European Arrest Warrant
ECHR   European Convention on Human Rights
ECtHR   European Court of Human Rights
EAW FD Framework Decision on the European Arrest Warrant
ICCPR   International Covenant on civil and political rights
LECrim Ley de Enjuiciamiento Criminal

1.   The Right to Liberty

The Spanish Constitution considers freedom foremost among the superior values of the Spanish legal system.[1] The major importance of freedom in a democratic society leads Spanish constituents to attribute to the public authorities the duty of primarily promoting the conditions so that the freedom of the individuals and groups of which it is comprised may real and effective, thereby removing obstacles that impede or hinder its fulfillment.[2]

During the course of a criminal procedure, when the final condemnatory decision has not yet been handed down and therefore the defendant is protected by the presumption of innocence, measures that limit or deny a person his or her right to freedom may be adopted while nonetheless complying with the constitutional clause establishing such freedom and with the provisions of the law.[3] The restrictive measures of the law provided in the LECrim refer to the different aspects of freedom – from the provisional denial of the right to drive motor vehicles to the most essential form of freedom, such as the right to move freely in society. This chapter especially refers to the latter, that is the right to personal

---

1 Art. 1.1 CE.
2 Art. 9.2. On this topic see *Moreno Catena* [3], pp. 281 ff. A complete and illustrative view of criminal procedure, from investigation to enforcement, including pre-trial measures, etc. may by seen in *Arnaiz Serrano et al.*, pp. 102 ff.
3 Art. 17.1 CE.

liberty recognized as a person's fundamental right,[4] and the limited precautionary measures jeopardising this right that may be agreed upon in the course
of a criminal proceeding.

The denial of the freedom of movement of a person may arise for very different reasons. Detention (*detención*), provisional imprisonment (*prisión provisional*) and pre-trial release (*libertad provisional*) are the measures that serve
the precautionary purpose.[5] Their purpose is to ensure that both the criminal
process be completed and any eventual criminal sentence handed down, and
may only be enacted under specific circumstances.

The right to personal freedom and security is, according to the consolidated
case law of the Constitutional Court, the right that all people enjoy to prevent any
undesired interference in their physical wellbeing, i. e. the absence of any arbitrary or illegal disturbance proceeding from a public authority or a private party
restricting their freedom to organize at any time and place their individual and
social life in accordance with their own options and convictions.[6] In other words,
personal liberty is the right to not be obliged to be where one does not want to
be.[7]

1.1.   History of the Right to Liberty

After the right to life and physical integrity, the right to personal liberty constitutes one of the most precious possessions of the human condition. The
recognition of this fundamental right was one of the most important achieve-
ments of the Liberal State. However, it was not definitively consolidated as a
fundamental right until well into the 19th century. The American Declaration of
Independence of 1776 and The Bill of Rights of 1789 were landmark achieve-
ments, as were international texts and statements such as Article 5 ECHR, Article
7 ACHR and Article 9 ICCPR.

Since then, all States of Law have been characterized by a search for the
perfect equilibrium to ensure the right to freedom but also to security. The right
to personal freedom historically appears to have been conceived in a "negative"
manner, i. e. with a view to excluding any possibility of it being unjustifiably
withheld. In the liberal state, for example, personal freedom was only the right to

---

4 *Ibid.*
5 In the opinion of *Moreno Catena* [3], p. 268, the police order for identification that may
   obligate the person whose identity is being ascertained to go to a police station for this
   purpose (Art. 20 Organic Law 1/1992) cannot be deemed a pre-trial measure of preventive
   detention.
6 Constitutional Court, Decision 15/1986.
7 *Gude Fernandez.*

obtain from the public powers a commitment of non-interference in the sphere of personal autonomy. This was subsequently completed by the democratic and social State of Law as a requirement to guarantee a sphere of personal autonomy.

The Spanish Constitution is founded along these lines. It has been argued that the public powers have a duty to respect the sphere of personal liberty and promote conditions such that the individuals and groups making up society achieve such freedom in a real and effective manner, by removing any obstacle that impedes this or renders its fulfillment difficult. Personal liberty is that freedom enjoyed by all individual humans with specific reference to physical freedom. By that same token it excludes any human activities that do not possess this characteristic.

The holder or active subject of the fundamental right of freedom is the individual, without restriction due to gender or nationality while the subject obligated by the constitutional rule is essentially the State, although private persons are also under the same obligation. Furthermore, the fundamental right to personal freedom recognized in Article 17 CE must not be confused with the freedom of a Spanish citizen to reside, enter, leave and move about the national territory provided in Article 19 CE.

1.2.   Pre-trial detention and Habeas corpus

1.2.1. Provisional imprisonment

Provisonal imprisonment of an individual is one of the first provisional precautionary measures the judiciary, police and even exceptionally, a private person, may adopt to limit the fundamental right to freedom of an individual. It has the essential objective of making that individual available to a judicial authority in order for a decision to be taken either reestablishing that individual's right to freedom, or adopting a less temporary precautionary measure in the form of provisional prison or pre-trial release, as will be discussed more fully below.

Provisonal imprisonment may not last for longer than is strictly necessary for the performance of the inquiries aimed to ascertain the facts. In any event, the detainee must be released or handed over to the judicial authority within a maximum period of 72 hours.[8] If the detained person is placed at the disposal of the judicial authority after 72 hours, such detention is illegal (except in exceptional cases where a request for an extension has been granted). Pre-trial detention is also illegal when the detainee, although placed at the disposal of the

---

8 Art. 17.2 CE.

judicial authority within 72 hours, has been detained for a longer time than strictly necessary.

The Constitution guarantees that all persons detained shall be immediately informed in a comprehensible manner of their rights and the reasons for their detention.[9] Detainees are furthermore under no obligation to make statements. The detainee is guaranteed a lawyer during police interrogation under the provisions of the law. Of course all detained persons or prisoners shall be informed especially of their rights and guarantees[10] and detention shall be exercised in a manner that least prejudices the detainee, their person, reputation or assets. To this end, the use of force or humiliating treatment, such as the use of handcuffs, is prohibited unless strictly necessary. The provisions governing detention guarantee the folowing rights: to remain silent; not to make statements unless the detainee so wishes; not to answer any questions or to state that he or she shall only make statements before a judge, to testify against him or herself or plead guilty; to designate a lawyer to assist him or her during the investigation being performed; to inform – at any time – a relative or a person of their choice of the detention and place of custody; and, to be assisted free of charge by an interpreter. In addition, the detainee has the right to communicate with the Ministry of Foreign Affairs and a foreign Embassy/Consulate; to be recognized by a forensic doctor or legal substitute, or in their absence, by the Institution in which he or she has been placed or by any other Public Administration employees. The detainee or prisoner shall be entitled to such amenities and occupations that are not incompatible with the reasons for detention and place of custody[11] and may receive visits and correspondence and make use of means of communication unless placed in solitary confinement.[12]

Nevertheless, some of the concrete guarantees and rights provided by this general framework may be restricted or diminished as in the case of crimes committed by a person belonging to or associated with an armed group, or if the detainee is a terrorist individual[13] or detained during an uprising. The period of detention may be prolonged to enable investigation up to a maximum limit of another 48 hours provided that such extension be requested during the first 48 hours of detention and be authorized by a judge within the subsequent 24 hours. The examining judge shall approve or deny the extension with a justified ruling. In addition, the detaining parties may request the detainee be committed to solitary confinement, in which case, the judge has to issue a reasoned decision within 24 hours. Once solitary confinement is requested, the detainee in any

---

9 Art. 17.3 CE.
10 Art. 520 LECrim.
11 Art. 522 LECrim.
12 Art. 523 LECrim.
13 Cf. *Moreno Catena / Catalina Benavente*, pp. 443 ff.; *Catalina Benavente*, pp. 171 ff.

event remains in solitary confinement without prejudice to his or her right to assistance by legal counsel until a formal decision is issued. In the event of solitary confinement being confirmed, the isolated detainee will no longer enjoy some of the rights and guarantees provided under the general regime. He or she shall no longer have the right to communicate his or her situation to a relative or another person designated, nor shall he or she be able to receive visits, correspondence, etc. In addition, the right to legal counsel may also be restricted, in the sense that such counsel shall be appointed by the court. In addition, the right to an interview with a lawyer may also be restricted.[14]

1.2.2. Habeas Corpus

The right to personal liberty is valued to such a point that the Constitution expressly establishes a specific legal instrument protecting the liberty of the individual known as *Habeas corpus*.[15] The *Habeas corpus* procedure was enacted to ensure that all persons detained be immediately brought before a judicial authority, thereby removing them from the custody of those who have hindered the exercise of this fundamental right. The *Habeas corpus* procedure is regulated by Organic Law 6/1984 with the aim of ensuring that the detainee be immediately brought before a court of law to ascertain the legality and conditions of detention.

The *Habeas corpus* procedure is very quick and simple. It is simple because it may be requested, without the need for a lawyer or procurator, in writing by the detainee him or herself, a spouse or legal partner, descendents, ascendants, brothers and sisters or legal representative, the Public Prosecutor's Office, Ombudsman and examining judge. It is rapid since it must be resolved within a maximum of 24 hours from the moment the procedure is filed.

As to the procedure, the request for *Habeas corpus* must be transferred to the competent examining judge who, after ascertaining that the procedure has been correctly filed, proceeds to accept or deny the application. The examining judge shall communicate the decision to allow or deny detention to the detainee, the requesting party and the Public Prosecutor. The decision is not appealable.

If the application procedure is accepted, the judge will then hear the testimony of the detainee, his/her legal representative or lawyer in the event such representative has been appointed. He will also subsequently summon the agents and authorities who practised the detention as well as the person under whose custody the detainee is held. The judge shall examine the evidence proposed and take a decision by means of a ruling either to release the detainee, uphold the

---

14 Art. 527 LECrim.
15 Art. 17.4 CE.

application or the constitutionality of the detention and the circumstances under which it is exercised, ordering the detainee to remain in detention, perhaps at a different center or under the custody of different persons or that the detained be placed at the disposal of the court. In the event of the interested party filing a request for *Habeas corpus* in bad faith, such parties may be ordered to pay the costs of the procedure.

1.3. Current situation

The Spanish National Institute of Statistics periodically publishes data relative to the prison population in Spain, distinguishing, among other factors, those persons provisionally detained. In 2009, 15,580 persons were in preventive custody, a slight fall compared to the previous two years when the highest rates were recorded of 16,137 and 17,849 for 2007 and 2008 respectively.

Provi-sional imprison-ment	*2000*	*2001*	*2002*	*2003*	*2004*	*2005*	*2006*	*2007*	*2008*	*2009*
	11,8	10,141	11,810	12,276	13,112	13,720	15,065	16,137	17,849	15,580

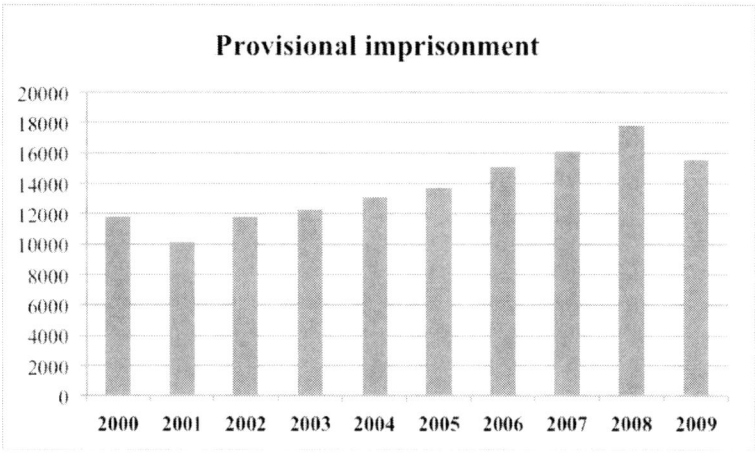

The table above illustrates prison population trends in the last decade. As shown by the graph and table below, most prison inmates (90 %) were males, with the female population barely reaching 10 %.

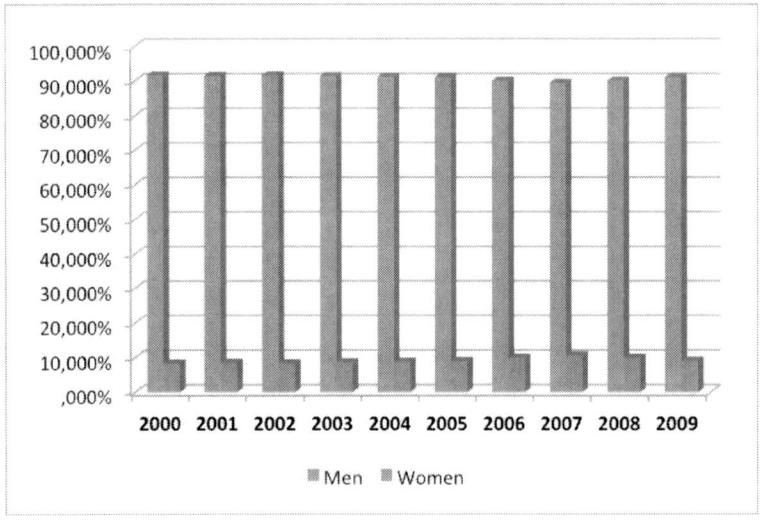

Most people in preventive detention are aged between 20 – 40 years. In short, provisional detention in Spain has risen by almost 32 % over the last ten years, even if a slight decrease was recorded in 2009. The profile of the typical person remanded in custody is that of an adult male generally between the ages of 20 – 30 years.

Preventive Detention	2000		2001		2002		2003		2004	
From 18 to 20 years old	847	7.17 %	669	6.60 %	847	7.17 %	792	6,45 %	832	6.35 %
From 21 to 25 years old	2,639	22.35 %	2,099	20.70 %	2,639	22.35 %	2,609	21,25 %	2,682	20.45 %
From 26 to 30 years old	2,944	24.93 %	2,617	25.81 %	2,944	24.93 %	3,165	25,78 %	3,340	25.47 %
From 31 to 40 years old	3,379	28.61 %	2,987	29.45 %	3,379	28.61 %	3,521	28,68 %	3,934	30.00 %
From 41 to 60 years old	1,822	15.43 %	1,618	15.96 %	1,822	15.43 %	2,022	16,47 %	2,131	16.25 %
More than 60 years old	179	1.52 %	151	1.49 %	179	1.52 %	167	1,36 %	193	1.47 %
Total	11,810	100.00 %	10,141	100.00 %	11,810	100.00 %	12,276	100.00 %	13,112	100.00 %

Preventive Detention	2005		2006		2007		2008		2009	
From 18 to 20 years old	756	5.51 %	894	5.93 %	1,006	6.23 %	1,184	6.63 %	965	6.19 %
From 21 to 25 years old	2.441	17.79 %	2,639	17.52 %	2,738	16.97 %	3,376	18.91 %	2,737	17.57 %
From 26 to 30 years old	3.336	24.31 %	3,587	23.81 %	3,643	22.58 %	4,168	23.35 %	3,551	22.79 %
From 31 to 40 years old	4.492	32.74 %	4,872	32.34 %	5,238	32.46 %	5,487	30.74 %	4,745	30.46 %
From 41 to 60 years old	2.486	18.12 %	2,840	18.85 %	3,209	19.89 %	3,315	18.57 %	3,300	21.18 %
More than 60 years old	209	1.52 %	233	1.55 %	303	1.88 %	319	1.79 %	282	1.81 %
Total	13,720	100.00 %	15,065	100.00 %	16,137	100.00 %	17,849	100.00 %	15,580	100.00 %

2.   Theoretical framework: significance and procedural purpose of interim measures in criminal proceedings

In today's society, court resolution of criminal disputes arising from apparent criminal events is achieved in a lawsuit conducted with public hearings, at the conclusion of which a final judgment is delivered publicly. In other words, in a State of law, judicial bodies are those entrusted with the task of adopting a final decision on the existence of a crime and on the defendant's guilt.

Thus, criminal proceedings require the State's response to a legally illicit and socially unacceptable action, i.e. a reaction to a crime, where the dispute is resolved with the application of criminal law. However, in addition to the issues arising between the offender and society, another dispute usually arises from the criminal facts between offender and victim that requires regulation, i.e. the subject who directly and personally suffers the damaging consequences of the acts. The victim cannot be deprived of his right to receive relief for the harm suffered,[16] be redirected to other civil proceedings in order to claim the relevant compensation, or be relegated to second, subordinate place in the criminal lawsuit, since this would be tantamount to leaving outstanding an important aspect of a case that the legal system is called to resolve.

In any event, in order to complete the proceedings and reach a judgment on criminal and civil liability under the provisions of Spanish law, a series of occasionally lengthy measures are required.

Before the hearing, which begins once the procedural positions of the accused and the defence are perfectly and definitively established, a series of prior stages must be completed, beginning with an investigation of the criminal acts. This investigation stage, which sometimes continues for a long period of time due to the complex nature of the acts themselves, exists because usually the public bodies in charge of the criminal prosecution (both the Police and the Public Prosecutor or investigating judge) are unaware, at the initial stage, of the way in which the events took place. Often, the offender tries to conceal the crime itself or, at the very least, usually tries to remove the sources of evidence leading to discovery of the acts and, especially, anything that might confirm his or her liability. This is why criminal proceedings include an initial stage to clarify the facts and justify the accusation, as well as to provide the defendant with elements he may use in his defence.

Once a judgment is delivered at the trial stage, the path is usually cleared for an appeal, which allows the party whose petitions have not been fully satisfied to

---

16 *Hassemer*, pp. 10, 37, 92; *Hassemer / Muñoz Conde*, p. 29.

address a higher court and request a new resolution, overruling or modifying the initial decision.

In fact, the mere passing of the time required first to prepare the trial and later, to reach a final judgment, may endanger both the trial itself and enforcement of the judgment in the event of conviction. This is because, on the one hand, in some legal systems, such as the Spanish system, a trial cannot be held without the presence of the defendant when the punishment sought exceeds two years' imprisonment; and on the other hand, the unavoidable delay in reaching a final judgment may endanger its effectiveness and full enforcement, either because the guilty party has evaded the law or because the assets required for an effective criminal sanction or civil liability no longer exist, thereby preventing resolution of the conflicts examined during the proceedings. As a result, the guilty party is not punished for his crime nor is the victim indemnified for the illegal and damaging acts perpertrated against him or her.

Precisely in order to ensure that these strictly procedural purposes are duly fulfilled, safeguarding the criminal lawsuit and ensuing it is correctly conducted and that an eventual conviction may be enforced, the law has foreseen the possibility of interim measures. Interim measures in a criminal lawsuit not only respond to the need to resolve disputes; they are also instrumental to the carrying out of public policies,[17] especially criminal policy. The aim of these measures is to prevent such time elapsing until the final judgment as to render the criminal lawsuit ineffectual on account of a state of affairs that would either hinder judgment or make enforcement unfeasible. The aim of preventive detention is also to prevent certain initiatives and actions being taken by the defendant, to prevent him from abandoning the proceedings if a judgment of conviction is likely or, once convicted, from taking measures to avoid the conviction.

In other words, interim measures include procedural steps aimed at preventing the criminal lawsuit from becoming ineffective on account of the State's *ius puniendi* being jeopardized, including any rights over assets held by those parties entitled to restitution for the harmful consequences of the criminal acts in question.

As a result, the need to protect the public interest when effectively prosecuting and imposing a conviction for crimes committed, and to provide victims with a remedy may sometimes require that the defendant sacrifice his / her own rights and liberties, both his / her personal freedom (including his freedom of movement) or patrimonial rights.

---

17 *Damaska*, pp. 125 ff., as well as, relating to the implementation of policies, pp. 253 ff. See also *Fiss*, pp. 21 ff.

2.1.   Instrumentality and provisional nature of interim measures

The procedural considerations justifying the adoption of interim measures require that these latter always be instrumental with respect to the specific
criminal lawsuit in question that is either being conducted or about to com-
mence. Only in this way can such measures fulfil their procedural aim, and they
not be invoked for any other purpose.

This instrumental nature reflects another essential characteristic of interim
measures which, according to majority legal opinion, has become one of its basic
prerequisites: the need for a reasoned court resolution ordering such measures.
This means that interim measures are part of a criminal lawsuit that is already
underway and may only be ordered by the judge in charge of examining the case.

One of the basic problems of the Spanish criminal system is the clear conflict
that arises with the permanence of a pre-trial judge, the judicial body in charge
of investigating the crime and clarifying the facts but who, at the same time, is
called upon to act as the judge safeguarding the rights of all citizens participating
in the process.[18] This includes safeguarding the specific rights of the person
whose freedoms may be hindered as a result of commencement of a criminal
lawsuit, i. e. the person charged with a criminal offence.

In my opinion, this two-fold role places incompatible duties on the pre-trial
judge, requiring him to exercise both tasks simultaneously while remaining
impartial. He who is in charge of an investigation may not also resolve the issue
of pre-trial detention,[19] nor should be in charge of enforcing the safeguarding
guarantees to ensure that citizens' rights and freedoms are strictly upheld during
a criminal lawsuit.

In any event, both the competent investigating judge during the first stage of
the procedure and the judicial body charged with hearing and deciding appeals
are made up of the same people, entitled to adopt any necessary interim
measures at the various stages of the lawsuit. Further risks or requirements may
also arise at later stages of the lawsuit when a conviction is handed down, even if
this is not the final outcome of the case. The judge or tribunal entrusted with
adopting interim measures is also legally entitled to order any such measures *ex
officio* (except for orders of provisional imprisonment or parole for which, since
1995, the law demands a hearing of the defendant). This means that the right to
provide interim relief is not always exercised in the interests of the defendant,
albeit with a prior hearing of both parties to the lawsuit.

---

18 Art. 117.4 CE.
19 See ECtHR, Decision of 1.10.1982, Piersack v. Belgium, Application No. 8692/79; ECtHR,
    Decision of 26.10.1984, Cubber v. Belgium, Application No. 9186/80. The Constitutional
    Court's application of both judgments led to an amendment of regulations concerning
    summary criminal proceedings and the criminal law applicable to minors.

The above comments are particularly relevant, as I will expand upon below, in light of the vogue enjoyed by interim measures, the frequency with which they are adopted and their effects on the defendant to the point of actually replacing the contents of the ruling itself when this is a conviction.

The instrumentality of an interim measure means it is directly linked to the pending nature of the main lawsuit. Therefore, the completion of the main lawsuit in any form provided for by law (i. e. by means of a judgment or final court order, not subject to appeal) should entail the cancellation of the interim measure.

Since it is not independent, no interim measure can subsist separately from the main lawsuit. If a final judgment of conviction is delivered, the interim measure must be replaced with an enforcement measure; if a stay of proceedings or acquittal is ordered, the interim measure should be lifted.

However, this instrumentality not only entails a link to a lawsuit but also a link to its object and to the background facts, i. e. a future enforceable conviction and its guaranteed processing.

Thus, an interim measure should adjust to the aims pursued in each case, which means that even the very content of the measure may be identical to the conviction eventually ordered in the judgment and the measures of enforcement. This is the case of measures eventually decreed by the pre-trial judge while the case is being examined and which are materially identical, not just homogeneous, to enforcement measures, such as the case of provisional imprisonment if there is a risk of absconding,[20] or the closure of a company or suspension of activities, adopted pursuant to the provisions established in Article 129.2 of the Criminal Code, which should, in any case, uphold certain basic human rights and freedoms, such as the right to information and communication.[21]

As an interim measure is aimed at ensuring the enforceability of a judgment, it must remain in force for a limited period of time, i. e. it is illogical for it to continue beyond the judgment of conviction that definitively completes the proceedings without the possibility of appeal. Given their link to the main lawsuit and the purposes pursued, interim measures are provisional, not only because they cannot remain as provisional once the main lawsuit is completed, regardless of the outcome, but also because interim measures may only continue insofar as the reasons for them continue. In other words, as soon as these cease to exist, such measures should be lifted.

Precisely because of this link to the justifying reasons, any interim measure may, in itself, be revoked. Therefore, if the factual situation giving rise to the

---

20 Art. 503.1(3) LECrim.
21 Criminal Division of the National Spanish Court, Decision of 12.4.2010, Egunkaria case, Sentence No. 27/2010.

measure ceases to exist or changes, the measure should follow the same fate and be cancelled, lifted, or replaced with another that better covers the change in circumstances.

Finally, since interim measures may deprive a subject of his or her right to freedom in the course of the criminal process, as in the case of arrest or provisional imprisonment, the Spanish Constitution[22] and the law establish, in any case, a maximum term for such interim measure, even if the circumstances remain unchanged.

2.2.   Preconditions of interim measures: *fumus boni iuris* and *periculum in mora*

In order to adopt an interim measure that is both instrumental to a main lawsuit and provisional, academics of civil procedure law[23] traditionally require at least two presumptions: apparent "legality," and a potential risk to the lawsuit's effectiveness if the measure is not adopted.

2.2.1. *Fumus boni iuris* and the presumption of innocence

The first presumption behind an interim measure is its apparent "legality" (*fumus boni iuris*). Such legality need only be apparent and does not require final verification. This will only be achieved with the judgment following the evidence and discussions held between both parties to the lawsuit.

However, the reasoning and principles governing a criminal lawsuit are very different from those applicable to civil proceedings.

First, because, in general, civil litigation deals with subjective rights in the sense that a person's capacity to act as party to a lawsuit is upheld when the subject is the main party to the legal relationship under dispute. The procedural claim includes individual rights of the party to the lawsuit. Second, because interim measures in civil proceedings are asset-related and do not entail restrictions to or limitations on personal freedom, i. e. if eventually the judgment does not uphold the plaintiff's arguments, any damage caused the defendant may be remedied in economic terms. Third, and as a result of the foregoing, interim measures in civil proceedings are adopted at the cost of the applicant, who affirms that his rights exist and remain in force. In the event, a lack of evidence confirming the plaintiff's arguments is remedied by demanding a counter-guarantee, i. e. a deposit to cover any potential loss and damage to the

---

22 Arts. 17.2 and 4 CE.
23 *Calamandrei*, pp. 59–63.

defendant if the judgment delivers an acquittal. Fourth, because the rights under dispute in civil proceedings are generally unrestricted, which means that the parties may forfeit, waive, abandon or reach a settlement in the proceedings, as suits their interests.

The approach in criminal proceedings is totally different. First, there is no subjective right to a criminal conviction, i.e. the prosecution in a criminal case does not pursue the recognition of individual rights and is not a main party to the legal relationship. Second, criminal law is not unrestricted, and notwithstanding the application of the principle of opportunity to criminal actions brought in many jurisdictions, at least in Continental Europe, the law has raised a solid barrier against total discretion, demanding that certain regulatory parameters be met in order to define the accusation's scope of action. Third, as criminal litigation does not examine personal rights there is no need for the applicant of the measures to provide a deposit or counter-guarantee (let alone the investigating judge who, in Spain, may order most of the interim measures *ex officio*) in order to cover any certain loss and damage suffered by the accused if a judgment of acquittal is delivered, in which case the State will be the indemnifying party, although it will not even cover a minimum part of the damage effectively caused the innocent party.

There are two important points to this regard. First, criminal proceedings examine issues related to the public interest, far beyond the object of civil proceedings. At issue is the question of deciding whether the State is entitled to impose a criminal sanction on the defendant. Second, criminal interim measures may affect the exercise of basic human rights, particularly the right to personal freedom, a right protected by law that is totally unrelated to the interim measures and the content of any judgment delivered in civil proceedings.

For both reasons, a criminal lawsuit is governed by a principle that does not exist in civil proceedings and which should be upheld at all times, from the beginning of the lawsuit until the final court decision: a presumption of innocence, which means that the accused becomes the protagonist of any steps taken, the focus of any decisions adopted; he or she is no longer the object of the lawsuit but the main subject.

This basic human right[24] has a two-fold meaning. On the one hand, as is generally known, the presumption of innocence is a trial rule, which means that somebody may only be considered guilty when the judge convicts him or her based on a belief as to the accused's guilt that is beyond all reasonable doubt and further to sufficient, legally obtained evidence. However, even though the presumption of innocence is upheld as a trial rule, it then becomes a rule governing

---

24 Art. 24.2 CE.

the treatment of the accused, i.e. being treated as innocent throughout the criminal process until a final judgment declares criminal liability.

Clearly, the presumption of innocence as a treatment rule is related to the moment in time when the interim measures are adopted, that is, during the processing of the criminal lawsuit and always prior to a final judgment of conviction, as such measures entail an interference or detriment to the freedoms or rights of an unconvicted subject, who, on the basis of the presumption of innocence principle, must be treated as innocent at that particular procedural moment.

It is therefore necessary to provide an adequate explanation of the relationship and compatibility between respect for this basic human right to a presumption of innocence, as a treatment rule, and the adoption of interim measures.

On the one hand, it is obvious that interim measures are only justifiable if there is a possibility of a criminal judgment of conviction. The measures try to guarantee the completion of the lawsuit and, in any case, assume that the party in question will be declared guilty. If it is assumed that the judgment will be one of acquittal, clearly the adoption of interim measures would be inappropriate as indeed would the continuation of criminal proceedings, which should immediately cease.

On the other hand, it is also clear that interim measures in any case restrict or deprive the defendant of certain assets or rights, since he or she is prevented from disposing of their personal freedom, freedom of movement or other freedoms, or is provisionally deprived of material assets, on the assumption that the judgment will be one of conviction.

Finally, very often criminal interim measures do not entail less sacrifice but a similar, albeit identical, detriment to that resulting from a criminal conviction. However, in such cases the presumption of innocence has been annulled by certainty of culpability.

It follows that clarification is needed on whether the soundness of the claim that presumption of innocence is generally upheld in a criminal lawsuit when interim measures are adopted against a defendant who is presumed likely to receive a judgment of conviction. The first issue to be resolved would be how the presumption of innocence works at the trial stage and how it ceases on conviction beyond all reasonable doubt. Importantly, presumption of innocence does not mean that the objective pursued in criminal proceedings is that of proving a person's innocence. On the contrary, as indicated by Vives,[25] criminal proceedings should only ensure that the person eventually punished is truly guilty. To this end, any judgment of conviction may not uphold likely versions of

---

25 In general terms see *Vives Antón* [1] and [2].

the facts or what is intuitively believed to be true but rather be based on that which may be affirmed as true without doubt. No penalty may be imposed if there remains any uncertainty as to the perpetrator of the crime. Judgment shall ensue only on the basis of the truth and objective, undisputed certainty in both factual and legal terms. This does not mean that the presumption of innocence should reflect what generally happens (even if this is in fact very often the case) but should, in principle, reflect what is accepted or deemed valid unless proved otherwise.

Such truth may only be reached if the procedural guarantees regarding the defence[26] and hearing of both parties to a lawsuit are upheld. The presumption of innocence as a trial rule works as "the accused party's right not to be convicted unless his culpability is ascertained beyond all reasonable doubt, further to evidence considered as accusatory and fully guaranteed."[27] Bearing in mind that the lawsuit should achieve a just decision, not only should applicable rules be adequately selected and interpreted, but the facts should be reliably determined and ascertained and a valid and just procedure pursued to attain a judgment.[28]

However, it is very clear that these guarantees are not upheld nor is this evidence conducted when the law allows interim measures to be adopted against the defendant who should be treated as innocent since culpability has not been proved. The judicial decision adopting such measures must therefore be justified on other grounds, without forgetting that the requirement that incriminating evidence exists suggesting the likelihood of a judgment of conviction.

Under Spanish procedural law, the principle of *fumus boni iuris* within the framework of criminal interim measures is described as "rational evidence of criminality." This leads to three conclusions.

First, evidence must consist of affirmations based on details and factual circumstances on court records that represent more than a mere possibility, even if not total certainty or the truth as declared in a judgment, of guilt.[29] It follows that evidence entails a judgment of attributed criminal conduct based on the facts of the lawsuit in compliance with the rules of logic, science and experience. This means that for interim measures to be implemented, the mere suspicion, hypothesis or speculation that may justify the commencement of criminal investigations,[30] should give way to certainties, albeit provisional, on the part of the public body adopting such measures.

---

26 *Moreno Catena* [2], pp. 17 – 40.
27 Constitutional Court, Decision 81 / 1998.
28 *Taruffo* [1], pp. 199 – 212; *Colmenero Guerra*, pp. 117 ff.
29 Constitutional Court, Order No. 289 / 1984.
30 *Moreno Catena* [1], pp. 13 – 54.

According to the ECtHR, these "reasonable suspicions" are necessary for the adoption and continuation of an interim measure.[31]

Second, these suspicions must be "rational," which means that no arbitrary or whimsical suspicions are allowed[32] In particular, the rule affirms the need to express the evidence justifying an interim measure decision in factual and legal terms. The justification must guarantee the solidity and reliability of the evidence and eschew all subjective impressions of the deciding party.

In order to justify the adoption of interim measures there needs to be rational suspicion of criminality, which entails a double accusation: an objective accusation of a criminal act; and a subjective accusation that the person covered by the measure seems to be responsible for the act. In this regard, rational suspicion of criminality will be pursued by the lawsuit, i. e. both those assuming the reality of a fact and those defending the contrary.

Moreover, with regard to the apparent legality of interim measures, the situation in criminal law terms should be taken into account as a whole, both objectively and subjectively. In other words, not only must the illicit nature of the facts be considered but also the entire circumstances giving rise to criminal liability, as well as any causes for non-attribution, justification or exclusion of illegal conduct, culpability or punishment, grounds for absolution or annulment of criminal liability, so that a final decision of conviction can be finally obtained in each specific case.

If these circumstances were not assessed, the decision to adopt interim measures would be unduly disconnected from the main lawsuit and could breach the basic principle of proportionality, since an interim measure should not only be proportional to the aims pursued but also to the facts being examined and to any potential conviction, i. e. the sacrifice entailed by the measure with respect to the rights of the defendant cannot be more burdensome for the person suffering the effects of the measure than the potential conviction delivered in the judgment.

As an interim measure represents a limitation or prohibition of the enjoyment of rights by the accused party (including the right to freedom) until a final judgment of conviction is obtained, there must be sufficient evidence to support the State in the exercise of its *ius puniendi* in the specific case.

---

31 ECtHR, Decision of 10.11.1969, Stögmüller v. Austria, Application No. 1602/62; ECtHR, Decision of 28.3.1990, B. v. Austria, Case's number 8/1989/168/224; ECtHR, Decision of 26.6.1991, Letellier v. France, Application No. 12369/86; ECtHR, Decision of 27.11.1991, Kemmache v. France, Application No. 12325/86, 14992/89; ECtHR, Decision of 12.12.1991, Toth v. Austria, Application No. 11894/85; ECtHR, Decision of 27.8.1992, Tomasi v. France, Application No. 12850/87; ECtHR, Decision of 26.1.1993, W. v. Switzerland, Application No. 14379/88.

32 In this sense Constitutional Court, Order 199/1982.

In criminal proceedings therefore, the principle of *fumus boni iuris* consists of a reasoned and plausible accusation, i.e. the attribution of criminal liability based on specific criminal facts brought against a specific person. This entails an, admittedly, indicative assumption, prior to a final judgment, that certain criminal acts have taken place (objective component) and that the person against whom the measure is ordered is responsible for the same (subjective component), regardless of whether a criminal or civil liability is at stake.

2.2.2. Periculum in mora

Together with the attribution of criminal acts to a specific person, the second presumption required for the adoption of interim measures is the need to avert the risk of the final resolution of conviction being delayed, which could render ineffective all the procedural steps taken.

The *periculum in mora* principle establishes the purposes to be fulfilled by interim measures and acts as a measurement of constitutionality, i.e. if the purposes pursued do not conform to the provisions of the Spanish Constitution, such interim measures will be considered illegitimate.

As already mentioned, the *periculum in mora* principle applies in those cases or situations where hindrance to a lawsuit or unenforceability of a judgment of conviction are highly likely.

The first scenario of *periculum in mora* is that of ensuring the procedural steps may be adequately taken and refers to those cases in which the gathering of evidence, particularly accusatory evidence supporting the charge or at trial leading to conviction, may be endangered. In this case, the interim measure aims to prevent action being taken by the accused or a third party with a view to hindering the contribution, both at the criminal investigation stage and at the public hearing, of instruments and effects of the crime, the so-called "elements of conviction," or the discovery of other sources of evidence, thereby avoiding any potential manoeuvres to conceal or remove evidence from the proceedings.

Alongside the presumed risk of delay in the adequate processing of the case, there is also the possibility of concealment or disappearance of the defendant. If the defendant absconds, no trial may be held if the punishment requested exceeds two years' imprisonment.

The *periculum* presumption may also be justified by the risk of unenforceability of any future judgment. It is clear that this will be the case if the convicted party is not available to the court, especially of the sentence handed down directly affects the convicted party, as is the case in most criminal sanctions.

Judgment would also be unenforceable in the event of material sanctions such as a fine or other financial obligations, including an order to pay the legal costs of private prosecution, if the material assets of the criminally liable party were no longer available for disposal.

Asset concealment would also render judgments unenforceable in the event of civil liability, eiher direct or subsidiary, being confirmed.

It follows that in the absence of any likely jeopardy to either the court case or enforcement of the final decision, the second requirement of an interim measure would not exist. The interim measure would therefore be unsustainable, even if there were solid, evident and rational signs of criminality.

Defined in negative terms, interim measures may not be enacted for any other considerations other than the presumption of guilt (i. e. that the defendant is guilty in principle). Interim measures may not be used to anticipate punishment, as a sanction, or as an intimidatory or exemplary measure, since this would constitute violation of the presumption of innocence, on the grounds that an interim measure may not be adopted to compensate for an infringement that has still to be legally established.

Neither may it be claimed that interim measures may be used simply to mitigate social alarm, there being always the requirement of presumption of guilt. The only true legal remedy to pacify social alarm (which may be described as a "thirst for collective vengeance" that unfortunately arises, and is even more unfortunately fomented in some cases) would be rapid judgment on the merits of the case, with conviction or absolution.

Nor may interim measures be used as an instrument in criminal investigations, in such a way as to entitle the pre-trial judge judge (or Public Prosecutor) to adopt a measure on the basis of the attitude of the accused party or his readiness to actively contribute to the clarification of the facts. This is why the LECrim expressly provides for that pre-trial detention may not be justified on the grounds of a right of defence or lack of cooperation in investigation proceedings entailing a risk of concealment or destruction of evidence.[33]

According to Spanish law, a remand measure may pursue the aim of avoiding criminal recidivism,[34] in compliance with the doctrine laid down by both the Constitutional Cour[35] and the ECtHR. This thesis is however tantamount to a presumption of guilt for which preventive detention may be invoked. The terminology itself, most often used to express the likelihood of "other" or "future" crimes being committed suggests that it is based on a presumption of culpability. Deprivation of freedom is thus used to remedy fear over the defendant's dangerous behaviour, although in fact effective danger may only be ordinarily justified if it is assumed that the accused party is actually guilty of the criminal

---

33 Art. 503.1(3b) LECrim.
34 Art. 503.2 LECrim.
35 Constitutional Court, Decisions 40/1987; 47/2000; 207/2000; 217/2001.

charges. In my opinion, this is an exaggerated interpretation of Article 5.1(c) ECHR, which allows a person to be detained (not provisionally imprisoned) "when it is reasonably considered necessary to prevent his committing an offence" (which in fact means that a criminal action is stopped when the consequences are imminent). The ECtHR has justified provisional imprisonment when potential criminal recidivism is considered to exist.[36] Nevertheless, as stated by Judge Zekia in his dissenting opinion in *Matznetter v. Austria*, the rule is unrelated to that particular case and does not comply with the provisional imprisonment of individuals who, merely based on their tendency to offend, may relapse or commit an offence, as otherwise all individuals with criminal tendencies would be required to remain in prison indefinitely.

2.2.3. Need for and proportionality of interim measures

Once these presumptions have been satisfied, the two basic guarantees required in order to adopt interim measures are specific need and guaranteed proportionality.

Specific need means that the existence of a crime, rational signs of criminality and the need to prevent procedural risk are all insufficient; the measure to be adopted must be necessary. This entails two requirements: on the one hand, that the measure be suitable to avoid any potential risk and satisfy the public interest to be upheld in criminal process. It is then necessary to ascertain whether the deprivation or limitation of rights derived from the interim measure is precisely and directly justified by the need to protect specific assets or constitutionally relevant public interests.

The principle of necessity requires that no other measure exist that would satisfy the aim pursued and be less burdensome for the accused. The interim measure requested will not be granted if it may be replaced by another, equally effective, provision that fits the circumstances of the case and is less detrimental for the defendant.

Proportionality will depend on the seriousness and impact of the facts being investigated or tried and requires that the interim measures conform to such facts. Interim measures may not be adopted to inflict a greater sacrifice on the accused than would result from a judgment of conviction. If this principle of proportionality is applied to restrictions on freedom imposed during the lawsuit, it seems clear that, since the prerequisite is to guarantee hearing of the

---

36 ECtHR, Stögmüller v. Austria (fn. 31); ECtHR, Decision of 10.11.1969, Matznetter v. Austria, Application No. 2178/64; ECtHR, Decision of 16.7.1971, Ringeisen v. Austria, Application No. 2614/65; ECtHR, Decision of 28.3.1990, B.v. Austria (fn. 31); ECtHR, Decision of 26.01.1993, W. v. Switzerland (fn. 31).

defendant and completion of the proceedings, provisional imprisonment will not apply in all criminal processes, imprisonment being the most serious punishment. Therefore applications to remand the accused party in custody throughout the lawsuit would be unconstitutional if the final judgment is unable to impose a custodial sanction in light of the circumstances and seriousness of the facts. This would run contrary to the proportionality required of any measure entailing restriction of rights.

3.   Limitations on the right to liberty

The normal status of an defendant must be that of liberty. However, under the circumstances mentioned above, it may be necessary during the criminal process to restrict that party's freedom and even exceptionally deny it.

3.1.   Pre-trial supervision measures other than custody

Provisional imprisonment is, in accordance with Article 520.2 LECrim, an exceptional precautionary measure to ensure, on certain occasions and with the guarantees provided by law, the completion of the legal procedure and the execution of the decision. Nevertheless if that aim may be reached with similar efficiency by other less serious precautionary measures that impinge less on the rights of the accused, these must be preferred.

In fact, the LECrim seems to consider implicitly the precautionary measure of pre-trial release as an alternative to preventive detention.[37] Nevertheless on this point, the doctrine has reproached Spanish legislators on various occasions for their failure to regulate on alternative measures to prison, such as permanent traceability or house monitoring as provided for by other legal orders.

Even though not exactly an alternative precautionary measure to provisional imprisonment, a provision under Spanish law called "reduced" detention may be applied in which the accused is confined to a place other than a penitentiary center. "Reduced" detention can be adopted in two circumstances. First, when the defendant is ill and imprisonment in a penitentiary center would endanger his or her health, he or she may comply with the precautionary measure at home. The home is equipped with the necessary security measures and any absence, such as leaving home to receive treatment, must be authorized. The judge or tribunal may also order reduced provisional imprisonment when the accused is following drug desintoxication or rehabilitation that would in any case have been

---

37 Art. 529.1 LECrim.

ordered after the crime and where prison confinement would be detrimental to such treatment.

3.2.1. Pre-trial release

Pre-trial release is a precautionary method consisting in the limitation of the freedom of the defendant to move about, and is adopted by the judge or tribunal when it is ascertained that there are sufficient reasons to consider that a person has committed the crime in question and, given the circumstances of the case and the demands of the proceedings, it is necessary to restrict his or her liberty.

The right to freedom of a subject on pre-trial release is limited and subordinate to the criminal process. Nevertheless, the restriction of liberty resulting from this precautionary measure may vary since it is a versatile measure offering different options. These include the discretion of the Judge to choose the most adequate and proportional version in the specific circumstances in light of the requests made by the accusing parties and defence on appearing before the Public Prosecutor.

Hence, the defendant on pre-trial release normally also remains subject to other obligations that in some way restrict his or her right to liberty and/or other rights. Such restrictions include the obligation to register on established days with a local authority and for as long as the judge may order (Art. 530 LECrim) with the aim of ascertaining at specified intervals the whereabouts of the defendant on pre-trial release. As a rule, those on pre-trial release have to present on the 1st and 15th day of every month.[38] Along these same lines, the judge or tribunal may agree to the withholding of a defendant's passport on pre-trial release in order to guarantee their presence at trial.[39]

Lastly, a pre-trial release ruling may also order posting of a bond. If this were the case, the same resolution ordering this precautionary method also determines the amount and type of bond,[40] again in accordance with the principle

---

38 However, if the defendant fails to appear without a legitimate reason at the first summons of a judge or at any time at which his or her commitment to prison is deemed necessary, the provisions of Article 504.4 LECrim may be adopted provided the remaining circumstances also apply.

39 In the abbreviated procedure for crimes arising from the use and circulation of a motor vehicle when subject to pre-trial release, the judge or court may authorize the defendant to leave Spanish territory if the defendant's domicile or normal residence is in a country enjoying diplomatic relations with Spain. A prior hearing with the Public Prosecutor must be held and the defendant be able to supply sufficient guarantee that the monetary damages arising from the fact shall be covered, designating a person with a fixed domicile in Spain to receive any correspondence. Finally, defendant must provide a non-personal guarantee that he/she shall present before the judicial body in question. On failure to appear the trial will proceed, the damages determined and a default judgment lodged (Art. 765.2 LECrim).

40 Art. 529.2 LECrim.

of proportionality. As a result, various factors must be considered such as the nature of the crime, the social condition and history of the defendant, as well as other circumstances that may influence to a greater or lesser degree the interest of the defendant to place him or herself beyond the reach of the judicial authority.[41]

Like any other precautionary method, pre-trial release may be ordered solely in cases in which *fumus boni iuris* and *periculum in mora* concur.

In accordance with *fumus boni iuris,* the judge or tribunal may only agree to pre-trial release when a criminal complaint presents aspects of a crime and there are also sufficient reasons or evidence in the view of the judge to believe that person affected by the precautionary measure is liable. The proportionary principle also demands that not even pre-trial release may be ordered if the facts of the case would not lead to an eventual custodial sentence. To this regard, it may be argued that both legislator[42] and the Constitutional Court[43] seem to implicitly admit this possibility.

On the other hand, *periculum in mora* plays a differnt role in pre-trial release that it does in provisional imprisonment. When considering pre-trial release of a defendant as opposed to allowing him or her complete liberty of movement, the Judge must assess the risk to the normal functioning of the criminal process and the effectiveness of the sentence in light of the grounds proposed by the applicant, and whether the interim measures requested are suitable to ensure attendance at trial, the criminal process and the enforcement of the sentence eventually handed down. In the event that the weight of circumstances seems to indicate a risk that the above conditions would be jeopardized, pre-trial precautionary provisions are justified. The same assessment method also serves to determine how intensive the restriction of personal freedom should be: whether it should entail appearance of the defendant before a legal authority at set periods, passport confiscation, etc.

3.2.   Custody

Pre-trial detention is considered a necessary evil in all legal orders and today represents the most serious interference the state authority may exercise in the sphere of individual liberty, in the absence of a firm criminal sentence. It consists of denying the defendant his or her fundamental right to move about freely by

---

41 Art. 531 LECrim.
42 See for example Art. 539 LECrim.
43 Constitutional Court, Decision 66 / 1989.

confining him or her to a penitentiary center during the development of a criminal proceeding.

Provisional imprisonment may only be justified to the extent that it is absolutely necessary in order to defend fundamental legally-protected rights and that there are no other less radical mechanisms to achieve this. It follows that preventive detention shall not last longer than necessary.[44]

It should not be forgotten that provisional imprisonment involves the denial of liberty during a criminal process, i.e., before a court decision has been handed down and therefore during a period the defendant is protected by his or her fundamental right to presumption of innocence. On this point, the case law of the Constitutional Court is very clear that the presumption of innocence must be considered not only as a trial rule at the moment of issuing the ruling, but also as a rule of treatment during the entire process, i.e. all charged persons shall be considered innocent until found guilty and convicted. As a result, in order to legally overcome this rule of treatment on the presumption of innocence, sufficient elements must be seen to concur (*fumus boni iuris*) which must also be conducive to the aims or demands of the process (*periculum in mora*). Although pre-trial precautionary measures may be necessary to ensure the presence of the defendant and the results of the procedure, pre-trial detention may not be adopted if a prison sentence is not the most serious punishment that may be delivered in the case in question.

3.2.1. Requirements for the application of remand detention

Provisional imprisonment may be decreed when the three circumstances demanded by all precautionary measures concur: that of *fumus boni iuris, periculum in mora* and the judicial decision confirming that the legal constitutional aim pursued is consistent with the nature of the measure, pursuant to Article 503 LECrim.[45] In the concrete case of provisional imprisonment noted below, these circumstances give rise to a relatively complex system due to the multitude of exceptions and specific points that we will now examine.

Fumus boni iuris or existence of valid grounds on which to order provisional imprisonment demands the concurrence of two elements, which are at the same time *objective* and *subjective*. The objective component of this first circumstance demands that the criminal complaint include one or several facts that present the characteristics of a crime.[46]

The type of sentence envisaged by for the crime in question plays an essential

---

44 Arts. 504.1 and 528 LECrim.
45 Constitution Court, Decisions 56/1997; 14/2000; 47/2000; 207/2000; 217/2001.
46 Art. 503.1(1) LECrim.

rule in this issue for a multitude of reasons. On the one hand, the principle of proportionality forbids a pre-trial measure of preventive detention when the toughest sanction for the case in question does not include a prison sentence. By the same token, the extent of the prison sentence envisaged by law serves to establish the limits of provisional imprisonment. In this sense, the alleged crime has to be punishable with a sentence of two years or more,[47] ii. e., when the prison sentence is fairly severe. Pre-trial detention may not be ordered if the eventual prison sentence is less than two years since the criminal fact in question lacks the gravity justifying such a serious precautionary measure.

However, the rule presents three exceptional cases, in which, despite the fact that the crime entails a prison sentence of less than the two year limit, the judge or tribunal may agree to provisional imprisonment if this is deemed objectively necessary on account of the repercussions for the defendant and the entity of the sentence that could be imposed:[48]

– when the defendant has a criminal record for an intentional crime not ex-punged nor susceptible to expunging;[49]
– when at least two judicial summons have been ordered in the previous two years;[50]
– to avoid criminal reiteration in the case of an intentional crime and when the defendant's police record or his/her actions infer activity within a criminal organization or habitual criminal activities.[51]

In the first and third case, the circumstances of *periculum in mora*[52] that we examine below, would also have to concur. The second case sets forth a cir-cumstance in which in addition to *fumus boni iuris, periculum in mora* would also apply, with the purpose of preventing the defendant absconding.

On the other hand, the subjective component of *fumus* demands that there be sufficient reasons in the complaint to believe that the person against whom the prison ruling is requested is criminally responsible for the crime.[53] Therefore, even though the fact and the participation of the defendant may be accredited, if

---

47 Art. 503.1(1) LECrim.
48 Art. 503.1(3) LECrim.
49 Art. 503.1(1) LECrim.
50 Art. 503.1(3a) LECrim.
51 Art. 503.2 LECrim.
52 As will be explained below, the only constitutional purposes that may justify pre-trial de-tention are those of avoiding absconding of the defendant, preventing hindrance to the investigation and the hiding or destroying of evidence. In any other circumstance, pre-trial detention would violate the constitutional authorization for denial of liberty during the process.
53 Art. 503.1(2) LECrim.

the crime was committed while there was a concurrence of justification, the precautionary measure would be absolutely inappropriate.[54]

The circumstance of *periculum in mora* centres on the concrete dangers that any adoption of a precautionary measure before an eventual decision tries to overcome. In provisional imprisonment, the circumstance of *periculum in mora* centres on the aims pursued, which must comply with constitutional provisions on pain of the precautionary measure being declared illegal.

Nevertheless, Article 17.4 of the Constitution is very succinct on this point stating only that "by law, the maximum period of duration or provisional imprisonment shall be determined." A hasty reading of this clause could lead to the view that for the Constituent Assembly the aim that provisional imprisonment plays is irrelevant insofar as the law regulates it and establishes a maximum period of duration; which is tantamount to saying that once these two conditions are satisfied, any aim would be constitutionally legitimate.

Nevertheless, the Constitutional Court has highlighted that this would be an erroneous conclusion because the essential content and respect of the fundamental rights to liberty and presumption of innocence guarantee that these may be waived only under exceptional circumstances to allow an effective criminal process. Hence, doctrine and case law have gradually discarded some of the aims which, if applied to provisional imprisonment, render this unconstitutional. Accordingly, the aim of provisional imprisonment can consist neither of anticipating the sentence[55] nor of alleviating social alarm following a particular criminal act. Nor can it be used as an instrument of criminal examination or to encourage the discovery of the crime since this would turn penal examination into something very similar to investigative torture.

As a result, the legislator has expressly denied that the danger of concealment or destruction of evidence may by itself infer exercise of the right of defense or lack of collaboration by the defendant in the course of the investigations.[56] The legislator further adds that in order to assess the existence of this danger, the capacity of the defendant to access by him or herself or through third parties the sources of evidence and influence other defendants, witnesses, experts or any other persons, must also be examined.

After the modification of Organic Law 13/2003, the LECrim provides for, in accordance with the Constitutional Court, that provisional imprisonment may only be ordered when some of the following aims are pursued:[57]

---

54 Art. 502.4 LECrim.
55 Constitutional Court, Decision 128/1995.
56 Art. 503.1(3) LECrim.
57 Art. 503.1(3) LECrim.

- to ensure the presence of the defendant, to avert absconding and being beyond the reach of justice, thereby jeopardizing its exercise.[58] The judge will have to examine all the different factors that may produce a risk of absconding, including the nature of the facts, the severity of the criminal sentence that may be imposed, the defendant's family, work and economic condition as well as the imminence of the trial. When considering the likelihood of absconding, the Law refers to the defendant's police record, citing at least two summons to appear as well as investigation by any judicial body of the defendant's record over the two previous years.
- to prevent the defendant from hiding, manipulating or destroying the sources of evidence, for which attention must be given to the ability of the defendant or third parties to access sources of evidence or influence other defendants, witnesses or experts in the event of the defendant being released.
- to prevent criminal reiteration. Although the Constitutional Court[59] and ECHR have guaranteed the legitimacy of this aim, as mentioned in the previous section, I disagree. In my view this starts from the erroneous position of presumption of guilt, which goes against the fundamental right to presumption of innocence.

3.2.2. Time Limits

One of the fundamental problems in refusal of pre-trial release is the issue of duration. It was not by chance that the Spanish Constituent Assembly decided to make express reference in Articles Art. 17.2 and 4 of the Constitution to this point in the case of the detention and provisional imprisonment.

Provisional imprisonment may only last for a prescribed time and for such as the reasons justifying it prevail. As a result, any precautionary measure must be immediately revoked if the aim pursued ceases to exist, if the provisional imprisonment no longer fulfills the aim for which it was ordered, or as soon as the innocence of the preventively detained prisoner is ascertained.

Article 504 LECrim establishes a complex system of maximum periods of provisional imprisonment that follow two parameters: the severity of the violation and the aim pursued when the provisional imprisonment was ordered.

- When the provisional imprisonment was ordered to avoid the concealment, alteration or destruction of sources of evidence, its duration may not exceed six months.

---

58 Constitutional Court, Decisions 33/1999; 14/2000; 169/2001.
59 Constitutional Court, Decisions 40/1987; 47/2000; 207/2000; 217/2001.

- When preventive imprisonment was ordered to avert the risk of absconding by the defendant or the danger of criminal reiteration, the measure may not last more than two years if the crime indicates a sentence denying liberty for more than three years. If the envisaged sentence for the crime is equal or less than three years, the pre-trial detention cannot last more than one year. In this case, when the defendant is remanded in custody to prevent him from absconding or repeating the crime, the precautionary measure may exceptionally be extended if circumstances exist whereby it is likely that the decision will not be issued in the maximum periods referred to. Accordingly, imprisonment may be extended, by means of a hearing of the defendant, Public Prosecutor and by means of a ruling, up to two years if the sentence indicated for the crime exceeds three years and up to six months if the sentence is equal or less than three years.

Naturally, once the periods referred to have elapsed, the defendant must be released[60] even if the criminal procedure has not been concluded. However, if subsequently the defendant fails to appear without a legitimate reason on being summoned by the judge or tribunal, a new pre-trial detention may be ordered.

These maximum periods are absolute and in no case may they be exceeded since they constitute a constitutional requirement that includes the guarantee established in Article 17.4 of the Constitution whereby exceeding the period would entail a violation of the right to liberty.[61]

4.   Procedures

Provisional imprisonment may be decreed by the competent judicial authority during the entire criminal procedure provided previously examined cases warrant this. This interim measure is an indispensable tool to ensure the defendant complies with the legal process and the criminal process is accomplished.

---

60 The Criminal Code provides for a sentence of disqualification or suspension of any judicial authority failing to decree release of the defendant once the maximum periods have been fulfilled (Arts. 530 and 532).
61 Constitutional Court, Decisions 127/1984; 40/1987; 103/1992; 37/1996; 48/1998; 142/1998; 49/1999; 71/2000; 147/2000; 206/2000; 231/2000; 305/2000.

4.1.   Domestic Procedure

In accordance with these cases, provisional imprisonment may be agreed to by various judges depending on the state and the phase of the criminal process. During the investigation phase, only the pre-trial judge may order provisional imprisonment.[62] However, if for any reason, the detainee has been placed at the disposal of a judge other than the official in charge of the process, and if the detainee cannot be transferred within 72 hours, this other judge, complying with the procedure discussed below, may rule on the personal situation of the detainee and decide whether to order provisional imprisonment, conditional release, release, etc. Once the trial begins, it is the criminal judge or tribunal that will have this responsibility. In the event of appeal against the final decision, the competence for deciding on pre-decision custody lies with the court or high court (*Juzgado de lo Penal, Audiencia Provincial* or *Juzgado Central de lo Penal, Audiencia Nacional*).

With regard to the concrete procedure required to adopt the precautionary measure of provisional imprisonment, as a rule the judge or relevant tribunal hears the testimony of the defendant[63] and, in the event of a decision to proceed with preventive detention, calls a hearing to decide on these points. The Prosecutor and detainee or defendant, assisted by counsel,[64] are summoned to appear.

Let us now examine in detail some of the aspects of this procedure. Since the LECrim amendment of 1995, the judge may only order provisional imprisonment if the Prosecutor or any accusing party request this interim measure. Previously, the pre-trial judge had the power to automatically determine the circumstances of the case, and without taking further steps, order the defendant be taken into custody.

In general, once the detained defendant has been placed at the disposal of the examining judge entrusted with hearing his or her testimony, there are three options available: a) the judge may ascertain that the facts do not constitute a criminal offence or that the defendant ws not party to any criminal offence, in which case he or she will be released, all complaints will be dropped and the defendant removed from the criminal process; b) the judge may ascertain that although the circumstances do not warrant an order of provisional imprisonment or pre-trial release on bond, the subject remains nonetheless a defendant in the case, thereby issuing an order establishing the periods or times at which the defendant must appear before the judicial authority; c) the judge deems it

---

62   Art. 502.1 LECrim.
63   As will be seen below, the defendant may or may not be detained.
64   Even if the criminal Judge is not competent. Arts. 499 and 505.6 LECrim.

necessary to order pre-trial detention or pre-trial release on bail, in which the same judge shall fix the date of a hearing.

Even if the defendant is not detained, the judge may subsequent deem one of these precautionary measures appropriate, in which case a hearing will be called. Likewise, when the accusing parties are informed that there is a procedure to adopt imprisonment or release on bond, they are likewise entitled to apply to the examining magistrate for a hearing.[65]

In the event of the defendant being released when the judge ascertains that the circumstances exist to adopt precautionary measure, a hearing must be called within 72 hours.[66] Furthermore, in the event of a provisional imprisonment order being issued, the accusing party must proceed to request the measure at the subsequent hearing, failing which the judge shall revoke the measure and release the defendant.[67]

The hearing, which must be held in order to confirm provisional imprisonment or pre-trial release on bond, is called "vistilla" in forensic practice. The procedure aims to determine the legitimacy of the measure in such a manner that if no one requests an intermim measure, the judge may not order such, with the result that if the defendant being held in custody, he or she will be immediately released.[68] This requirement is a tribute to the adversarial principle and the principle of contradiction. It also slight redefines the role of the judge in the criminal examination process. The hearing to which the Prosecutor's Office, the accusers and defendant (assisted by counsel) shall be summoned, has to be held within the shortest timeframe possible and in any case within seventy-two hours following the moment in which the detainee is placed at the disposal of a judge. At that time, allegations may be made and evidence proposed that is pertinent to the matter in question and the adoption of the precautionary measure, which may be ordered and executed within 72 hours from the moment the defendant was placed at the disposal of the judge.[69]

After the hearing, the judge shall issue a justified decision in the form of a ruling which, in the event of commitment to prison, shall also contain the reasons why the measure is considered necessary and proportional.[70] The preventive detention order may be appealed against within five days following notice of the ruling, by means of a document laying down the reasons for the challenge.

As described at length above, the procedure and system for pre-trial custody

---

65 Art. 505.2 LECrim.
66 Art. 539.4 LECrim.
67 Art. 505.4 LECrim.
68 Art. 505.4 LECrim.
69 Art. 505.3 LECrim.
70 Art. 506.1 LECrim.

are eminently reviewable. In addition, all actors must ensure that preventive detention is not prolonged more than necessary.[71] Accordingly, the time spent in prison by the defendant prior to trial must be considered as well as the considerations leading to the order, with particular attention to the fact that the simple passage of time lessens the danger of the defendant absconding even in the event of a severe sentence[72] and, by the same token, if the aim pursued has already been achieved. When the justification for preventive detention no longer subsists, the judge shall issue another ruling. On this occasion, there is no need for a special hearing. Similarly, the judge may replace preventive detention with a more lenient interim measure. Continued refusal of pre-trial release beyond the existence of the aim it serves constitutes a violation of the Constitution.[73] Like a pre-trial detention order, a ruling to lift preventive custody is also appealable. Obviously in the event of acquittal, even if the case is not concluded, any pre-trial imprisonment measure will be lifted.

4.2.   Court resolution granting an interim measure

A court resolution adopting a criminal interim measure must be sufficiently reasoned since it limits the rights of the accused or deprives him or her of the right to freedom at a moment when a final judgment on any alleged guilt has still be taken.

Clearly, the rule must be very cautious when establishing the means of assuming a defendant party's culpability because, in material terms, the conviction is effectively anticipated. This is borne out by the fact that compensation may be recognised in the event of an interim measure being applied inappropriately.

The court order (the form given to the judge's decision) should explain in appropriate length and detail on what basis it complies with all the presumptions and requirements imposed by law for issuing the interim measure in question. The use mere "standards" or formulae for all situations, i. e. so-called "standard forms," are forbidden, as this would be a breach of the obligation to provide reasoned grounds. This duty is imposed by the Constitution on all judgments[74] and also applies to any orders entailing a restriction of rights.

However, given the relatively wide range of interim measures, from lien on assets and withdrawal of a driver's licence to the curtailing of personal freedom, the requirement for reasoned grounds may be adjusted. Clearly, even though a

---

71 Arts. 504.1 and 528.3 LECrim.
72 Constitutional Court, Decisions 128 / 1995; 14 / 1996; 37 / 1996.
73 Constitutional Court, Decision 178 / 1985.
74 Art. 120.1 CE.

lack of grounds is not permitted, in order to adopt certain measures, particularly those affecting basic human rights and freedoms, a higher degree of reasoning is required. According to the Constitutional Court, an order of provisional imprisonment must be sufficiently and reasonably justified. Failure to ascertain and explain all the elements justifying such a measure would not only jeopardize an individual's right to effective court protection but also the right to personal freedom.[75]

Thus, the need for reasoned grounds not only arises from a need to uphold the right to be informed of the reasons for judicial resolutions, legitimating the decision adopted, but also ensures the law is exercised to the benefit of the accused party. Only in this way may decisions regarding interim measures be challenged. If the grounds for a measure are not made known to the parties, their chances of bringing a challenge are reduced to a pure formality or must be based on mere conjecture or supposition, to the detriment of effective court protection and the effective guarantee of rights.

In any event, when ordering an interim measure, whether at the request of the prosecution or *ex officio*, the judge must ascertain that clear, rational signs of criminality exist, that the criminal process is at risk were the measure not adopted, and that the specific pre-trial measure is both required and proportional to the circumstances.

It is clear that, unlike the case of a final judgment where the judge makes a decision on past events based on a reasoned conviction of culpability beyond all reasonable doubt, a decision on interim measures is much more complex.

In fact, an interim measure order delivered by a judge must necessarily provide grounds on three types of issues: first, *fumus boni iuris* and evidence of criminality; whether the facts took place; if they amount to criminal acts, and whether there is a likelihood that the defendant is guilty, i.e. the same issues covered by the final judgment.

Secondly, the judge must also make a prediction on a future event: *periculum in mora*, the potential risk to the lawsuit if the interim measure is not adopted, e.g. that the defendant will abscond, evidence manipulated or destroyed or an asset removed from the reach of the court.

This requires that one or more reasonably possible hypotheses be drawn up according to the knowledge available to the judge; any hypotheses not likely to be confirmed or unrelated to the situation at hand, or manifestly absurd, should be excluded. *Periculum in mora* should be examined on the grounds adopted (and explained) by the judge to confirm that the hearing of the accused during the proceedings is guaranteed and to what extent, whether the investigation may

---

75 Constitutional Court, Decisions 37/1996; 62/1996; 158/1996; 98/1997; 107/1997; 146/1997; 206/2000.

be adequated conducted and any eventual penalty complied with; an assessment of these circumstances will determine the type and degree of the measure to be imposed.[76]

Finally, the court resolution will examine the specific interim measure adopted and justify the need for its adoption, i. e. its suitability and, *a contrario*, any another measure that is less burdensome for the defendant.

Since the circumstances and facts available to the judge when drawing a conclusion have not been subject to a hearing with the parties to the lawsuit and are incomplete (very often the decision is adopted at the beginning of the investigation stage to obtain the necessary evidence), and since the judge is called to make an assessment of future events, the reasons adduced cannot evidently be based on a conviction beyond all reasonable doubt.

Although the judge ordering the interim measures cannot assure certainty, he must nonethless not be arbitrary in his decision as this would be in outright conflict with the need for reasoned grounds. The measures must be justified on the reasonable likelihood within the context of a lawsuit, and with the knowledge available to the judge, provided this knowledge confirms that the requirements applicable to interim measures are met.

For this reason and since the initial understanding of the facts by the judge will be subsequently part of the criminal lawsuit, the judge ordering the interim measures must, if necessary, gradually adjust his initial decision, i. e. if reasons arise to remove the defendant subject to interim measures from the criminal process, such measures should be immediately lifted.

The same will apply if the circumstances of the crime, the liability or risk to the lawsuit change, in which case the judge will adjust his decision accordingly on pain of breaching the principle of necessity or proportionality.

The LECrim, as established by Article 17.4 of the Spanish Constitution, provides for a maximum duration for provisional imprisonment. Therefore, at the expiry of this time-frame, even if all other components of the case remain unchanged, the defendant's freedom must be declared *ex officio*.

In practice, the Spanish criminal law system makes excessive recourse to interim measures without adequate justification in many cases and without heed to the fact that the harm arising from a measure of this kind usually greatly exceeds the benefits of a judgment of conviction. All parties to a lawsuit should be forewarned to ensure that the principle of necessity is strictly applied to avert a situation in which enforcement of punishment is voided of any real content and the day of conviction becomes the day of release of somebody who has been temporarily imprisoned.

---

76 *Taruffo* [2], pp. 303–317.

4.3.   International Procedure

The denial of the liberty of movement of a person may also be ordered in relation to a criminal process not heard before a Spanish Tribunal, but at the request of foreign judges – European or otherwise – as in the case of the EAW[77] or extradition.[78]

The EAW replaces the instrument of extradition within the European Union while arrest requests from other States continue to be treated as an extradition matter. The EAW is essentially a more agile, simple and strictly judicial procedure than the former and based on the principle of mutual confidence and recognition of judicial decision. Spain was the first EU Member State to transpose the EAW FD into its legal system. The Spanish law of transposition is essentially characterized[79] by its literal following of the FD, to such a degree that instead of a transposition it at times seems like a translation.

In the case we now address the precautionary measures restricting the right to liberty of a person may also be upheld in the course of the procedure of execution of a EAW. In Spain, the judicial authority executing the European arrest warrant is the Central Examination Courts, which handle the initial process and adopt the decision on delivery if the summoned person consents and if the Prosecutor does not communicate a reason for denial of the request. Should these two conditions fail to exist, the Criminal Chamber of the National Court becomes competent. Accordingly, if a person is arrested in Spain by virtue of EAW, the individual must be taken in the shortest period possible, and in any case within 72 hours, from their place of detention and brought before the Central Examination Court. There he or she shall be informed of his or her rights, of the contents of the EAW and the possibility of consenting irrevocably to delivery to the issuing State. This hearing shall be held with the assistance of the Prosecutor's Office, the lawyer of the detainee and if necessary, an interpreter, and must be performed in conformity with the provisions governing testimony of the detained persons of criminal procedural law.

In the course of this hearing the Central examining judge shall decide on the personal situation of the detainee, and in light of the allegations of the Prosecutor and the defense, on the adoption of provisional imprisonment, pre-trial release or another precautionary measure that will ensure the availability of the person in question. The Central Examining Judge, having considered the circumstances of the case, shall decide by means of a ruling aimed at ensuring

---

77 See Law 3/2003. On the EAW cf. *Castillejo Manzanares* [1], pp. 1–3; *Jimeno-Bulnes*.
78 Law 5/1985 on Response to extradition requests.
79 *Oubiña Barbolla*, pp. 473–596.

execution of the European warrant. An appeal may be filed against this decision on the interim measure before the Criminal Chamber of the National Court.

The duration of provisional imprisonment and pre-trial release remain subject to the decision that ends the procedure for the enforcement of the EAW. On this point, when the person in question does not consent to being handed over and the Public Prosecutor indicates a cause for mandatory refusal, the Central examining judge shall send the decision to the Criminal Chamber of the National Court ("Audiencia Nacional") that shall have a maximum of 60 days from the issuing of the detention order to approve or reject the handing over to the issuing State. In any case, the handing over of the person requested must be physically effective within 10 days[80] following the judicial decision of surrender. If this maximum period of surrender expires without the person being received by the issuing state, that person shall be released.

As a primary instrument of European judicial cooperation in the criminal procedural framework, the EAW has been in force for more than seven years. It is therefore time to assess its effective operation, the various transpositions that Member States have made, the problems which may inhibit this instrument of cooperation as well as verify the degree of confidence in the judicial decisions of other Member States, the respect of fundamental rights etc. Evaluations and studies[81] of this type are highly valuable and a means of allowing the design of more and better instruments of judicial criminal cooperation, the reformulation of the instruments already in existence and more effective judicial cooperation between Member States in the hope of developing an effective space of liberty, security and justice.

---

80 Exceptionally, Article 20 Law 3/2003 provides for the possibility of an extension of another 10 days in two cases. The first when, for reasons beyond the control of any of the issuing State or executing State, the execution cannot be verified in this period. Also when due to serious humanitarian reasons the surrender has been suspended, but surrender must take place as soon as these grounds have ceased to exist; in this case the surrender shall take place within ten days of the new date agreed when these grounds have ceased to exist.

81 In this sense we point out *The European Arrest Warrant in Law and in Practice: a comparative study for the consolidation of the European law-enforcement area*, Coimbra, 2010, available at http://opj.ces.uc.pt/pdf/EAW_Final_Report_Nov_2010.pdf in a European research project JLS/2007/JPEN/245 and ABAC 30-CE-0178645/00–20 made by the Centro de Estudos Sociais (CES) of Coimbra University (Portugal) and the collaboration of Utrecht School of Law (Netherlands), L'Istituto Ricerca sui Sistemi Giudiziari (Italy) and the Association Jueces para la Democracia and Institute Alonso Martínez de Justicia y Litigación of Carlos III University (Spain).

5.   Recent Reform and Proposals of Reform

The range of interim measures foreseen by the LECrim is certainly scant: provisional imprisonment, parole with or without bail, certain accessory measures
such as withholding of a passport or the surveillance of the accused, as well as
asset-related measures. Indeed immediate reform of Spanish law should be
envisaged to incorporate alternatives to imprisonment and other, more tech-
nically feasible measures that do not infringe personal freedom so drastically.

5.1.   Preventive Detention

As has been advanced, Organic Law 13 / 2003 reformed provisional imprisonment in compliance with the LECrim. The case-law of the Constitutional Court
to date demands a modification of this respectful institution within the framework of fundamental rights to liberty and to the presumption of innocence. As
indicated in the Introduction on provisional imprisonment, reform had to
balance the state's duty to effectively pursue crime, on the one hand, with its
duty to ensure wide-ranging freedom of the citizen[82].

The essential points of the reform were the circumstances, duration and
procedure necessary for adopting provisional imprisonment. In the case of the
circumstances, without referring to the previous points, the minimum limit of
provisional imprisonment was established: two years except in exceptional
cases. Equally important is the specification that preventive detention may only
be justified by constitutionally valid aims,[83] i. e. that the defendant is likely to
place him or herself beyond the reach of judicial action, conceal, alter or destroy
evidence or may commit further criminal acts. In this last case, there is the
further essential requirement of the principle of proportionality that prevents
provisional imprisonment being imposed on the basis of any generic or abstract
risk of committing a crime.

As to the duration, the legislator echoes the foresight shown by the Constitution whereby provisional imprisonment cannot last more than the time
necessary and in any event, may be enforced solely while legitimate constitutional purposes justify its continuing existence. This places directly or indirectly
a burden on the administration of criminal justice to act without due delay to
ensure that any provisionally detained person be judged in reasonable time and
may be released during the proceeding.

Finally, with regard to the procedure, the reform maintains the general rule

---

82 Constitutional Court, Decision 41 / 1982.
83 Art. 503 LECrim.

that Organic Law of 22. 05. 1995 had previously introduced, whereby the judge or tribunal may only agree to provisional imprisonment when the Public Prosecutor or an accusing party requests this and in any case, by means of a justified ruling after holding a contradictory hearing in order to hear the allegations of all the parties.[84]

This is the first extensive reform of provisional imprisonment system. It was long awaited and therefore availed itself of the doctrine. This does not, however, signify that provisional imprisonment necessarily comply with the requisites demanded or may not extended for more than the reasonable period. This is the case, for example, of extensions of provisional imprisonment ordered at the last minute, less than two days before the provisional imprisonment period ends, or in the case of the almost automatic provisional imprisonment imposed on subjects requested by a EAW.

5.2.   Interim measures, protective measures and other measures

Apart from strictly interim measures, the LECrim provides for other protective measures that pursue other purposes – no longer the guarantee an effective lawsuit and enforceable judgment, but rather to ensure the safety of the victims of criminal conduct who would probably be unable to defend themselves from future attacks of the offender with their own legal resources. For this reason, Article 13 LECrim establishes that protection of parties attacked or harmed by a crime, including their relatives or third parties, should be the first measure conducted in a criminal lawsuit.

Since 2004 these measures have focused on protecting women suffering gender violence. The Law attempts to protect victims while the criminal lawsuit is being processed and until definitve judgment is delivered establishing liability and determining the accessory consequences of the crime. As a consequence, protective measures, in the same way as interim measures,[85] relate to an ongoing criminal lawsuit and their content in either case may be identical. Furthermore, they entail limitations or prohibitions on rights, which is why the requirements (including a reasoned court resolution) to adopt such measures should be identical.

However, even if regulated in the same Article[86] provisional imprisonment as an interim measure and imprisonment ordered to protect the victim are two

---

84 Art. 505 LECrim.
85 *Colomer Hernández*, pp. 131 – 151; *Castillejo Manzanares* [2] pp. 2026 – 2034; *Fernández Fustes*.
86 Art. 503 LECrim.

conceptually different regulatory provisions and must comply to two different sets of requirements.

The aim of these measures, which include, among other, orders to abandon the home, prohibitions on residence, movement or communication, as well as the so-called protection order under Article 544ter LECrim, is not to avoid concealment of the crime or the flight from Justice, but rather to protect the victim from probable future attacks. The legislator authorizes these measures if there is accusatory evidence brought by a judicial authority against a party protected by the presumption of innocence.

As a result, in this case the *fumus boni iuris* principle is fulfilled by the court's appreciation. It is not *periculum in mora* (danger for the orderly progress of the lawsuit due to delay) that is here fulfilled but rather *periculum in damnum* (a founded danger of recidivism), based on a presumption of guilt.

It follows that these measures are similar to provisional civil protection (e. g. measures foreseen in matrimonial cases) since they stress the danger of recidivism, a feature that individual interim measures have largely tried to avoid for the reason that it is an assumption, that somehow, anticipates the effects of the judgment. As a result, rather than an interim measure, it is more of a protective and exceptional instrument, to the extent that it affects basic human rights and is therefore limited in scope (though the requirements applicable to interim measures are still valid).

Together with the provisional effects and protection of the victim, in Spanish criminal lawsuits there are other different measures aimed at protecting society, and which are somehow unrelated to a strict guarantee of procedural development or enforcement of the judgment, i. e. unrelated to the very purpose underpinning interim measures.

In effect, apart from measures to protect the victims, the LECrim allows the withdrawal of a driver's licence and the provisional closure of businesses, premises or establishments. It is highly debatable, however, whether these really constitute authentic interim measures, i. e. are a sort of anticipatory protection, amounting to measures that will be brought in once the pending case finally reaches the judgment stage and executes the measures anticipated in the interim order. Anticipatory protection is a unique type of protection with its own, separate *raison d'être* compared to interim protection, and it is especially common in civil proceedings but is unheard of in criminal proceedings, which traditionally hold that the content of a judgment of conviction, i. e. the penalty, cannot be anticipated on the grounds of mere suspicion.

Naturally these measures, which are materially identical to penalties, are not justified on strictly procedural grounds. Nor may they hinder basic human rights, particularly the right to freedom. Therefore curtailing freedom of movement may never be justified on the grounds of defending society for whatever reason: the demand for vengeance or on account of the social alarm caused by the crime (e. g. suspension of a public post), nor on the basis of the public interest and the need to prevent certain conduct from being reproduced or reiterated. However these measures may affect the exercise of other rights, such as forbidding a person to drive a motor vehicle by withdrawing his or her driver's licence.

Whatever the legal instrument, for any of these measures to become effective, the party in question must be heard and allowed to plead in his or her own defence. Furthermore, as in all (probabilistic) prognoses, there is a high likelihood of error, which requires rapid correction.

Furthermore the guarantees, surrounding the decision and the cautionary measures adopted by the judge, should be stricter as there is a risk that the consequences of the measure may be more burdensome than the criminal sanction.

Bibliography

Arnaiz Serrano et al., Derecho procesal penal, Tirant lo Blanch (2005).

Calamandrei, Piero, Introduzione allo studio sistematico dei provvedimenti cautelari, Cedam (1936).

Castillejo Manzanares, Raquel, [1] El procedimiento español para la emisión y ejecución de una orden de detención y entrega europea, in: 587 Actualidad Jurídica Aranzadi (2003), pp. 1 – 3; [2] Cuestiones que suscita la Ley Orgánica de Medidas de Protección Integral contra la Violencia de Género, in: La Ley: Revista jurídica española de doctrina, jurisprudencia y bibliografía (3 / 2005), pp. 2026 ff.

Catalina Benavente, María Ángeles, Los supuestos de detención en los casos de terrorismo: propuestas para una reforma, in: Faraldo Cabana, Patricia et al. (eds.), Derecho penal de excepción: terrorismo e inmigración, Tirant lo Blanch (2007), pp. 171 ff.

Colmenero Guerra, José Antonio, Ciudadanía y Justicia. Eficacia y Legitimidad de la Administración de justicia, in: Nuevas Políticas Públicas: Anuario multidisciplinar para la modernización de las Administraciones Públicas (5 / 2009), pp. 117 ff. Available in http://www.juntadeandalucia.es/institutodeadministracionpublica/anuario/articulos/descargas/anuario_n5_2009/05_EST_04_COLMENERO.pdf.

Colomer Hernández, Ignacio, El Ministerio Fiscal y la lucha contra la violencia de género, in: La Administración de Justicia en la Ley Integral contra la Violencia de Género, Ministerio de Justicia (2005), pp. 131 ff.

Damaska, Mirjan, Las caras de la Justicia y el Poder del estado. Análisis comparado del proceso legal (Translation from English into Spanish by Morales Vidal and Ruiz-Tagle Vial), Edición Jurídica de Chile (2000).

Fernández Fustes, María Dolores, La intervención de la víctima en el proceso penal, Valencia, Tirant lo Blanch (2004).

Fiss, Owen M., El derecho como razón pública (Translation from English into Spanish by Restrepo Saldarriaga), Marcial Pons (2007).

Gude Fernández, Ana, El *Habeas Corpus* en España, Tirant lo Blanch (2008).

Hassemer, Winfried, Fundamentos de Derecho Penal (Translation from English into Spanish by Muñoz Conde and Arroyo Zapatero), Bosch (1984).

Hassemer, Winfried / Muñoz Conde, Francisco, Introducción a la Criminología y al derecho penal, Tirant lo Blanch (1989).

Jimeno-Bulnes, Mar, European Judicial Cooperation in Criminal Matters, in: European Law Journal (9 / 2003).

Moreno Catena, Víctor, [1] La garantía de los derechos fundamentales durante la investigación penal, in: Problemas actuales del proceso penal y derechos fundamentales, 7 Cuadernos penales (2010); [2], Sobre el derecho de defensa: cuestiones generales, 8 Teoría y Derecho: revista del pensamiento jurídico (2010), pp. 17 – 40; [3] Manual de derecho procesal penal, 4ᵗʰ ed., Tirant lo Blanch (2010).

Moreno Catena, Víctor / Catalina Benavente, María Ángeles, Limiting Fundamental Rights in the fight against Terrorism in Spain, in: Wade, Marianne / Maljevic, Almir (eds.), A War on Terror? The European Stance on a New Threat, Changing Laws and Human Rights Implication, Springer (2010), pp. 443 ff.

Oubiña Barbolla, Sabela, The European arrest warrant in law and in practice: a comparative study for the consolidation of the European law-enforcement area, Permanent Observatory of Portuguese Justice (2010). Available in English at http://opj.ces.uc.pt/ pdf/EAW_Final_Report_Nov_2010.pdf.

Taruffo, Michele, [1] Ideas para una teoría de la decisión justa, in: Sobre las fronteras. Escritos sobre la Justicia civil (Translation from Italian intro Spanish by Quintero de Prieto), Temis (2006), pp. 199 ff.; [2] El juicio pronóstico del juez entre ciencia privada y prueba científica, *ivi*, pp. 303 ff.

VVAA, The European Arrest Warrant in law and in practice: a comparative study for the consolidation of the European law-enforcement area, Permanent Observatory of Portuguese Justice (November / 2010), European research project JLS / 2007 / JPEN / 245 and ABAC30-CE-0178645 / 00 – 20. http://opj.ces.uc.pt/pdf/EAW_Final_Report_Nov_2010.pdf.

Vives Antón, Tomás Salvador, [1] La reforma del proceso penal. Comentarios a la ley de medidas urgentes de reforma procesal, Tirant lo Blanch (1992); [2] La libertad como pretexto, Tirant lo Blanch (1995).

III. Comparative Analysis

Stefano Ruggeri

Personal Liberty in Europe. A comparative analysis of pre-trial precautionary measures in criminal proceedings

Table of Contents

Table of Abbreviations

ACHR	American Convention on Human Rights
CPP	*Codice di procedura penale* (Code of Criminal Procedure)
EAW FD	Framework Decision on the European Arrest Warrant
EU FRCh	Charter of Fundamental Rights of the European Union
ECHR	European Convention on Human rights
ECtHR	European Court of Human Rights
EU	European Union
FD	Framework Decision
GC	German Constitution
IC	Italian Constitution
ICCPR	International Covenant on Civil and Political Rights
JFS area	Area of justice, security and freedom
LECrim	*Ley de enjuiciamiento criminal* (Code of Criminal Procedure)
RStPO	*Reichsstrafprozessordnung* (Code of Criminal Procedure of the *Reich*)
SC	Spanish Constitution
StPO	*Strafprozessordnung* (Code of Criminal Procedure)
StPÄndG	*Strafprozessänderungsgesetz* (Act amending the Code of Criminal Procedure)
TEU	Treaty on the European Union
TFEU	Treaty on the Functioning of the European Union
UDHR	Universal Declaration of Human Rights
UK	United Kingdom
US	United States (of America)

1. Introduction. Pre-trial precautionary measures in a multilevel system of protection of personal freedom in Europe

Over recent years most of the criminal justice systems in Europe have witnessed a rising tendency to enhance the role of pre-trial inquiries. Paradoxically, this trend has been accompanied in many continental countries[1] by structural legislative reforms and case-law developments aimed at strengthening the adversarial character of criminal procedures. Despite the centrality of trial decisions,

---

1 For instance, in Italy Law 63/2001, while domesticating the principles of due process enshrined in the Constitution through the Constitution Amendment Act 2/1999, has strengthened the pre-conviction assessment of the suspicion of guilt. On this constitutional reform see *Marzaduri* [6], pp. 762 ff.

the criminal justice systems in the common law world have seen equally significant developments with the granting of unprecedented investigative powers to prosecution authorities in the pre-trial stages aimed mostly at fighting new forms of serious and organized crime.[2] Such phenomena have considerably increased the use of different kinds of pre-trial measure for diverse purposes and have had a heavy impact on the fundamental rights of individuals involved in criminal procedures.

In this context, a comparative study on pre-trial precautionary measures impacting the right to personal liberty in Europe provides a unique vantage point, and by the same token raises crucial questions. What is meant by precautionary measures in Europe? What is meant by pre-trial means, i. e. what chronological-procedural extension can be attached to the pre-trial stages within the criminal process? And, above all, what is meant by personal freedom in Europe? Are European countries rooted on a uniform notion of this classical liberty and has it remained unchanged over recent years even within the same legal system? What suggestions or limitations derive from ECtHR case-law and what challenges is the EU facing in this field? What results can a comparative analysis be expected to achieve in the current tangled web of legal sources?

These questions show some of the aims of this research and I will deal with them in detail on a comparative basis. In the introduction I will attempt to address two issues regarding the method and boundaries of the study that are thus of crucial importance for facilitating understanding of its objectives.

From a methodological standpoint it is evident that research into such a delicate issue within the current European framework of the different legal systems and traditions of Member States that aim to ensure justice, freedom, security, and respect fundamental rights[3] must go beyond mere single-level comparison of the most significant solutions adopted by the various domestic criminal justice systems. The legal force attached to the EU FRCh[4] and the process of accession of the EU to the ECHR promoted by the Treaty of Lisbon[5] clearly mark the cultural development of the former European Communities towards a Union endowed with its own heritage of shared fundamental values enshrined the standards of protection laid down by the ECHR.[6]

This process of integration is cogently demonstrated especially by the importance attached to the rules on interpretation of the rights and freedoms of the EU FRCh[7], perhaps more so than the formal recognition of the fundamental

---

2 On this topic see *Ashworth / Redmayne*, pp. 116 ff.
3 Art. 67.1 TFUE.
4 Art. 6.1(1) TEU.
5 Art. 6.2 TEU.
6 On this topic see recently *Hecker*, pp. 110 f.; *Manacorda*, pp. 147 ff.
7 Art. 6.1(3) TEU.

rights guaranteed by the ECHR as general principles of the EU.[8] It follows that any comparison of the way four national legal systems deal with the most intrusive measures of coercion must be approached from a multilevel perspective. It is widely recognized that while always dealing with a concrete case, ECtHR case-law has over recent years acquired an increasingly important role especially in the protection of human rights in the pre-trial phases of the criminal process, and has significantly changed its decision-making techniques. This has been achieved mainly in two very different ways: a) by requiring legislative reforms of the domestic legal order in question where the violation of the Convention is due not to misuse of procedural guarantees but to structural deficiencies of the legal order examined;[9] and b) through the consolidation of standards of protection of human rights that can be widely shared by the Member States. This latter role has undoubtedly been strengthened within the EU area since the Union has not succeeded in establishing common procedural rights in criminal matter.[10] This has led some observers to speak, somewhat hastily, of the harmonization role of the Strasbourg jurisprudence in establishing minimum levels of protection of due process guarantees.[11] In any event, apart from this common basis of procedural rights,[12] the EU has over recent years strongly enhanced the instruments of cross-border cooperation in the JFS area, and extended its mutual recognition policy to the field of pre-orders. The right of liberty in the pre-trial stages was already a key focus for the introduction of the EAW FD,[13] widely considered the cornerstone of the EU's mutual recognition policy. More recently, concerns about the use of custodial means in cross-border cooperation in Europe has led EU institutions to launch a new legislative instrument regarding supervision measures as an alternative to pre-trial detention.[14]

In such a complex context, a cross-cutting analysis cannot be limited to verifying the compatibility of national regulations and/or case-law with the standards of protection imposed by ECtHR case-law and EU legislation, i.e. a merely vertical approach aimed at ascertaining whether and to what extent domestic laws fulfil supranational requirements. This would oversimplify the complex web of legal and jurisprudential sources we are nowadays witnessing in the field of fundamental freedoms. These issues require a more flexible analysis.

---

8 Art. 6.3 TEU.
9 On this topic see, among others, *De Salvia*, pp. 73 ff.
10 The Proposal for a Council FD on certain procedural rights in criminal proceedings of 5.6. 2007 has failed to make headway.
11 In critical terms on the subject relating to the role of harmonization of the ECtHR case-law, see *Allegrezza*, p. 575.
12 For the risks arising from the extension of the mutual recognition policy without a proper basis of common procedural rights, see *Gleß*, pp. 606 f.
13 Council FD 2002/584/JHA.
14 Council FD 2009/829/JHA.

The well-known phenomenon of multilevel integration is especially marked in the area of protection of personal liberty, which remains unique among fundamental freedoms in the way ECtHR case-law deals with domestic laws. As we will see, the two-fold relevance of the requirement of lawfulness in the ECHR system has allowed the Court of Strasbourg to extend its oversight to a field usual beyond its remit, and there is no doubt that in many cases this has elevated the standard of protection of personal liberty to a degree beyond what may be defined as a minimum standard. As Trechsel points out, this singular approach by supranational case-law in the field of individual freedoms is in line with the "character of human rights involved in this context", which "differs markedly from those in relation to the guarantee of the fair trial", being designed not to create a duty for the State "to organize proceedings" but to "restrain the prosecution authorities and to ensure that measures such as detention [...] are based on appropriate legal regulation", and "to restrict any interference to a degree which can reasonably be accepted as necessary."[15]

Furthermore, the impact of human rights instruments and supranational jurisprudence is not limited to domestic legal orders. EU law governing the right to personal liberty has been clearly influenced by ECtHR case-law, as is apparent from the inclusion, by the FD EAW, of the retrial requirement, in the case of *in absentia* procedure, among the guarantees the executing authority may request for the execution of an EAW.[16] This raises the question of whether at supranational level EU legislation satisfies the standards of protection of fundamental rights required both by its own Charter and the ECHR. The picture becomes even more complicated by an interesting phenomenon: the circular and mutual influence of different sources in which a leading role is often played by both domestic and supranational case-law and the increasingly frequent dialogue between the two.[17] In Italy, we have recently witnessed an interesting case in which the Court of Cassation re-interpreted a national Law transposing EU legislation in the light not only of ECtHR case-law but also of Recommendation Rec(2006)2 and Recommendation Rec(2006)13 of the Committee of Ministers of the Council of Europe, despite their non-binding character.[18]

In this context, the question may be asked as to what is meant by precautionary measures and what room they should occupy among pre-trial measures. Significantly, neither EU legislation nor the ECHR system contains any explicit reference to the precautionary character of pre-trial measures. Nor does this notion appear in countries like England and Germany that are strongly focused

---

15 *Trechsel*, p. 405.
16 See Oubiña Barbolla, *supra*, § 4.
17 See recently *Martinico*, pp. 7 ff.; *Ferrari*, pp. 23 ff.
18 See below, § 2.2.

on the distinction between remand detention and alternatives to custody. The concept of precautionary means appears in Spain and Italy where it clearly alludes to the aim of certain pre-trial measures to address specific risks within the criminal process. Unifying a wide range of coercive means pursuing common objectives in the criminal proceedings was one of the core challenges of the 1988 Italian CPP, and may explain why reference to the precautionary character of interim measures appears only in the Italian text of the FD 2009/829/JHA (*misure alternative alla detenzione cautelare*), whereas the same legislative act in other languages specifies their aim of either supervision (the English and the German texts of the FD 2009/829/JHA) or control (the Spanish and the French texts of the FD 2009/829/JHA).

What in Italy is meant by "precautionary" largely corresponds to the classical grounds for remand detention (or *Haftgründe*). The issue of definition is only apparently insignificant since it raises further questions. What incidence can the extension of the grounds for detention to non-custodial measures have on the appreciation of personal freedom? Does the widening of the justification of pre-trial measures suffice to avoid abusive interference with the sphere of personal liberty? Is pursuance of the scopes of the criminal process compatible with supervision and control objective? And what is the scope today of the criminal process? These are all questions this study has tried to answer.

2.   The right to liberty in Europe

2.1.   The historical development of the right to liberty in Europe

2.1.1.   The physical liberty of the individual

A comparative analysis of measures affecting personal liberty in the pre-trial stages presupposes that the main features of this fundamental right in Europe have been clarified in advance. Undoubtedly, after the right to life and physical integrity, personal freedom constitutes "one of the most precious possessions of the human condition,"[19] although, unlike the right to life and physical integrity, it is a right "which the authorities regularly and lawfully interfere with."[20]

This can explain the enshrinement of the right to liberty in England and Wales as early as 1215 in the *Magna Carta* as the right of every "free man" not to "be arrested or imprisoned […] except by the lawful judgment of his peers or by the law of the land". Subsequently this right was included in other constitutional

---

19 *Moreno Catena, supra*, § 1.1.
20 *Trechsel*, p. 407.

enactments. The 1998 Human Rights Act, which domesticated the ECHR, made the full contents of Article 5 part of UK law.[21] In continental Europe, personal freedom is recognized at constitutional level and occupies a key position on the list of individual fundamental values enshrined in the Constitutions of the countries included in the study.

Constitutional sanction of the right to freedom is, however, generally the result of a long historical process that has unfolded in many different ways. In Italy, the former Constitution, the 1948 Albertine Statute, did not – in contrast to other rights – consider individual freedom inviolable.[22] The right to liberty was generically guaranteed but the terms of such guarantee were entrusted to the law, which was entrusted with laying down the "cases" and "forms" for lawful arrest. Moreover, the flexible character of the Albertine Statute, which ranked only on a par with other sources of law, debilitated protection of the right to personal liberty.[23] Personal liberty only became inviolable with the Italian Constitution of 1948. Article 13 accords it first place among the civil rights enshrined therein. Furthermore, the Constitution's new position of having precedence over the law explains the much more detailed provisions regulating personal freedom than hitherto delegated to law. The German Constitution ranks personal freedom among the fundamental freedoms provided for by Article 2.2, thus making an explicit distinction between this and the right to free development of the personality laid down in Article 2.1. No explicit qualification of personal liberty in provided for by the Spanish Constitution, which does, however, include rules that appear neither in the Italian nor in the German Constitution. On the other hand, the Spanish Constitution – the most recent in our study sample (1978) – is the only constitutional text that couples the right to liberty with that of security,[24] in line with most international human rights charters and notwithstanding almost all the guarantees laid down in Article 17 manifestly address only the right to liberty.

None of these constitutional texts actually defines personal freedom. Rather than affirmative statements, their approach is that of defining personal freedom in the typically negative terms. In a liberal State this was conceived as the right to obtain a commitment from the public powers of non-interference in the sphere of personal autonomy.[25] Personal liberty is therefore primarily conceived as freedom from arrest,[26] which explains the prominence given to the guarantees regarding deprivation of liberty.

---

21 *Vogler, supra,* § 1.
22 *Di Chiara, supra,* § 1.1.
23 *Ibid., supra,* § 1.1.
24 Art. 17.1 SC.
25 See *Moreno Catena, supra,* § 1.1.
26 See *Amato,* p. 6; *Di Chiara, supra,* § 2.1.

This appreciation of the right to liberty is entirely consistent with the approach of the Court of Strasbourg. Since its earliest rulings, the Court has considered personal freedom in terms of physical liberty,[27] pointing out that the scope of the provisions laid down in Article 5 ECHR include protection of the right to freedom against arrest and detention.[28] This is further borne out by a detailed list of the grounds required to deprive and individual of his or her liberty (Art. 5.2), a fact that distinguishes the ECHR from other international instruments such as the ICCPR and ACHR. At first sight, these grounds appear as exceptions to the right to liberty. However, ECtHR case-law has always considered the cases listed in Article 5.2 as exhaustive and has consistently followed a very narrow interpretation of its provisions.[29] Significantly, since these provisions are concerned only with right to liberty with a view to preventing unlawful and arbitrary deprivation of liberty, they are to be seen as upholding the right to liberty rather than exceptions under which this freedom may be waived.

2.1.2. The evolution of the right to liberty and the widening of its scope of application

Starting from this basic notion of liberty, a comparative analysis of the four legal systems highlights how the scope of application of this fundamental right has been broadened and the concept of personal freedom profoundly changed over recent decades. I will deal with the latter question by examining the justifications posited for pre-trial measures.[30] As to the former, I will follow the historical development of personal freedom in the pre-trial stages in the four countries examined in this study, a development that is reflected in the Strasbourg case-law and EU law.

2.1.2.1. The perspective of the domestic legal systems
A) The concept of personal freedom has clearly been broadened in England, where protection of physical freedom from detention during the criminal process has always been of such significance that the entire bail system is construed on the basis of conditional release. This system, significantly considered as old as English law itself,[31] has been deeply rooted for centuries and remains of fundamental importance to its criminal justice system, as is apparent from the

---

27 ECtHR, Decision of 8.6.1976, Engel and others v. Netherlands, Applications No. 5100/71; 5101/71; 5102/71; 5354/72; 5370/72, § 58.
28 See *Trechsel*, p. 409.
29 *Marzaduri, supra*, § 1.
30 Below, § 3.2.
31 *Vogler, supra*, § 1.1.

enactment of a presumption in favour of unconditional bail in s. 4(1) of the Bail Act 1976.

Nevertheless, the bail system in England and Wales has been subjected to considerable changes over time. The Bail Act of 1976 testifies to the revolutionary replacement of the historical free-market relationship between State and bailee for the payment of a money bond or security with an unprecedented penal approach based on the offence of failing to answer bail.[32] This legislation clearly demonstrates the significant change in the use of bail in two ways. Firstly, it provides a statutory basis for refusing bail on grounds of risk of reoffending, a provision that had appeared in English law for the first time in the 1950s.[33] Secondly, by amending the Criminal Justice Act 1967, it grants the courts completely new powers to impose conditions other than financial sureties on the grant of bail. In general terms, s. 3(6) of the Bail Act 1976 empowers courts granting bail to impose any condition they consider necessary to address exceptions to bail.[34]

Since then, the increase in recourse to bail conditions has deeply changed the way bail is used and expanded the area of pre-trial measures that had hitherto consisted solely of bail (whether unconditional or a money bond and personal sureties), and remand in custody. In a deeper sense, this phenomenon has radically changed the way the right to liberty is conceived. Since the increasing use of conditions has led to more restricted use of unconditional bail,[35] it may be said that the right to personal liberty has itself become a much more complex freedom, not only in the sense of freedom from detention but also from other types of restriction.

B) Most continental European countries have seen similar shifts in the very concept of personal freedom. They differ markedly from English law, however, with the use of alternative measures narrowing the scope for remand detention rather than the area of personal freedom. Significantly, supervision measures have largely been welcomed in continental Europe as a means of enhancing the presumption of innocence of the accused in criminal proceedings. However, despite this positive feature, there is little doubt that the right to liberty has also been broadened in continental Europe.

Bearing in mind the historical context in which both the Italian and German Constitutions were drawn up, it is no surprise that both constitutional texts focus on the requirement of lawfulness not only for detention but also for any form of restriction of personal freedom.[36] In Italy, at the time of the constitu-

---

32 *Ibid.*, *supra*, § 1.1.
33 *Ibid.*, *supra*, § 1.1.
34 *Ibid.*, *supra*, § 2.1.
35 *Ibid.*, *supra*, § 2.1; *Ashworth / Redmayne*, p. 236.
36 See respectively arts. 13.2 IC and 104.1 GC.

tional reform, criminal procedure was mainly regulated by the CPP 1930, which surprisingly contained specific rules on personal liberty, unlike the subsequent code. The CPP 1930 was, however, issued by then new fascist regime and thus permitted complete deprivation of personal liberty with different types of detention warrants. The systematic inclusion of the rules on both arrest and remand detention in CPP 1930 at the beginning of the Book on the second phase of proceedings, concerned with gathering of evidence (*istruzione*), was clearly in line with the inquisitorial character of pre-trial custody, considered as the most appropriate means of forcefully achieving the collaboration (if not confession) of the defendant, who was thus viewed as an instrument in the successful conclusion of criminal inquiries rather than as a right holder.[37] Although at the time of the previous code defendants were normally detained in prison, however, remand detention was paradoxically directly connected with the primary purposes of the criminal process. The liberal concept of a need for deprivation of liberty, strongly advocated by the Italian legal Enlightenment,[38] was turned into the brutal need to keep the defendant in custody as a prerequisite for taking evidence, whose main scope in the procedure was explicitly the search for truth.[39]

The constitutional reform of 1948 was not sufficient to overhaul a criminal justice system so deeply rooted in this cultural background. Indeed at the beginning of the 1970s, remand detention was still the basis of the system, be it via a mandatory (*mandato di cattura obbligatoria*) or discretionary detention warrant (*mandato di cattura facoltativa*), which was however unconnected with the aims of the criminal process. Meanwhile, the lack of any definition of personal freedom in the Constitution led to endless debates on the general features of this right and consequently the area of application of the constitutional guarantees. These debates progressively shifted away from the classical notion of freedom from arrest to a more general right to free development of an individual's moral personality and social dignity.[40] This broader concept of personal freedom overlapped with the introduction for the first time of alternatives to custodial sentence (*misure alternative alla detenzione*) with Penitentiary Law 354/1975. Uncertainty over the meaning of personal liberty continued during the 1980s and coincided chronologically with the enactment in law of specific grounds for detention, extended to house arrest and supervisory measures of a purely prescriptive nature.[41] The upshot was Law 532/1982 and the introduction of a new

---

37 See *Marzaduri* [5], p. 61.
38 See *Di Chiara, supra*, § 1.
39 Art. 299 CPP 1930.
40 In the same sense *Barbera*, pp. 98 ff.; *Mortati*, p. 955; *Martines*, p. 610. For a general view of different opinions on this topic, see *Pace*, pp. 287 ff.
41 Art. 254 CPP 1930 as amended by the Law 532/1982.

complaint procedure (*riesame*) against pre trial orders that significantly encompassed not only remand detention but also all pre-trial measures restricting personal freedom.[42]

This may explain why the issue of personal liberty was not expressly included in the 1988 adversarial CPP, even if many pre-trial measures directly affect this freedom. As noted above, one of the core reforms of the current code was to unify all precautionary interim measures under a risk prevention umbrella. Attributing a common purpose to a series of very different pre-trial measures had the effect of placing these measures in the much wider frame of "freedom of the person."[43] The adoption by the Italian CPP of this expression, certainly equivalent to the concept of personal liberty indicated in most international human rights texts, was due to the inclusion in the rules on "personal precautionary measures" (*misure cautelari personali*) of two different types of interim means: coercive measures (*misure cautelari coercitive*) and control measures (*misure cautelari interdittive*), which do not even indirectly jeopardize physical liberty. In the case of coercive measures, this approach paradoxically achieved two quite opposite results. It considerably narrowed the area of coercion in contrast to other countries, by including the interim means aimed at the same risks addressed by remand detention, and extended the notion of personal liberty to situations in which freedom of movements suffers very little restriction (e. g. expatriation prohibition) on the grounds that all the coercive measures in some way potentially affect personal liberty.[44]

C) The phenomenon of broadened personal freedom at first sight appear more limited in Germany, which has never had a similar system of precautionary measures in the pre-trial phases. Yet, the StPÄndG 1953 introduced new supervision measures into German law that went beyond the furnishing of a security (*Sicherungsmittel*), which the RStPO provided for as the only means of suspending the execution of an arrest warrant in case of risk of absconding. Since then, German legislation has undergone important reforms that have widened the catalogue of alternatives measures to the arrest warrant (StPÄndG 1964) over and above the flight risk.[45] Significantly, there is a requirement to assess *ex officio* the effective need to apply these judicially set conditions in all phases of the detention procedure[46] and an arrest warrant must be suspended in the event mitigating measures are sufficient to prevent the risk at stake.[47] In the 1960s, Federal constitutional case-law had already pointed out that the pro-

---

42 See *Marzaduri* [2], pp. 776 ff.
43 Art. 272 CPP.
44 See *Marzaduri* [5], pp. 62 f.
45 See *Paeffgen*, § 116, point 1.
46 *Ibid.*, § 116, point 4.
47 See *Beulke*, point 228.

portionality principle plays a decisive role in the choice of conditions to be applied even after suspension of an arrest warrant, taking into account the limitation of personal liberty deriving from the application of any supervision measure provided for in § 116 StPO.[48] This ruling revealed an awareness of the changing concept of personal liberty, a phenomenon to which the non-exhaustive character of the pre-trial measures mentioned by § 116 StPO[49] and the rising application of new means of control have surely contributed. Moreover, since some of the explicitly mentioned conditions affect fundamental rights other than individual physical freedom, this has led to a blurring of the traditional distinction between freedom of movement and restrictions on personal freedom.[50]

D) Compared with these countries, Spain remains unique in the way it assesses personal liberty. Supervision measures are few, basically detention and pre-trial release, a shortcoming that the doctrine has on various occasions blamed on the legislator.[51] Moreover, the constitutional rules on the duration of remand detention and the *Habeas corpus* proceeding clearly testify to the importance protection of physical freedom still enjoys in Spain, with a sharp distinction being made between personal freedom and freedom of movement within the national territory.[52] Finally, the Spanish Constitution includes personal liberty among those freedoms the public powers have a precise duty to promote by ensuring the necessary conditions to achieve them effectively, which is tantamount to the requirement to guarantee the sphere of personal autonomy in a democratic and social State.[53]

2.1.2.2. The supranational context

A) In this scenario, ECtHR case-law seems at first sight to offer a fairly well defined concept of personal liberty, especially if compared with the vague notion of security. As mentioned above, protection of the right to liberty is, as in other international texts, described more in terms of its deprivation and hence depends on the interpretation given to this expression. ECtHR case-law has consistently ruled that simple restrictions of the freedom of movement are not significant in this area being separately regulated under Article 2.1 of Protocol No. 4 to the ECHR.[54]

Nevertheless the Court of Strasburg has pointed out on numerous occasions

---

48 See BVerfG, Decision of 15.12.1965 – 1 BvR 513/65, in: BVerfGE 19, pp. 342 ff. (351).
49 See *Paeffgen*, § 116, point 9.
50 In this respect cf. *Müller-Franken*, point 29.
51 See *Moreno Catena, supra*, § 3.1.
52 Art. 19 SC.
53 See *Moreno Catena, supra*, § 1.1.
54 See *Marzaduri, supra*, § 2.

that the distinction between restrictions of the freedom of movement and deprivation of liberty is merely one of degree or intensity, not one of nature or substance.[55] Thus, as in other fields, the Court has construed an autonomous interpretation of the notion of deprivation of liberty, starting from the analysis of the concrete situation of the individual concerned and of a whole range of factors arising in a particular case.[56] Defining the line separating deprivation of freedom of movement, restriction on and finally deprivation of personal liberty also requires very complex ascertainment of numerous elements such as the type, duration, effects and manner of implementation of the measure of coercion.[57] Moreover, whereas the action of depriving an individual of his or her liberty certainly implies the use of, or threat to use, force by limiting the space of movement of that individual,[58] account must also be taken of factors that are not directly related to the type of interference but rather concern the living conditions and degree of freedom the individual has previously enjoyed.

This fluidity of ECtHR case-law,[59] which has increased since the beginning of the 1980s,[60] has led to relativization of the Court's notion of deprivation of liberty,[61] which has diverged markedly in its assessment of personal liberty from that of some countries. An emblematic case was *Vittorio and Luigi Mancini v. Italy* in which the two applicants were kept in prison notwithstanding a decision to change the prevention measure to house arrest.[62] In this case, a situation of continued serious restriction of the freedom of movement did not prevent the Court from envisaging a violation of Article 5.1 ECHR, thus largely departing from the Italian law view that remand detention and house arrest are equivalent.[63] An even more considerable shift away from the Italian concept of personal liberty emerged in *Guzzardi v. Italy*,[64] which has rightly been defined "the most critical borderline case decided" by the ECtHR.[65] Despite the relatively wide area (2.5 square km.) in which the applicant was free to move, the Court held that he had been deprived of his liberty due to the general characteristics of his forced stay on the island of Asinara.[66]

---

55 *Ibid., supra*, § 2.
56 See *Trechsel*, p. 412.
57 See *Marzaduri, supra*, § 2.
58 See *Trechsel*, pp. 412 ff.
59 For a general approach to the fluidity of the ECtHR case-law, see *Vogliotti*, pp. 851 ff.
60 See ECtHR, Decision of 21.6.2011, Shimovolos v. Russia, Application No. 30194/09, § 49, with further references to the ECtHR case-law.
61 In the same sense *Trechsel*, pp. 417 ff.
62 ECtHR, Decision of 2.8.2001, Vittorio and Luigi Mancini v. Italy, Application No. 44955/98, § 19.
63 Art. 284.5 CPP. See below, § 3.1.
64 ECtHR, Decision of 6.11.2001, Guzzardi v. Italy, Application No. 7367/76.
65 In this sense *Trechsel*, p. 407.
66 See *Marzaduri, supra*, § 2.

B) Within this framework, how is the right to liberty in EU law likely to develop? It is well known that the EU FRCh explicitly enshrines the right to personal liberty,[67] thus providing it with a clear legal basis at the level of primary EU law.[68] Despite its succinct wording, the provision is to be interpreted as having at least the same meaning and scope as the provisions of the ECHR.[69]

This assumption leads to different conclusions. Like the ECHR, the EU FRCh aims to protect personal freedom in a strict sense, which implies that personal freedom may not be extended to include the right to free development of personality.[70] Moreover within the area of physical freedom (*liberté d'aller et de venir*), personal freedom is to be distinguished from other freedoms, such as freedom from slavery, forced labour or the right to free movement.[71] Doubtless, the general clause laid down by Article 52 EU FRCh implies that at EU level too, the right to liberty may not suffer limitations other than those lawfully allowed pursuant to the provisions listed in Article 5.1 ECHR.[72] Nor can EU law allow ascertainment of the deprivation of liberty to dispense with an assessment of the concrete situation. Consequently, as in the ECHR system,[73] even short-term detention may fall within the scope of protection of personal freedom.[74]

This could further close the gap personal liberty and freedom of movement also at EU level. Indeed this is apparent from the objectives pursued by the above-mentioned FD 2009/829/JHA, which explicitly aims at enhancing the right to liberty and the presumption of innocence in the European Union by promoting, where appropriate, the use of non-custodial measures as an alternative to provisional detention.[75] As has occurred in most countries of continental Europe, the introduction of pre-trial measures alternative to custody aims, also at supranational level, to markedly reduce the area of remand detention, a measure subject to misuse in the absence of any legislation on non-custodial measures especially with regard to non-residents accused of offences in other Member States on the assumption of a greater risk of flight.[76] Indeed, the FD EAW, one of the cornerstones of EU cooperation and mutual recognition, has paradoxically placed the right to personal liberty in jeopardy on account of the absence of an analogous legislative instrument governing non-custodial instruments. A rapid overview of the interim measures explicitly covered by the

---

67 Art. 6 EU FRCh.
68 Art. 6 TEU.
69 Art. 52 EU FRCh.
70 See *Bernsdorf*, p. 161 fn. 9.
71 *Ibid.*, p. 161.
72 Explanations to Art. 6 EU FRCh (2007/C 303/02).
73 See *Marzaduri, supra*, § 2.
74 See *Bernsdorf*, p. 162.
75 Recital No. 4 FD 2009/829/JHA.
76 See *Rafaraci, supra*, § 1.

FD 2009/829/JHA[77] shows a rising tendency to use the supervision procedure envisaged by EU cross-border cooperation for policing and control purposes. That the area of physical freedom has been extended to include other non-custodial limitations of different types of freedom is even more evident in respect of the measures other than those provided for by Art. 8.1 FD 2009/829/JHA, which the Member States can additionally decide to monitor.[78]

C) In a wider perspective, the shift in Europe away from the classic conception of personal liberty is also evident in the above-mentioned Recommendation Rec (2006)13 of the Committee of Ministers of the Council of Europe. Although not binding, the Recommendation's core objectives aim to promote non-custodial measures as a means of reducing the use of remand detention. Some of the alternatives to custody clearly limit the sphere of the free development of personal autonomy and so jeopardize defendant's rights to continue his or her profession, the right to work, etc., which at the domestic level have been excluded from the area of personal liberty in the strict sense.[79] Notwithstanding the exceptional character of remand detention, which must be considered a measure of last resort,[80] the alternatives to custody provided for, albeit not exhaustively, under point 2 of this Recommendation give cause for concern. Indeed, the different levels of intrusiveness of the various measures are such as to question whether they can really address the specific concerns for which the pre-trial detention is deemed as necessary and, at the same time, whether pre-trial detention can be considered as necessary in cases when non-intrusive measures would suffice.[81]

2.2. The fundamental guarantees of protection of the right to liberty in Europe

2.2.1. The guarantee of lawfulness

The guarantees protecting the right to liberty have been closely linked with the development of the notion of personal freedom over the years. They therefore vary according to the historical development of the different legal orders.

Certainly, the main guarantee that all continental European Constitutions have in common is the requirement of a formal law as a precondition for a

---

77 Art. 8.1 FD 2009/829/JHA.
78 Art. 8.2 FD 2009/829/JHA.
79 On this topic, with specific regard to the Italian measures of control, see *Marzaduri* [5], pp. 62 f.
80 Point 3.2 of the Recommendation Rec(2006)13 of the Committee of Ministry of the Council of Europe.
81 On the issue of justification of pre-trial means see, with more detail, below, § 3.2.

legitimate intrusion into the sphere of personal freedom. The consecration of this classical principle, whose origin in continental Europe can be traced back to the Enlightenment, acquired an entirely new meaning as a result of the historical developments that led to the promulgation of the Constitutions. It is readily understandable, therefore, that unlike the Spanish Constitution, the German and the Italian Constitutions aim to provide the widest protection for personal freedom and extend the requirement of lawfulness to any restriction on freedom, even if this does not entail deprivation of liberty in a strict sense. The fact that the German Constitution only calls for a legal basis to warrant restriction on freedom does not signify waiver of this fundamental requirement in the more intrusive cases of deprivation of liberty.[82] Although neither of these constitutional texts defines the substantive requirements of law, it is significant that both the German and Italian Constitutions expressly prohibit any form of mental and physical mistreatment of persons restricted in their liberty.[83] The Italian Constitution treats this as a punishable offence. In English law, notwithstanding the *Magna Carta's* provision that "no free man shall be arrested or imprisoned [...] except by the lawful judgment of his peers or by the law of the land," the requirement of law has clearly always had an entirely different meaning than that enshrined in the formal legislation of continental Europe. As a result, the ECtHR has had the difficult task of adapting the meaning of law to the characteristics of the common-law system on the basis that all law, even if unwritten, fulfils the basic requirements of foreseeability, "to a degree that is reasonable in the circumstances," of the "consequences which a given action might entail."[84]

The requirement of lawfulness is key to the ECHR's protection of personal freedom and, to a certain extent, overlaps with the general need for a "procedure prescribed by law" laid down in Art. 5.1.[85] Surprisingly, the only case among those provided for by Article 5.1 ECHR, which in the French version does not contain any reference to the lawful deprivation of liberty, is the arrest or detention of a person in the pre-trial stages for the purposes of initiating a criminal process[86]. The lacuna is only apparent, however, since the requirement of lawfulness certainly applies to all the cases listed in this paragraph.[87]

Bearing in mind the top priority given to personal liberty among the fun-

---

82 In the same sense *Müller-Franken*, point 55.
83 See respectively Arts. 104.1 GC and 13.4 IC.
84 In this sense ECtHR, Decision of 5. 10. 2004, H.L. v. United Kingdom, Application No. 45508/99, § 114. On this topic see *Marzaduri, supra*, § 1.
85 ECtHR, Decision of 5. 10. 2004, Winterwerp v. the Netherlands, Application No. 6301/73, § 39.
86 Art. 5.1(c) ECHR.
87 ECtHR, Decision of 24. 11. 1994, Kemmache v. France (No. 3), Application No. 17621/91, § 42.

damental freedoms of the individual, the provision of this requirement in the Convention has enabled the ECtHR from the outset to extend its ascertainment to a field normally outside its remit, i.e. compliance of the substantive and procedural rules of domestic law.[88] This has been decisive in the assessment by the Court of Strasbourg of the lawfulness of the deprivation of liberty and has even facilitated its task since a finding of non-compliance with domestic law is tantamount in principle to violation of the Convention.[89]

2.2.2. Protection against arbitrariness

An overview of ECtHR case-law shows clearly, however, that mere compliance with domestic law cannot always rule out a declaration of unlawfulness under the ECHR system, since any deprivation of liberty must additionally be in line with the purpose of Article 5, namely to protect individuals from arbitrariness.[90] Surprisingly, the ECHR is perhaps the sole international human rights instrument not to contain an explicit reference to arbitrariness, although the ECtHR has always held that even the purpose of the consecration of this fundamental right is to protect individuals from arbitrary intervention by public authorities.[91]

The link between the requirement of lawfulness and the aim of avoiding arbitrariness is very close in the ECHR system of protection of personal freedom, since in a "democratic society subscribing to the rule of law, no detention that is arbitrary can ever be regarded as lawful."[92] Furthermore it must also be ascertained whether lawful detention is compliant with both the procedural and substantive rules of national law as well as with the aims of Article 5.1 ECHR. A clear distinction between the requirement of lawfulness and absence of arbitrariness emerges from the provisions regarding the right to personal freedom contained both in the ICCPR and the ACHR,[93] which clearly demonstrate that protection against arbitrary forms of deprivation of personal liberty is one of the core objectives of international instruments. Within the frame of the ECHR, the Court of Strasbourg considers the two notions as autonomous, surprisingly from two different viewpoints. In one instance the Court ruled out a breach of the Convention in cases of unlawful detention according to domestic law since "the core task of the Court is to detect manifest cases of arbitrariness."[94] On the other

---

88 *Ubertis*, p. 100.
89 *Ibid.*, p. 100.
90 See *Marzaduri*, *supra*, § 1.
91 *Ibid.*, *supra*, § 1; *Trechsel*, p. 407.
92 ECtHR, Kemmache v. France (No. 3) (fn. 87), § 42.
93 See respectively Art. 9 ICCPR and Art. 7 ACHR.
94 *Marzaduri*, *supra*, § 1.

hand, where deprivation of liberty fails the test of necessity,[95] the court ruled, albeit in isolated cases, that it was arbitrary.[96]

To be sure, the requirement of necessity is not expressly included among the cases provided for by Article 5.1, in contrast to other rights enshrined in the ECHR.[97] This apparent oversight can be explained by the considerable differences between the grounds for deprivation of liberty envisaged, in respect of which the assessment of necessity would sometimes be inadequate.[98] However, this test plays a crucial role in the field of remand detention especially with a view to avoiding excessive duration of the curtailment of personal freedom.[99]

It is worth noting that neither the requirement of necessity nor the aim of avoiding arbitrary detention explicitly appears as a general precondition for interferences with personal freedom in most domestic Constitutions of continental Europe. This is probably because it is thought that the principle of lawfulness provides a sufficient barrier against the risks of arbitrariness. The Spanish Constitution is significant since it expressly prohibits preventive detention lasting any longer than the time strictly required to carry out the necessary investigations to establish the facts.[100] The guarantee of necessity, which in this constitutional provision clearly links the length of remand detentions with the objectives of the criminal process, is of such importance in the Spanish legal system that it has been included in the LECrim law and extended to all grounds justifying the application of preventive detention.[101] Notwithstanding the wording of the second sentence of Article 17.2 of the Spanish Constitution, handing over the individual to the judicial authority within 72 hours does not in itself allow the continuation of remand detention for an unnecessary period.[102] Another significant aspect of Spanish protection of personal liberty is that both Constitution and LECrim make a distinction between the requirement to avoid unnecessary duration of the remand detention and the need for a legal definition of maximum time limits for provisional imprisonment.[103]

Despite the emphasis during the Italian Enlightenment on the requirement of necessity as a general precondition for granting and extending pre-trial detention,[104] the Italian Constitution paradoxically makes no express reference to this. Instead it draws attention only to the need for legal regulation of the

---

95 *Trechsel*, p. 421.
96 See *Trechsel*, p. 435.
97 See Art. 8.2 ECHR concerned with the right to respect for private life.
98 *Trechsel*, p. 434.
99 *Ibid.*, p. 435.
100 Art. 17.2 SC.
101 Art. 504.1 LECrim.
102 See *Moreno Catena*, *supra*, § 1.2.
103 See respectively Arts. 17.4 SC and 504.2 LECrim.
104 See above fn. 39.

maximum duration of preventive detention.[105] Moreover, it cannot be ruled out that this lacuna, which, unlike the case of Spain, has not been filled by the CPP, may have led in practice to a considerable shift in the normal duration of remand detention and other custodial measures towards the maximum time limits established in the detailed provision of Article 303 CPP.

Compared to these constitutional texts, the German Constitution proves, at first sight, rather scant in terms of guarantees, since it contains no reference to the requirement to avoid unnecessary restrictions on personal liberty or to the need for legal rules establishing a maximum duration of remand detention. This lacuna has recently caused some problems in cross-border cooperation with Italy due to the fact that the Italian Law implementing the FD EAW included in the grounds for refusal to surrender a maximum duration provision of remand detention in the issuing Member State. This led to the above mentioned ruling of the Court of Cassation, which re-interpreted the domestic provision in light of consistent ECtHR case-law that requires constant reviews of remand detention, an orientation that has been also confirmed by Recommendation Rec(2006)13 of the Committee of Ministers of the Council of Europe.[106]

This ruling is of great systematic importance in that, although confirming the complexity of the multilevel tangled web of legal rules of different origin, it contradicts the assumption that the German law remains indifferent to the requirement to use remand detention for the time strictly necessary by considering the requirement of periodical reviews of custody as tantamount to establishing maximum detention duration by law. Indeed, the StPO grants the defendant, as long as a judgement has not been given imposing imprisonment or a custodial measure of reform and prevention, the right to obtain judicial review of his or her pre-trial detention after six months and subsequently, in the case of extended remand detention, every three months.[107] In practice this leads to short remand detention durations. Compared with other continental countries, detention in Germany in 2009 was one month in the majority of cases (8151), between six months and one year in 4918 cases, and over one year in only 1428 cases. Moreover, an analysis of German law shows clearly that the requirement to avoid arbitrary intrusions into the sphere of personal liberty is very much linked to a dynamic control mechanism. This conclusion can be extended to those countries that have no predefined legal maximum time limits for remand detention but nonetheless provide the instruments with which to check constantly whether measures curtailing personal freedom are in effect justified.[108]

---

105 Art. 13.5 IC.
106 Cass. (SU), Decision of 30.1.2006, Ramoci, in: Cass. pen. 2007, p. 911. On this decision see *De Amicis*, pp. 1435 ff.
107 See respectively §§ 121.1 and 122.3 – 4 StPO. On this topic cf. *Sinn*, *supra*, § 3.1.3.
108 On this topic cf., for an overall analysis of the European countries, *Kamlthout*, pp. 64 ff.

A particular solution for avoiding a unnecessarily lengthy remand detention has been adopted in England and Wales, which, unlike Scotland, do not provide for effective time limits of either the main proceedings or the length of remand in custody.[109] Moreover the Bail Act 1976 restricts the right of the remanded defendant to ask for bail each time he or she appears in court to two hearings within the space of one week, i.e. the first when the defendant appears in court, the second at the subsequent hearing, if he or she has not been granted bail. Yet, as we will see, it is the judicial authority that is charged with checking whether the requirements for conditional bail or custody exist or not. Furthermore the second application for bail can be sustained on the basis of the same circumstances previously examined. Subsequent bail applications require a change of circumstances and any defendant who has not been granted bail does not have to be produced in court within 28 days.[110] In any event, the average duration of remand detentions is very short in England and Wales and has even fallen over the last few years (from 58 days in 2006 to 55 days in 2007).[111] The opposite has occurred in continental Europe, as the Spanish experience clearly demonstrates, despite the slight fall between 2008 and 2009.[112] This situation in England and Wales, which is largely due to the "relative rapidity (in most cases) of the strongly adversarial pre-trial,"[113] is a clear signal demonstrating that the absence of rigid time limits does not impede drastic reduction of the time of deprivation of liberty.

2.2.3. The judicial guarantee

Another fundamental guarantee that the cross-cutting analysis of four legal orders examined against the supranational Europe backdrop concerns the increasing role of judicial control in pre-trial procedures.

Compared with other constitutional texts, the Italian Constitution provides for strict rules. These include the requirement that the police authorities have substantive grounds for adopting "temporary measures"[114] and, as we have seen, the issuing of a judicial warrant in the event of restricting an individual's personal freedom. Although Article 13.2 IC has certainly contributed to transferring the power to limit someone's liberty from the criminal prosecution authorities (Prosecutor and the police) to the judiciary in the field of pre-trial measures

---

109 See *Vogler, supra,* § 2.2.
110 *Ibid., supra,* § 3.1.
111 *Ibid., supra,* § 2.2.
112 *Moreno Catena, supra,* § 1.3.
113 See *Vogler, supra,* § 2.2.
114 According to Article 13.3 IC the police may adopt such measures only "in exceptional cases of necessity and urgency."

aimed at preventing precautionary risks, Italian criminal procedural system has still not completely achieved full jurisdictionalization of all forms of restriction on personal freedom in the pre-trial inquiries.[115] Furthermore, the wording of this provision might have generated the belief that only the application of measures limiting the right to liberty requires a judicial order and that, in the case of preventive imprisonment, the introduction of legal time limits is sufficient to keep duration within reasonable boundaries. In contrast, the fact that the German Constitution requires judicial control, albeit limited to cases of deprivation of liberty, both to impose and continue any form of deprivation has led to the introduction of a system of automatic judicial controls of remand detention.

There is a strict link between the requirements of lawfulness and jurisdictionality, and there is no doubt that in all those countries where judicial order is a precondition for the restriction on personal freedom, the requirement of lawfulness tends to acquire more specific significance. The link between the two guarantees is very clear in the Italian Constitution since the judge may order restriction on liberty "only in the cases and manner provided for under law."[116] In other words, judicial power must remain within the broader circle previously traced by the law.[117] The full functioning of judicial control therefore presupposes a clear definition under the law of the limits and terms according to which restriction of personal freedom is permissible.[118] As we have seen, the requirement of certainty in the legal regulation of permissible restrictions on personal freedom has great importance in the ECHR system as well,[119] even if the Court of Strasbourg has sometimes refrained from declaring a violation of the Convention in cases of clear domestic case-law,[120] thus adopting a substantive than formal notion of law,[121] a ruling that has rightly been considered not entirely satisfactory.[122]

---

115 For instance, both physical inspection (Art. 246 CPP) and body search are ordered, during the preliminary inquiry, by the Public Prosecutor's Office, although they clearly affect personal freedom and are expressly mentioned by Article 13.2 IC. However, Law 85/2009 has recently introduced a new provision to the CPP, according to which – where an expert examination requires the use of measures potentially affecting personal freedom, such as the taking of blood or other body samples in order to ascertain someone's DNA, and the interested party does not consent – the judge will be able, even *ex officio*, to order the measures strictly necessary to carry out the investigations aimed at establishing the facts (Art. 224bis CPP).

116 Art. 13.2 IC.

117 On the image of the concentric circles see *Di Chiara, supra*, § 1.2.1.

118 Particular weight is attached to this requirement by the Germany case-law. See BVerfG, Decision of 13.10.1970 – 1BvR 226/70, BVerfGE 29, p. 196.

119 See *Trechsel*, pp. 429 f.

120 See, for instance, ECtHR, Decision of 8.11.2001, Laumont v. France, Application No. 43626/98, §§ 50–1.

121 An explicit reference to the formal character of law is provided for by Article 104.1 GC.

2.2.4. The *audi alteram partem* rule

Most European countries have become aware that judicial control cannot in itself suffice to ensure full protection of personal freedom without strengthening the *audi alteram partem* rule and the rights of the defence. This awareness has grown progressively over the last decades. A decisive contribution has been given by the ECHR system, which entails specific provisions connecting judicial control with the right to effective defence. Significantly, like other international human rights instruments, the ECHR grants any person deprived of his liberty the right to be "informed promptly, in a language which he understands, of the reasons for his arrest and any charge against him."[123] This fundamental guarantee supplements the general duty of information provided for by Article 6.3(a) ECHR and cannot be replaced therewith, as it relates to a previous stage in the proceedings and has the different purpose of allowing for the lawfulness of the detention to be challenged effectively.[124] This right is a natural precondition for the effective exercise of the right to defence once the detainee is brought before the judge under Article 5.3 ECHR.[125] It also enables the judicial authority to fulfil its control tasks properly.

Although the duty of information according to the ECHR applies to all the grounds for detention under Article 5.1,[126] its main field of application is without doubt detention on remand.[127] Similarly the German Constitution expressly links the duty to inform the person deprived of his or her liberty of the reasons for his or her arrest, as well as the duty to examine the detainee and give him or her the opportunity to raise objections, only with provisional detention on suspicion of having committed a criminal offence, the sole reason justifying the immediate hand-over of a detainee to the judicial authority.[128] According to the German doctrine, this guarantee applies also to cases in which by ordering an arrest warrant, the judicial authority has already examined the question of urgent suspicion and checked the permissibility of the deprivation of liberty. It demonstrates that Germany has enshrined at constitutional level the right of the

---

122 See *Trechsel*, p. 420.
123 Art. 5.2 ECHR. On this topic see *Maggio, supra*, § 1.
124 See *Trechsel*, p. 458.
125 *Ibid.*, p. 514.
126 The reference to "any charge" makes it clear "that the duty to give reasons for the detention also arises in cases of arrest based on other grounds than a suspicion." In this sense *Trechsel*, p. 455. The ACHR appears to lead to a different conclusion by providing for a duty to notify the charge or charges against the detainee (Art. 7.4).
127 See *Trechsel*, p. 458.
128 Art. 104.3 GC.

remanded defendant to obtain re-assessment of the lawfulness of the pre-trial detention on the basis of his or her eventual reasons.[129]

The *audi alteram partem* rule is not expressly provided for in remand cases in the Spanish Constitution. However, the right of the remanded defendant to an oral hearing is implicit in the provision prohibiting any form of compulsion to make statements, a provision of crucial importance in that it breaks the historical use of remand detention to obtain the confession of the suspect.[130] Moreover, the Spanish Constitution attaches great weight to the contents of the information to be given to the individual deprived of his or her liberty, as shown by the detailed provisions under Article 17.3 that largely reproduces the contents of Article 5.3 ECHR. Furthermore, by using the general wording "grounds for arrest" rather than specifying a given charge, the Spanish provision does not refer just to remand detention but to any form of deprivation of liberty. The Constituent Assembly drawing up the 1978 Constitution was well aware that merely referring to information of the detainee would not suffice to grant him or her lawful defence. It therefore expressly guaranteed this, in contrast to other Constitutions, the right to be assisted by a lawyer, a right significantly applying both to police and judicial proceedings.

Compared to these constitutional texts, at first sight the Italian Constitution appears the least specific on the rights of those restricted in their liberty, seemingly satisfied with the existence of a judicial warrant as a precondition for limiting someone's freedom accompanied by the guarantee of judicial control in the event of temporary measures adopted by the police authorities. Moreover the broad interpretation of the expression "judicial authority" in Article 13 IC contributed to the 1930 CPP approach being maintained for over almost forty years, i.e. that both validation of the police arrest and issuing of the remand order be delegated to the Prosecutor.[131]

Reacting against this system, the 1988 CPP, following the precise indications of the Parliament Act containing the legislative delegation for the drafting of the code (Law 81 / 1987), transferred power of validating a police arrest and issuing a precautionary order from the prosecutor to the judiciary. This new approach formed the basis for strengthening the participation of the arrested person and the role of the defence in both these pre-trial procedures. Under the new procedure, the judge is charged with hearing the suspect during the validation procedure and the interview of his or her lawyer is now mandatory.[132] Remand detention and further custodial measures are even more innovatively dealt with.

---

129 See *Gusy*, point 66; *Müller-Franken*, point 103.
130 On this topic see *Serrano Alberca*, pp. 360 ff.
131 See Art. 246 CPP 1930.
132 Art. 391.3 CPP.

The judge competent for the preliminary inquiry must now hear the remanded suspect within five days of execution of the remand order,[133] after which the measure must be lifted and the person released.[134] Subsequent legislative reform overturned the rule that allowed the remanded suspect to be heard by the Prosecutor before the judicial interview,[135] and introduced the duty for the judge to hear the suspect within ten days in the event of further measures restricting his or her personal freedom or imposing any form of control.[136] More recently the presence of a defence lawyer during the remand hearings has become mandatory.[137]

It is worth noting that although the Italian Constitution still lacks clear provisions regarding the right of a detainee to be heard and enjoy effective defence, by domesticating the due process principle, Constitutional Amendment Act 2/1999 has contributed to providing a clearer justification for this legislative approach in that it has codified the *audi alteram partem* rule as a basic tenet of "every process,"[138] a wide notion that encompasses not only remand proceedings but all precautionary proceedings. Moreover, in the absence of an explicit reference to the right of information, the enshrinement in the Constitution of most of Article 6 ECHR,[139] has paradoxically led to a broader interpretation of the notion of "accusation" than that advocated, albeit not always clearly, by ECtHR case-law.[140] As a result, the duty of information provided for by Article 111.3 IC would also apply to all the cases in which the suspect is charged in the preliminary phase with a criminal offence, including by means of a precautionary order.[141]

2.2.5. The *Habeas corpus* proceedings

A time-honoured means of avoiding arbitrary deprivations of liberty is the *Habeas corpus* proceeding, whose origins are usually traced back to England and the Habeas Corpus Act of 1679. In English law, this procedure has for centuries constituted a powerful device for obtaining prompt assessment by the administrative authorities of lawfulness of detention. In this way any person deprived of his or her own liberty is afforded a quick and effective remedy consisting of a

---

133 Art. 294.1 CPP.
134 Art. 302 CPP. See *Di Chiara, supra*, § 2.2.2.
135 See Art. 294.6 as amended by Law 332/1995.
136 See Art. 294.1bis as amended by Law 332/1995.
137 See Art. 294.4 as amended by Law 63/2001.
138 Art. 111.2 as amended by Constitution Amendment Act 2/1999.
139 Art. 111.3 as amended by Constitution Amendment Act 2/1999.
140 See ECtHR, Decision of 19.12.1989, Kamasinski v. Austria, Application No. 9783/82,
       §§ 79–80. In the same sense cf. *Trechsel*, pp. 196 ff.
141 *Marzaduri* [6], pp. 776 f.

summons of the custodian demanding that the person be handed over to the judicial authority for the lawfulness of detention to be examined.[142] Interestingly, a similar procedure to the Habeas Corpus Act 1679 existed in the Kingdom of Aragon between 1428 and 1552.[143]

Undoubtedly *Habeas corpus* is one of the most significant instruments the ECHR, and other human rights Charters has enacted, albeit not explicitly, to ensure protection of personal liberty, which is defined as a "preferential freedom."[144] However, in continental Europe only a few countries have enshrined this fundamental guarantee in their Constitutions.[145] Only Spain of the countries considered here has, for historical reasons, included an explicit reference to *Habeas corpus* in its Constitution of 1978 that significantly supplements the provisions relating to the arresting authority's duty to promptly hand over the arrested person to the judicial authority. Paradoxically, whereas in England and Wales *Habeas corpus* can, as any common law instrument, be overruled by statute law and therefore is nowadays used for matters not specifically addressed by the Bail Act 1976,[146] the Spanish constitutional provision has given rise to a *Habeas corpus* procedure established under the Organic Law 6/1984. According to the Constitutional Court, *Habeas corpus* is neither a recourse nor an abbreviated procedure, but a special procedure[147] "susceptible of being requested by the detainee or his or her relatives without a lawyer and whose purpose is to bring the arrested person before a judicial authority."[148]

The role of *Habeas corpus* has probably been steadily decreasing in Europe as most legal systems have progressively extended the area in which a judicial order is required to justify interference with the sphere of personal freedom. The Italian experience confirms this assumption. The 1948 Constitution does not in fact mention *Habeas corpus* but rather provides a detailed provision on the duty of the police to hand over the arrested person to the judicial authority. Moreover, the only remedy against measures on personal freedom enshrined in Constitution is the appeal on a point of law to the Court of Cassation (*ricorso in cassazione per violazione di legge*). This remedy constitutes a minimum guarantee that must always be always allowed in the event of decisions or measures limiting personal freedom ordered by ordinary and special courts. The rule is so fundamental that it can only be waived in the case of decisions by military

---

142 See *Vogler, supra*, § 1.1.
143 See *Gimeno Sendra*, p. 537.
144 *Trechsel*, p. 462.
145 Apart from Spain, the only exception is the Portuguese Constitution (Art. 31).
146 See *Vogler* (Questionnaire), under § 1.2.
147 Constitutional Court, Decisions 21/1996; 21/1994.
148 In this sense *Moreno Catena* (Questionnaire), § 1.2. For more details see *Moreno Catena*, *supra*, § 1.2.1.

tribunals in time of war.[149] This entitlement to appeal, which was long deemed appropriate to comply with the requirements of the ECHR, proved an unsatisfactory device especially in the case of interim measures.[150] This led to the introduction of a new remedy – i. e. a judicial complaint – aimed at achieving re-examination of the merits of the pre-trial order.

While providing for the duty of the judicial authority to question the individual restricted in his or her freedom by a personal precautionary measure within the aforementioned time-frames, the 1988 CPP grants the person subject to a coercive measure the right to lodge a judicial complaint challenging the interim measure. It may therefore be affirmed that the guarantee of judicial control under Italian law, respectively by the same judge ordering the precautionary measure and a higher court, aims to ensure re-examination of the merits of the pre-trial order in compliance with the *audi alteram partem* rule. Significantly, however, these devices provide instruments for correcting errors and in the event providing a remedy for violations committed not by the administrative authorities but by the same judiciary. This is of special importance since interim orders are issued in the pre-trial stage by single judges without previous examination of the defendant.

2.3.   Presumption of liberty and presumption of innocence

Starting from the premise that as a rule, the defendant has the right to await the outcome of the criminal process as a free person, the question arises as to whether and how restrictions on personal freedom are compatible with the presumption of innocence, a rule of a crucial significance in all modern criminal justice systems. I will deal with this issue from the perspective of the ECHR, where the presumption of innocence has, like other human rights charters, been significantly recognized in a separate provision to that governing the fair trial guarantees granted persons charged with a criminal offence and the rules on deprivation of liberty.[151] This autonomous position of the presumption of innocence was viewed, especially in the past, as confirming the lack of any connection between this principle and the sphere of personal freedom. This conclusion, based on explicit reference to proof of guilt in all international instruments, was surprisingly advocated by scholars of continental background[152] on the assumption that the ECHR wording would have limited itself to reproducing

---

149 Art. 111.7 IC.
150 On this topic, for an in-depth analysis of the Italian remedy and a comparison with the *habeas corpus* procedure laid down in the ECHR, see *Chiavario*, p. 292 ff.
151 Cf. Arts. 6.2 ECHR, 14.2 ICCPR, 8.2 ACHR.
152 *Amodio*, p. 867.

the Anglo-Saxon version of the presumption of innocence, and that the presumption of innocence in English law applies exclusively to trial decisions.

Were this approach to be followed, the role of the presumption of innocence in continental Europe as the most basic rule governing the treatment of the defendant throughout the criminal process[153] would not apply to the ECHR system, with the consequence that the entire regulation on personal freedom would be completely uncoupled from the issue of the condition of the defendant in criminal proceedings. Significantly, countries that have embodied the presumption of innocence in their Constitutions have also included it in different provisions to those relating to personal freedom. In Italy this led in the past to the regulation on personal freedom being considered as having a "lack of purpose."[154] In addition Italian Constitutional Court recently ruled out that the presumption of innocence could in anyway impinge on the regulation of the means of restriction on personal freedom.[155]

On the other hand, scholars of the ECHR system from continental Europe tend to consider pre-trial coercive measures as definitely compatible with the presumption of innocence. Despite the apparent *contradiction in adjecto* consisting of considering someone innocent even if charged with an offence,[156] the presumption of innocence does not prevent suspicion of guilt being raised. Since the application of any pre-trial measure of deprivation of liberty presupposes such suspicion pursuant to Article 5.1(c) ECHR, this would place it legitimately within the sphere of interference with personal freedom.[157]

In my view neither of these approaches can be shared. Methodologically it does not appear coherent that an international text be interpreted so as to make it compatible only with a specific legal tradition. However, it is highly questionable that the field of application of the presumption of innocence in UK law is circumscribed within the area of the burden of proof and the rules on decision-making. The prevailing Anglo-Saxon and American literature is well-aware of the potential of this principle to extend its guarantee function from the trial to the wider area of the treatment of the defendant throughout the criminal proceedings, implying not only rules governing standard of proof but also how the State should treat citizens. In this sense it exerts exceptional restraint on the coercive measures that may be ordered at the pre-trial stages.[158] Ashworth and

---

153 See *Moreno Catena, supra*, § 2.1.1; *Sinn, supra*, § 2.2.1; *Di Chiara, supra*, § 1.1.2.
154 See *Di Chiara, supra*, § 1.1.2.
155 Constitutional Court, Decision 450/1995. See *Marzaduri* [7], p. 218.
156 *Trechsel*, p. 154.
157 *Ibid.*, pp. 434.
158 In this sense *Ashworth/Redmayne*, p. 154. In the same sense *Hamilton*, pp. 155 ff.; *Stumer*, p. 43; *Sanders-Young-Burton*, pp. 520 f. For an overview of the role of the presumption of innocence in the pre-trial stages in US criminal justice, see *Stuckenberg*, pp. 342 ff.

Redmayne clearly affirm that the "starting point for discussion of remand should be Article 5 of the Convention, which declares the right to liberty, and Article 6, which declares the presumption of innocence."[159] The US Supreme Court pointed out in *Stack v. Boyle* in 1951, i. e. at a time when common law considered the risk of flight as the sole legitimate justification for pre-trial remand, that "unless the right to bail is preserved, the presumption of innocence, secured after centuries of struggle, would lose its meaning."[160]

Nor can it be affirmed that the inclusion by international human rights instruments of the presumption of innocence among the due process guarantees, such as the right to a public hearing and the right to a defence, signifies that its only field of application is limited to trial activities.[161] This link between the presumption of innocence and the right to defence is perhaps most clearly spelt out in the UDHR, for which "everyone charged with a penal offence" is to be presumed innocent "until proved guilty according to law in a public trial at which he has had all the guarantees necessary for his defence."[162] However, the fact that the possibility of using all the defence tools in a public trial is a *condicio sine qua non* for reversing the presumption of innocence[163] does not rule out its application in the pre-trial stages. This is apparent in the wording of Article 11.1 UDHR, which confirms that the defendant is, until proved guilty in a public trial, to be considered and treated as innocent throughout the criminal process. Moreover, if the trial were the only field of application of the presumption of innocence, we would still have the question of the condition of the defendant in the pre-trial phases as well as in the alternative procedures aiming to achieve a decision on the merits of the case outside a public trial. At any rate, although the condition of the defendant can manifestly not be considered equivalent to that of a guilty person, his somewhat undefined status, as provided for by the definition of presumption of innocence in the Italian Constitution,[164] could pose more of a danger to the individual's fundamental rights than if the individual were generally treated as guilty, as the Italian experience unfortunately demonstrates.[165]

These conclusions certainly apply to the ECHR, and the Strasbourg Court's constant reiteration that presumption of innocence is the most significant implication of the right to a fair trial[166] cannot imply that this falls exclusively

---

159 *Ashworth/Redmayne*, pp. 252 f.
160 342 U.S. 1 (1951) at 4, cited by *Vogler, supra*, § 1.1.
161 *Amodio*, p. 868.
162 Art. 11.1 UDHR.
163 *Trechsel*, p. 154.
164 Art. 27.2 IC.
165 See *Ruggeri* [1], pp. 134 ff.
166 The leading case can be considered ECtHR, Decision of 27. 2. 1980, Deweer v. Belgium, Application No. 6903 / 75. The same conclusion has been repeated on several occasions. See,

within the area of the trial decision. Indeed the same wording of the provision under Article 6.2 ECHR makes it very clear that the presumption if innocence applies to "everyone charged with a criminal offence." Although the French text contains a different expression (*toute personne accusée d'une infraction*), the English version suggests a reading compatible with the technical meaning of the term "charge," which in English law marks the beginning of criminal investigations on suspicion of commission of a criminal offence, and which, once suspicion is corroborated, can lead to a formal "accusation."[167] Of course there can be various forms of charging someone with a criminal offence depending on the diversities of the legal orders. However, it should be noted that in English law the 2003 Criminal Justice Act has transferred the decision to charge to the Crown Prosecution Service (CPS) with the exception of the most trivial offences. The reform is justified "on the basis that the police, not being lawyers, make mistakes as to the correct charge."[168] It is significant that in Italy the Parliament Act containing the legislative delegation for the drafting of the new code adopted a similar notion of charge with regard to any initiative of the Prosecutor during the preliminary inquiry aimed at applying not only a coercive measure but also a means of interference in the assets.[169]

This confirms the need to broaden the field of application of the presumption of innocence, and justifies its separate status as seen in the ECHR, to rights granted any person "charged with a criminal offence" under Article 6.3, some of which, by presupposing a formal accusation, apply to a later stage of the proceedings.[170] Thus, the presumption of innocence forms a fundamental value aimed at defining the general status of the defendant and subsequently the fashion in which public authorities competent for the various stages of the criminal process must treat such persons until proved guilty.[171] Furthermore, the ECtHR has on numerous occasions pointed out the strict link between the right to liberty and the presumption of innocence. When assessing the justification of continued detention in a concrete case, the Court has required there be "specific indications of a genuine requirement of public interest which, notwithstanding the presumption of innocence, outweighs the rule of respect for individual liberty."[172]

---

for instance, ECtHR, Decision of 3. 10. 2002, Böhmer v. Germany, Application No. 37568/ 97. This assumption is repeated also in the German literature. See *Sinn, supra*, § 2.2.1.
167 *Trechsel*, p. 196.
168 *Darbyshire*, p. 86.
169 See the Directive No. 36 of Law 81 / 1987. On this topic see *Marzaduri* [4], p. 282 f.
170 *Trechsel*, p. 196.
171 In the same sense *Pradel*, p. 300.
172 See, for instance, ECtHR, Decision of 6. 4. 2000, Labita v. Italy, Application No. 26772/95, § 152.

Assuming that as a consequence of this fundamental rule, the defendant maintains the right to be treated as a free person as long as he or she enjoys presumption of innocence, the subsequent question is what decision must be considered as asserting proof of guilt, and consequently, whether the defendant loses both right the right to freedom and presumption of innocence after conviction in first instance. Despite the confused formulation, the chronological extension of the presumption of innocence is very clear in the Italian Constitution, and the many attempts to blur the notion of "final conviction" have all failed.[173] Although it is almost unanimously accepted that a final decision is required, no explicit reference to the type of decision capable of reversing the presumption of innocence appears in other constitutional texts from the continental area.[174] Within the ECHR system, however, the Court of Strasbourg has always viewed deprivations of liberty subsequent to the first instance as allowed by lit. (a) rather than (c) of Article 5.1.[175] This approach has been strongly criticised,[176] and it cannot be excluded that the ECtHR may adapt its case-law to the new orientation emerging within the Council of Europe whereby Art. 1(2) of the Recommendation Rec(2006)13 of the Committee of Ministers of the Council of Europe lays down in very clear terms that "remand in custody also includes any period of detention after conviction whenever persons awaiting either sentence or the confirmation of conviction continue to be treated as unconvicted persons."[177] This should not, in my view, lead to considering the condition of the defendant after the conclusion of the first instance as equivalent to his or her pre-trial status. Even the narrowest notion of presumption of innocence[178] does not preclude a distinction between the defendant's pre-trial condition and his status following a decision of the first instance, provided that his or her right to full enjoyment of liberty is protected.[179]

On the other hand, assuming that the presumption of innocence must guide the treatment of the defendant throughout the process, giving him or her a "protection umbrella" against any form of restriction of freedom,[180] is not the same as saying that coercive measures are compatible with the presumption of innocence because of being based on suspicion of commission of a criminal offence. Indeed this suspicion varies widely, even within the same country, ac-

---

173 See *Ruggeri*, pp. 78 ff. and further references therein.
174 See *Moreno Catena, supra,* § 2.2.1.
175 See above, § 1.2.
176 See, especially, *Trechsel*, pp. 519 f.
177 On this topic *Marzaduri, supra,* § 2.
178 For the classical distinction between the psychological and the normative version of the presumption of innocence see *Orlandi*, pp. 123 ff.
179 See, on this topic, *Marzaduri* [7], pp. 213 ff.; *Ruggeri* [1], pp. 65 ff.
180 In this sense *Marzaduri* [7], p. 223.

cording to the weight of the different types of coercion. In continental Europe, where it is unanimously accepted that neither the presumption of innocence nor the right to liberty prevent the criminal prosecution authorities from making a pre-conviction assessment of suspicion of guilt,[181] it is noteworthy that German case-law rejects the duty to give reasons laid down in § 114 StPO, also implying the obligation to disclose to the defendant the quality of evidence collected up to that point, as this disclosure might influence the trial decisions and thus infringe presumption of innocence.[182] Significantly, in Italy, the elevation of the threshold of suspicion with CPP 1988[183] and the subsequent strengthening of the reasoning of the precautionary order through a reform in 1995[184] led the Constitutional Court to overrule its previous case-law[185] and recognize that the pre-conviction assessment of strong suspicion of guilt may jeopardize the impartiality of the judge, a crucial element for ensuring the full protection of the presumption of innocence.[186] The procedural code has thereby inserted further grounds affirming the incompatibility of the pre-trial judge with regard to the trial decision-making.[187]

Thanks to appropriate rules aimed at preserving the impartiality of the trial judge, suspicion of guilt can thus perform an important guarantee function *vis-à-vis* the presumption of innocence. It reduces the risk of restrictions on personal freedom on account of a mere charge of a criminal offence that may result in acquittal for lack of evidence.[188] The requirement that there be a strong likelihood that the defendant has committed a criminal offence is a fundamental to prevent inappropriately severe measures in respect of nature of the offence and expected punishment,[189] a concept referred to by both the Italian CPP and German StPO, albeit in different terms,[190] as proportionality.

---

181 See *Sinn*, § 2.2.1.
182 OLG Düsseldorf, Decision of 23.7.1991 – 1 Ws 588/91, Strafverteidiger 1991, p. 522.
183 The "sufficient evidence of guilt" (*sufficienti indizi di colpevolezza*) under the CPP 1930 (Art. 254) became "strong evidence of guilt" (*gravi indizi di colpevolezza*) under the CPP 1988 (Art. 273.1). See *Di Chiara*, § 2.3.1.
184 See below, § 3.2.
185 See Constitutional Court, Decision 502/1991.
186 See *Trechsel*, pp. 164 ff.
187 See Constitutional Court, Decision 502/1991. On this topic see *Di Chiara*, pp. 111 f.; *Negri*, pp. 16 ff.
188 In this sense *Marzaduri* [5], p. 64.
189 *Moreno Catena*, supra, § 2.2.1.
190 On this topic cf. respectively *Di Chiara*, supra, § 2.3.3 and *Sinn*, supra, § 2.2.3.5.

2.4. The requirement of proportionality

The requirement of proportionality is of crucial significance in the doctrine of fundamental rights and has numerous and important implications on the sphere of individual freedoms.[191] There is a close link between presumption of innocence and the proportionality principle. This is particularly manifest in the field of pre-trial means of coercion, where compliance with the requirement of strong suspicion does not always suffice to avoid disproportionate measures, which in turn violate presumption of innocence.

In the ECHR system this can occur with particular regard to the length of the remand detention. It has been argued that the Court of Strasbourg, notwithstanding the confusing wording of Article 5.1(c) ECHR, tends to focus ascertainment of reasonable duration of pre-trial detention not only on initial suspicion of offence but also on a "genuine requirement of public interest justifying [...] a departure from the rule of respect for individual liberty."[192] This assessment must be conducted "with due regard to the principle of presumption of innocence,"[193] in the light of which reasonable suspicion of guilt, although sufficient to deprive someone of his or her liberty, is "a condition *sine qua non* for the lawfulness of the continued detention. However, after a certain lapse of time this no longer suffices in the absence of "other grounds given by the judicial authorities to justify the deprivation of liberty."[194]

Thus, whereas reasonableness is manifestly one of the core elements of proportionality,[195] presumption of innocence is of paramount importance in the assessment of the duration of pre-trial measures despite the fact that the ECtHR tends to focus on violation of Article 5.3 ECHR. Indeed, although an infringement of this *lex specialis* rule makes it procedurally unnecessary to examine the issue posited by Article 6.3 ECHR,[196] the study evidenced how the investigation of further grounds for detention presupposes respect for the presumption of innocence.

Duration of pre-trial measures is, however, not the only area where the proportionality requirement in light of the presumption of innocence may impinge. All the continental systems assessed in this study require more justification than suspicion of guilt to condone pre-trial measures. Significantly, custody decisions under English law require a two-fold assessment. Both the nature and seriousness of the offence or default and the strength of the evidence of commission of

---

191 On this topic see, among others, *Bernar Pulido*, pp. 81 ff.
192 In this sense ECtHR, Decision of 6.4.2000, Labita v. Italy (fn. 156), § 152.
193 *Ibid.*, § 152.
194 *Ibid.*, § 153.
195 See *Epping*, pp. 42 f.
196 See *Trechsel*, p. 180.

an offence or default must be examined by courts ascertaining whether there are substantial grounds for believing that the defendant, if released on bail, would either (a) fail to surrender to custody, (b) commit an offence while on bail, or (c) interfere with witnesses or otherwise obstruct the course of justice, whether in relation to himself or any other person.[197]

At any rate, it would be hasty to conclude that the ECtHR has always been alien to this evaluation of justification of an initial period of detention. Since any form of deprivation of liberty must always comply with the requirement of lawfulness, the specific grounds for detention other than suspicion of guilt maintain their importance for the Convention in an indirect way, thus requiring the Court to examine their existence insofar as the domestic law in question prescribes this.[198] Furthermore, ECtHR case-law has evidenced a new and interesting approach in the delicate issue of the fight against organized crime with greater emphasis being placed on the principle of proportionality.[199] Without prejudice to its former case-law, the Court of Strasbourg has acknowledged that although legal presumption of risk may be initially justified in cases concerning the most serious forms of organized crime, it must, however, be given "specific substantiation" to "be accepted in the context of the whole period."[200] At any rate, it cannot be ruled out that we will see further developments of ECtHR case-law in this perspective on the basis of the Recommendation Rec(2006)13 of the Committee of Ministers of the Council of Europe, which requires both suspicion of guilt and justification co-exist for a person to be remanded in custody initially or held for a longer time.[201]

As well as these requirements, this fundamental test requires a third precondition to be ascertained before remanding someone in custody without infringing "both the presumption of innocence and the presumption in favour of liberty,"[202] i.e. the impossibility of applying any different measure to address concerns that would justify the pre-trial detention. Although not a separate precondition, since it is strictly linked to justifications for remand in custody, it further demonstrates how detention must not only be appropriate to prevent a specific risk but also the only measure capable of countering it. While this requirement is apparently not entertained by the ECHR system, which focuses

---

197 See extensively *Vogler, supra*, § 1.2.

198 In this sense *Trechsel*, pp. 425 f.

199 In this sense *Marzaduri, supra*, § 6.

200 In this sense ECtHR, Decision of 3.3.2009, Hilgartner v. Poland, Application No. 37976/06, § 32.

201 Point 7 Recommendation Rec(2006)13 of the Committee of Ministry of the Council of Europe.

202 Point 3.1 Recommendation Rec(2006)13 of the Committee of Ministry of the Council of Europe.

only on deprivation of liberty, it nonetheless occupies a strong position in ECtHR's assessments of compliance with the presumption of innocence, which always include examination of the need to remand someone in custody. From this viewpoint, the requirement of necessity plays a double role in the application of pre-trial detention, marking the external and internal boundaries of deprivation of freedom in its insistence that the measure in question be strictly necessary to achieve the aim pursued and never exceed that purpose.[203]

Using pre-trial detention as a last resort is not tantamount to asserting that *any* pre-trial measure must be the most appropriate to counter a given concrete risk. The aforementioned Recommendation does not go as far as to require that the adopted measure, whichever it is, be strictly necessary to achieve its purposes. Our comparative analysis of the four domestic legal orders evidenced a different approach. The Italian CPP has perhaps mostly explicitly codified the principle of least necessary sacrifice,[204] specifying the need for an examination of the type and degree of the precautionary risk at stake before adopting the most adequate measure.[205] Unlike the German StPO,[206] the Italian code does not make an *a priori* distinction between the alternatives to custody on the basis of different precautionary needs, but rather entrusts the judicial authority with the task of selecting the most adequate means in respect of the particular risk.

A superficial overview of the Italian regulation might lead to the conclusion that the principle of adequacy entails an entirely different assessment than that required to ascertain proportionality. I do not share this conclusion, bearing in mind the approach of this study to presumption of innocence and the potential of the proportionality principle. First, pre-conviction assessment of suspicion of guilt in light of the presumption of innocence prevents from the adoption of excessively intrusive and thus inadequate measures.[207] Second, the application of a less intrusive measure than remand detention highlights another fundamental side of the principle of proportionality, which requires, in view of the requirement of necessity, that limitations be ordered with the least possible sacrifice for personal freedom. As we have seen, the German federal constitutional case-law has, in line with German doctrine,[208] shared this approach.[209]

---

203 In this sense *Trechsel*, p. 181. In the latter sense, it may also be affirmed that the Court has somewhat blurred its own case-law on Article 5 ECHR as traditionally concerned only with deprivation of liberty, not with the modalities and conditions of detention.
204 See *Di Chiara, supra*, § 2.3.3.
205 Art. 275.1 CPP. On this topic see *Di Chiara, supra*, § 2.3.3.
206 Art. 116 StPO.
207 In this sense *Marzaduri* [5], p. 73.
208 *Paeffgen*, § 116, point. 2; *Meyer-Goßner*, § 116, point 1.
209 See above, fn. 48.

3.   Interim restrictions on personal liberty

3.1.   Pre-trial measures aimed at preventing precautionary risks

Taking into account the link between the right to liberty, the presumption of innocence and the proportionality principle, it is clear that any interference with personal freedom must be the exception rather than the norm. In the following paragraphs I will deal with the whole issue of pre-trial measures aimed at preventing certain precautionary risks that most countries provide for with uniform regulation introduced for either structural or teleological reasons.

In the case of Italy, the 1988 CPP establishes a *numerus clausus* of pre-trial measures affecting the "liberty of the person." This broad freedom may thus be limited only by precautionary measures listed in Book IV, Part I, Title I, of the code. This systematic premise does not include certain coercive measures clearly affecting personal freedom, like police arrest even if some of these measures were at least initially of a precautionary nature.[210] By contrast, Book IV of the code contains rules on the provisional application of safety measures that differ significantly in nature and function from precautionary measures.[211] The main justification for such a heterogeneous group of pre-trial means is functional, i. e. to unify all pre-trial measures pursuing precautionary aims. With specific regard to the area of coercion, as seen above, this has led to the establishment of common grounds justifying all measures affecting the freedom of the person. Thus, all pre-trial means other than custody satisfying such justification are deemed potentially able to counter the same risks that would be prevented through pre-trial detention. There is no link between these supervision measures and police arrest except that validation of the latter may lead to the application of any of the coercive measure set out in Article 391.5 CPP. Further forms of detention, such the trial arrest provided for by CPP 1930 have been abolished.

The need for a uniform approach to pre-trial measures limiting the right to liberty certainly applies to Germany as well. Although not providing for a similar frame of rules governing "precautionary measures" – a category that does not even exist – Germany law has progressively included, as seen above, new forms of pre-trial conditional release. On the other hand, Germany, unlike Italy, still provides for several forms of pre-trial and trial detention, some of which pursue

---

210 According to the original version of Article 381 CPP, subsequently modified by Legislative Decree 12/1991, discretionary arrest (*arresto facoltativo*) aimed at satisfying the "need for interrupting a criminal activity." Another form of provisional arrest (the so-called "*fermo d'indiziato di delitto*") is still today aimed at countering the risk of absconding of a person seriously suspected of having committed certain offences (Art. 384 CPP).

211 *Grevi*, p. 470.

aims that are completely unconnected with precautionary needs.[212] Understandably, the judicially imposable measures listed under § 116 StPO are deemed alternatives to remand detention alone (*Haftsurrogate*). English law, on the other hand, still conceives of precautionary measures in terms of bail and custody.[213] Likewise the same decision-making process following the first court appearance of the defendant[214] is adopted for both bail (with or without conditions) and custody. Although bail can nowadays be granted in several forms and entail very different conditions, the purposes pursued by remand detention and conditional bail practically always coincide.[215] In the case of Spain, although Spanish law does not have a list of precautionary measures as comprehensive as other countries, the regulation of the measures that do exist is fairly uniform. For example, provisional release, although included under a different Title (VII) of the II Book of the LECrim, remains strictly linked to the grounds justifying the application of remand detention.[216]

In light of the presumption of innocence enshrined in Article 5.1 ECHR, it is clear that any limitation of the right to liberty, where needed, must be considered in terms of restriction rather than deprivation. Supervision measures should therefore not be deemed as alternatives to custody, rather custody should be considered as the extreme alternative to all other measures. This is borne out by all the countries studied, each of which evidences an embedded rule whereby remand detention is an *extrema ratio*. In continental Europe this has been achieved through a long historical process. An example is the Italian experience. The 1930 CPP provision of provisional release[217] illustrates clearly the extent to which personal freedom was considered a concession of the State rather than an individual right.[218] Indeed this concession was waived in the event of mandatory detention warrants.[219] Although Law 773/1972 changed this, it took another twelve years before pre-trial detention could only be permitted if deemed an authentic means of countering precautionary risks. Even after the amendment of the previous code by Law 398/1984, the principle of adequacy played a role only from a reverse perspective, since pursuant to Article 254bis CPP 1930 a man-

---

212 For more details see *Sinn, supra*, § 2.
213 See *Vogler, supra*, § 1.
214 Under English law, although a single lay magistrate sitting alone can grant bail (whether conditional or not), he cannot remand a defendant in custody. See *Vogler, supra*, § 3.1.
215 *Law Commission*, Bail and the Human Rights Act 1998: Item 10 of the Seventh Programme of Law Reform, Law Commission 2001, pp. 65 ff.
216 *Moreno Catena, supra*, § 3.1.1.
217 On this topic see *Marzaduri* [1], pp. 912 ff.
218 *Marzaduri* [1], p. 912.
219 Art. 277 CPP 1930.

datory detention warrant could only be avoided where there did not manifestly exist any precautionary need.[220]

In English law, provisional release developed very differently, deriving from a very particular approach to the sphere of personal liberty, which led to the codification in 1976 of the aforementioned presumption in favour of bail. As a result, the defendant must, unless the court has substantial grounds for believing that some risks may arise if he or she is released, be granted bail. It is also significant that, except the cases provided for in s. 3 of the Bail Act 1976, bail shall not, as a rule, imply the imposition of any condition, i. e. bail must be unconditional.[221] To be sure, the defendant may be required to provide a security or sureties to secure his or her release from custody,[222] and conditions may be imposed each time the court deems them necessary to secure certain results that in large measure significantly correspond to the purposes established for custody.[223] Thus, judicially set conditions belong to the field of bail and do not constitute exceptions to the rule laid down in s. 4 of the Bail Act 1976, as is apparent from Schedule 1, Part I, paragraph 2 of the same Act on exceptions to the right to bail, be this unconditional or conditional. In this regard, only Spain has the system comparable to English law with its inclusion of most judicially set conditions in the sphere of pre-trial release. By implying limitations that in other legal systems assume an autonomous position, such as the posting of a bond and the withholding of the defendant's passport, this measure has proved very versatile in offering different options[224] and allowed the Spanish criminal justice system to compensate for the relative deficiency of alternatives to custody.

The divide between continental European and common law remains deep, however. It has been argued that although all countries assessed in this study share the fundamental principle that the defendant has the right to await the outcome of the criminal process as a free person, the introduction of new alternative means of coercion has had a very different impact on English and continental law, i. e. respectively restricting and broadening the area of personal freedom. Nor is this conclusion contradicted by the fact that in the English system it is the defence that often proposes conditions as a means of encouraging the grant of bail.[225] In the absence of such conditions the presumption set out in s. 4 of the Bail Act 1976 would in fact oblige decision-makers to grant unconditional bail rather than issue a remand order. The presumption in favour of bail still plays a crucial role where English law does not allow the imposition of

---

220 *Marzaduri* [3], p. 286.
221 S. 3(3) of the Bail Act 1976.
222 S. 3(4) of the Bail Act 1976.
223 S. 3(6) of the Bail Act 1976.
224 *Moreno Catena*, § 3.1.1.
225 See *Vogler, supra,* § 2.1; *Ashworth / Redmayne,* pp. 235 f.

conditions to counter certain risks in relation to which the defendant can be remanded in custody.[226] Moreover, taking into account the special characteristics of the English system, the exponential rise of the use of conditions has remained within the sphere of bail and significantly has not thus prompted, in the period assessed between 1994 and 2008, a rise in remand decisions. Although this depends largely, as we have seen, on the relative rapidity of the pre-trial in English law, it can also explained by reasons, not necessarily connected with the priorities of the trial process, related with Government concerns about prison overcrowding.[227]

These concerns are certainly shared by continental countries, which however attempt to ease prison overcrowding by means other than interim custodial measures. Significantly, whereas the number of defendants remanded in custody has progressively diminished in England and Wales, in continental Europe, as we have seen, the average percentages of remand detentions have progressively risen despite recent stabilisation.[228] As we have seen, a considerable rise in remand detentions has also occurred in the field of EU cross-border cooperation, thus leading to the adoption of a new legislative instrument aimed at preventing further misuse of custody. An opposite trend in Germany[229] is probably largely due to a judicial review system aimed at keeping the duration of pre-trial detentions under strict control. At any rate, it should be borne in mind that pretrial detention in continental Europe usually entails forms of detention that can even last over the first instance.

It should also be noted that even when new alternative means have been added to continental law outside the field of remand detention, not always have these broadened the sphere of freedom. This paradoxical situation is largely due to the fact that the boundaries between supervision measures and deprivation of personal liberty are not univocally defined at national level and that, even within the same domestic legal systems, any rigid demarcation lends itself to abuses. Italy's application of so-called windows of freedom to house arrest[230] has in practice led to a blurring of the distinction between this measure and prohibition or obligation of residence, even if very different rules apply to each with serious consequences for the individual's fundamental rights. For example, time limits are twice as long for custodial compared to non-custodial measures including house arrest.[231] This extremely broad concept of custodial measures in Italian law has led legislators to include in the regulation on custodial measures even

---

226 *Law Commission* (fn. 215), pp. 70 ff.
227 In this sense *Vogler, supra*, § 2.2.
228 As to Spain, see *Moreno Catena, supra*, § 1.3.
229 *Sinn, supra*, § 1.3.
230 See *Di Chiara, supra*, § 2.2.
231 Art. 308 CPP.

means, such as electronic tagging,[232] which in other countries[233] and supranational texts[234] are viewed as alternative measures.

3.2. Justification of pre-trial measures

Justification is of crucial importance when ordering pre-trial measures limiting personal freedom. Indeed there is no doubt that the requirement of specific grounds for restricting personal liberty has generally provided more adequate protection of the individual's rights. I will deal with justification of both remand detention and supervision measures, as justification constitutes one of the main features pre-trial precautionary measures have in common in many countries. At first glance, this does not appear the case for the ECHR system, which by providing that "release may be conditioned by guarantees to appear for trial,"[235] seems to indicate appearance at trial as the only legitimate ground for conditional bail. This is clearly not the case. If the Convention allows for the defendant to be detained where it is necessary to avert further risks of crime, it is "reasonable to assume that those risks can also justify the imposition of bail conditions, as this entails a lesser encroachment on the defendant's liberty."[236]

German law does not admit all conditions when allowing alternative measures to remand detention. Although the means mentioned in § 116 StPO do not form a restrictive list, pre-trial measures are, as we have seen, grouped on the basis of the different purposes of detention they aim to eliminate or reduce. In Italy, neither the suspicion of guilt nor the justifications laid down in Article 274 CPP relate to any specific measure. Consequently, to speak of extending the grounds for detention (*Haftgründe*) to non-custodial measures would be in principle inappropriate, as there are general grounds for limitation of liberty that also apply both to coercive and control measures. In English law, the grounds for justifying remand detention and conditional bail are not exactly the same. Thus, not only may the defendant be remanded in custody for reasons that are extraneous to the aims of the trial process[237] and that would not justify conditional bail (e. g. for the protection of the defendant or, in the case of a child or young person, for the child's own welfare), but also conditional bail may be

---

232 According to Art. 275bis CPP, electronic monitoring constitutes a modality of execution of house arrest. See *Di Chiara, supra*, § 2.2.
233 With regard to England and Wales, see s. 3AA of the Bail Act 1976.
234 See point 2.1 Recommendation Rec(2006)13 of the Committee of Ministry of the Council of Europe.
235 Art. 5.3 ECHR.
236 *Law Commission* (fn. 215), p. 66.
237 *Vogler, supra*, § 1.2.

granted for reasons that would not justify the defendant being remanded in custody; for example, for the purpose of enabling inquiries or a report to be made to assist the court in the case, a purpose that in continental inquisitorial tradition would in the past have justified automatic detention of the defendant.

The first ground for limiting personal liberty is the suspicion of guilt. Unlike some European countries,[238] all the national laws assessed provide for a uniform degree of suspicion with regard to precautionary means that does not vary with the severity of the alleged offence. Nor does the level of suspicion change with regard to limitations to personal freedom in relation to the type of measure to be applied. Nevertheless, in England and Wales the fact that the strength of the evidence that the defendant committed the offence or defaulted[239] is to be assessed when remanding the defendant in custody could lead to the conclusion that such an assessment is not required for granting bail, with or without conditions. If this were the case, the individual's freedom would clearly be jeopardised given the restrictions that conditional bail implies. However, the wording of the provisions under Schedule 1, Part I, para. 2 of the Bail Act 1976 gives decision-makers a general criterion that has to be followed for the whole bail / custody decision.

It should be noted that all the domestic systems examined herein require, albeit with a certain variety of legal expressions, a higher level of suspicion than the reasonable degree provided for by the ECHR. As we have seen, far from infringing the presumption of innocence, this approach aims to provide broader protection of individual freedom, as is apparent in the tendency of many countries to require a graver degree of suspicion the more intrusive the coercive measure.[240] Yet, the higher the degree of suspicion, the more likely is the risk that pre-conviction assessments of guilt will influence the trial decision. In England and Wales, research evidence has shown a significant impact of the initial police advice on the Crown prosecutor's recommendations for bail, conditional bail and custody, as well an impact of these recommendations on court decision-making, with the consequence that "a refusal of bail may well set up a chain of perceptions, which will lead ultimately to a conviction."[241] As mentioned above, this risk has been largely countered in Italy through the introduction of a new ground for judicial incompatibility, although its field of application does not cover the entire proceedings. Especially when the Prosecutor applies for a precautionary measure during the trial phase, the same judge or bench of judges

---

238 Both in Sweden and Denmark provide for two degrees of suspicion of guilt according to the severity of the alleged offence. See *Kalmthout*, pp. 56 ff.
239 Schedule 1, Part I, para. 9(d) of the Bail Act 1976.
240 See, from Italian perspective, the comprehensive analysis of *Negri*, pp. 84 ff.
241 In this sense *Vogler*, *supra*, § 1.2.

seized with the provisional assessment of guilt will then sit on the decision of the case.[242]

Moreover, unlike England and Wales,[243] all continental countries presuppose that this assessment will be required only for an offence punishable with a sentence of imprisonment. This is the result of a crucial principle of general theory of process that forbids provisional restrictive measures being more severe than the punishment that could be metered out with a final decision. Special forms of provisional imprisonment for offences bearing only pecuniary punishment have been abolished in Italy, although disproportionate pre-trial measures may also arise if these exceed the time frames provided for by an imposable sentence.[244] Within the field of imprisonable offences, most continental legal orders provide for specific sentence thresholds upon which pre-trial measures may be ordered.[245] As a consequence, charging someone with a one offence rather than another becomes an important and delicate matter.[246]

The contents of the pre-conviction assessment of the suspicion of guilt vary considerably among the legal systems. Its features are generally those of prognosis and undoubtedly "in almost no other circumstances is the court called upon to make predictions about future conduct rather than to determine and to punish events which have taken place in the past."[247] In Germany, urgent suspicion relates to the probability (*Wahrscheinlichkeit*) of the defendant either having committed an offence or, where punishable, having attempted to do so. The analysis thus entails a prognosis, but not a statement of the likelihood of conviction.[248] Moreover, whereas urgent suspicion is usually stronger than the sufficient suspicion to open the trial, the former does not necessarily presuppose the latter. In more general terms, they entail different types of assessment in that urgent suspicion does not require the conclusion of the pre-trial inquiries and is conducted on the basis of the current results of the investigations as a typically *rebus sic stantibus* decision.[249]

A higher degree of suspicion is required in Italy and entails, according to the prevailing opinion, a two-fold assessment: a prognosis and a decision on the basis of the current investigation. However, unlike the German system, the prognosis relates to the probability not only of guilt but also of conviction, encompassing the most likely sentence and its enforceability, e. g. with regard to

---

242 On this topic *Di Chiara*, pp. 184 ff.
243 See Schedule 1, Part II of the Bail Act 1976.
244 On both topics see *Ruggeri* [1], pp. 151 ff.
245 For a comprehensive overview of the different thresholds, see *Kamlthout*, pp. 56 ff.
246 On this topic see *Negri*, pp. 75 ff.
247 In this sense *Vogler*, *supra*, § 1.
248 See *Sinn*, *supra*, § 2.2.3.1.
249 In this sense *Meyer-Goßner*, § 112, point 6.

the possibility of a suspended sentence decision.[250] On the other hand, the fact that judges conduct this provisional assessment usually on the basis of the results of uncompleted investigations implies that *per se* the decision cannot prove the suspect's involvement beyond all reasonable doubt. At any rate, the prognosis must be extended to the capability of evidence already filed to lead to sufficient further developments in the trial process.[251] In light of this, Italian law has included, albeit in a rather contradictory manner,[252] some of the rules of evidence that apply to the trial phase, such as the corroboration rule in the assessment of statements by accomplices,[253] in the evaluation of the strong suspicion of guilt within the precautionary proceedings.

Despite its merits, such a high degree of suspicion gives cause for concern for at least two reasons. First, it does not seem appropriate that the degree of suspicion be the same level irrespective of the different levels of incidence of pretrial measures on the sphere of personal freedom. Second, even a high degree of suspicion does not exonerate decision-makers from their responsibility of ensuring that limitations to fundamental rights do not exceed a reasonable time frame. Thus, a high level of initial suspicion cannot become the justification for any excessive duration of restrictions on liberty. Moreover, Italian law has in principle[254] a rather static system where the degree of suspicion does not vary depending on the stages of the criminal process, nor on the duration of the pretrial means. By contrast, in Germany, at the time of the accusation (*Anklageerhebung*), urgent suspicion must always be stronger than sufficient suspicion.[255]

This point is of the highest importance and casts into question the common assumption that the ECHR is always satisfied with a lower degree of suspicion and thus provides only a minimum standard of protection of personal freedom. Undoubtedly the Charter's enshrinement of the notion of "reasonableness" is due to the need to apply the provision laid down in Article 5.1(c) also to police arrests, which clearly at the time of arrest do not presuppose sufficient evidence to bring charges.[256] However, the Court of Strasbourg has stressed that the "object of questioning during detention [...] is to further the criminal investigation by way of confirming or dispelling the concrete suspicion grounding the

---

250 Art. 275.2bis CPP.
251 In this sense *Di Chiara, supra*, § 2.3.1.
252 Cf. *Negri*, pp. 143 f.
253 Art. 273.1bis CPP.
254 It is quite obvious that the suspicion of guilt based on the evidence gathered in the trial phase cannot be deemed as equivalent to that assessed during the preliminary inquiry.
255 *Meyer-Goßner*, § 112, point 7.
256 See *Marzaduri, supra*, § 3.

arrest,"[257] with evident repercussions on the continuation of detention. To be sure, the concept of "reasonableness" has allowed the ECtHR to adopt, even with regard to assessment of the suspicion of guilt, an extremely flexible and dynamic perspective. It appears significant that – whereas Italian case-law has somehow blurred the application of the trial rules of assessment applicable to complicity in the serious evidence of guilt,[258] although domestic law requires their corroboration – the Court of Strasbourg has acknowledged, with regard to statements made by *pentiti*, that they could, according to the Convention, justify the initial detention of the suspect, but could not subsequently constitute valid grounds for its continuation.[259]

As we have seen, this reasoning has been transposed by ECtHR case-law to the whole assessment of the reasonable length of remand detention, in the light of the need for further grounds for detention other the mere suspicion of guilt after the initial period, grounds that have been envisaged either as the risk that the defendant fail to appear for trial, or that the defendant, if released, would take action to prejudice the administration of justice, commit further offences or cause public disorder. It has been argued that, through the requirement of lawfulness, importance can be attached to these reasons also for justifying the initial period of deprivation of liberty when required by domestic law. Significantly, whereas there is little room for autonomous application of the two further reasons laid down in Article 5.1(c) of the ECHR, namely the risk of repeat offence and the risk of absconding,[260] the risk of tampering with evidence as a form of obstructing the course of justice has assumed a role in justifying deprivation of liberty in Strasbourg case-law.

It is worth noting that thanks to this jurisprudence, the ECHR in fact covers a wider range of grounds for restriction on liberty than all the countries assessed in this study, which, like most other European legal systems, have not included in their laws the risk of posing a serious threat to public order.[261]

All the legal orders examined provide for both the risk of the defendant absconding and tampering with evidence. In Italy, the risk of flight is linked to a sentence threshold of two years' imprisonment, under which the sentence would be ordinarily suspended.[262] It is significant that in Germany the risk of ab-

---

257 ECtHR, Decision of 5.1.2010, Lexa v. Slovakia (no2), Application No. 34761/03, § 50.
258 Cass. (SU), Decision of 30.5.2006, p.m. in c. Spinnato, in: *Ced Cass.*, No. 234598. See *Di Chiara, supra*, § 2.3.1.
259 In this sense ECtHR, Decision of 6.4.2000, Labita v. Italy (fn. 156), § 159. See *Marzaduri, supra*, § 3.
260 See *Marzaduri, supra*, § 4.
261 Of the 27 EU Member States, only France, the Netherlands, Poland and Portugal have enacted this ground for detention. See *Kamlthout*, pp. 61 ff.
262 Art. 274(b) CPP.

sconding has retained a leading position in practice and led in 2009 to the ordering of remand detention in 25779 cases of the overall 28309 suspects remanded that year.[263] This result, which characterizes pre-trial detention as a precautionary measure linked to the purposes of the criminal process, can largely be explained if it is remembered that German law requires the defendant to be personally present for the duration of the trial[264] and therefore provides coercive means either to assure that he or she attends trial or to facilitate the criminal investigations.[265]

The risk of tampering with evidence is generally construed as a real risk of obstructing justice and leaves no room for limiting the defendant's freedom either to ensure that he or she is present in court or to facilitate facilitates the course of the criminal investigations.[266] As we have seen, this constitutes a reason in English law for granting conditional bail, but not for refusing bail. Nor can the defendant be deprived of his or her liberty against a declaration or confession, an instance that has, albeit in different ways, been prohibited in Italian and Spanish law.[267] Even where remand detentions justified on the basis of this risk are permitted for a fixed period, usually shorter than in other cases,[268] it is clear that a prompt evidence-gathering would prevent individual's liberty being excessively restricted.

At any rate, the risk of reoffending remains the most controversial ground for detention and still gives cause for concern in terms of presumption of innocence and its corollary of forbidding any form of anticipating the punishment.[269] In a deeper sense, the commonly shared tendency to use pre-trial measures for countering the risk of reoffending testifies to the mutation preventive means has undergone,[270] a phenomenon that linked to the fact that "security has become a constant requirement, tapped into by every ruling class to increase its political consensus and leverage."[271]

In Italy the need for the protection of collective rights (*tutela della collettività*) – an expression included in the Parliament Act containing the legislative delegation for the new code, following an approach shared also by the Constitutional Court at the beginning of the 1980s[272] – was specified for the first

---

263 *Sinn, supra*, § 1.3.
264 *Ibid., supra*, § 3.1.1.
265 *Ibid., supra*, § 2.2.1.
266 See *Marzaduri* [5], p. 71.
267 See respectively Art. 274(a) CPP and Art. 520.2(b) LECrim (related to the Art. 24.2 SC).
268 See, with regard to Spain, Art. 504.3 LECrim.
269 On this topic see *Moreno Catena, supra*, § 2.2.2.
270 In sense, with regard to provisional imprisonment in Spain, *Montero Arroca et al.*, pp. 500 ff.
271 See *Orlandi, supra*.
272 See Const. Court, Dec. 1/1980. See *Marzaduri* [5], pp. 71 f.

time[273] by the CPP 1988 mainly through a provision establishing that the risk of reoffending in certain types of serious offences justifies restriction on personal freedom. The risk of repeating an offence of the same nature, which had caused serious disquiet among Italian scholars,[274] was specified by Law 332/1995 for crimes with a minimum sentence threshold of four years' imprisonment. Such specifications are certainly useful in view of wider protection of the individual's freedom and can perhaps help attenuate all the concerns relating to this ground of detention. From this viewpoint, the lack of precision of international texts such as the Recommendation Rec(2006)13 of the Committee of Ministers of the Council of Europe regarding the types of offence that can be committed by the defendant if released, appears thus censurable.

This comparative analysis also evidences further devices for avoiding an infringement of presumption of innocence on account of the risk of repeat offence. Significantly, German law attributes, albeit in different terms, a subsidiary role to the risk of reoffending as a justification for pre-trial detention. Thus, risk of reoffending cannot be adduced when the risk of absconding or of obstructing justice exist or when the preconditions for suspending execution of the arrest warrant are evident. Moreover, as in Italy and other EU countries, the risk of recurrence is linked in Germany to specific serious offences and can anyway justify shorter detention than other remand needs.[275] It is worth noting that, whereas the Spanish literature radically rules out the possibility of ordering pre-trial detention for the purpose of alleviating social alarm (*alarma social*),[276] the German literature shows that the risk of reoffending is aimed at general public safeguard. Hence, this kind of pre-trial detention is known as "preventative detention" (*Sicherungshaft*) and its legitimacy has been confirmed by federal constitutional case law.[277] However, the doctrine has raised strong criticism of this ground for detention.[278] This, in addition to its subordinate position in law, may explain its rather limited application in practice. In fact in 2009, only 380 and 1553 suspects were remanded in custody respectively for alleged sex crimes and other serious offences.[279] The quite opposite trend in England and Italy confirms a clear shift of remand detention from the aims of the trial process to control and policing purposes.[280]

Of course, the burden of establishing that a substantial risk exists and con-

---

273 Art. 274(c) CPP.
274 See *Marzaduri* [5], p. 72.
275 See § 122a StPO. On this topic cf. *Sinn, supra*, § 3.1.3.
276 In this sense *Moreno Catena, supra*, § 2.2.2.
277 See *Sinn, supra*, § 2.2.3.4.
278 See references in *Sinn, supra*, § 2.2.3.4.
279 *Ibid., supra*, § 1.3.
280 See *Vogler, supra*, § 1.2. On this topic, see also *Ashworth/Redmayne*, p. 249.

tinues to exist, as well as demonstrating that such risk cannot be allayed, shall lie with the prosecution or investigating judge, as is clearly laid down by the Recommendation Rec(2006)13 of the Committee of Ministers of the Council of Europe.[281] As a result, taking into account the presumption in favour of bail, under English law, even speaking of "bail application"[282] appears inappropriate.[283] Among the continental countries, German law, which requires application of mitigating measures to be assessed *ex officio* at any phase of the detention procedure, and at the same time provides for rigid time-limits for this re-assessment,[284] appears to satisfy the presumption of innocence much more than the solution adopted in the Italian CPP, where the initiative both for lifting remand detention and its replacement with alternative measures lies generally with the remanded defendant.[285]

3.3.   Reasoning of pre-trial orders imposing precautionary measures

Undoubtedly justification constitutes a powerful instrument against abuses of powers in the pre-trial stages. It is of great importance that the Spanish Constitutional Court has required that, as well as the traditional preconditions required to apply precautionary measures, a constitutional aim must also be pursued that is consistent with the nature of the measure to be adopted.[286] The most significant effectiveness test of the justification requirement consists of the reasons adduced for pre-trial orders. This is another fundamental guarantee to which, as we have seen, most constitutional texts attach great importance. Clearly the duty to give reasons fulfils a crucial aim since the more pre-trial measures impinge on personal freedom, the more strict justification of these can avoid misuse. This happened unfortunately in Italy under the previous code, since the prevailing case-law continued, even after the reform of provisional release, to consider the pre-trial judge as having almost arbitrary power to order

---

281 Point 8.2 Recommendation Rec(2006)13 of the Committee of Ministers of the Council of Europe.
282 Schedule 1, Part IIA, para. 2 of the Bail Act 1976 as inserted by the Criminal Justice Act 1988.
283 In the same sense *Vogler, supra*, § 3.
284 See above, § 2.1.2.
285 See Art. 299 CPP. Indeed, the mere fact that the judicial authority has, after the indictment, the possibility of assessing the need for either lifting the precautionary measure or replacing itwith less intrusive means does not imply that it has a duty to do so. However, an obligation of re-examining the status of the defendant limited of his or her liberty has been provided for with regard to decision-making both in first and second instance.
286 See references in *Moreno Catena, supra*, § 3.2.1.

provisional release, starting from the premise that these rulings did not have to be analytically reasoned.[287]

At any rate, appreciation of the protection granted personal liberty largely depends on the contents of this duty and the manner in which it is fulfilled in practice. At first sight, this marks a considerable difference between English law and continental systems, where judicial reasoning has acquired increasing importance in the field of pre-trial orders. In Germany, the StPÄndG 1964, following harsh criticism raised by the German doctrine against the former version of § 114 StPO,[288] introduced a stricter duty to give reasons when ordering remand detention. In Italy, after the reform of most rules on precautionary means with Law 332 / 1995, the duty to give reasons when ordering these measures has become of such overwhelming complexity that it contains rules (especially regarding the methods to be followed and the validity of the pre-trial order) that are not even provided for in relation to the trial decision.[289]

In English law, despite the exceptional character given to custody, the duty to give reasons applies to both remand decisions and pre-trial orders granting conditional bail.[290] By requiring reasons to be given when a magistrates' or Crown Court either withholds bail or imposes conditions in granting bail or varies the conditions imposed, s. 5(3) of the Bail Act 1976 apparently does not specify the contents of such reasoning. However, it should be recalled that in England and Wales conditions may only be imposed for the purpose of preventing conduct that could be prevented by refusing bail altogether and that, even in order to prevent such conduct, "conditions may not be imposed unless they are necessary for that purpose."[291] Thus, to achieve a proper decision, the reasons given by decision-makers for imposing bail conditions "should include the purposes for which the conditions were imposed, so as to enable" both "the ECtHR, if need be, to see what informed the imposition of those conditions" and "a court dealing with the defendant following his or her arrest to address properly the reason for detention arising from any actual or anticipated breach of the condition".[292]

In Germany the contents of the judicial reasoning are differently regulated between remand decisions and pre-trial orders imposing conditions. Indeed, if the suspension of the execution of the arrest warrant clearly presupposes the indication of the facts demonstrating the strong suspicion of the offence and the

---

287 *Marzaduri* [1], pp. 913 f.
288 See especially *Jescheck*, p. 68.
289 On this topic see, among others, *Vogliotti* [1], pp. 64 f.
290 See *Ashworth / Redmayne*, p. 250.
291 *Law Commission* (fn. 215), pp. 68 p.
292 *Ibid.*, p. 80.

ground for issuing the warrant,[293] imposition of conditions does not require demonstration that the risks which detention aims to avoid cannot be averted by any alternative means. The wording of § 116 StPO testifies to a considerably lower degree of justification (*hinreichend begründet*), namely an expectation that the ground for detention may be achieved (risk of absconding) or can be at least attenuated through different measures (risk of tampering with evidence),[294] even if the requirement of proportionality requires the arrest warrant to be, where indispensable, suspended.[295]

Of the other countries assessed, Italy is unique in structuring the duty to give reasons. As mentioned above, notwithstanding the intention of introducing a "systematic scale of precautionary measures of increasing severity,"[296] the 1988 code submits in principle all precautionary measures affecting individual freedom, irrespective of their intrusiveness, to the same general preconditions for application laid down for custody. As a result, even control measures are nowadays subject to heavier requirements than provided for by the previous code in the matter of remand detention. However, with specific regard to precautionary needs, the guarantee function of the principle of adequacy – which, as we have seen, constitutes one of the core implications of the proportionality principle, thus supplementing the provision on the role of remand detention as *extrema ratio*[297] – is considerably attenuated by the rules on reasoned precautionary orders that require the judicial authority to state, only when remanding someone in custody, the reasons whereby no other means can counter the specific risk in question.[298] Moreover it should be considered that in practice, judicial pre-trial rulings are strongly focused on the evidence justifying suspicion of guilt and therefore generally leave very little room for precautionary risks, which are often reasoned on the basis of standardized expressions. Nor can it be ruled out that such deficiencies have been accentuated by the dissemination in Italian case-law of the thesis relating to the composite legal basis of the pre-trial measure,[299] which would thus consist of the pre-trial order, on one hand, and the ruling of the competent court for the complaint under Article 309 CPP (*tribunale del riesame*), rejecting the appeal filed against the first order, on the other hand. The fact that the decision ruling on the lack of reasoning the precautionary needs in the pre-trial order does not entitle the defendant to lodge a

---

293 See § 114.2(4) StPO.
294 *Hilger*, § 116, points 12 ff.
295 In this sense *Meyer-Goßner*, § 116, point 14.
296 *Di Chiara, supra*, § 2.
297 Art. 275.3 CPP.
298 Art. 292.2(cbis) CPP.
299 See references in *Ceresa-Gastaldo*, pp. 35 ff., 183 ff.

remedy for false imprisonment under Article 314 CPP has probably further contributed to impoverish the duty to give reasons on precautionary risks.[300]

3.4.   Special regulations relating to serious crimes

The comparative analysis of the domestic legal orders carried out in this study shows there is a common awareness that the general rules governing pre-trial orders cannot be applied to all criminal offences and that there is a need for procedural mechanisms to counter the risks connected with the most aggressive forms of crime. As a result, almost all legal systems have enacted special regulations that derogate from ordinary law, albeit with considerable differences due to the diverse impact of serious offences in their countries.

However, the search for procedural mechanisms must, in light of the ECHR system, remain compatible with the basic rules of due process. In this regard credit must be given to the ECtHR for its constant efforts to ensure the difficult balance between social needs and individual freedoms. This is especially apparent from the manner in which, as we have seen in the case *Labita v. Italy*, the Court of Strasbourg has dealt with the evidence supporting the strong suspicion of guilt required to order personal precautionary measures. The need for an appropriate balance is even more evident in the fight against terrorism, where the ECtHR, while recognising that the notion of reasonableness "cannot always be judged according to the same standards as are applied in dealing with the conventional crime," has ruled out that the need to fight terrorist crime may "justify stretching the notion of 'reasonableness' to the point where the essence of the safeguard secured by Article 5.1(c) is impaired".[301] And even "in some circumstances, for example where the suspect allegedly belongs to a gang implicated in violent crimes, or, probably, in terrorist cases, the 'unavailability of bail' can be self-evident,"[302] thus legitimising "a legal presumption of risk, in particular when this is not absolute but may be countered with evidence to the contrary,[303] the Court has ruled out that detention is automatic[304] and that legal presumption can justify the whole period of detention.[305]

---

300 Cass. (SU), Decision of 12.10.1993, Durante, in: CP 1994, p. 283. On this remedy *Di Chiara, supra*, § 3.1.4.
301 ECtHR, Decision of 30.8.1990, Fox, Campbell and Hartley v. United Kingdom, Application no. 12244/86, 12245/86, 12383/86, § 32. See *Marzaduri, supra*, § 3.
302 EctHr, Decision of 31.5.2011, Khodorkovskiy v. Russia, Application No. 5829/04, § 196.
303 In this sense *Marzaduri, supra*, § 3, relating to the case ECtHR, Decision of 6.11.2003, Pantano v. Italy, Application No. 60851/00, § 69.
304 ECtHR, Decision of 31.5.2011, Khodorkovskiy v. Russia (fn. 273), § 196.
305 ECtHR, Decision of 3.3.2009, Hilgartner v. Poland (fn. 182), § 32.

Bearing in mind these premises, it appears questionable whether the regulation contained in the Terrorism Act 2006, according to which alleged terrorism defendants can be subject to a maximum pre-trial detention of 28 days before appearing before a judicial authority, is compatible with the aforementioned standards of protection of individual freedom. Moreover, it is equally manifest that the rule prescribing written reasons to be given for granting bail to the defendant charged with serious offences under the Criminal Justice Act 1988 has ended up reversing the presumption in favour of bail.[306]

In continental Europe, the fight against serious and especially organised crime has led to different solutions. In Italy, Article 275.3 CPP provides for a very controversial regulation with regard to mafia-related crimes (mafia-type association, crimes committed using the typical conditions of mafia association and crimes of mafia abetting). A recent attempt to extend this provision to the area of sexual offences and other serious crimes has been largely countered by the Constitutional Court, which has further narrowed the application of the exceptional mechanism.[307] It would appear that the Italian solution provides for proper balancing, since it introduces a device based on a rebuttable presumption of dangerousness of defendants charged with these crimes. This exonerates the judicial authority from assessing the real existence of any precautionary need, thus making remand detention the only permissible solution. Nevertheless, the possibility of overturning this presumption of adequacy of the most intrusive pre-trial measure depends on the existence of specific elements demonstrating that none of the ordinary precautionary needs apply to the case in hand.[308] Moreover, proof must be furnished by the defendant. This clearly overturns the burden of proof which Recommendation Rec(2006)13 of the Committee of Ministers of the Council of Europe states must lie, as we have seen, with the prosecution or investigating judge. Finally, proof of the inexistence of any precautionary risk is manifestly more difficult for the defence to demonstrate than the proof lying with the Prosecutor, who shall only demonstrate the existence of one risk.[309] And even if in the field of mafia-related crimes it would be extremely difficult for the Prosecutor to demonstrate a specific risk, for defendants it is sometimes impossible to adduce proof that they are not dangerous at all, since according to prevailing case-law they should prove the criminal organization no longer exists or they are no longer part thereof. As a result, legal presumption becomes in practice almost irrebuttable.

In Germany, despite the wording of § 112.3 StPO, the Constitutional Court has

---

306 In this sense *Vogler, supra,* § 1.2.
307 *Di Chiara, supra,* § 2.3.3.
308 *Ibid., supra,* § 2.3.3.
309 *Ruggeri* [2], pp. 440 ff.

found a more appropriate balance between personal liberty and the need for prevention of the risks connected with serious offences, requiring that for defendants charged with serious crime to be remanded in custody, the likelihood they might abscond or destroy evidence must at least not be excludable.[310] To be sure, this is a considerably lower threshold than that provided for in § 112.2 StPO, in that only a relatively mild or remote danger of this sort need be claimed.[311] Unlike the Italian solution, however, the German system leaves no leeway for presumptions or reversal of the burden of proof,[312] which still lies with the criminal prosecution authorities.

4.   Procedural safeguards

In light of the approach of this study, the cross-cutting analysis of the procedural features of the pre-trial measures provided for by the domestic legal systems assessed highlights some fundamental aspects regarding the fairness of two phases of the interim proceedings: application of provisional means of coercion and their subsequent controls.

We have seen that most European Constitutions issued after the Second World War have strongly promoted a process of jurisdictionalization of the measures of coercion affecting fundamental freedoms, and considerably reduced the powers of the police to interfere with the sphere of personal liberty. Although not yet completed, this process has significantly reinforced the duty to give reasons for pre-trial orders. More recently, countries like Italy and Spain have felt the need to further enhance jurisdictional guarantees by introducing the principle of application as a form of ensuring the impartiality of decision-makers.[313] Judges have been deprived of the power to autonomously order restrictions on the personal freedom of defendants, a prerogative they still retain in Germany, albeit only in particular circumstances, due the essentially inquisitorial features of German procedures.[314]

However, the application requirement has been enacted in very different ways in Italy and Spain. In deference to the adversarial principle and the *audi alteram partem* rule,[315] Spain, unlike Italy, requires a hearing (*vistilla*) prior to the adoption of precautionary measures. In Italy, the requirement of a previous request from the Public Prosecutor's Office has, despite its institutional role as

---

310 BVerfG, Decision of 15.12.1965 – 1 BvR 513/65, BVerfGE 19, pp. 342 ff.
311 In this sense *Sinn, supra,* § 2.2.3.3.
312 *Meyer-Goßner,* § 112, point 38.
313 See, respectively, *Di Chiara, supra,* §§ 3.1 and 3.1.1, and *Moreno Catena, supra,* § 4.1.
314 On this topic *Sinn, supra,* §§ 2.2.2 and 3.1.1.
315 See *Moreno Catena, supra,* § 4.1.

guarantor of both substantial and procedural legality,[316] paradoxically lent itself
to abuses. Indeed, the Prosecutor, whereas has the duty to include with his
request all evidence collected in favour of the defendant, can legitimately select
the information deemed appropriate to support the request for a pre-trial
measure.[317] This has a huge influence on judicial assessments. Despite strict
procedural code requirements on a wide range of precautionary means, the pre-
trial judge is nonetheless called to determine the existence of strong evidence of
guilt and alleged risks on the basis of the information attached by the Prosecutor.
The risk of partial judicial evaluation is unavoidable and is further aggravated by
the lack in Italy[318] – unlike Spain – of an adversarial precautionary procedure
prior to the issue of pre-trial orders. This vacuum is only in part filled by the
requirement that the pre-trial judge question the remanded defendant within
strict time frames, at the expiry of which the measure becomes ineffective.[319] In
applying for a remand order, the Prosecutor still can request that the interview
between defendant and his or her lawyer be postposed[320] and that the judicial
hearing of the defendant be brought forward. The repercussions of this choice on
the sphere of personal freedom are apparent and can render mandatory appearance of the defendant's lawyer at the remand hearing, which must then take
place within forty-eight hours from implementation of the measure,[321] a mere
formality. Moreover, the defence is highly unlikely to be able to undermine the
initial assessment during this examination given the short time-limits provided
for under Article 294 CPP, which do not allow the defence, especially in case of
sudden remand orders issued against suspects previously unaware that a preliminary inquiry was being conducted, to collect sufficient evidence and prepare
an adequate defence strategy.

The issue of the information available to the competent court for bail decisions is of the highest importance in England and Wales as a fundamental
element of their strongly rooted adversarial procedures. In comparison to
continental criminal justice systems, English law has not enacted the principle of
request and has over recent decades even strengthened the role of the police,
which since 1984 have acquired new powers to attach conditions to granting bail
and can even remand defendants in custody, albeit only for a very brief period in

---

316 Art. 73.1 of the Real Decree 12/1941.
317 *Di Chiara, supra*, § 3.1.1.
318 However, as we have seen above (§ 2.2.2), where the precautionary order (especially a
     remand order) is issued in the course of the procedure aimed at the validation of a pro-
     visional arrest, the suspect must be interviewed by the pre-trial judge prior to the adoption
     of the precautionary means.
319 See above, § 2.2.2.
320 Art. 104.3 CPP.
321 Art. 275.1ter CPP.

order to appear before the next available Magistrates' Court. Moreover, in contrast to a single lay magistrate, a Magistrates' court can both grant bail (conditional and unconditional) and remand the defendant in custody. The court's strong powers to take all bail or custody decisions is justified by the presumption in favour of bail and the adversarial character of what is inappropriately called "remand hearings," i. e. a procedure in open court in which the defendant is entitled to be represented by a duty lawyer.[322] This can also explain why the question of evidence to decide on pre-trial measures is of such importance to prevent judicial assessment turning into "a speculation at best" rather than an examination of hard evidence.[323] Objective Bail Information Schemes along the lines of the Vera Institute in the US have been introduced since the 1990s with the purpose of providing "factual, verified information," relating also to the "defendant's character, antecedents, community ties," in addition to "that otherwise available to the Crown Prosecution Service (and the defence) to assist it to decide whether there are grounds for asking the court to release a defendant on bail rather than remand him or her in custody".[324]

It is significant that, whereas continental Prosecutors can continue to interview the remanded defendant,[325] in England the defendant, once remanded, "may no longer be interviewed by the police or any other authority in connection with the case except in exceptional circumstances." We have seen that the defendant has the right to apply for bail each time he or she appears in court and, although since 1988 he or she has lost the possibility of supporting the same arguments after the first two hearings, it still remains "the court's duty to consider, at each subsequent hearing while the defendant is a person to whom s. 4 of the Bail Act 1976 applies and remains in custody, whether he ought to be granted bail."[326] In practice, however, "the position of the defendant at trial is materially undermined by custody and the wearing of handcuffs and the presence of escort officers is very likely to prejudice a court in their disfavour."[327] Moreover remand in custody has "a strongly negative impact on the capacity of the defence to mount a successful defence in an adversarial setting,"[328] mostly due to the difficulties to access legal advisers, a problem which tends to be aggravated with particular regard to young female detainees.[329] This shows that

---

322 See *Vogler, supra*, § 3.1.
323 *Ibid., supra*, § 3.1.
324 *Ibid., supra*, § 3.1.
325 In Italy Law 332 / 1995, by reversing the rule that allowed for the Prosecutor to interview the remanded defendant before the judge (Art. 294.6 CPP), has confirmed this practice.
326 Art. 154 of the Criminal Justice Act 1988.
327 In this sense *Vogler, supra*, § 2.2.
328 *Ibid., supra*, § 2.2.
329 On this topic *Ashworth / Redmayne*, p. 248.

the lack of the necessary preconditions for collecting evidence and preparing an appropriate defence can strongly undermine even an adversarial procedure and affect the whole decision-making process.

The awareness of such risks was probably what led Germany recently to reform the law on pre-trial detention of 2010 and introduce, *inter alia*, the requirement that participation of the defence counsel is mandatory where remand detention is to be executed against the accused.[330] It should be noted, however, that the previous failure to appoint a counsel for the remanded defendant was in part compensated for by a provision whereby after three months' remand detention during which the accused had neither applied for review of detention nor lodged a complaint against remand detention, a review was conducted on the court's own initiative.[331] This typically inquisitorial instrument allows the judge to "order specific investigations which may be important for the subsequent decision concerning continuation of remand detention, and he may conduct a further review after completion of such investigations."[332] It is also a means of ensuring verification of the reasonableness for continuing remand detention.

Italian law provides a similar instrument whereby a defendant subject to any precautionary measure (whether coercive or control measures) may apply at any time for a judicial review to amend or revoke the measure.[333] Despite the great potentialities of this instrument, which is not in principle linked to the emergence of new facts or circumstances, the possibility for the defendant to obtain a review on the basis of the same elements nonetheless suffers, as in English law, from a limitation that in Italy derives from the co-called "precautionary *ne bis in idem*," i.e. a final ruling on the same facts or circumstances within the appeal procedures against pre-trial orders.[334] Moreover, unlike Germany, the Italian competent judge for judicial review has, apart from the exceptional case laid down in Article 299.4ter CPP, no power in the event of insufficient information either to conduct autonomous investigations or to order the prosecution authorities to do so. Finally, the fact that the judge may, in certain instances during the preliminary inquiry and in any case after the accusation, re-examine *ex officio* the grounds for restriction of personal freedom, does not imply any duty to do so after certain periodical intervals, as is the case in other countries. This in my view undermines the ability of judicial review, as set down in Article 299 of

---

330 See § 140.1(4) StPO. On this topic cf. *Sinn, supra*, § 3.1.3.
331 See § 117.5 StPO (fv).
332 See § 117.3 StPO.
333 *Di Chiara, supra*, § 3.1.3.
334 On this topic see *Ruggeri* [3], pp. 425 ff.

the CPP, to ensure constant re-examination of the factual and legal grounds for limiting personal freedom.[335]

In the light of the aforementioned aim of creating a "microsystem" of precautionary means, Italy provides for an extremely complex range of remedies against pre-trial orders. The most powerful means of challenging coercive measures in Italian law is the judicial complaint, provided for under Article 309 CPP. Very similar to the German remand complaint (*Haftbeschwerde*), this instrument aims to provide an overall re-examination of the grounds for pre-trial orders. There is no doubt that this remedy provides a higher level of protection of the right to liberty than that achieved by the above-mentioned appeal on a point of law to the Court of Cassation provided for by the Constitution as a mandatory remedy against pre-trial orders limiting personal freedom.[336] There are at least two reasons for this: a) it allows for re-assessment of the grounds for restriction within fixed time-limits, at the expiry of which the measure becomes ineffective;[337] b) it grants the defendant the right to challenge the pre-trial measure in a hearing, albeit *in camera*, before a collegial body. Nevertheless, the wide-ranging powers of the competent court in respect of this complaint allow it to remove eventual defects of the pre-trial order but also confirm the measure by amending the reasons initially adduced. Thus, the thesis of the composite legal basis of the pre-trial measure[338] attaches enormous value to the ascertainment of this ruling, against which only an appeal to the Court of Cassation pursuant to Article 311.1 CPP can be lodged. Given its strictly devolutive limits,[339] this remedy cannot offer a proper protection of individual freedom.

5. Conclusive remarks. The development of pre-trial precautionary measures and the approximation of the notions of personal liberty and security

Although several changes have occurred in the way personal freedoms are conceived over the last decades, protecting the right to liberty remains today a priority concern of both domestic criminal justice systems and supranational institutions in Europe. The comparative analysis of the four legal systems has shown the strong growth of individual guarantees like legality and juris-

---

335 Of a different opinion *Di Chiara*, § 3.1.2.
336 On this topic see recently *Spagnolo*, pp. 131 ff., 287 ff.
337 Art. 309.9–10 CPP.
338 See above, § 3.2.
339 See *Di Chiara*, *supra*, § 3.1.3.

dictionality, thereby fulfilling requirements provided for by the various Constitutions.

The situation in practice is unfortunately very different and the ECtHR appeals to enhance the effectiveness of procedural rights have largely gone unheeded. Structural guarantees have not succeeded in avoiding the risk that pre-conviction assessments of guilt lead to adopting different means of coercion, which, although completely unconnected with the criminal process, may have serious repercussions in terms of individual freedoms. This risk is perceived almost everywhere. In England and Wales it has recently permitted the use of remand detentions and conditional bail for preventive purposes even in minor cases[340] and with discriminating effects.[341] In Spain, new means have been introduced aimed either at protecting different rights to those safeguarded by personal precautionary measures, such as the safety of the victims of criminal conduct, or to protect society (e.g. withdrawing a driver's licence, provisional closure of businesses, premises or establishments). Both groups of measures have given cause for serious concern: the former due to their impact on the right to personal liberty; the latter, because they are based on a presumption of guilt and become anticipatory forms of punishment.[342]

This result is largely due to the need to provide a prompt (albeit provisional) response to criminal offences. This is particularly apparent in countries like Italy where the length of the criminal process prejudices the possibility of effective sanctions. It must however be very clear that the use of pre-trial instruments of coercion for preventive purposes brings with it the danger of misuse of procedural devices for policing and control purposes,[343] a danger to which even countries like Germany are constantly exposed, despite the limited application of the risk of re-offending in its legal system.[344]

The changes in pre-trial measures testify to a deep mutation of criminal justice, which cannot be countered by simply invoking the traditional aims of the process and thus trying to restrict within this context new coercive means that have often been introduced in response to the urgent call for adequate devices capable of fighting new forms of crime. Indeed, like criminal punishment,[345] the process itself has undergone radical changes over the last few decades, acquiring unprecedented preventive purposes. These are thus reflected in the coercive measures adopted in the pre-trial stages and subsequently in the way precautionary interventions in the sphere of fundamental freedoms are

---

340 *Vogler, supra*, § 4.
341 On this topic *Ashworth / Redmayne*, p. 251 f.
342 *Moreno Catena, supra*, § 5.2.
343 *Vogler, supra*, § 4.
344 *Sinn, supra*, § 5.
345 On this topic see *Donini*, pp. 1035 ff.

nowadays conceived. The traditional perspective aimed at balancing individual freedoms with the repressive needs of the state has been largely replaced by the increasing demand for security.[346] As a result, both punishment and the criminal process itself have become tied to "affirmed and contingent individual needs," rather than to "abstract state interests."[347] Of paramount importance is the requirement that any jeopardy to the fundamental freedoms of the individual during preliminary enquiries must be carefully assessed in the light of the presumption of innocence, which remains the most powerful instrument to prevent coercive measures becoming punitive.

Bibliography

Allegrezza, Silvia, Critical remarks on the Green Paper on obtaining evidence in criminal matters from one Member State to another and securing its admissibility, in: ZIS (9/2010), pp. 569 ff.

Amato, Giuliano, Individuo e autorità nella disciplina della libertà personale, Giuffrè (1976)

Amodio, Ennio, La tutela della libertà personale dell'imputato nella Convenzione europea dei diritti dell'uomo, in: Rivista italiana di diritto e procedura penale (1967).

Ashworth, Andrew/Redmayne, Mike, The Criminal Process, 4th ed., Oxford University Press (2005).

Barbera, Augusto, I principi costituzionali della libertà personale, Giuffrè (1967).

Bernar Pulido, Carlos, El principio de proporcionalidad y los derechos fundamentales, 3rd ed., Centro de estudios políticos y constitucionales (2007).

Bernsdorf, Norbert, Article 6, in: Meyer, Jürgen (ed.), Charta der Grundrechte der Europäischen Union, 2th ed., Nomos (2006).

Beulke, Werner, Strafprozessrecht, 10th ed., C.F. Mueller Verlag (2008).

Ceresa-Gastaldo, Massimo, Il riesame delle misure coercitive nel processo penale, Giuffrè (1993).

Chiavario, Mario, Processo e garanzie della persona, II, Le garanzie fondamentali, 3rd ed., Giuffrè (1984).

Darbyshire, Penny, Report on England and Wales, in: Vogler, Richard/Huber, Barbara (eds.), Criminal procedure in Europe, Duncker & Humblot (2008).

De Amicis, Gaetano, Mandato di arresto europeo e limiti massimi di custodia cautelare: incostituzionalità o "interpretazione costitutionalmente orientatata" del motive di rifiuto alla consegna?, in: Giurisprudenza di merito (2007), pp. 1435 ff.

De Salvia, Michele, L'obbligo degli Stati di conformarsi alle decisioni della Corte europea e del Comitato dei Ministri del Consiglio d'Europa, in: Kostoris, Roberto K./Balsamo, Antonio (eds.), Giurisprudenza europea e processo penale italiano, Giappichelli (2008), pp. 67 ff.

---

346 In this sense *Orlandi, supra.*
347 *Ibid., supra.*

Di Chiara, Giuseppe, L'incompatibilità endoprocessuale del giudice, Giappichelli (2000).

Donini, Massimo, Non punibilità e idea negoziale, in: Indice penale (2001), pp. 1035 ff.

Epping, Volker, Grundrechte, 4th ed., Springer (2010).

Ferrari, Giuseppe Franco, National Judges and Supranational Laws. On the Effective Application of EU Law and ECHR, in: Martinico, Giuseppe/Pollicino, Oreste (eds.), The National Judicial Treatment of the ECHR and EU Laws. A Comparative Constitutional Perspective, Europa Law Publishing (2010), pp. 21 ff.

Gimeno Sendra, Vigente, Derecho procesal penal, 2nd ed., Colex (2007).

Gleß, Sabine, Europäische Beweisanordnung, in: Sieber, Ulrich et al. (eds.), Europäisches Strafrecht, Nomos-Beck (2011), pp. 596 ff.

Grevi, Vittorio, Il sistema delle misure cautelari personali nel nuovo codice di procedura penale, in: Grevi, Vittorio (ed.), La libertà personale dell'imputato verso il nuovo codice di procedura penale, Cedam (1989).

Gusy, Christoph, *Article 104, in: von Mangoldt, Hermann et al. (eds.), Kommentar zum Grundgesetz, III vol., 5th ed., Vahlen (2005).*

Hamilton, Claire, The Presumption of Innocence and Irish Criminal Law. "Whittling the Golden Thread", Irish Academic Press (2007).

Hecker, Bernd, Europäisches Strafrecht, 3rd ed., Springer (2010).

Hilger, Hans, §§ 112 ff., in: Erb, Volker et al. (eds.), Löwe-Rosenberg. Die Strafprozeßordnung und das Gerichtsverfassungsgesetz, 26th ed., IV vol., De Gruyter (2007), pp. 1 ff.

Jescheck, Hans-Heinrich, Recht und Praxis der Untersuchungshaft in der Bundesrepublik Deutschland, in: Goltdammer's Archiv für Strafrecht (1962), pp. 65 ff.

Meyer-Goßner, Lutz, Strafprozessordnung mit GVG und Nebengesetzen, 54th ed., C.H. Beck (2011).

Manacorda, Stefano, Carta dei diritti fondamentali dell'Unione europea e CEDU: una nuova tipografia delle garanzie penalistiche in Europa?, in: Manes, Vittorio/Zagrebelsky, Vladimiro (eds.), La Convenzione Europea dei diritti dell'uomo nell'ordinamento penale italiano, Giuffrè (2011), pp. 147 ff.

Martines, Temistocle, Diritto costituzionale, 2rd ed., Giuffrè (1981).

Martinico, Giuseppe, National Judges and Supranational Laws: Goals and Structure of the Research, in: Martinico, Giuseppe/Pollicino, Oreste (eds.), The National Judicial Treatment of the ECHR and EU Laws. A Comparative Constitutional Perspective, Europa Law Publishing (2010), pp. 7 ff.

Marzaduri, Enrico, [1] Libertà provvisoria (diritto processuale penale), in: IV Novissimo Digesto italiano (1983); [2] Riesame dei provvedimenti restrittivi della libertà personale, in: Novissimo Digesto italiano (1986), VI App.; [3] Custodia cautelare nel diritto processuale penale, in: III Digesto delle discipline penalistiche (1989); [4] Imputato e imputazione, in: VI Digesto delle discipline penalistiche (1989); [5] Misure cautelari personali (princìpi generali e disciplina), in: VIII Digesto delle discipline penalistiche (1994), pp. 59 ff.; [6] Art. 1, Legge costituzionale 2/1999, in: Legislazione penale (2000), pp. 762 ff.; [7] Accertamenti non definitivi sulla responsabilità dell'imputato ed attenuazione della presunzione di non colpevolezza, in: VVAA, Presunzione di non colpevolezza e disciplina delle impugnazioni, Giuffrè (2000), pp. 213 ff.

Montero Arroca, Juan et al., Derecho jurisdiccional III. Proceso penal, 15th ed., Tirant lo Blanch (2007).

Mortati, Costantino, Istituzioni di diritto pubblico, 8th ed., II, Cedam (1969).

Müller-Franken, Sebastian, Article 104, in: Stern, Klaus/Becker, Florian (eds.), Grundrechte-Kommentar, Carl Heymanns Verlag (2010).

Negri, Daniele, Fumus commissi delicti. La prova per le fattispecie cautelari, Giappichelli (2004).

Orlandi, Renzo, Provvisoria esecuzione delle sentenze e presunzione di non colpevolezza, in: VVAA, Presunzione di non colpevolezza e disciplina delle impugnazioni, Giuffrè (2000), pp. 123 ff.

Paeffgen, Hans-Ullrich, §§ 112 ff., in: Wolter, Jürgen (ed.), Systematischer Kommentar zur Strafprozessordnung mit GVG und EMRK, 4th ed., II vol., Carl Heymanns Verlag (2010), pp. 635 ff.

Ruggeri, Stefano, [1] Giudicato penale ed accertamenti non definitive, Giuffrè (2004); [2] Art. 2, Decreto legislativo 11/2009, in: LP 2009, pp. 429 ff.; [3] Giudicato cautelare, in: III Annali Enciclopedia del diritto (2010).

Sanders, Andrew/Young, Richard/Burton, Mandy, Criminal Justice, Oxford University Press (2010).

Serrano Alberca, José María, Article 17, in: Garrido Falla, Fernando (ed.), Comentarios a la Constitución, 2nd ed., Civitas (2001).

Spagnolo, Paola, Il tribunale della libertà tra normativa nazionale e normativa internazionale, Giuffrè (2008).

Stuckenberg, Carl-Friedrich, Untersuchungen zur Unschuldsvermutung, Walter de Gruyter (1998).

Stumer, Andrew, The Presumption of Innocence. Evidential and Human Rights Perspectives, Hart Publishing (2010).

Trechsel, Stefan, Human Rights in Criminal Proceedings, Oxford University Press (2005).

Ubertis, Giulio, Principi di procedura penale europea, 2th ed., Raffaello Cortina Editore (2009).

van Kamlthout, Anton, Introductory Summary, in: Kamlthout, Anton et al. (eds.), Pre-trial Detention in the European Union. An Analysis of Minimum Standards in Pre-trial Detention and the grounds for Regular Review in the Member States of the EU, Wolf Legal Publishers (2009).

Vogliotti, Massimo, [1] La motivazione dei provvedimenti giurisdizionali, in: Marzaduri, Enrico, Atti del procedimento penale. Forma e struttura, Utet (1996), pp. 33 ff.; [2] La logica *flue* della Corte europea dei diritti dell'uomo tra tutela del testimone e salvaguardia del contraddittorio: il caso delle testimonianze anonime, in: Giurisprudenza italiana (1998), pp. 851 ff.

Vogler, Richard, Introduction, in: Vogler, Richard/Huber, Barbara (eds.), Criminal procedure in Europe, Duncker & Humblot (2008).

The chapter contributions of this book are quoted with the only reference to the Author's surname, *supra*, and the number of the paragraph concerned.

IV. Annex

Questionnaire on Pre-trial Precautionary Measures in Criminal Proceedings. A comparison between England and Wales, Germany, Italy and Spain[1]

1. The right to liberty and security
    1.1. What protection does the right to liberty and security receive in your legal system?
    1.2. Does your law grant the right to *Habeas Corpus* proceedings?
2. Types of pre-trial precautionary measures
    2.1. What is meant by "pre-trial precautionary measures" in your legal system?
    2.2. What position does remand detention occupy in your legal system in relation to the presumption of innocence?
    2.3. Does your law provide for alternatives to custody? In the affirmative case, what kind of alternatives does your law permit and which fundamental rights do such measures limit or prejudice?
    2.4. Does your legal system provide for special pre-trial measures and / or any special regulation of pre-trial measures with regard to specific forms of crime (juvenile crime, terrorism, organized crime etc.)?
3. Competent authority
    3.1. Which kind of authority is competent to order pre-trial precautionary measures?
    3.2. If your system requires judicial intervention, does the judge intervene before or may he or she intervene after pre-trial measures have been ordered?
    3.3. If your system requires the intervention of a judicial authority, is it a different authority from the one competent for the criminal proceedings? If not, does your law contain any provision guaranteeing the impartiality of the judicial authority in both criminal and remand proceedings?
4. The procedure for ordering precautionary measures
    4.1. May pre-trial measures be ordered *ex officio?* If not, does your law provide for any request to be made by the Prosecutor?

---

1 The questionnaire has been answered by Prof. Dr. Richard Vogler (England and Wales), Prof. Dr. Arndt Sinn (Germany), Prof. Dr. Stefano Ruggeri (Italy) and Prof. Dr. Víctor Moreno Catena (Spain).

4.2. Does your law provide for any hearings for the person subject to pre-trial measures? In the affirmative case, which procedure does your law establish for such hearings?

4.3. Does your law grant the defendant the right to legal assistance during remand proceedings?

4.4. What kind of information does your law grant the defendant on remand and / or subject to alternatives to custody?

5. Justification

5.1. Which pre-conditions does your law require as a basis for ordering precautionary measures?

5.2. Are the conditions established for ordering pre-trial measures proportionate to the different limitations of fundamental rights imposed by them?

5.3. Do legal conditions have the same relevance throughout the remand proceedings?

6. The duration of precautionary measures

6.1. Which provisions ensure the continued lawfulness of pre-trial precautionary measures?

6.2. Does your law provide for periodic review of pre-trial precautionary measures by the judicial authorities?

6.3. Does your legislation provide for maximum time limits of pre-trial measures?

7. Remedies

7.1. What remedies does your law grant to a defendant subject to a deprivation / restriction of his or her right to liberty?

7.2. Which rights are granted to the defendant subject to a deprivation / restriction of his or her right to liberty during appeal proceedings?

7.3. May the appeal against a remand order coexist with a judicial review of the remand detention?

8. Pre-trial precautionary measures and criminal proceedings

8.1. May pre-trial precautionary measures be ordered at any stage of the criminal proceedings?

8.2. What influence do pre-trial orders and / or decisions of the criminal proceedings have on pre-trial precautionary measures?

8.3. Do the legal conditions governing pre-trial measures have the same relevance throughout criminal proceedings? If not, how does their effect vary according to the stage of the criminal proceedings?

8.4. Does the length of the criminal proceedings influence that of the precautionary measures?

8.5. May the duration of the precautionary measures influence that of the criminal proceedings?

8.6. Does a charge always accompany the imposition of pre-trial measures?

1.   The right to liberty and security

1.1.   What protection does the right to liberty and security receive in your legal system?

ENGLAND AND WALES: England and Wales, in common with the other parts of the United Kingdom, has no written constitution and therefore no specific constitutional right to liberty and security. However, as early as 1215, clause 39 of *Magna Carta* held that "no free man shall be arrested or imprisoned, or disseised or outlawed or exiled or in any way victimized, neither will we attack him or send anyone to attack him, except by the lawful judgment of his peers or by the law of the land." This right has been repeated in subsequent constitutional enactments, most recently in the Human Rights Act 1998 which domesticated the ECHR, including the Article 5 right to liberty and security, directly into UK law. The protection of liberty and security in criminal process was reinforced by the Bail Act 1976 which creates in s. 4 a presumption in favour of release. Practical and detailed provisions relating to the rights of persons arrested in connection with a criminal investigation are set out in the Police and Criminal Evidence Act 1984 (PACE) and its associated Codes of Practice.

GERMANY: A custodial sentence represents a restriction of a person's freedom of movement. This basic principle is all the more important in cases of pre-trial measures. The German Constitution (hereinafter GG), provides a few provisions to protect fundamental rights like the right to liberty. Art. 104 GG is central to this issue. Article 104.1 GG asserts that "liberty of the person may be restricted only pursuant to a formal law and only in compliance with the procedures prescribed therein."

According to Article 104.2 GG, "only a judge may rule upon the permissibility or continuation of any deprivation of liberty. If such a deprivation is not based on a judicial order, a judicial decision shall be obtained without delay. The police may hold no one in custody on their own authority beyond the end of the day following the arrest. Details shall be regulated by a law." Article 104.3 GG states the aspect of time more precisely. Article 104.3 GG also contains the right to be heard. Concerning the right to liberty see moreover Articles 2.1 and 11 GG.

According to the GG, the German code of criminal procedure (hereinafter StPO) – as a formal law – provides corresponding regulations. The requirement of a judicial order is found expressly in § 125 StPO [Competence for issuing the arrest warrant] and § 115 StPO [Examination by a judge] as well as § 115a StPO [Examination by the judge of the nearest local court]. The procedure is particularly determined in §§ 114–130 StPO. For more details see below.

ITALY: The right to personal liberty constitutes the first liberty among those recognized and protected by the Italian Constitution, which defines it as inviolable (Art. 13.1 of the Constitution). It implies firstly that nobody may be restricted or deprived of his personal liberty without a reasoned judicial order and beyond the limits established by law (rule of law and jurisdiction) (Art. 13.2 of the Constitution). Moreover, all judicial orders restricting or depriving anybody of his or her personal liberty are subject to an appeal on a question of law (Art. 111.7 of the Constitution).

In contrast to the code of criminal procedure of 1930, the current one (1988) does not contain any regulation explicitly concerned with personal liberty. Instead, Book IV of the code contains a catalogue of pre-trial measures sharing the common precautionary character, albeit with significant subdivisions. The first group of pre-trial means contained in this Book encompass all the measures concerned with the protection of the "liberty of the person" (Art. 272 CPP), although not all these measures impinge on personal liberty and only the "custodial measures" (*misure custodiali*) entail a deprivation thereof. See 2.2 below.

SPAIN: The Spanish Constitution considers freedom foremost among the essential values of the Spanish legal system (Art. 1.1). Precisely for this reason does the Spanish constituent impose upon public authorities the positive duty to promote the necessary conditions, which ensure that the freedom and the equality of the individuals and the groups to which they belong be real and effective, thereby removing the obstacles that impede or hinder its fulfilment (Art. 9.2).

In the Spanish legal system, the right to personal liberty and security is a fundamental right and therefore receives maximum protection. Legal protections govern all public authorities and private parties and only by Organic Law, which in any case must respect its essential content, may the exercise of this right be regulated. The responsibility for safeguarding of the right to personal liberty lies with the ordinary courts by means of a procedure based on the principle of preferential and summary treatment and where appropriate through an appeal to the Constitutional Court (Art. 53 of the Constitution).

1.2.   Does your law grant the right to *Habeas Corpus* proceedings?

ENGLAND AND WALES: No, except in certain circumstances. This is an ancient Common Law right and therefore statute law (such as the Bail Act 1976) takes precedence. *Habeas Corpus* is still used for matters not specifically addressed by the Act, such as abuse of process, as in R. (on the application of Hauschildt) v

Highbury Corner Magistrates Court [EWHC 3494 (Admin); [2009] Crim. L.R. 512 (QBD (Admin)] to halt proceedings where (in this case) false promises of the grant of bail were given to induce a defendant to return to the jurisdiction.

The Divisional Court of the High Court issues writs of *Habeas Corpus* and the procedure is initiated by filing a writ.

GERMANY: The GG contains specific guarantees against an improper detention, which are deemed as equivalent to those deriving from the writs of *Habeas Corpus*. As to the requirement of a judicial warrant for arrest as well as of a judicial control of any arrest carried out by the police, see Articles 104.2–3 and, generally, 2.2 GG. Moreover, Article 19.4 GG provides a statutory basis for a judicial control (which, if no other jurisdiction has been established, must be carried out by the ordinary courts) to be ensured where any person's right is violated by public authority.

These rights are enshrined in the StPO (see, in particular, 3.2 and 5.1 above).

As regards the competent authority for issuing an arrest warrant, the Public Prosecutor's Office is competent in the first instance (§ 125.1 StPO). The arrest warrant is issued by the competent court/judge. During the investigative proceedings the local court judge (*Amtsgericht*) will have jurisdiction (§ 125.1 StPO; see also § 116.1 of the Judicature Act). The competence changes after the indictment (§ 125.2 StPO). Judges are required to be independent pursuant to Articles 92 and 97.1 GG.

The procedure consists in the following steps:
- Application for the issue of a remand order.
- Issue of remand order.
- Arrest of the suspect.
- Immediate presentation (maximum period 1 day) before the custodial judge (usually through committal to an institution for remand detention and information for the judge and the public prosecution office) (§ 115 StPO). The expiry of the time-limits established for such a committal does not imply that the arrest warrant must be revoked and the remanded defendant released.
- Not later than the day after committal the remanded defendant is to be heard.
- If the person is arrested without a warrant, the judge must issue the warrant (§ 128 StPO).

As regards detailed information about obligations see §§ 114a ff. StPO.

See also 2.1 and 5.1 below, as well as § 126a StPO.

According to § 127.2 StPO, provisional arrest is not subject to this procedure, as the suspect is caught in the very act and this procedure could not be performed.

Further procedures are conducted pursuant to § 128 StPO.

ITALY: Italian law does not provide for *Habeas Corpus* as a procedure aimed at granting the person deprived of his or her liberty by administrative authorities the right to challenge the detention by taking proceedings for the lawfulness of his or her detention to be speedily checked by a judicial authority.

The Constitution allows, as an exception to the rule of law and the jurisdiction requirements explained above under 1.1, the authority responsible for public safety to provisionally deprive an individual of his or her right to liberty, but obliges it to inform the judicial authority within 48 hours, which within another 48 hours must confirm a provisional deprivation of liberty or release the arrested individual. Pursuant to the general rule laid down by Article 111.6 of the Constitution, this judicial decision must also be reasoned.

The code of criminal procedure contains much more detailed regulation. Any arrested individual must be brought before the Prosecutor within 24 hours from the moment of being detained (Art. 386). After the arrest the police must promptly provide legal assistance for the arrested person. The prosecutor will hear the arrested person and inform him or her about the reasons for the arrest and any charge against him or her (Art. 388 CPP). If all the legal conditions are not fulfilled, the arrested person must be immediately released. Otherwise the prosecutor must apply for judicial confirmation within 48 hours from the moment of the arrest. This procedure includes the hearing of the arrested person, except in case of impossibility or a suspect's refusal of the hearing (Art. 391 CPP). Judicial confirmation can lead to the adoption of a precautionary measure after the detainee has been heard (Art. 294 (1) CPP). However, in this case, if the suspect was arrested pursuant to Article 381.2 or for an offence which was not *in flagrante*, the ordinary penalty thresholds established by Articles 274(c) and 280 CPP may be exceeded.

The competent authority for judicial confirmation is the pre-trial judge, except in case of the so-called "direct proceedings" (*giudizio direttissimo*), where judicial confirmation is entrusted to the competent trial court.

These guarantees are supplemented, at constitutional level, by the provision of an appeal on a question of law which any person deprived of his or liberty can always lodge to the Court of Cassation. However this guarantee has proved unsatisfactory with the time and has been integrated by the introduction of a judicial complaint against any coercive measure (see below, § 7.1).

SPAIN: Spanish law establishes a procedure for controlling the restriction of liberty by administrative authorities.

The arrested suspect must be brought before the judicial authority within 72 hours (although the length of this detention has to be restricted to the time strictly necessary for police enquiries), with some exceptions in the case of terrorism (5 days and the request to the judicial authority within 72 hours from the moment of prolongation).

The investigating judge has jurisdiction. If a pre-trial measure was ordered by the investigating judge, this can be appealed.

The right to *Habeas Corpus* is laid down in the Organic Law 6/1984, which contains a simple proceeding, susceptible of being requested by the detainee or his or her relatives without a lawyer and whose purpose is to bring the arrested person before a judicial authority.

2. Types of pre-trial precautionary measures in criminal proceedings

2.1. What is meant by "pre-trial precautionary measures" in your legal system?

ENGLAND AND WALES: The most important legislation in this area is the Bail Act 1976 which provides for the following three pre-trial measures:
- Bail (Conditional release)
- Bail with Conditions
- Remand in Custody

In addition, the Policing and Crime Act 2009 provides for the seizure of assets on arrest.

GERMANY: In order to protect the integrity of criminal proceedings, German criminal procedural law provides for remand detention in ordinary criminal proceedings (§§ 112 ff. StPO), provisional committal in security proceedings (§ 126a StPO) and trial arrest (§ 127b StPO) in accelerated proceeding (§ 417 StPO). Numerous other measures are ancillary to the conduct of the proceedings, although they principally aim at the achievement of investigative goals (see, for instance, physical examination of the defendant, § 81 StPO; custody for establishing the defendant's identity, § 163c StPO; fingerprinting measures, DNA-Analyis, § 81a ff. StPO; seizure of assets etc., § 94 ff.). With some measures there is a dominant safety goal (see, for example, withdrawal of the driving license, § 111a StPO; prohibition of certain occupations, § 132a StPO).

In cases of international legal assistance there is the possibility of extradition detention, §§ 15 ff. IRG.

ITALY: The Italian code of criminal procedure distinguishes between real and personal precautionary measures. The former include two types of seizure of assets. The latter include two groups of measures, i.e. the measures of coercion (*misure coercitive*) and the measures of control (*misure interdittive*). Remand detention (*custodia cautelare in carcere*) is the most significant coercive measure. Moreover, the Italian code of criminal procedure establishes a legal equivalence between remand in custody and house arrest (Art. 284.5 CPP), which implies that, unless the code indicates otherwise, the latter is considered as remand detention as to maximum time-limits (Art. 303 CPP), remedies (Art. 309 ff. CPP), remand hearings (Art. 294 CPP), etc. Fur these purposes, Italian law does not thus distinguish, within the personal precautionary measures, between coercive and control measures, but between remand detention and house arrest, which form the so-called "custodial measures" (*misure custodiali*), on one hand, and the rest of personal precautionary measures, irrespective of their coercive or control character. Furthermore, house arrest may consist of very different forms of "pre-trial detention" (in the case, for example, of AIDS patients or patients with immuno-deficiencies – see the provisional committal procedure laid down under Art. 275.4ter CPP) and can be ordered with or without electronic monitoring (Art. 275bis CPP), which thus doesn't constitute an alternative to custody but a form of implementation of any type of pre-trial detention. As regards alternatives to custody and the other custodial measures, see 2.3 below.

SPAIN: Spanish law basically provides for two types of precautionary measures in order to ensure the integrity of the process: personal precautionary measures, which affect the liberty of the accused, and real precautionary measures, which relate to assets.

The first group includes preventive detention, remand detention and provisional release, which deprive or limit the exercise of freedom of movement, as well as suspension from office or official duties or professional activities, the temporary withdrawal of permits or licenses (to drive, to bear arms), the closure of businesses or establishments, or the seizure of publications and a broadcasting ban.

The second group includes measures designed to secure, on one hand, the *corpus delicti* and, on the other hand, eventual civil liabilities and liabilities *in rem* arising from the commission of criminal offences. The seizure of assets and deposits belong to the former group, whereas the latter include a bail bond, freezing of assets, seizure of goods and things, as well as setting a provisional allowance in criminal cases when insurance for civil liability exists.

2.2.   What position does remand detention occupy in your legal system in relation to the presumption of innocence?

ENGLAND AND WALES: It is an exception. S. 4(1) of the Bail Act creates a presumption in favour of bail, although some exceptions have been introduced subsequently (see 2.4 below).

GERMANY: It is firstly worth mentioning the presumption of innocence. From the constitutional point of view the presumption of innocence derives from the rule of law (Art. 20 GG). Moreover, the presumption of innocence is based on Article 11.1 of the UDHR of 1948.

Moreover, the presumption of innocence is enshrined by Article 6.2 ECHR.

Finally, the presumption of innocence is explicitly mentioned by various state laws: see, for instance, the Prison Law of Niedersachsen: "Legal Status of Prisoners: (1) Prisoners shall be presumed innocent" (§ 135).

ITALY: Article 275.3 CPP deems it exceptional, since it can be ordered only where no other pre-trial measure is adequate to prevent any substantive precautionary risk. It also implies that by ordering remand detention the judicial authority must explain the "real and specific grounds which indicate that the purposes provided for in Article 274 CPP cannot be satisfied through different measures" (Art. 292.2(c-bis) CPP).

SPAIN: It is an exceptional measure which may be ordered only when there is a reasonable suspicion of guilt, provided the circumstances of the case are compatible with legal requirements. Therefore it must be issued, according to the procedure established by law and in conformity with the criterion of necessity and the principle of proportionality, and for constitutionally legitimate purposes such as preventing the escape of the accused or interference with the investigation by concealing or destroying evidence.

More generally the adoption of precautionary measures requires that the competent judicial authority verifies, together with other circumstances, whether a sufficient suspicion of guilt exists or not, i.e. whether there is a high probability that the presumption of innocence may be overruled. This criterion has also been taken into account by the legislator, implying that the preferment of criminal charges for certain offences is not sufficient for ordering precautionary measures, as each situation requires a concrete evaluation of the degree of suspicion depending on the various stages of the investigative proceedings.

Remand detention can be more easily ordered when a conviction, albeit a non-final one, has already been recorded at first instance. Indeed, although the presumption of innocence has not been overruled, a stronger suspicion is deemed to derive from the conviction issued by a court after assessing evidence collected during the public hearing. Therefore, in the case of conviction, the criteria for assessment of evidence are different from those adopted during the investigative proceedings, as regards the maintenance and duration of the precautionary measures.

2.3.   Does your law provide for alternatives to custody? In the affirmative case, what kind of alternatives does your law permit and which fundamental rights do such measures limit or prejudice?

ENGLAND AND WALES: Yes. All the following potentially prejudice the Right to Liberty enshrined in Article 5 ECHR, which is enacted directly into English Law by the Human Rights Act 1998.
    The most common alternatives to custody are as follows:
    Bail (Conditional Release)
    Bail with Conditions, which include *inter alia*, residence, curfew, reporting to the police station, surrender of passport, money security (surety) paid by another person (but not be the defendant), keeping away from particular places or persons (including prosecution witnesses), monitoring by electronic tagging (introduced in 2005), and drug testing.

GERMANY: Yes, especially the suspension of execution of the arrest warrant (§ 116 StPO).
    The judge shall suspend the execution of the arrest warrant issued on the basis of a risk of flight, if less intrusive measures can be employed to achieve the purpose of the remand detention. In particular, the following measures may be considered:
– a requirement to report at certain times to the office of the judge, the prosecuting authority, or to a specific office to be designated by them (§ 116.1(1) StPO);
– a requirement not to leave his or her place of residence without permission of the judge or the prosecuting authority (§ 116.1(2) StPO);
– a requirement not to leave his or her private premises except under the supervision (§ 116.1(3) StPO);
– provision of an adequate security by the accused or another person (§§ 116.1 (4) and 116a StPO).

The judge may also suspend the implementation of the arrest warrant based on the risk of intereference with evidence, if less intrusive measures can be employed to reduce this risk. In particular, requirements to have no contact with co-accused, witnesses, or experts may be considered (§§ 116.2 StPO).

In respect of arrest warrants justified by an alleged danger of reoffending (§ 112a StPO), the defendant may be subject to other conditions (§ 116.1(1) StPO).

Depending on the contents of the judicial order, different restrictions of fundamental rights come into consideration. In particular, the following fundamental rights are important: "general freedom of action" (Art. 1.1, 2.1 GG), "freedom of movement" (Art. 11.1 GG), "occupational freedom" (Art. 12 GG), "freedom of expression" and "freedom of assembly" (Art. 5.1, 8.1 GG), as well as "property rights" (Art. 14.1 GG).

As regards the primacy of remand in custody before extradition detention, see § 116b StPO.

The possibility of the introduction of an electronic ankle bracelet as an alternative to custody or imprisonment has been discussed and even piloted in Germany. Nevertheless no general regulation has been issued yet.

ITALY: Together with the distinction explained under 2.1 above, the Italian code of criminal procedure has introduced different regulations for custodial measures and the other personal precautionary measures (for instance, as to the defendant's hearings, see Art. 294.1 – 2 CPP). Therefore alternatives to custody include also measures of control, which are the suspension of the care and custody of a child (Art. 288 CPP), the compulsory suspension from office (Art. 289 CPP) and from a specific profession (Art. 290 CPP). According to Article 276.1 CPP, the infringement of conditions concerning any personal precautionary measure may lead to its substitution with or the addition of another one The same rule applies in the case of infringement of the conditions concerning any control measure, which may result in its substitution by another or in the addition of a coercive measure.

Moreover Italian legislation provides for different coercive non-custodial measures, such as the requirement to reside at a specific address, or report to the police station and the prohibition of leaving his or her own country. From 2001 other precautionary measures have been introduced, such as keeping away from the family home (Art. 282bis CPP) and, more recently, from places frequented by the victim (Art. 282ter CPP).

In light of the extension of the field of the personal precautionary measures, the equivalence between remand detention and house arrest might be considered as inappropriate and unrealistic. Nevertheless, according to Art. 276.1ter CPP, the infringement of conditions concerning house arrest consisting in the requirements not to leave the defendant's residence, may lead to its substitution with or the addition of remand detention.

All these measures prejudice more or less directly the right to liberty, although they often limit other fundamental rights.

SPAIN: In principle alternatives to remand detention are admissible where their constitutional purposes may be secured through them, provided other less restrictive measures cannot achieve the same result as remand detention can.

Remand detention is also admissible in the form of a provisional committal to a psychiatric centre or prison, even a hospital, but only as far as necessary to ensure the health of the accused and always within the penal system, whenever the purposes of the pre-trial detention could not be achieved through other forms of enforcement.

Therefore Spanish law, differently from other legal systems similar to ours, does not provide for alternatives to prison such as a residence condition or residential supervision, although in principle there would be no resistance (from a doctrinal or political point of view) to the introduction of such alternative measures.

Instead, a particular type of pre-trial detention is the so-called "extenuating custody" due to illness, or in order to avoid the possibility that imprisonment may frustrate the outcome of a therapeutic treatment for drug addiction which was begun after the offence. In this case, extenuating custody is enforced by committing the accused to his or her place of residence, provided that there was appropriate monitoring and his or her release may be allowed only for the treatment of the disease, or, in the case of therapeutic treatment, to an official centre for further detoxification.

In consideration of the restrictions related to remand detention, as well as its exceptional nature, provisional release, with or without bail, may be ordered to ensure the presence of the accused during the proceedings. This measure limits the freedom of movement of the defendant. If the defendant, without just cause, fails to appear in court at the first hearing or whenever the judicial authority deems it necessary, the judge shall order his imprisonment, provided that all other conditions exist.

Along with this restriction of freedom there are ancillary measures such as requirements to surrender a passport, which prevent the defendant from leaving Spain and therefore affect freedom of movement under Article 19 GG.

Along with precautionary measures restricting liberty, Spanish law allows the adoption of further measures for different purposes, which lead to the limitation or deprivation of certain rights of the accused. There are very different measures, which involve various legal interests, sometimes related to the enjoyment of fundamental rights, such as the freedom of movement and residence or the right to exercise a public office, or, in other cases, the freedom of establishment by ordering the suspension of activities or the closure of businesses.

However, pre-trial measures which are both less intrusive for the defendant and more effecetive for the purpose of the criminal proceedings, such as the permanent supervision of the defendant, are missing from the Spanish legal system.

In no case may precautionary measures affect the fundamental right to life and physical or psychological integrity.

2.4.   Does your legal system provide for special pre-trial measures and / or any special regulation of pre-trial measures with regard to specific forms of crime (juvenile crime, terrorism, organized crime etc.)?

ENGLAND AND WALES: For alleged Terrorism defendants, the maximum pre-trial detention (without appearance before a judicial authority) is 28 days [Ss. 23 – 24 of the Terrorism Act 2006.]. Where a defendants has allegedly committed one or more serious offences (murder, manslaughter, and rape, for example) and has a record of similar offences, the courts are required to provide written reasons for granting bail [S. 153 of the Criminal Justice Act 1988].

A defendant who has been charged with a serious offence which was allegedly committed while on bail for another serious offence, cannot be granted bail unless the court believes that there is no significant risk of offences being committed on bail [S. 25 of the Criminal Justice and Public Order Act 1994 as amended by the Criminal Justice Act 2003].

A defendant for whom there is drug test evidence of Class A drug use need not be granted bail if the offence is drug-related and he or she does not agree to undergo assessment and / or follow-up treatment for drug dependency [S. 4(9) of the Bail Act 1976, as inserted by s. 58 of the Criminal Justice and Court Services Act 2000].

In the 1990s the government attempted to reverse the presumption in favour of bail in respect of serious offences but was obliged to withdraw this provision before it was the subject of an unfavourable judgement in the ECtHR. There have been no subsequent attempts to reverse completely the presumption in favour of bail but the above provisions nevertheless come very close.

GERMANY: Following the Law on combating illicit drug trafficking and other forms of organized crime (Federal Law Gazette I 1992, p. 1302 – 1312) numerous special investigative measures have been introduced into the code of criminal procedure in the field of the organized crime. During the few last years the lists of offences containing rules enabling the adoption of such measures have been greatly expanded, so that a restriction to organized crime is no longer tenable.

Moreover, there are specific restrictive measures aimed at the preparation for trial. The need to counter terrorist threats, with regard to the activities of the Red Army Faction, led to the enactment of the Contact Barrier Law (Art. 31 ff. of the Introductory Law of the Judicature Act), which is still in force. Contact block is the interruption of any communication of suspects or prisoners with other prisoners and the outside world, including the contact with his or her own counsel.

On 1st January 2010 further restrictions during pre-trial detention were introduced into § 119 StPO and into the Rules for the execution of a remand order, including a joint management arrangement between the provincial States. This regulation was not introduced through national Parliamentary legislation.

The recent reform of remand detention (Federal Law Gazette I 2274 of 1.1. 2010) relates, *inter alia*, to the new rules on the execution of pre-trial detention. Before 1st January 2010, despite legislative competence of the Federal State, the enforcement of remand detention was not regulated. A few areas had been addressed in the code of criminal procedure, but a much more exhaustive regulation was laid down by a remand executive order, which aimed to provide guidance to the appropriate authorities.

As part of the federalism reform, the previous contents of § 119 StPO were repealed, as the new Article 74.1, 1 of the Constitution (Law amending the GG of 28 August 2006, Federal Law Gazette I, p. 2034) has transferred the legislative competence on the execution of remand detention to the provincial states.

As the provincial states (*Bundesländer*) had adopted only a partial regulation at the time of the reform, the Federal Legislator decided to introduce a transitional arrangement in order to avoid a legal hiatus.

Art. 13 of the Introductory law of the code of criminal procedure establishes that, until the introduction of rules on the enforcement of remand orders by the provincial states, the former version of § 119 StPO, in addition to the new version, shall regulate the field of remand in custody.

Restrictions established to maintain order in prisons continue therefore to operate under the former provisions. By contrast, further restrictions apply according to the new version in order to combat the risk of interfering with evidence as well as the risk of committing another offence (previously: "The purpose of pre-trial detention"). This regulation will apply until 31st December 2011.

As to remand detention, see the current version of § 119 StPO.

By certain serious offences (international law crimes, crimes against life, terrorism) the ground for arrest under § 112.2 StPO is not required (see § 112.3 StPO). Yet the Federal Constitutional Court has called for a restrictive interpretation of this provision, according to which even in these cases, the possibility of an arrest warrant must be linked to a risk of absconding or interfering with evidence which the circumstances of the case do not exclude.

Imprisonment based on a risk of interfering with evidence is not admissible in the case of petty crime (imprisonment up to six months and 180 days penalty rates) and exceptionally for risk of flight only under strict conditions (§ 113 StPO).

For grounds based on a risk of recurrence, German law provides for a list of specific offences (sexual offences and crimes against the physical integrity, crimes against assets and property, arson offences, drug offences). See § 112a StPO as well as the case-law of the Constitutional Court (BVerfGE 19, 342; BVerfGE 35, 185).

ITALY: Yes. For instance, according to Art. 19 of the Decree of the President of the Republic 448 / 1988 (containing the procedural rules on juvenile crime), juveniles may be subject only to those pre-trial measures provided for by this Act (prescriptions, house detention, remand in community, custody) and only on the condition that these measures do not prejudice the educational development of the defendant.

Moreover, the Italian StPO contains specific rules concerning the most serious crimes. According to Article 275.3, defendants charged with various serious offences (mafia-related crime, terrorism, sexual crimes, slavery etc.) may be remanded in custody when a strong suspicion of guilt arises (Art. 273.1). Instead, the so-called "precautionary risks" do not need to be proved. Remand in custody can be avoided only by proving the failure of any risk laid down for by Article 274. In this case no pre-trial measure may be ordered. However, this provision has been declared partially unconstitutional by the Constitutional Court, Decisions 265 / 2010, 164 / 2011, 231 / 2011 and 331 / 2011.

SPAIN: No specific measure is provided for with regard to certain criminal offences, except in the case of final indictment accompanied by the issue of a remand order for a crime committed by individuals forming part of or in connection with an armed group or alleged terrorists and rebels. In this case the person holding a public office at the time of the indictment shall be automatically suspended from such an office for the duration of the pre-trial detention.

There are, however, some exceptions, in the field of the precautionary measures relating to the nature of the criminal offences allegedly committed by the accused. Thus pre-trial detention is generally compatible with communications with the outside world, but exceptionally such communications will be excluded if there is sufficient justification, for a very short period of time.

This involves a significant infringement of the rights of the accused, who in any case will have a court-appointed counsel and may not meet privately with him or her after giving evidence, neither will he or she be entitled to let his or her relatives or other people know about his or her deprivation of liberty and the place of custody. Moreover, all communications with the outside world will be completely prohibited.

These restrictions may not exceed five days, although there are exceptions for crimes committed by individuals forming part of or in connection with an armed group or individual terrorists or rebels, or crimes committed by organized criminals.

In this case such restrictions may be extended for another period not exceeding five days, and with sufficient grounds the judge may order that no communications will be permitted, but this second restriction must never exceed three days.

3.   The competent authority

3.1.   Which kind of authority is competent to order pre-trial precautionary measures?

ENGLAND AND WALES: Three types of authority have this responsibility, one non-judicial and two judicial.

Non judicial: The police, acting under s. 47(3) of the Police and Criminal Evidence Act 1984 (PACE) can (a) release a suspect on bail during the course of an investigation, requiring him or her to attend at such police station at such time as the custody officer may appoint [with no maximum time limit despite a Recommendation from a Standing Committee of the House of Commons. See http://www.parliament.the-stationery-office.co.uk/pa/cm200203/cmselect/ cmhaff /83/8306.htm], or (b) where the investigation has been completed, can bail a defendant to appear before a Magistrates' Court at such time and such place as he or she shall appoint. Since 1994 the police also have been authorised to attach conditions to these two types of bail [with the exception of residing at a bail hostel] under s. 27 of the Criminal Justice and Public Order Act 1994 and s. 37 of PACE respectively [as amended by s. 28 and schedule 2 of the Criminal Justice Act 2003]. The Police can also remand a defendant in custody overnight to appear at the next available court.

Judicial: The Magistrates' Court, sitting with three lay magistrates or one (professional) District Judge, can remand a defendant in custody, impose conditional or unconditional bail subject to the conditions set out below. A single lay magistrate, sitting alone can order bail or conditional bail but not custody.

A Judge of the Crown Court, sitting alone hears appeals from decisions on bail, conditional bail or custody from the Magistrates' Court and can also rule on bail, conditional bail or custody in respect of defendants appearing in the Crown Court.

GERMANY: An arrest warrant may be issued only by a judge (§§ 81.2, 125, 126a I, StPO). Provisional arrest pursuant is possible to § 127.2 StPO also by the Public Prosecutor's Office / the police. However, note to § 128 StPO (as to the new obligation to caution, *inter alia*, see also § 127 IV in conjunction with §§ 114a ff. StPO).

Furthermore see §§ 163b, 163c StPO (Public Prosecutor's Office / police). See also § 127b.1 StPO for trial detention.

Further coercive measures may also be authorised by the Public Prosecutor / police, i. e. (the so-called "investigative bodies"), especially in cases of imminent danger (for instance, under § 98 StPO by seizure; § 81a II StPO by blood sample collection, etc.).

ITALY: Precautionary measures may be ordered only by the judicial authority, pursuant to the general principles enshrined in Article 13 of the Constitution. See 1.2. above.

Moreover, the police and the Public Prosecutor are competent for the provisional arrest. Italian law provides for two different forms of provisional arrest, i. e. *arresto* (Arts. 380 and 381 CPP) and *fermo di indiziato di delitto* (Art. 384 CPP), which, despite pursuing different purposes, share the common character of needing a subsequent judicial confirmation. As to the procedure see 1.2 below.

SPAIN: According to Spanish law the competent authority for ordering precautionary measures is the investigating judge (*juez de instrucción*). As precautionary measures affect fundamental rights, they need a reasoned judicial order ("*auto*"), in which the judge has to ascertain whether all conditions for the adoption of the requested measure exist or not.

Exceptionally, where the charges have been brought, the police or any person may order the preventive detention allowed by the Constitution under Article 17.2. Yet, such a measure has a very short duration (max. 72 hours) and is for the immediate purpose of conducting investigations aimed at clarifying the facts. Moreover, the judicial authority must always review it subsequently or during its execution.

One of the most serious problems of the Spanish system in the area of precautionary measures is that the code of criminal procedure, by maintaining the figure of the investigative judge, entitles him to order *ex officio* any precautionary measure, except pre-trial detention and provisional release, for which the request of the Prosecutor is required.

3.2.   If your system requires judicial authority, does the judge intervene before or may he or she intervene after pre-trial measures have been ordered?

ENGLAND AND WALES: All pre-trial measures, with the exception of Police Bail (see 3.1 above), may be ordered only by a judicial authority. This is not a retrospective but a prior intervention. Appeal against a decision by the police to impose conditions on bail can be made to a Magistrates' Court in the first instance throughout the period during which these conditions are in effect (see The Criminal Procedure Rules 2010, No. 60 (L2) part 19.2). Appeal against a decision on bail, conditional bail or custody made by a Magistrates' Court is to a Crown Court Judge sitting alone (see The Criminal Procedure Rules 2010, op. cit., part 19.7). Appeal against a decision by a Crown Court Judge is to the Court of Appeal. Alternatively, decisions of either of these courts may be reviewed for their legality by an appeal "by way of case stated" to the Divisional Court of the High Court or by Writ of *Habeas Corpus* in some circumstances.

GERMANY: The adoption of remand detention requires a judicially issued arrest warrant.

After the suspect's provisional arrest on grounds of imminent danger (§ 127.2 StPO), he or she shall be promptly brought by the Prosecutor / police before the judicial authority competent for the arrest (not later than the day after the arrest) (§ 128.1 StPO).

After the suspect's arrest on the basis of an arrest warrant, he or she must be produced immediately before the competent court (§ 115.1 StPO).

Following the 2010 reform of pre-trial detention, the defendant must now be assisted by a court-appointed counsel during the preliminary proceedings (see § 140.1(4) StPO). This will usually be a court-assigned defence lawyer.

As a consequence of this reform, the provision laid down by § 117.5 StPO, which stated that the issue of remand detention had to be reviewed *ex officio* after 3 months if the defendant had no legal assistance, is no longer effective.

If remand detention continues after the defendant's hearing, he or she may lodge a complaint and further remedies (§§ 117.1 – 2, 118.1 – 2, 119.5, 119a.1 StPO). § 304.4 – 5 StPO remain unaffected.

As long as the defendant is on remand detention, he or she may at any time apply for a court hearing as to whether the arrest warrant is to be revoked or whether its execution is to be suspended in accordance with § 116 (review of detention) (see § 117.1 StPO).

Complaint against the detention (*Haftbeschwerde*) will be inadmissible where the defendant has applied for a review of remand in custody (*Haftprüfung*). The right of complaint against the decision following the application remain unaffected (see § 117.2 StPO).

The judge may order specific investigations, which can be important for the subsequent decision about the continuation of remand detention, and undertake a further review after the completion of such investigations (§ 117.3 StPO).

As long as a judgment imposing imprisonment or a custodial measure of reform and prevention has not been made, remand detention for the same offence, upon expiry of a period of six months, may be executed only if the particular difficulty or the particular extent of the investigation or some other important reason does not permit the pronouncement of a judgment while justifying the maintenance of remand detention (§ 121.1 StPO).

The arrest warrant must be revoked, upon expiry of a six-month period, unless its execution is suspended (§ 116 StPO) or the Higher Regional Court (*Oberlandesgericht*) authorizes the continuation of remand detention (§ 121.2 StPO), according to the procedure established by § 122 StPO. However, the Higher Regional Court must rule again within three months.

Pre-trial detention may be continued no longer than one year by the Higher Regional Court, if it is based on the grounds for arrest under § 112a StPO (risk of recurrence) (see § 122a StPO). Upon expiry of the maximum period of detention, the arrest warrant will be revoked.

ITALY: The ordering of any pre-trial precautionary measure restricting the right to personal liberty need always the previous intervention of the judicial authority, which is normally called upon to assess the preconditions for the issue of the requested measure *inaudito reo* and only the basis of the evidence and documents attached to the application by the Public Prosecutor. A re-assessment of the conditions for the application of the precautionary measure will usually follow the questioning of the suspect pursuant to Article 294 CPP. On this topic see 4.2 below.

SPAIN: One of the presuppositions for the valid adoption of any precautionary measure in criminal proceedings is a reasoned judicial order.

As a result, the precautionary measures form part of criminal proceedings which have already been instituted and may be ordered only by the investigative judge. Moreover they will be reviewed by the competent judicial authorities at various stages of the proceedings. Finally Spanish law provides for remedies before the superior court.

Thus the intervention of the judicial authority is always prior to the ordering of any precautionary measure. If requested by any prosecuting party, both remand detention and provisional release may be adopted only by the competent judicial authority from the time of the lodging of the charge. The judicial authority can reject the request of the prosecutor, but it cannot order *ex officio* any measure, unless there is a risk of flight or, conversely, when there is the need to modify a precautionary measure in favour of the defendant.

By ordering *ex officio* a precautionary measure (pre-trial detention or provisional release with bail), the judicial authority must fix a hearing (which is called "*vistilla*" in forensic practice) within seventy-two hours, so that any party can apply for the adoption of the measure (which is a prerequisite for its continuation).

3.3. If your system requires the intervention of a judicial authority, is it a different authority from the one competent for criminal proceedings? If not, does your law contain any provision guaranteeing the impartiality of the judicial authority in both criminal and remand proceedings?

ENGLAND AND WALES: Normally it will not be the same bench of magistrates in the Magistrates' Court which will make the decision on bail and custody as the bench of magistrates which will eventually adjudicate on the case. However a court which is unable to complete a trial and must adjourn the matter to another day, is competent to decide on bail / custody for the adjournment. Crown Court judges are competent to review decisions on bail / custody and then sit as a trial judge on the same case. However, it must be remembered that the Crown Court judge does not decide the outcome of the case. That is a matter for the jury.

GERMANY: Before any charge is brought, the local court judge within whose District the place of jurisdiction is established by law, or where the accused is residing, will issue an arrest warrant upon application by the Public Prosecutor or, if a public prosecutor cannot be reached or there is an imminent danger, even *ex officio* (§ 125 StPO).

After the charge has been lodged, an arrest warrant will be issued by the court seized of the case (see particularly §§ 125.2, 126 StPO).

The code provides for a review of detention. Before charging, the judge who issued the warrant of arrest will have jurisdiction. After the public charges have been preferred, the court seized of the case will have jurisdiction (§ 126 StPO).

A complaint against detention is admissible against the arrest warrant, any amendment and any decision ordering the continuation of the pre-trial detention (in principle it should be addressed to the Regional Court, § 304 StPO; while further complaints shall be addressed to the Higher Regional Court, § 310 StPO).

The code of criminal procedure does not contain any provision barring the remand judge from participating in the subsequent hearing of the case (see § 22 StPO). However, if the trial judge acted in the case as an official of the Public

Prosecutor's Office, as a police officer, as attorney for the victim, or as defence counsel, he will be barred by law from exercising judicial office in the case (see § 22.1(4) StPO).

ITALY: The Italian code of criminal procedure does not provide for a judicial authority with exclusive competence in the field of pre-trial precautionary measures. It implies that the competent judicial authorities for the various stages of the criminal proceedings (with the exception of the Supreme Court) will order precautionary measures and review their implementation before trial (see Art. 279 CPP).

However, this double competence of the same judicial authorities both for criminal and remand proceedings has led to many declaratory judgments of unconstitutionality of Article 34 CPP. Thus the Italian Constitutional Court has, by the means of the so-called "integrative judgments of unconstitutionality" (*sentenze additive*), added new grounds for judicial incompatibility, which however concerns the pre-trial phases. As a result, a judge who ordered any precautionary measure, or who ruled on the appeal lodged against a judicial order imposing a precautionary measure, in the pre-trial stages may not decide the outcome of the case (both for a regular trial and in accelerated proceedings). However, a significant exception is provided for in the case where a precautionary measure is ordered pending trial, since here the requirements for concentration and the speediness of the trial take precedence over the need for a different judge.

SPAIN: Remand detention may be ordered only by the competent judicial authorities at the various stages of criminal proceedings. During the preliminary inquiry (depending on the type of proceedings and on the seriousness of the offence) it will be the competent judicial authority for the investigation, which is different from the one dealing with the trial.

After the opening of the trial it will be the judge of the Criminal Division or the trial court.

However, in case of appeal the same authority competent for prosecution will have jurisdiction in the field of precautionary measures.

Moreover, the Spanish legal system has provisions for the withdrawal from the case and disqualification of judges and magistrates in order to ensure their impartiality as well as their independence from the parties and the subject matter of the proceedings, which means the absence of any personal interest in resolving the dispute.

Precautionary orders are reviewable by a higher court through appeal.

It can occur that the trial court is required to decide on an appeal against a precautionary measure and thus to assess its legitimacy, although the rules laid down for the allocation of the cases between various courts usually establish that the court competent for appeals against the orders of the investigative judge shall be different from the one having competence for the trial.

4. The procedure for ordering precautionary measures

4.1.   May pre-trial measures be ordered ex officio? If not, does your law provide for any request to be made by the Prosecutor?

ENGLAND AND WALES: Only the authorities named above can order pre-trial measures and only in the circumstances set out under 6 below. Clearly the Crown Prosecutor can request that an order be made by one of the competent authorities set out above.

GERMANY: In principle a request by the Public Prosecutor is mandatory during investigative proceedings. Indeed during the investigative proceedings the Public Prosecutor's Office is competent to apply for an arrest warrant and any extension/modification of the charges or the grounds for detention (§ 125.1 StPO). The judicial authority, at least during the investigative proceedings is thus bound by the requests of Prosecutor. This follows from § 120.3 StPO, according to which the arrest warrant must be revoked when the Prosecutor requests it before the charge is preferred. After the accusation, the court may issue an arrest warrant on its own initiative, having heard from the Prosecutor.

Exceptionally, according to § 125.1 StPO, the arrest warrant may be issued *ex officio* by the judge, if a public prosecutor cannot be reached or in exigent circumstances.

ITALY: No precautionary measure can be ordered *ex officio*, except in the case of the substitution of the imposed measure with a more intrusive one due to the infringement of the conditions set out in the judicial order (Art. 276 CPP). Therefore all pre-trial precautionary measures need the prior request of the Prosecutor and may be ordered only within the limits established by the request. It follows that the judicial authority cannot order a more intrusive measure than the one requested by the Prosecutor, although it can order a milder one or no measure at all. Moreover, according to Article 299.4 CPP, also the substitution of any pre-trial measure with a more intrusive one requires an application by the Prosecutor.

Of course, once the original justification of the measures ceases to exist, they must be immediately set aside by the judge (Art. 299.1 CPP).

SPAIN: The investigating judge has competence to order precautionary measures, even *ex officio*, although an important restriction was introduced by a reform of 1995, by which the issue of pre-trial measures *ex officio* was considerably limited and a request of the prosecutor was required for pre-trial detention and provisional release with bail (Art. 505 LECrim).

Moreover the judicial authority is bound by the request of any prosecutor in ordering a precautionary measure, i. e. restrictive measures may be adopted only after the request of any prosecuting party. However a less intrusive measure may be ordered without such a request.

In case of emergency, if there has been no hearing to enable the prosecutor to apply for a pre-trial measure, it may be ordered *ex officio*. However a hearing in the presence of the defendant must be held within 72 hours and the precautionary measure will be continued only if, during such a hearing, the prosecutor requests it.

4.2.   Does your law provide for any hearings of the person subject to pre-trial measures? In the affirmative case, which procedure does your law establish for such hearings?

ENGLAND AND WALES: Yes. This is mandatory, except in the case of Police Bail (see above). These are full adversarial hearings with representation for the defendant if required (provided free of cost if eligible). These are known as "Remand Hearings." The Magistrates' Court and the Crown Court are the competent authorities for conducting these hearings. A hearing is automatic but will be brief if either bail, conditional bail or custody is not opposed. No intervention is necessary for a first or second consideration of pre-trial measures. Subsequent re-hearings must be requested.

GERMANY: In principle the right to be judicially heard derives from Article 19.4 of the Constitution. During the investigative proceedings a hearing is not mandatory for all coercive measures. In particular, in the case of issuing secret investigative measures, the hearing of the defendant is prohibited, as it would conflict with the purpose of these measures.

However defendants must always be informed about their right of silence and the nature of any charge against them (see especially §§ 136, 163a StPO).

In an application for remand detention the defendant must be heard by the judge.

The StPO provides for oral proceedings by a review of remand in custody or improper detention if the defendant requests it or the Court deems it necessary.

The review of the decision to remand in custody and the judicial complaint against detention (§§ 117, 118, 304 StPO) can be made on the files only.

Hearings conducted before the Prosecutor or the police (see § 163a StPO) take place without a judge. Defence counsel has the right to be present.

As to the competent authority, it depends on the type of the hearing. In the case of a review of remand in custody it is the judge unless it is a "simple" first hearing conducted by the police or the Prosecutor. In the case of a complaint against detention, the defendant must be heard by the competent court.

The court, the police or the Prosecutor call the hearings and conduct them. There is no duty for the defendant to appear (see § 163a.3 StPO).

German law provides for no adversarial procedure before the issue of a remand order. This does not exclude a hearing of the defendant by the police or the Prosecutor before the issue of an arrest warrant. However, in case of a risk of flight, this strategy might be inappropriate. See 6.3 below.

ITALY: Art. 294 CPP provides for two types of hearing the suspect subject to a precautionary measure according to its character (i. e. custodial measures and alternatives to custody). This questioning aims to evaluate the legal conditions necessary for ordering pre-trial measures and both are mandatory, so that by exceeding the time limits provided for by Art. 294.1 – 2) CPP (5 days in case of pre-trial detention and 10 days for the rest of the personal precautionary measures) pre-trial measures become ineffective. After the opening of the trial such a hearing is not required, including in relation to pre-trial measures ordered after judicial confirmation of provisional arrest (Art. 294.1 CPP).

The hearing is conducted *in camera*. The Public Prosecutor may appear, while the defence counsel must attend (Art. 294.4 CPP). However, it can happen that the defence counsel has not had the opportunity to contact the remanded suspect before the hearing. In particular, the CPP allows the Public Prosecutor, by requesting a custodial measure, to ask the judge both to hear the individual within 2 days from the enforcement of the measure (294 – 3ter) and to postpone any contact between the remanded person and his or her lawyer (102.3), which ends up jeopardizing the effectiveness of the defence in the context of this hearing.

The competent judge for the preliminary inquiry (*giudice per le indagini preliminary* or GIP) conducts the hearing.

Moreover, according to Art. 294.6 CPP, the Prosecutor cannot conduct the hearing of the remanded defendant before the judicial authority. Legal assistance must be granted to the defendant. Indeed ithis is a case of mandatory legal assistance, on which the legitimacy of the hearing depends (Arts. 178(c) and 179 CPP). It cannot be considered as a full adversarial hearing, to the extent that the hearing is conducted by the judicial authority which in general has not a full knowledge of the investigative results.

In principle the defendant may not be heard before being remanded in custody, except when a custodial measure is adopted after the remand order has become ineffective upon expiry of the time-limits established by Article 294 (Art. 302 CPP) or when a precautionary measure is ordered after the judicial confirmation of provisional arrest (Art. 391 CPP).

SPAIN: The defendant subject to any precautionary measure must always be heard and may defend himself or herself personally or through legal assistance. Moreover the parties may make submissions and offer further evidence (Art. 505 LECrim). The hearing is conducted by the investigative judge. In case of remand detention or provisional release the defendant must always attend a hearing where a pre-trial measure against him or her is requested.

4.3.   Does your law grant the defendant the right to legal assistance during remand proceedings?

ENGLAND AND WALES: Yes.

GERMANY: Yes, see § 137 I StPO, according to which the defendant may apply for legal assistance at any stage of the proceedings. The assistance of a court-appointed counsel is provided for by §§ 140 ff. StPO and is mandatory on remand. See also the advice requirements under §§ 136.1; 163a.4 StPO, which include the defence consultation.

ITALY: See 4.2 above.

SPAIN: Always and it cannot be waived.

4.4.   What kind of information does your law grant the defendant on remand and / or subject to alternatives to custody?

ENGLAND AND WALES: Information will be provided by the police to the Prosecutor who represents the Crown at the remand hearing. The defence lawyer will have taken his or her instructions directly from the defendant. Further information will be provided by the Probation Service. Bail Information Schemes were introduced in the 1990s on the model of the Vera Institute in the US to provide factual, verified information, in addition to that otherwise available, to the Crown Prosecution Service (and the defence) to assist it to decide whether there are grounds for asking the court to release a defendant on bail rather than remand them in custody. Although these early court-based schemes were discontinued for lack of funding they have continued to operate successfully in prisons [see Prison Service Order 6101, *Bail Information Scheme*. Issued 02/09/1999] primarily in order to support the Bail Accommodation and Support Scheme (BASS) and the Effective Bail Schemes (EBS) set up in 2007. Bail information schemes address the specific concerns expressed in opposition to bail and also aim to draw attention to the defendant's character, antecedents, community ties which are relevant to the remand decision. Bail information is not, simply a case of providing details of suitable accommodation, but also looks for factors such as the defendant's reliability, employment record, family responsibilities and support services in the community.

GERMANY: The provisions of Article 5.3 ECHR are enshrined in § 115 StPO. For details see 1.2 below.

Execution of the arrest warrant may be suspended in some circumstances by the provision of an adequate security under § 116.1(4) StPO. See for other alternatives 2.3 above.

ITALY: According to Article 293 CPP, the remand order must immediately be handed over to the defendant. The judicial order relating to non-custodial measures must be notified to the defendant. The defence counsel, if existent, must be promptly informed and is entitled to examine the dossier containing the results of preliminary inquiry attached to the request of the Public Prosecutor. However, no provision establishes a deadline, so that it can occur that the defendant's lawyer attends the hearing without sufficient preparation.

SPAIN: Spanish law grants the defendant legal assistance and guarantees the participation of defence counsel at the hearing where the pre-trial measure will be adopted. In cases involving alternative measures, the accused must be informed. The most common possibility is that pre-trial detention is avoided by paying a bond (provisional release on bail).

5.   Justification

5.1.   Which pre-conditions does your law require as a basis for ordering precautionary measures?

ENGLAND AND WALES: Under Schedule 2, paragraph 2 of the Bail Act 1976, a defendant charged with an imprisonable (eg serious) offence must be granted unconditional bail unless

the court is satisfied that there are substantial grounds for believing that the defendant, if released on bail (whether subject to conditions or not) would –

"(a) fail to surrender to custody, or

(b) commit an offence while on bail, or

(c) interfere with witnesses or otherwise obstruct the course of justice, whether in relation to himself or any other person.

(2 A) The defendant need not be granted bail if –

(a) the offence is an indictable offence or an offence triable either way; and

(b) it appears to the court that he was on bail in criminal proceedings on the date of the offence."

(3) The defendant need not be granted bail if the court is satisfied that the defendant should be kept in custody for his own protection or, if he is a child or young person, for his own welfare.

(4) The defendant need not be granted bail if he is in custody in pursuance of the sentence of a court or of any authority acting under any of the Services Acts.

(5) The defendant need not be granted bail where the court is satisfied that it has not been practicable to obtain sufficient information for the purpose of taking the decisions required by this Part of this Schedule for want of time since the institution of the proceedings against him."

Guidance on the criteria for applying these conditions is given by Paragraph 9 of this Schedule:

"In taking the decisions required by paragraph 2 [or 2 A] of this Part of this Schedule, the court shall have regard to such of the following considerations as appear to it to be relevant, that is to say –

(a) the nature and seriousness of the offence or default (and the probable method of dealing with the defendant for it),

(b) the character, antecedents, associations and community ties of the defendant,

(c) the defendant's record as respects the fulfilment of his obligations under previous grants of bail in criminal proceedings,

(d) except in the case of a defendant whose case is adjourned for inquiries or a report, the strength of the evidence of his having committed the offence or having defaulted, as well as to any others which appear to be relevant."

There is strong evidence of considerable diversity in the application of these criteria.

GERMANY: Remand detention is a pre-trial measure designed exclusively to ensure the integrity of the trial process and the achievement of the purposes of the trial, i.e. it has no tactical purpose.

Remand detention is subject to the following conditions.

The first one is that there should be a strong suspicion that the defendant committed the offence. Such a "strong suspicion" means a high degree of probability that the culpable commission of the offence by the defendant can be proven. The strong suspicion may be always reviewed *ex officio* during the period of remand detention.

Furthermore a ground for arrest is required. This is a formal requirement for detention and includes flight, risk of flight based on concrete circumstances as well as the risk of interfering with evidence, i.e. the risk that the defendant may destroy, alter, remove, suppress, or falsify evidence, or improperly influence co-accused, witnesses, or experts. In the case of a strong suspicion of having committed certain serious offences, such as sexual offences, further limiting circumstances are required for pre-trial detention, even in case of danger of recurrence. Finally, it is worth mentioning that in cases of serious crimes (§ 112.3 StPO) the so-called "trial arrest" (§ 127b StPO) is possible, which may last only a week. In practice, however, this has little significance.

If a defendant, albeit duly summoned, fails to appear in court for trial, remand detention can be ordered, regardless of the existence of a strong suspicion or a ground for a bench warrant (§ 230.2 StPO).

In any event, the principle of proportionality applies to all types of detention. Pre-trial detention must not be disproportionate to the seriousness of the offence and the nature and extent of the threat of legal consequences for the accused. Therefore remand detention is not permitted generally in cases of trivial and petty crime.

From a formal perspective the issue of an arrest warrant presupposes that the arrested defendant has already been brought before the judge and has had the opportunity of being notified by the judge of the grounds for arrest and on any charge preferred against him or her. In case of flee, the suspect will be brought for the hearing not later than the day after arrest before the judge who issued the arrest warrant or, if it is not possible because of the distance, the judge of the next District Court.

ITALY: The Italian code of criminal procedure provides for two general conditions applicable to all personal precautionary measures (coercive measure and measure of control). It requires both a "serious evidence of guilt" (Art. 273 CPP) and (at least) one of the "precautionary risks" provided for by Article 274 CPP, i. e. the risk of interference with evidence (lit. a), the risk of absconding, provided the defendant is facing a charge which carries a sentence of over 2 years (lit. b), and the risk of committing other serious offences (*inter alia* offences which imply the use of weapons, crimes against constitutional order etc.).

Both these conditions are required, although they lead to two different evaluations, laid down by Article 275 CPP. All precautionary measures must be proportionate to the seriousness of the offence and the sentence which can be imposed or has been imposed (principle of proportionality). All precautionary measures must be appropriate to the type and the seriousness of the risk involved (principle of adequacy).

An important exception is provided for in regard to mafia-crimes and, to a certain extent, to many other serious offences as well. See 2.4 above. Article 275.3 CPP establishes a double presumption. Firstly the judicial authority does not need to ascertain a specific precautionary risk, but only the strong suspicion of guilt, which implies that the defendant will be almost automatically remanded in custody. However, in case there are grounds for excluding all the specific risks provided for by Article 274 CPP (i. e. the suspect or the defendant succeeds in proving that so such risks exist), no measure will be ordered and the defendant must be immediately released. In any event, neither house arrest nor alternatives to custody are allowed in respect of mafia-crimes (presumption of adecuacy), whereas this possibility has been re-introduced by the above mentioned judgments of unconstitutionality with regard to other serious crimes (murder, drug-related crimes, etc.).

SPAIN: Spanish law lays down the requirements for the adoption of each precautionary measure. The criteria of proportionality, legality, temporality, instrumentality must always be respected.

5.2. Are the conditions established for ordering pre-trial measures proportionate to the different limitations of fundamental rights imposed by them?

ENGLAND AND WALES: Yes.

GERMANY: Yes. There are more onerous requirements for measures that are more intrusive. For instance, an arrest warrant is used only under strict conditions (§§ 112 ff. StPO).

ITALY: In principle both general conditions established by Articles 273 and 274 CPP apply to all personal precautionary measures (see 5.1 above). Yet, the principle of adequacy aims to avoid a restriction of liberty that is not capable of addressing the specific precautionary risk.

SPAIN: The principle of proportionality is the main principle in respect of all pre-trial measures.

5.3.   Do legal conditions have the same relevance throughout the remand
        proceedings?

ENGLAND AND WALES: Yes.

GERMANY: Yes. However, for example the level of suspicion required (initial suspicion, reasonable suspicion, strong suspicion) may change because of new findings during the investigative proceedings.

The court and the Prosecutor are required to exercise constant vigilance *ex officio* to ensure that the legal justifications of the detention are still in effect and, if necessary, to revoke the imposed measure.

ITALY: In principle yes, albeit with same exceptions due to the dynamic structure of the precautionary proceedings. In particular a strong suspicion of guilt can be much better assessed at trial, due to the adversarial method of collecting evidence. Indeed, according to Italian criminal procedure, the results of the preliminary investigation conducted by the Prosecutor and the police cannot be generally admitted as evidence of guilt at trial and neither are their files generally available to the trial judge who must decide the outcome of the case – as a matter of principle – exclusively on the basis of evidence heard in open court. However, even after the beginning of the trial the investigative files may be utilized for remand proceedings (as well as for other interlocutory proceedings), although they must be assessed in the light of the evidence presented during the trial, which can lead to different conclusions.

SPAIN: In order for any precautionary measure to continue, the circumstances which have justified its original adoption must continue throughout the pre-trial proceedings. For example, if pre-trial detention was based on the risk of destruction of evidence, once this risk disappears, this measure should be lifted. Precautionary measures may vary according to the circumstances and be made more or less intrusive as the situation demands.

6. The duration of precautionary measures

6.1. Which provisions ensure the continued lawfulness of pre-trial precautionary measures?

ENGLAND AND WALES: The Bail Act 1976 guaranteed the right of a remanded defendant to ask for bail each time he or she appeared in court (which was formerly every week until trial). This was considered to be wasteful of resources if exactly the same issues were being addressed on each occasion. S.154 of the Criminal Justice Act 1988 codified the practice of restricting effective bail applications to two, unless new circumstances arose. As a result, defendants are entitled to an automatic remand hearing when they first appear in court (a "duty-lawyer application") and a subsequent, usually more detailed consideration, after a week, if they are not granted bail on the first occasion. Thereafter the defendant will not have to be produced in court for 28 days, albeit with a right of appeal against the decision to remand in custody (see 3.2 above).

GERMANY: See 3.2 above.

ITALY: The Italian code of criminal procedure does not provide for judicial reviews of the lawfulness of pre-trial measures at specific time intervals, without prejudice to the right of the defendant on remand (or subject to other pre-trial measures) to request a judicial review of the lawfulness of the measure, at any time from the preliminary inquiry onwards.

SPAIN: The system of controls aims at ensuring that no measure is maintained if circumstances have changed. It implies no limitation to the right of the parties to apply for the modification or the revocation of a pre-trial measure through a judicial decision itself subject to appeal.

The judge may also modify *ex officio* the imposed measure by making it less onerous or even aggravating it, unless a party's request is required by law, such as in the case of remand detention.

6.2. Does your law provide for periodic review of pre-trial precautionary measures by judicial authorities?

ENGLAND AND WALES: Only where "new circumstances" arise after the first two remand hearings or where there is an appeal.

The competent authorities are the Magistrates' Court and/or Crown Court, usually the same court that ordered the original pre-trial measure. In the case of the Magistrates' Court the court will certainly be differently constituted. The lawfulness of pre-trial measures is not reviewed *ex officio*.

GERMANY: See 3.2 above. In the case of a review of pre-trial detention, in principle, the court or judge which issued the remand order (the pre-trial judge of the District Court) is competent to review the imposed measure. Depending on the stage of the procedure or the legal organization and management decisions etc., other institutions may have competence. The pre-trial judge has a "neutral" position in the code of criminal procedure and is not specifically assigned to any criminal proceeding. His or her jurisdiction is based in principle on local factors, including the place of arrest / districts of the local court judge (see § 125.1 StPO). It can therefore change and more pre-trial judges may be involved in the same proceedings.

After charging, jurisdiction passes to the court competent to decide the outcome of the case (see especially § 125.2 StPO).

After six months of remand detention, it is the Higher Regional Court which is competent to extend its duration, according to §§ 121 and 122 StPO.

Moreover it is worth mentioning that the Court and the Public Prosecutor's Office are required to ensure *ex officio* the lawfulness of the pre-trial detention at any time. During the investigative proceedings the same rule applies for all investigative measures.

ITALY: In the case of safety measures (*misure di sicurezza*), periodical review (every 6 months under Article 72 CPP) is required by Article 313 CPP. These measures, which may be provisionally ordered at any stage of the criminal proceedings within the limits laid down by Article 206 of the criminal code. For purely historical reasons the regulation of these pre-trial measures has been included in the same Book IV of the CPP which is concerned with precautionary measures, although the nature of the former is very different from that of the latter.

The authorities competent for the review of pre-trial measures are described at 3.3 above.

As regards the legitimacy of a judicial intervention *ex officio*, it must be remembered that Italian law has not entrusted the direction of the preliminary inquiry to a judicial authority but in principle to the Prosecutor and the police as investigative bodies. The competent judge for the preliminary inquiry may intervene only in specific contexts which enable him to verify the lawfulness of the precautionary measures on his own initiative. After charging, the judicial authorities dealing with the case at the various stages of the proceedings may always review the continuing legailty of the imposed measure (Art. 299.3 CPP), although, as explained under 6.1 above, no provision imposes a re-examination at regular intervals.

SPAIN: Yes. The Spanish code of criminal procedure establishes that, from the moment that the grounds which have led to the remand order no longer apply, the judge must issue another order in the same way and even *ex officio*, without the need to fix a hearing as explained above. Through this order the defendant will be released or the pre-trial measure will be substituted with another less intrusive measure. The issue of remand detention is always reviewable and everybody must prevent it from being prolonged more than necessary. Furthermore, pre-trial detention expires in the case of acquittal, even if it has not yet acquired legal finality. See 8.2 below.

A remand order may be appealed, just as the order of withdrawal of a pre-trial measure.

The authority competent to review pre-trial measures is the same judge who adopted the precautionary measure. In the case of appeal, the competence passes to the Superior Court.

Judicial authorities may request any files on the implementation of pre-trial measures that they consider appropriate. Moreover, where the defendant is required to appear *apud acta*, every interview or questioning of the defendant conducted before the competent court (which may not be the same one that ordered the precautionary measure) must be forwarded to the competent authority for the pre-trial measure.

6.3.   Does your legislation provide for maximum time limits of pre-trial measures?

ENGLAND AND WALES: Yes, under the prosecution of Offences Act 1985, as amended but these are easily extended.

In principle the enacted time-limits are proportionate, but they are ineffective in practice. Nevertheless, the average time spent in custody awaiting Crown Court trial (which deals with the most serious offences) was 55 days in 2007 [MINISTRY OF JUSTICE (2008). Offender Management Caseload Statistics 2007 London, Ministry of Justice] and delays before trial are generally shorter than in many other European jurisdictions. Time limits do not in practice prevent the renewal of a pre-trial measure.

GERMANY: Before the beginning of the trial, remand detention may last longer than six months only under strict conditions (§ 121 StPO). After a year, in the circumstances laid down by § 112a StPO, the remand order will automatically be revoked (§ 122a StPO).

Moreover during investigative proceedings time-limits are provided for by law relating to certain investigative measures such as the interception of tele-communications.

Once the legal conditions established for the remand detention cease to exist, the arrest warrant will be set aside. This will be the case if the precautionary intervention is no longer proportionate, see also § 120 StPO. Review by the court and the Public Prosecutor's Office aims to prevent the pre-trial measure becoming disproportionate at any time.

Where there is a change of circumstances, a new arrest warrant may be issued. If remand detention can be based on another ground for custody, a new arrest warrant may be issued.

ITALY: As to custodial measures see 2.1 above. Article 303 CPP establishes basically two different types of time-limits, related to the various stages of the criminal proceedings and to the whole course of the remand proceedings, including eventual suspension. All time-limits are proportionate to the severity of the maximum punishment established by law, although after the conviction of first instance the time-limits provided for with regard to the appeal proceedings must be proportionate to the punishment actually imposed. In view of the various levels of seriousness of different types of criminal offences, time-limits related to the whole course of the remand proceedings may be 2, 4 and 6 years, without prejudice to any subsequent prolongation of them as established by Article 304 CPP. Under Article 308.1 CPP these time-limits are doubled for all non-custodial coercive measures. Finally the pre-trial measures of control (see 2.3 above) have normally a duration of two months, according to Article 308.2 CPP.

In principle time-limits are proportionate to the limitations of fundamental rights produced by pre-trial measures. Yet the equivalence between custody and house arrest laid down by the Italian legal system, as well as the various types of restriction of liberty referred to by the complex regulation in the field of house arrest (see 2.1 above), can lead to contradictory results. For instance, although non-custodial pre-trial measures include requirements to reside at a specific address, this alternative measure may also be ordered with additional conditions, such as the obligation not to leave the address at certain hours (Art. 283.4 CPP). However a very similar result can be achieved also by ordering a house arrest (Art. 284 CPP), whose duration varies considerably.

Moreover, as a rule, after the lapse of a remand order on the expiry of the time-limits, only non-custodial pre-trial measures may be ordered (Art. 307 CPP). A new custodial measure may ordered in case of infringement of the conditions imposed by an alternative measure as well as in the case of a non-final conviction, but in the latter case only for risk of flight.

SPAIN: One of the main characteristics of precautionary measures is their provisional nature. Therefore, as the pre-trial measures aim at ensuring the integrity of the trial process, they have to be necessarily limited in time, so that it would not make sense maintaining them beyond the final decision. Precautionary measures may only be maintained as long as the reasons which have led to their adoption continue to exist, so that as soon as the grounds disappear, the measures must be revoked as well.

As a result, this connection with the reasons which justified the adoption of the original pre-trial measure implies that it will be always revocable. When the factual basis disappears or changes, the pre-trial measure will be lifted or replaced by another one, according to the changing circumstances. However, even if the circumstances have not changed, the Spanish Constitution (under Art. 17.2 and Art. 17.4) and the LECrim provide for a maximum duration of precautionary detention.

For preventive detention, the Constitution establishes a maximum period of seventy-two hours and it may never last longer than the time strictly necessary to carry out the investigation.

One of the fundamental problems of remand detention is its potentially excessive length. Notwithstanding that it may last only as long as required and as long as the reasons that have justified its adoption continue to exist, Spanish law provides for maximum time periods, which can be neither exceeded nor extended. These time limits are set out according to two parameters: a) the seriousness of the offence and, b) the purpose of the pre-trial detention. Maximum time limits constitute a constitutional requirement that gives effect to the guarantee enshrined in Article 17.4. As a consequence, exceeding the time limits results in a disproportionate limitation of the right to liberty and consequently a Constitutional violation.

Where remand detention has been adopted in order to avoid the risk of flight or the danger of recurrence, the precautionary measure may not exceed two years, if the offence is punishable with a sentence of imprisonment exceeding three years. If the potential sentence for the alleged offence does not exceed three years of detention, the pre-trial measure may not exceed one year.

With regard to these cases, Spanish legislation provides for the exceptional possibility of an extension of the precautionary measure if factual circumstances prevent the resolution of the case within the prescribed time limits. In this case the remand detention may be extended for up to two years, if the potential sentence for the alleged offence exceeds three years, and to six months, if the potential sentence is equal to or less than three years. The defendant and the public prosecutor must always be heard and an order must be issued.

An infringement of a precautionary measure creates a new offence and in the new proceedings instituted as a result, other precautionary measures may be ordered.

As to further pre-trial measures, time limits relate to the duration of the grounds which have justified their adoption and to the maximum time limit of the sentence that can be potentially imposed (for example, if the potential sentence consists of the deprivation of the right to drive a motor vehicle, the precautionary measure shall not exceed the maximum time limit provided for with regard to the deprivation of such right).

7.   Remedies

7.1.   What remedies does your law grant to a defendant subject to a deprivation / restriction of his or her right to liberty?

ENGLAND AND WALES: See 3.2 and 4.2 above.

GERMANY: The review of a remand in custody and complaint against the detention are different forms of judicial revision on either a factual or a legal basis (§§ 117, 121, 122, 304, 310 StPO).

During investigative proceedings the Prosecutor will examine the case and, if necessary, apply for a judicial decision as to whether the warrant of arrest is to be revoked (§ 120 StPO).

ITALY: It should first be remembered that it is exceptional for the defendant to appear in court before the issue of a judicial order imposing a precautionary measure. As a general rule, the adoption of a pre-trial measure presupposes only the request of the Prosecutor, so that the remanded defendant will be granted the right to challenge the legitimacy of the restriction of his or her freedom. As to the time limits laid down by Article 294 CPP, see 4.2 above.

As explained under 1.2 above, all judicial orders imposing a deprivation or restriction of someone's right to liberty must be reasoned and are always subject to an appeal on a question of law addressed to the Court of Cassation (Art. 111.6 – 7 of the Constitution). For a long time appeal on a question of law has constituted the only remedy for the remanded defendant.

The code of criminal procedure provides for different remedies against judicial orders imposing precautionary measures. The typical remedy against a custody remand order or the imposition of coercive measures is a judicial complaint under Article 309 CPP, which is addressed to the court, sitting en banc, of the provincial capital of the court of appeal in whose district the judge who issued the contested measure is based (*tribunale della libertà*). This is a very special remedy since it does not introduce a second instance into the precautionary proceedings, does not need to be reasoned and usually leads to the re-examination of the whole issue of the restriction of liberty. However, as it is a purely defensive remedy, it will never lead to the adoption of a more intrusive measure than that already imposed.

As an alternative, an appeal on a question of law may be addressed to the Court of Cassation (Art. 311.2 CPP).

Another opportunity for a remanded defendant to take proceedings against the judicial order imposing a precautionary measure is judicial review provided for by Article 299 CPP. This is a collateral procedure to that established for the complaint under Article 309 CPP and, as explained above, aims at the re-examination of the legal basis of the measure imposed.

At first sight judicial review and complaint are very different remedies and during the first years after the entry into force of the code of criminal procedure, case-law considered them as alternative proceedings by assuming that the judicial review could not permit a re-examination of the initial limitation of liberty. This conclusion seems to be contradicted by the provision laid down by Article 299.1 CPP, according to which a pre-trial measure may also be reviewed on the basis of new circumstances, which should mean that the review could be conducted on the basis of the findings initially assessed.

Judicial orders imposing non-coercive personal measures (i. e. the measures of control) are subject to appeal under Article 310 CPP, which, moreover, constitutes the only remedy against any other judicial order issued during the "precautionary proceedings" (e. g. rejection of the request for revocation of the imposed measure, suspension of the maximum time-limits etc.). Finally this remedy can be also lodged by the Prosecutor applying for a precautionary measure, if the request for its adoption was rejected by the judge for the preliminary inquiry.

SPAIN: Spanish law provides for an appeal which will have preferential treatment in the listing of cases (Art. 507 LECrim).

7.2. Which rights are granted to a defendant through appeal against a remand decision?

ENGLAND AND WALES: See 3.2 above.

GERMANY: § 117 StPO contains a legal remedy called "review of detention." during pre-trial custody the defendant "may at any time apply for a court hearing as to whether the warrant of arrest is to be revoked or its execution suspended in accordance with § 116". That means that the right to be heard is largely independent of any procedural event.

§ 304.1 StPO holds that "a complaint shall be admissible against all orders made by the courts at first instance or in appellate proceedings on fact and law". This provision of course includes orders relating to pre-trial custody.

If pre-trial custody for the same offence lasts longer than six months, review of detention is officially required (*ex officio*). That does not depend on other remedies.

If certain conditions are fulfilled, pre-trial custody may not extend for longer than one year (§ 122a StPO).

ITALY: It very much depends on the type of remedy. The procedure of judicial review provided for by Article CPP grants the defendant the right to be heard each time a change or substitution of the imposed measure is sought on the basis of new circumstances. Moreover, the very fact that the competent authority for intermediate proceedings, trial and appeal proceedings may review *ex officio* and at any time the justification of the ongoing measure, constitutes a guarantee for the defendant deprived of or restricted in his or her liberty.

With regard to complaint under Article 309 CPP, its defensive character implies, as explained above, that it will never lead to the worsening of an existing measure. Moreover, the procedure provided for by Article 309 CPP contains very short time-limits within which the competent authority must submit to the court in charge with the complaint the documentation on which the judicial order was based (5 days) and this court must adjudicate on the complaint (10 days from that submission), otherwise the precautionary measure becomes ineffective.

SPAIN: The defendant subject to a restriction of his or her right to liberty has the right to appeal the order which imposed it within the five days after notification of the order. Within the same period the Prosecutor and other parties also have the right to appeal an order refusing the interim precautionary measures. In the first case, the appeal procedure includes the guarantee that if the appellant is the person held in provisional incarceration, he or she may request a hearing, which must be granted, before the Appeal Court (see Arts. 507.1 and 766.5 LECrim as well as Constitutional Court, Decision 3/1992). Moreover, preference will be given to an appeal against an order of imprisonment. Likewise, an appeal against an order of imprisonment must be resolved within 30 days.

7.3.   May the appeal against a remand order coexist with a judicial review of the remand detention?

ENGLAND AND WALES: The right of appeal in respect of a decision made by a Magistrates' Court or by a Judge of the Crown Court is collateral to any proceedings for Judicial Review or for a writ of *Habeas Corpus* in the High Court.

GERMANY: There is no conflict. During the preliminary investigation the public prosecution office dominates the proceedings. However it requires judicial (control) measures without which detention is not possible.

ITALY: Italian case-law has recognized a very close relationship between the remedies provided for by Articles 309 – 311 CPP and judicial review under Article 299 CPP. It is known as "precautionary *ne bis in idem*" ("*ne bis in idem* cautelare"), according to which the judicial review must in principle be restricted to different issues from those addressed in the decision issued on appeal. Instead, they could be re-examined only in the case of new circumstances.

SPAIN: Not applicable.

8.   Pre-trial precautionary measures and criminal proceedings

8.1.   May pre-trial precautionary measures be ordered at any stage of the criminal proceedings?

ENGLAND AND WALES: The issue of bail, conditional bail or remand in custody can be considered at any stage.

GERMANY: Yes. Pre-trial detention may be ordered throughout the criminal proceedings. Investigative proceedings end with the beginning of the trial. However, the arrest warrant or accommodation warrant may also be ordered later (see § 125.2 StPO) and further evidence can be) collected.
    Remand detention may be ordered during appeal proceedings (*Berufungsverhandlung*). Here further evidence can be collected, which is not admitted pending the appeal on a question of law (*Revisionsverfahren*). However

the arrest warrant may be revoked by the court competent for the latter appeal (§ 126.3 StPO).

ITALY: Yes. All precautionary measures may be ordered at any stage of the criminal proceedings, albeit with the exceptions discussed under 8.3 above.

SPAIN: In principle, precautionary measures will be adopted during investigative proceedings, both in regard to the personal situation of the defendant and with regard to potential civil liabilities arising from the criminal offence. However there are no exceptions depending on the change of circumstances as the procedure continues. Even the trial court may order such measures at any time, so that the various judicial authorities seized of the case will have functional competence to order pre-trial measures.

8.2. What influence do pre-trial orders and / or decisions of the criminal proceedings have on pre-trial precautionary measures?

ENGLAND AND WALES: Only those which are likely to extend or abbreviate the length of time before trial, for example, case management decisions about the listing of the case, the need for extra time for preparation etc. The institution of new proceedings would enable the court dealing with those proceedings to consider the issue of bail / conditional bail or custody in the light of the existing proceedings. Moreover withdrawal of one of the charges would represent a "change of circumstances" enabling a defendant in custody or subject to bail conditions to make a fresh application for release or variation of bail conditions under the Criminal Justice Act 1988 (see 6.1 above).

On conviction the defendant may be remanded either on bail, conditional bail or in custody to a sentencing date, pending the completion of Pre-Sentence Reports. Once the defendant is sentenced, bail or custody no longer applies unless a released defendant appeals. Acquittals, which are final in England and Wales, result in the immediate release of the defendant.

GERMANY: Acquittal, dismissal of criminal proceedings and refusal to open the trial lead to the release of the remanded defendant (§ 120.1 StPO). See 4.2 above.

As regards accommodation in an psychiatric hospital see § 126a.3 StPO.

The hearing of evidence may also lead to the conclusion that a strong suspicion or any other condition of the arrest warrant (see 8.3 below) no longer exists.

Once the defendant is charged there is a change in the competence for ordering an arrest warrant and review of detention, § 125.2 StPO (see, for instance, 3.2 above).

The preferment of the charges and the opening of the trial define the subject of the proceedings (see §§ 199 ff., 264 f. StPO).

Moreover it can occur that, as a result of certain defects relating to the indictment, the Prosecutor may withdraw the charge before the beginning of the trial.

When the defects lead to the conclusion that a conviction is no longer probable (process impediments, changes in factual basis, new investigative elements, etc.), the Prosecutor must apply for the withdrawal of the arrest warrant, § 120.3 StPO. At the same time, the Prosecutor may order the release of the defendant.

However, if necessary, the Prosecutor can amend the charge and reissue it. In this case, provided there is the same factual basis and the same grounds for remand, the arrest warrant will remain.

After the opening of oral proceedings, the charge can no longer be withdrawn, § 156 StPO.

The code of criminal procedure distinguishes between three different degrees of suspicion: initial suspicion (initiation of the investigative proceedings), reasonable suspicion (preferment of the charge, commencement of the trial), strong suspicion (remand detention).

Additionally special investigative measures may be ordered only if the suspicion relates, for example, to particularly serious offences. At the time of preferring the charge, strong suspicion is always stronger than reasonable suspicion. After the accusation a strong suspicion of guilt may exist despite the inexistence of a reasonable suspicion. Moreover, the suspicion degrees may continually change during the course of the investigation or even disappear. At the opening of the trial (§ 207.4 StPO) and by reaching judgement (§ 268b StPO), the trial court will also determine whether the conditions of detention still exist or not.

As to the influence of non-final acquittals, see 8.2 and 4.2 above.

In the case of non-final judgments pre-trial detention can be continued. However, the sentence will not be enforced (see § 449 StPO).

ITALY: Criminal proceedings may influence the course of the precautionary measures at different levels. As regards their duration, the particular complexity of the preliminary inquiry can firstly justify an extension of the time-limits established for custodial measures (Art. 305.2 CPP). Moreover, the same time-limits are suspended during the trial when there is an adjournment applied for by the defendant or his or her lawyer, or resulting from his or her failure to appear before the court, or arising from his or her failure to appear before the court or because of the removal of one or more defence counsel results in a lack of legal assistance (Art. 304.1 CPP).

Moreover, several rulings issued during the criminal proceedings may influence the course of the precautionary measures as follows.

The opening of a preliminary inquiry is prerequisite for the legitimate ordering of any precautionary measure, since only a suspect may be subject to pretrial measures. The indictment does not automatically result in the issue of a precautionary order. However, if the rules on judicial competence provide for the institution of intermediate proceedings, during this phase the judicial authority (which is a single judge belonging to the same GIP) can much better ascertain the issue of precautionary measures by having access to all investigative records. As to the assessment of the strong suspicion of guilt pending trial, see 5.3 above.

The prosecution may not be withdrawn according to Article 112 of the Constitution, which states that, as a rule, the Prosecutor is required to institute penal action. Of course it does not mean that criminal proceedings will always be instituted independently of the findings obtained through the preliminary inquiry, which instead aims to verify whether or not sufficient evidence to prefer a charge has been gathered (Art. 326 CPP). If not, the Prosecutor will apply for an order of discontinuance of the proceedings (*archiviazione*), pursuant to Article 408 CPP. This order would make the precautionary measure immediately ineffective (Art. 300.1 CPP).

Criminal proceedings are collateral to any precautionary proceeding, albeit that they are closely linked. In the middle of the 1990s case-law went so far as to consider the assessment and even the re-examination of the reasonable suspicion provided for by Article 273 CPP unnecessary after the opening of the trial. The Constitutional Court declared the provisions laid down in Arts. 309 and 310 CPP as unconstitutional through another "integrative decision of unconstitutionality" by assuming that they did not provide for the possibility of assessing reasonable suspicion after the commencement of the trial (Decision 71 / 1996).

Once the defendant is acquitted, any precautionary measure becomes ineffective (Art. 300 (1) CPP).

As to non-final convictions, see 6.3 and 8.3 above. Moreover, according to Article 275.2ter CPP, the issue of precautionary measures must always be examined concurrently with the conviction issued on appeal when it concerns an offence for which the code provides for a mandatory arrest and the defendant has been convicted for a similar offence at least once during the last five years.

SPAIN: If the indictment has been dismissed or the defendant has been acquitted, pre-trial measures must be lifted. In some cases where during the proceedings the suspicion against the defendant increases, pre-trial measures may be aggravated.

There is no rule imposing pre-trial measures on the ground of decisions made in the main proceedings. Neither the preferment of the charge nor the opening of the trial lead to a modification of the precautionary measures imposed. In the case of discontinuance of the proceedings (*"archivo"*) no precautionary measure may be adopted and, if already ordered, it must be lifted. Any precautionary measure is subsidiary to the main proceedings, so that without pending proceedings no measure may exist.

In the case of provisional dismissal of the indictment (*"sobreseimiento provisional"*), pre-trial measures can survive until the order becomes final, but afterwards they lapse. In the case of a re-opening of the proceedings, there should be a new decision on precautionary measures for them to have effect.

The main consequence of an acquittal is the withdrawal of any pre-trial measure, which therefore ceases to be operative.

On the other hand, our system provides for three forms of state liability arising from the administration of justice, one of which aims at a compensation for wrongful detention. This compensation may be claimed by those who, after being remanded, have been acquitted on the grounds of the inexistence of the alleged offence, provided that they have suffered damages. The same applies in case of final dismissal of the indictment (*auto de sobreseimiento libre*). Nevertheless, according to a constitutional interpretation, the right to compensation will be granted in the cases of provisional dismissal of the indictment, final dismissal of the indictment, acquittal decision due to different reasons from the inexistence of the offence, as well as in the case of conviction for a non-custodial sentence or for a sentence of imprisonment but for a shorter period than the one spent on remand.

Non-final conviction may justify the maintenance or the adoption of pre-trial measures based on requirements partly different to those provided for during the investigative proceedings (see the above explanation relating to the time limits for pre-trial detention).

Once the conviction becomes final, precautionary measures are converted into enforcement measures.

8.3.   Do the legal conditions governing pre-trial measures have the same
        relevance throughout criminal proceedings? If not, how does their effect
        vary according to the stage of the criminal proceedings?

ENGLAND AND WALES: Yes.

GERMANY: See above.

ITALY: In principle yes, albeit with some exceptions. For instance, after or
concurrently with conviction following an appeal against acquittal lodged by the
Prosecutor, pre-trial measures cannot be ordered on the basis of a risk of interference with evidence, as no evidence can be collected before the Supreme
Court adjudicates on the appeal on a question of law (Art. 300.5 CPP). Moreover,
after the pronouncement of a conviction (albeit non-final) a consideration of the
proportionality of pre-trial measures (by way of derogation from the general rule
laid down by Article 278 CPP) must be conducted taking into account the severity of the sentence actually imposed, i.e. taking into account all the eventual
extenuating or aggravating circumstances of the case.

SPAIN: See above. As to remand detention, Spanish law lays down different
maximum time-limits depending on the various stages of the proceedings (first
instance, trial or appeal). In any event the circumstances which have justified the
pre-trial measure must continue to exist (for instance, risk of absconding, risk of
committing another offence etc.).

8.4.   Does the length of the criminal proceedings influence that of the
        precautionary measures?

ENGLAND AND WALES: Yes.

GERMANY: See also 3.3.1 above.
    After six months (see § 121 StPO, for the provisional committal see § 126a.2
StPO) or one year (§ 122a StPO) without judgement, the pre-trial detention may
be continued only under strict conditions.

ITALY: Yes. See 8.2 above.

SPAIN: In the Spanish legal system the length of criminal proceedings may
influence the duration of the precautionary measures, to the extent that, in case

of the expiry of the maximum period established for pre-trial detention, the remanded defendant must be released.

Moreover, there is a limit for pre-trial detention after conviction at first instance, i. e. to half of the sentence imposed, so that by exceeding this limit the defendant must be released.

If criminal proceedings are delayed for reasons not imputable to the re- manded defendant, it is generally understood that pre-trial measures are less justifiable.

8.5.   May the duration of the precautionary measures influence that of the criminal proceedings?

ENGLAND AND WALES: No.

GERMANY: In practice the time limits (see above) may affect the commencement of the trial and possibly of the judgement as well. For instance the Public Prosecutor's Office will often try to prefer a charge within the six months / one year time limit in order to avoid an eventual release of the defendant. The same may apply to the trial.

Moreover, in particular for pre-trial detainees, a claim for expedited trial derives from Articles 2.2 GG and 5.3 ECHR.

ITALY: Not traditionally. However, Law 125 / 2008 recently introduced a new system of "immediate proceedings" (*giudizio immediato*), which provides for a different length both for the preliminary inquiry and for criminal proceedings. As a consequence, the defendant may be subject to different time limits for the investigative phase from those established by Article 454 CPP (180 days from the execution of the custodial order instead of 90 days from the institution of the preliminary investigation) and effectively forfeits the guarantees provided by the intermediate proceedings, which aim at the judicial examination of the accusation.

SPAIN: In principle no, albeit that proceeding against remanded defendants will have precedence, so that judgements and decisions are made during the period of implementation of the precautionary measures.

They may have some influence as to the conviction (if undue delay is de- tected) and its enforcement (reduction of the sentence in regard to the time spent on remand).

The period of pre-trial detention is to be computed at the time of enforcement of the custodial sentence eventually imposed.

However, Spanish legislation establishes that, where pre-trial detention exceeds two-thirds of its maximum duration, the judge or court seized of the case and the Prosecutor must notify the Chairman of the Board or the chief prosecutor of the tribunal concerned, in order that these may adopt the measures necessary to expedite the proceedings. For this purpose, these proceedings have precedence over all others.

8.6.   Does a charge always accompany the imposition of pre-trial measures?

ENGLAND AND WALES: Yes.

GERMANY: Despite the adoption of remand detention, a charge may not always be preferred, as new evidence may arise during the investigation that would indicate that a conviction is more or less likely. Yet by ordering an arrest warrant (§ 112.1 StPO) a charge is often preferred.

However it can occur that a "sufficient ground for suspicion," which is prerequisite both for the preferment of the charges and the opening of the trial (§§ 170 and 203 StPO), exists when an arrest warrant (where there is "strong suspicion") has been ordered.

ITALY: In principle no. See Article 409.1 CPP, which states that the order of discontinuance of the proceedings shall be notified to the remanded defendant and makes it clear that the option between applying for the discontinuance of the proceedings and preferring the charges would however remain open to the Prosecutor.

However, notification of the charge provided for by Article 129 of the CPP Implementing Rules (in cases where the defendant is a public employee, a member of the ecclesiastic personnel, as well as in the case that the offence has caused damage to the Public Treasury) must take place when the suspect is arrested or remanded in custody.

However the new type of "immediate proceeding" introduced in 2008 (see 8.4 above) provides that within of 180 days from the execution of the remand order, the prosecutor must apply for these proceedings, unless this would prejudice the course of the investigation. Therefore, in the field of custodial measures, this alternative procedure, until then facultative, has become almost mandatory *rebus sic stantibus*. Moreover, according Art. 132bis of the CPP Implementing Rules, as reformed by Law 125 / 2008, criminal proceedings where the defendant has been arrested or subject to a personal precautionary measure must have absolute precedence.

SPAIN: In the case of remand detention, prosecutors must indicate in the indictment the continuation of the measure imposed and its justification. However, the inclusion of this information in the indictment does not mean that such a measure should in fact be imposed.

The Authors

Di Chiara, Giuseppe, Full Professor Dr. iur., Head of the Chair of Criminal Procedure at the University of Palermo, dichiara@unipa.it

Maggio, Paola, Dr. iur., Researcher of Criminal Procedure at the University of Palermo, paola.maggio@unipa.it

Marzaduri, Enrico, Full Professor, Head of the Chair of Criminal Procedure at the University of Pisa, marzend@interfree.it

Moreno Catena, Víctor, Full Professor, Head of the Chair of Procedural and Litigation Law at Carlos III University, Director of the Research Institut "Alonso Martínez" of Justice and Litigation, vmoreno@der-pu.uc3m.es

Orlandi, Renzo, Full Professor, Head of the Chair of Criminal Procedure at the University of Bologna, renzo.orlandi@unibo.it

Oubiña Barbolla, Sabela, Dr. iur., Visiting Professor of Procedural and Litigation Law at Carlos III University, Member of the Research Institute "Alonso Martínez" of Justice and Litigation, soubina@der-pu.uc3m.es

Rafaraci, Tommaso, Full Professor Dr. iur., Head of the Chair of Criminal Procedure at the University of Catania, trafaraci@lex.unict.it

Ruggeri, Stefano, Titular Professor Dr. iur., Head of the Chair of Criminal Procedure at the University of Messina, steruggeri@unime.it

Sinn, Arndt, Professor Dr. iur., Head of the Chair of German and European Criminal Law and Procedure, International Criminal Law and Comparative Criminal Law at the University of Osnabrück, Director of the ZEIS, sinn@uos.de

Vogler, Richard, Dr. iur., Senior Lecturer in Law, Solicitor, at the University of Sussex, r.k.vogler@sussex.ac.uk

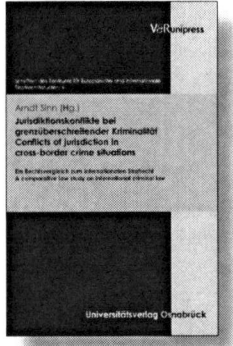